Atlantic Canada

Benoit Prieur

Fifth Edition

There was a freshness in the air as of a wind that
had blown over the honey-sweet fields of clover...
Beyond lay the sea, misty and purple,
with its haunting, unceasing murmur.

Lucy Maud Montgomery
Anne of Green Gables

Travel better, enjoy more

ULYSSES
Travel Guides

Offices

Canada: Ulysses Travel Guides, 4176 St. Denis Street, Montréal, Québec, H2W 2M5, ☎(514) 843-9447, ⇔(514) 843-9448, info@ulysses.ca, www.ulyssesguides.com

Europe: Les Guides de Voyage Ulysse SARL, 127 rue Amelot, 75011 Paris, France, ☎01 43 38 89 50, ⇔01 43 38 89 52, voyage@ulysse.ca, www.ulyssesguides.com

U.S.A.: Ulysses Travel Guides, 305 Madison Avenue, Suite 1166, New York, NY 10165, info@ulysses.ca, www.ulyssesguides.com

Distributors

U.S.A.: Hunter Publishing, 130 Campus Drive, Edison, NJ 08818, ☎800-255-0343, ⇔(732) 417-1744 or 0482, comments@hunterpublishing.com, www.hunterpublishing.com

Canada: Ulysses Travel Guides, 4176 St. Denis Street, Montréal, Québec, H2W 2M5, ☎(514) 843-9882, ext. 2232, ⇔514-843-9448, info@ulysses.ca, www.ulyssesguides.com

Great Britain and Ireland: Roundhouse Publishing, Millstone, Limers Lane, Northam, North Devon, EX39 2RG, ☎1 202 66 54 32, ⇔1 202 66 62 19, roundhouse.group@ukgateway.net

Other countries: Ulysses Travel Guides, 4176 St. Denis Street, Montréal, Québec, H2W 2M5, ☎(514) 843-9882, ext.2232, ⇔514-843-9448, info@ulysses.ca, www.ulyssesguides.com

Library and Archives Canada Cataloguing in Publication

Benoit, Prieur, 1965–

    Atlantic Canada

    (Ulysses travel guide)
    Includes index.

    ISSN 1704-4634
    ISBN 2-89464-723-9

    1. Atlantic Provinces – Guidebooks. I. Title. II Series.

FC2004.P7413   917.1504'5   C2002-301420-2

© May 2005, Ulysses Travel Guides.
All rights reserved.
Printed in Canada
ISBN 2-89464-723-9

Research and Writing
Benoit Prieur

Collaboration
Alexandra Gilbert

Publisher
Claude Morneau

Production Director
André Duchesne

Translator
Jennifer McMorran

Copy Editor
Pierre Ledoux

Artistic Director
Patrick Farei (Atoll)

Editing Assistants
Julie Brodeur
Pierre Ledoux
David Sirois

Cartographers
Marie-France Denis
David Sirois

Illustrators
Pascal Biet
Myriam Gagné
Lorette Pierson

Photography
Cover page
Cliff LeSergent / Alamy

Inside pages
John Sylvester
P. Quittemelle, Megapress
Nova Scotia Tourism
New Brunswick Department of Tourism and Parks
Gilles Daigle / New Brunswick Department of Tourism and Parks

Graphic Designer
Marie-France Denis

Acknowledgements

We acknowledge the financial support of the Government of Canada through the Book Publishing Industry Development Program (BPIDP) for our publishing activities. We would also like to thank the government of Québec for its SODEC income tax program for book publication.

Write to Us

The information contained in this guide was correct at press time. However, mistakes can slip in, omissions are always possible, places can disappear, etc. The authors and publisher hereby disclaim any liability for loss or damage resulting from omissions or errors.

We value your comments, corrections and suggestions, as they allow us to keep each guide up to date. The best contributions will be rewarded with a free book from Ulysses Travel Guides. All you have to do is write us at the following address and indicate which title you would be interested in receiving (see the list at the end of the guide).

Ulysses Travel Guides

4176 St. Denis Street
Montréal, Québec
Canada H2W 2M5

305 Madison Avenue
Suite 1166, New York
NY 10165

www.ulyssesguides.com
E-mail: text@ulysses.ca

Table of Contents

Table of Contents *(continued)*

List of Maps

Map Symbols

?	Tourist Information	▲	Mountain
🚗⛴	Car Ferry	🚶	Golf Course
⛴	Passenger Ferry	◍	Beach
★	Provincial Capital	☀	Lookout

Symbols

≡	Air conditioning
bkfst incl.	Breakfast included
⊗	Fan
⇄	Fax number
ℑ	Fireplace
⊘	Fitness centre
fb	Full board (lodging + 3 meals)
K	Kitchenette
🐕	Pets allowed
≈	Pool
pb	Private bathroom
≈	Pool
ℝ	Refrigerator
ℜ	Restaurant
⌂	Sauna
✿	Spa
sb	Shared bathroom
☎	Telephone number
🛶	Ulysses' favourite
⊛	Whirlpool

Attraction Classification

★	Interesting
★★	Worth a visit
★★★	Not to be missed

Hotel Classification

$	less than $60
$$	$61 to $100
$$$	$101 to $150
$$$$	$151 to $225
$$$$$	more than $225

Unless otherwise indicated, the prices in this guide
apply to a standard room for two people in peak season.

Restaurant Classification

$	less than $10
$$	$11 to $20
$$$	$21 to $30
$$$$	more than $30

The prices in the guide are for a full meal for one
person, not including taxes, drinks or tip.

All prices in this guide are in Canadian dollars.

🌐 Where is Atlantic Canada?

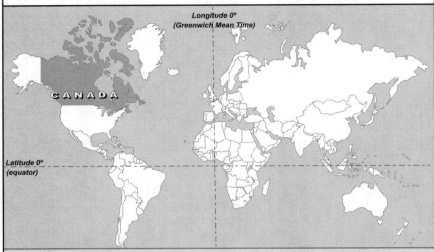

New Brunswick
Capital: Fredericton
Population: 751,449 inhab.
Area: 72,908km²

Nova Scotia
Capital: Halifax
Population: 938,134 inhab.
Area: 55,284km²

Prince Edward Island
Capital: Charlottetown
Population: 137,744 inhab.
Area: 5,660km²

Newfoundland and Labrador
Capital: St. John's
Population: 516,875 inhab.
Area: 405,720km²

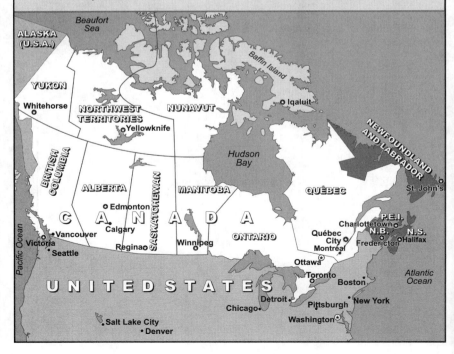

New Brunswick,

Nova Scotia, Prince Edward Island and Newfoundland and Labrador make up a picturesque region that combines thousands of kilometres of splendid coastal scenery with rich local traditions and a fascinating way of life.

The Atlantic provinces boast some of the most beautiful natural sites in eastern North America, including the spectacular Cape Breton Highlands, the magnificent sand dunes and beaches of Prince Edward Island, the cliffs and fjords of Newfoundland and Labrador's Gros Morne National Park, and the stunning landscapes along the Bay of Fundy, sculpted by the highest and most powerful tides in the world. The area's unique charm, however, is also largely due to its simple scenes of everyday life, like the sight of a fleet of colourful ships heading out in the morning fog from a little fishing port along the coast.

A trip to Atlantic Canada thus offers visitors an opportunity to view the region's magnificent scenery while getting to know its rich local culture and history. These are not the area's only pleasures, however. Among the most delightful memories will certainly be the beaches, washed by the warmest waters north of Virginia (U.S.A.), and the feasts of lobster and other fresh seafood.

Geography

Canada's territory covers 9,093,507km² of land and 891,163km² of fresh water, for a total area of 9,984,670km². The Atlantic provinces lie in the eastern part of this huge country, second largest in the world after Russia. These four provinces—New Brunswick, Nova Scotia, Prince Edward Island and Newfoundland and Labrador—all have shorelines along the Gulf of St. Lawrence, the Atlantic Ocean or the Bay of Fundy.

New Brunswick

New Brunswick covers an area of 72,908km² and shares a border with Québec to the north and Maine (U.S.A.) to the west; its coast is linked to Nova Scotia by the Chignecto Isthmus. To the east, the province is separated from Prince Edward Island by the Northumberland Strait. New Brunswick is bound by water on two sides; its northern and northeastern shores look out on the Baie des Chaleurs and the Gulf of St. Lawrence, its south shore on the Bay of Fundy. There are two major waterways that run through the heart of the territory—the St. John and Miramichi rivers. The north of New Brunswick has highlands reaching up to 820m that form the end of the Appalachians, and its centre is studded by several hills. A dense forest, consisting mostly of coniferous and some deciduous trees, covers approximately 85% of the territory and constitutes an important natural resource, enabling the province to become an exporter of pulp and paper. New Brunswick's capital is Fredericton.

Nova Scotia

Nova Scotia is only linked to the rest of Canada by a narrow strip of land, the Chignecto Isthmus. Its shores are washed by the Bay of Fundy to the northwest, the Atlantic Ocean to the south, the Gulf of St. Lawrence to the northeast and the Northumberland Strait to the north. The province also boasts no fewer than 3,000 lakes and many little streams and rivers. It covers an area of 55,284km^2, about 10% of which is arable land. Like New Brunswick, Nova Scotia also has a

dense forest consisting mainly of conifers. The province's landscape is relatively flat, except for Cape Breton Island which is much rockier. Nova Scotia's capital is Halifax.

Prince Edward Island

Prince Edward Island, which has an area of only 5,660km^2, is the smallest but most densely populated province in Canada, with an average of 21 inhabitants per km^2. Its economy, unlike that of New Brunswick and Nova Scotia, is largely based on agriculture; nearly 50% of its territory is covered with extremely fertile soil. The potato is one of the island's most important crops. Vast fields stretch across land once occupied by a forest of beech, birch, maple, oak and pine trees. This island, separated from Nova Scotia and New Brunswick by the Northumberland Strait, lies in the Gulf of St. Lawrence. Its inland waters are limited to small ponds and narrow rivers. Prince Edward Island's capital is Charlottetown.

Newfoundland and Labrador

The province of Newfoundland and Labrador is made up of two distinct parts: the island of Newfoundland and the immense territory of Labrador. The island covers an area of 111,390km^2. As North America's easternmost island, Newfoundland started playing a

pivotal role in communications between Europe and the New World at a very early date. It is separated from the mainland by the Strait of Belle Isle and also has shores on the Gulf of St. Lawrence and the Atlantic Ocean. Unlike the other Atlantic provinces, Newfoundland is almost entirely unfit for farming. Its population is thus concentrated along the shore, where fishing is the mainstay of the economy, and in a few inland urban centres, where the cutting and processing of wood are the main activities. The western part of the island is rimmed by the Long Range Mountains, whose highest summit rises to an altitude of 815m; the rest is either flat or has a gently rolling landscape. Spectacular cliffs tower over the coastline in many spots.

Labrador, nearly three times the size of the island of Newfoundland, covers 294,330km^2. Most of this territory has a gently undulating landscape strewn with countless lakes and rivers, which is typical of the Canadian Shield. Farther north, the terrain is shaped by the Torngat Mountains, which soar 1,729m into the sky at their highest point. Labrador is covered with subarctic forest and, in its northernmost part, tundra. Its shoreline stretches nearly 8,000km along the Strait of Belle Isle and the Atlantic Ocean. To the east and south, Labrador shares a long border with Québec. The capital of Newfoundland and Labrador is St. John's.

History

The arrival of European explorers in the 15th and 16th centuries did not mark the beginning of human history in the region now known as the Atlantic provinces. It was actually a moment of rupture, since the territory had already been inhabited for over 10,000 years by descendants of nomads who crossed the Bering Strait at the end of the ice age. Furthermore, John Cabot and Jacques Cartier were not the first Europeans to set foot in this part of North America. Legend has it that at the end of the fifth century, **St. Brendan**, an Irish abbot, crossed the Atlantic in search of new peoples to convert to Christianity, coming ashore on this island. The first Europeans whose presence here can actually be proved, however, are the **Vikings**, who, toward the year 1000, apparently used the island as a base for exploring the continent. Leif's Camp, in L'Anse-aux-Meadows (Newfoundland and Labrador), is the oldest known European settlement in North America. It wasn't until several cen-

turies later that Europeans rediscovered Newfoundland.

In the 15th century, Europeans learned of the teeming waters around the island from Basque fishers. Each summer, the Basques would come to this region to fish cod in the Grand Banks and hunt whales in the Strait of Belle Isle. The voyages of Cabot and Cartier nevertheless represented a decisive moment in history, heralding an era of European colonization in this region and the rest of North America.

In 1497, after securing financial support in England, **John Cabot** (born Giovanni Caboto) set out from Bristol in search of a direct route to the riches of the Orient. On June 24, 1497, he reached the coast of North America, most probably the northern shores of the island of Newfoundland, then returned to England. His voyage was not in vain, however, as he helped spread the word about the tremendous natural riches in this part of the world– an apparently inexhaustible supply of cod off the northern coasts of the New World. From that moment on, even larger numbers of English, French, Basque and Spanish fishers started heading out from the ports of Europe to fish cod off the coasts of Newfoundland and Nova Scotia.

In 1534, Breton navigator **Jacques Cartier** launched the first of his three voyages to North America. Commissioned by King

Francis I of France to seek out gold and a passage to Asia, he found neither. These expeditions did, however, enable Cartier to discover the shoreline of a huge territory. On his first voyage, he explored the coast of the Atlantic provinces, from the western point of present-day Prince Edward Island to the mouth of the Miramichi River in New Brunswick. Farther along, in the Baie des Chaleurs (Québec), he met the local Aboriginal people. He erected a cross here, symbolically claiming this land in the name of the King of France.

The Aboriginals Cartier encountered in the Baie des Chaleurs belonged to the Algonquian-speaking Mi'kmaq (Micmac) First Nation.

The **Mi'kmaq** inhabited not only this region but also, in greater numbers, what are now Nova Scotia, New Brunswick and Prince Edward Island, - territories they shared with another Algonquian-speaking nation, the **Malecites**. The direct ancestors of these Aboriginal people settled in the region about 2,500 years ago. In the summer, the Mi'kmaqs and Malecites lived in fairly large groups along the coast, surviving mainly on fish. In winter, they would leave the coast and head into the forest to hunt game. The island of Newfoundland, for its part, had been inhabited since the second century by the **Beothuk**, whose lifestyle was similar to that of the Mi'kmaq and the Malecite.

This traditional way of life was profoundly altered by the arrival of the European explorers and fishers.

By the second half of the 16th century, the Europeans were trading more intensely with the Aboriginal people. Fur garments were becoming fashionable in Europe, creating an extremely lucrative market. In response to this trend, many European fishers became merchants, trading metal objects, for the most part, for furs. The Mi'kmaqs, Malecites and Beothuks, who lived near the shore, profited the most from this trade. However, they were also the first to succumb to various illnesses transmitted by the Europeans, which their immune system could not defend against. Before long, these diseases claimed the lives of vast numbers of Aboriginals. Around the year 1600, for example, it is estimated that a mere 3,500 Mi'kmaqs remained in the Maritimes, a mere 10% of their population a century earlier, before their first contact with Europeans.

Acadia and Early Settlement

The development of fisheries prompted the Europeans to establish trading posts on the shores of Newfoundland. The English founded their first outpost in Trinity in 1558, on the Bonavista Peninsula, then officially took possession of the port of St. John's in 1583. The French also started establishing footholds on the shores of Newfoundland to support their seasonal fishing activities. However, the fur trade being carried out with Aboriginal suppliers required a much more permanent European presence on the continent.

Most efforts to set up trading posts along the coast of this part of North America were made by the French. Several fruitless attempts were made, namely on Sable Island (Nova Scotia) and in Tadoussac (Québec). Then, in 1604, one year after receiving authorization from King Henry IV of France, **Pierre du Gua, sieur de Monts**, founded

the first real French colony in North America. It was christened Acadia *(Acadie)*, a term probably derived from the word "Arcadia" (the name of a region in ancient Greece), which the explorer Verrazano had already used to designate this part of the North American coast.

In March 1604, de Monts set out from the port of Le Havre, in France, for Acadia; he was accompanied by about 80 men, including Samuel de Champlain, who would found the settlement of Québec a few years later. De Monts and his men decided to spend their first winter on the little island of Sainte-Croix, at the mouth of the Sainte-Croix River (in the present-day state of Maine), in the Bay of Fundy. This proved to be an error in judgment, because as soon as winter set in, the men could no longer cross the strait between the island and the continent to go hunting, cut firewood or find potable water. At least 35 of the original colonists perished before spring arrived.

As soon as the ice melted, the survivors hurried off to make another attempt at colonization somewhere else. They crossed the Bay of Fundy and settled at the mouth of the river now known as the Annapolis, where they founded the colony of Port-Royal (in present-day Nova Scotia). The site had a safe, natural harbour and was advantageously located on the territory of a Mi'kmaq

Mi'kmaq cradle

Portrait

The Beothuks

Before the arrival of European colonists, Newfoundland was inhabited by the Beothuks, an Aboriginal people that settled in the area around 200 AD. Unfortunately, this Aboriginal group was totally decimated by the early 19th century.

First weakened by diseases brought by the Europeans, they were then forced out of their ancestral lands by the arrival of the Mi'kmaq, themselves displaced by the colonists. The Beothuks found themselves with limited access to the sea, their primary means of subsistence, and they slowly died out. Shawnawdithit, the last known Beothuk, died of tuberculosis in 1829, bringing with her the last of their secrets.

community that was friendly towards French settlers. Its chief, **Membertou**, was in favour of trading with France, believing that his people could thereby increase their power by acting as commercial intermediaries between the Europeans and other Aboriginal peoples. Before long, a close personal relationship had developed between Membertou and one of the colony's most important officers, Baron **Jean de Biencourt de Poutrincourt**. Without the direct assistance of the Mi'kmaq, Port-Royal probably never would have existed.

In France, however, the settlers' efforts made little impression on Henry IV, who, in the spring of 1607, cancelled the fur-trading monopoly he had granted to de Monts. In the wake of this royal decree, Port-Royal was temporarily abandoned only to be re-inhabited some time later, mainly as a result of Baron de Poutrincourt's efforts. In order to start colonizing Port-Royal again, de Poutrincourt joined forces with wealthy French Catholics, promising to try to convert the Aboriginals to Christianity. In 1610, he left the French port of Dieppe accompanied by a priest named **Jessé Flesché** and about 20 men. Upon arriving at Port-Royal in June, he found the settlement he had abandoned three years earlier almost entirely intact. In an effort to satisfy the baron's Catholic allies, Jessé Flesché baptised some 20 Mi'kmaqs, including Membertou, who were quite cooperative, apparently consider-

ing their conversion to be a mere adjunct to their own traditional religious beliefs. In France, however, news of the Aboriginals' conversion was greeted with such great enthusiasm that Jesuit missionaries **Pierre Biard** and **Edmond Massé**, along with about 40 men, came to bolster the population of Port-Royal the following year.

Nevertheless, sustaining the French presence along this part of the North American coast was never an easy task. Due to its location, isolated from both France and New France (present-day Québec), the settlement was particularly vulnerable to attacks from Great Britain and its fledgling colonies farther south along the Atlantic coast. In 1613, an adventurer from Virginia named **Samuel Argall** seized Port-Royal and drove out most of the colonists. It wasn't until 1632, with the **Treaty of Saint-Germain-en-Laye**, that France was able to regain possession of Acadia.

This episode was but the first of a long series in which the Acadians were often the primary victims of the rivalry between the French and British empires. Acadia fell into British hands again in 1654, and was returned to the French in 1667 under the Treaty of Breda. The British seized Acadia once more in 1690, in the wake of a naval attack led by General Phips, and then again relinquished it to the French in 1697, under the

Treaty of Ryswick. Finally, in 1710, Acadia was appropriated by the British once and for all. In 1713, its status as a British colony was confirmed by the **Treaty of Utrecht**.

During this time, the little colony continued to grow. Most of the original settlers, who had arrived in the 1630s, 1640s and 1670s, came from the southern part of the Loire valley, mainly from Poitou. The Acadians quickly became self-sufficient, supporting themselves through farming, breeding livestock, fishing and hunting as well as through trade. They initially remained in the immediate vicinity of Port-Royal, but were then attracted by the excellent farmlands along the Bay of Fundy, where they established new settlements in the 1670s and 1680s. The most important of these was Grand-Pré, on the Minas Basin. The Acadians were successful as farmers because they managed to develop an ingenious system of dikes and *aboiteaux* (sluice gates) that made it possible to drain excellent farmlands and protect them from the tides of the Bay of Fundy.

The Deportation

With the signing of the Treaty of Utrecht in 1713, Acadia came under British rule once and for all. This loss, along with that of the port of Plaisance in Newfoundland and Britain's control of Hudson Bay, weakened France's position in North America

considerably. To counterbalance the British presence on the Atlantic coast, French authorities decided to develop Île Saint-Jean (Prince Edward Island) and Île Royale (Cape Breton Island), which they still controlled. The first became a settlement devoted solely to agriculture. On Île Royale, however, France erected the largest network of fortifications in its North American possessions—the fortified city of **Louisbourg**, which had 10,000 inhabitants at its peak.

The struggle between Great Britain and France for control over North America put the Acadians in a difficult position. Having French roots, they were subjected to increasing pressure from colonial authorities anxious to make them swear an unconditional vow of allegiance to Great Britain. The Acadian leaders were willing to accept British authority, provided that they would be allowed to remain neutral in the event of a conflict between the two colonial powers. British governor **Philips** (1729-1731) accepted the Acadians' neutrality. Life went on under the British regime, and the Acadian population grew from about 2,500 inhabitants in 1713 to some 14,000 by 1755.

During the first half of the 18th century, however, there continued to be a great deal of tension between the two colonial powers, and a face-off for control of North America was clearly imminent. In

1745, troops from New England scored a decisive blow with the swift and stunning capture of the fortress of Louisbourg on Île Royale. To the great disappointment of British colonists, however, Louisbourg was returned to France three years later under the **Treaty of Aix-la-Chapelle**. In 1749, in an effort to reinforce their hold over Nova Scotia (formerly Acadia), whose population was still mostly Acadian, 2,500 British soldiers landed on the Atlantic coast and built the citadel of Halifax. The French accelerated their own war preparations by erecting Fort Beauséjour (New Brunswick) on the Chignecto Isthmus in 1750. The British responded the following year by building Fort Lawrence just 3km east of Fort Beauséjour.

Given the context, British authorities found the Acadians' neutrality increasingly troubling. They feared that the Acadians would help the French in one way or another in the event of a conflict. In 1755, the Legislative Council of Nova Scotia, led by **Charles Lawrence**, decided to settle the issue once and for all by ordering the deportation of all Acadians. Between 1755 and 1762, the majority of Acadian villages were destroyed: houses and churches were burned and livestock was confiscated. About half of the 14,000 Acadians were put on boats and deported to England, France and other parts of North America. The others managed to escape, seeking refuge in the woods. When the signing of the **Treaty of Paris** brought the war between France and Britain to an end in 1763, Acadia had already been wiped from the map. Under the terms of the treaty, France ceded New France and its other North American possessions, including Île Saint-Jean and Île Royale, to Great Britain. Of her empire in North America, France kept only the two small islands of Saint-Pierre and Miquelon, as well as fishing rights on the coasts of Newfoundland.

The deportation scattered the Acadians, and in many cases split up families. Many took up residence along the eastern and northeastern coasts of New Brunswick, which now has the highest proportion of Acadians in the Maritimes. Others settled elsewhere in the Maritimes, in Québec, in Louisiana, where they would become the ancestors of today's **Cajuns**, and elsewhere in North America or Europe. It would take the Acadians of the Maritimes more than a century to establish their own institutions once again.

The Arrival of the Loyalists

Following the Franco-British wars for control of North America, another conflict had significant repercussions on the Atlantic provinces. The **American Revolution**, in the beginning at least, was a veritable civil war that

pitted supporters of independence against the Loyalists who wished to maintain colonial ties with Great Britain. Over 350,000 of these Loyalists became active participants in the conflict by joining the British forces. In 1783, after a long, agonizing battle, the British admitted defeat. The victory of the American revolutionary forces prompted about 100,000 Loyalists to leave the United States to seek refuge elsewhere. Of this number, approximately 35,000 chose the Atlantic provinces as their new home.

Within a few months, the impact of this massive influx of new colonists was felt all over the region, whose population had previously been no more than 20,000. The major ports of entry for the Loyalists were Shelburne, on the Atlantic coast of Nova Scotia, and the mouth of the St. John River, on the Bay of Fundy. Shelburne suddenly became one of the most populated towns in North America, with about 9,000 inhabitants. More than 14,000 Loyalists headed up the St. John River in New Brunswick, most settling on the fertile lands of the valley. Several other ports, including St. Andrews by-the-Sea, St. Stephen, Annapolis Royal and Halifax, were also flooded by large numbers of Loyalists.

The political and economic repercussions of this influx of Loyalists varied from one region to another, depending on the size of the local population. For

example, the several hundred Loyalists who settled on Île Saint-Jean (renamed Prince Edward Island in 1798) and on Cape Breton Island quickly blended into the existing population, causing very few changes. In New Brunswick, however, the Loyalists represented more than three quarters of the population and soon occupied positions of political and economic power. In Nova Scotia, where they made up about half of the population, their integration caused a certain degree of friction for the first few years. Be that as it may, the arrival of the Loyalists was a key moment in the history of the Atlantic provinces and radically transformed the profile of the region with a sudden increase in the local population.

The Golden Age and Canadian Confederation

For the first half of the 19th century, the Atlantic provinces experienced an economic boom as well as a remarkable growth in population. In less than a century, the natural growth of the population, combined with substantial immigration (mainly from the British Isles) caused a 10-fold increase in the number of inhabitants.

This population explosion was sustained by a dramatic increase in the region's economic activity, due in large part to the export value of local products. Many people profited from this boom, but merchants, shipowners and shipbuilders were especially well-positioned to amass immense fortunes. Foreign markets were found for many products, including agricultural produce from Prince Edward Island, coal ore from Cape Breton and the Chignecto Isthmus, wooden billets from the area around the Miramichi River and fish from Nova Scotia and Newfoundland. All this exportation was made possible by the large fleet of Atlantic Canada's merchant navy, which crisscrossed the seas of the world. Shipyards could be found in many towns and villages along the coast. This was a glorious era for the region.

The second half of the 19th century, however, proved less prosperous for the region, whose economy gradually slowed down. This decline was caused by a number of different factors, an important one being the development of new technologies in the transport industry. Traditional vessels, until then one of the mainsprings of the local economy, began to face fierce competition from steamships. The era also witnessed the development of the railway, a new, highly efficient transportation network in which Atlantic Canada played only a minor role. The decline of the region's economy and political powers was probably accentuated by the **Canadian Confederation** (1867), which Nova Scotia and New Brunswick joined immediately, de-

spite considerable controversy, followed by Prince Edward Island in 1873. The province of Newfoundland didn't join the Confederation until 1949. Confederation soon led to the creation of a large domestic market, stretching from the Atlantic to the Pacific. The central regions were at an advantage, since they served as transportation and communication centres for the entire country. The political powers of the Atlantic provinces greatly diminished with Canadian Confederation, and their economies became controlled by the central provinces.

The 20th Century

The 20th century was marked by several bursts of economic growth, particularly during the two **World Wars**, in which the region played an important role. Most of the military convoys transporting Canadian troops to Europe set out from the city of Halifax, which is still the Canadian Navy's principal home port in the eastern part of the country. Newfoundland, for its part, was used as a base for the Allied naval and air forces defending the North Atlantic. The period between the two wars was much more difficult for Atlantic Canada, however. The **Great Depression** of the 1930s dealt a crushing blow to the local economy, perhaps hitting harder here than elsewhere in the country, given the region's dependence on the decisionmakers in central Canada.

The most significant political event in the post-war period took place in New Brunswick in the 1960s and 1970s, when the Acadian community was accorded more rights and began to advance economically. In 1968, in the heat of this campaign to promote equality, the New Brunswick government passed the **Official Languages Law**, which required public services to be available in both French and English. The government's efforts had a concrete effect, for Acadians now play a very active role in the economy and politics of the province. In the last decade of the 20th century, however, current events were above all marked by difficulties encountered in certain traditional and important sectors of the local economy. This was particularly true for the fisheries, where a poor management of resources forced authorities to declare a moratorium on the fishing of certain species such as cod. The local economy was seriously affected, especially in Newfoundland and Labrador, a province heavily dependent on fishing. The Atlantic provinces have reacted and are making concerted efforts to diversify their economy and develop new areas of expertise.

Politics and the Economy

Politically speaking, New Brunswick is different from the other Maritime provinces because of its

Official Languages Law, which makes it the only officially bilingual province in Canada. French-speakers make up about 33% of the province's total population, and government services are available here in both French and English. This law, along with the promotion of equality for Acadians in general, has been upheld by every provincial government since the 1960s. However, the Confederation of Regions, a political party opposed to official bilingualism in New Brunswick, has had eight deputies in the province's Legislative Assembly since 1991.

New Brunswick's economy revolves around forestry, the chemical and oil industries, farming, fishing, mining and tourism. The Prime Minister of the province from 1987 to 1997, **Frank McKenna**, was able to boost his province's economy by attracting foreign investments through his dynamic public relations efforts.

The province's extremely efficient telephone system and skilled workforce allowed New Brunswick to persuade several large companies to set up their telephone exchanges here. Also, in recent years, the province's Acadian community has demonstrated a dynamic entrepreneurial spirit. **Bernard Lord**, of the Progressive Conservative Party, is presently premier of the province. The population of New Brunswick totals about 751,449 inhabitants.

Of the four Atlantic provinces, Nova Scotia is the most prosperous and has the most diversified economy. Its capital, Halifax, is the region's main seaport, as well as its most important financial and commercial centre. Halifax is also the Canadian Navy's main home port on the east coast.

The fishing, mining and shipbuilding industries, cornerstones of the local economy for many years, now represent only a small share of the province's gross domestic product. Today, the service and manufacturing sectors predominate. In 1995, the city of Halifax was chosen to host the delegates of the G-7, a union of the seven most economically powerful countries in the world. The premier of Nova Scotia is **John F. Hamm**, of the Progressive Conservative Party. Nova Scotia is the most populous of the Atlantic provinces, with a population of 938,134.

Industrialization only began in Prince Edward Island at the end of the Second World War. Located far from the big urban centres and cut off from the major transportation networks, the island has always been slow to develop a strong manufacturing industry. Hopefully, the newly inaugurated Confederation Bridge, which joins the island to New Brunswick, will remedy some of its problems. Presently, a large portion of the economy is based on agriculture (especially potato farming) as well as the fishing,

tourist and service industries. Prince Edward Island is the least populated province of Canada, with 137,744 inhabitants. The current premier is **Patrick George Binns**, of the Progressive Conservative Party.

Newfoundland and Labrador's economy, still largely dependent on the fisheries, has been hard hit since the government imposed a moratorium on cod fishing. Years of commercial fishing had nearly exhausted the supply of cod in the Grand Banks. Newfoundlanders are frustrated by this situation, since it is difficult for them to exercise control over fishing activities in the Grand Banks, which lie in both Canadian and international waters.

In addition to fishing, the province has a large wood-cutting and -processing industry and one of the biggest iron mines in the world, located in Labrador. Newfoundlanders have also started to capitalize on Labrador's tumultuous rivers by building huge hydroelectric dams. Furthermore, they have high hopes for an offshore drilling operation over 300km from the coast of the island. The Hibernia platform, the biggest ever built, exploits this oilfield, estimated to contain over 600 million barrels of petroleum. The total population of Newfoundland and Labrador is 516,875. The province is currently led by Premier **Danny Williams** of the Conservative Party.

Architecture

Aided by favourable winds, a few Viking boats reached the shores of Newfoundland in the year 1000, carrying hale and hearty fellows with thick, blond mustaches. Before long, these men had built villages near the beaches. Their houses, made of wood and stone, were roofed with thick layers of earth, with thick blankets of wild grass sprouting out of them. Around 1950, archaeologists excavated one of these villages, **L'Anse-aux-Meadows**, in the northern part of Newfoundland. The village then became the object of a restoration campaign and was equipped with its own interpretation centre. Thanks to this discovery, the Atlantic provinces can justly take pride in being home to the oldest European settlement in all of North America.

When the Vikings arrived, Newfoundland's hinterland was inhabited by Aboriginal peoples. Iron objects left by the Vikings were later discovered here. In those days, many nations, such as the Beothuk, survived on fishing and hunting. These nomads would move from one region to another depending on the season and the availability of food, rebuilding their camp each time. They used lightweight materials, like branches and birch bark to make **wigwams**. The Labrador Inuit, for their part, lived in dome-shaped **igloos** made of ice and snow during winter and in tents made of animal hides during summer. Nowadays, these traditional dwellings are reconstructed periodically for folk festivals. In the 19th century, missionaries encouraged Aboriginals to settle in one place. They now live in the west, in small aluminum-roofed wooden houses, clustered in villages on federal reserves.

Once the Vikings left, there were no new European settlements in North America for over 500 years, at which point the Spanish and the Portuguese started establishing a foothold in the south, and Basque and French fishers set up camp on the coast of Newfoundland and in the St. Lawrence River Valley. The few remaining traces of their annual summer stays are few, and little effort has been made to turn them into attractions. It wasn't until 1605, with the founding of the colony of Port-Royal, that any permanent architecture was erected in the Atlantic provinces.

The **Abitation de Port-Royal** has been successfully reconstructed (Annapolis Royal, Nova Scotia, see p 152). Its main buildings, with their walls made of squared-off tree trunks, are grouped around a courtyard with a drinking well in the middle. They have few doors and windows and are clustered together to ward off the cold, the wind coming off the sea and possible attacks by Aboriginals or the British. These buildings fall into the medieval tradition, with their high–boarded roofs and massive chimneys made of big stones gathered from the surrounding fields. A palisade ran along one edge of the site, so that the men could safely leave the central courtyard to watch out for the enemy. The peasants who worked the surrounding land lived in hovels with walls made of posts planted straight into the ground instead of foundations. The only stone portion of these structures was a central hearth.

The 18th century saw the emergence of much more substantial buildings. The French, after losing part of Acadia to the British in 1713, consolidated their position in their remaining territory along the coast. Meanwhile, the British wasted no time founding villages in Acadia, thus reinforcing their own hold. The French built the **fortress of Louisbourg** at the mouth of the Gulf of St. Lawrence. Much more than a simple fort, Louisbourg was a veritable fortified town with a large harbour. Begun under the French Regency, it was not completed until 1745. The Royal Treasury spent over three million *livres* on the project, the largest ever undertaken in New France. At its peak, in 1745, the town had some 10,000 inhabitants—2,000 more than Québec City, the capital of the French colony. Vauban-style ramparts with bastions and baroque gates made of hewn stone hemmed in a town that was not just a cluster of half-timbered houses; it had some prestigious buildings, like the king's barracks, a long rectangle of rubble stone and French bricks in the spirit of Louis XV. Unfortunately, Louisbourg was destroyed by the English army during the French and Indian War (or Seven Years' War). Thanks to archaeological excavations begun in 1960, a portion of the fortress was rebuilt and is open to the public (see p 184).

To counterbalance Louisbourg, the British founded Halifax in 1749. Right from its first few years of existence, its civilian architecture was far more impressive than its meager fortifications, thus conveying the confidence and strength of the British colonies, who had little fear of the feeble flotillas sent out by the French. The landscape was dominated by several white, wooden, Georgian-style churches similar to those already scattered across New England. These buildings are as elegant as they are simple. **St. Paul Church** in Halifax, built in 1750, is representative of this era (see p 127). The comfortable

houses, for their part, all had sash windows subdivided into little squares.

With the massive influx of Loyalists in 1783, the population of the mainland maritime territories doubled. These new arrivals, who came from urban areas, sought to refine the local architecture even further by adorning the facades with Palladian decorations made of carved wood, for example. Palladian windows (a central arched window with a small, rectangular window on either side) are definitely the most characteristic feature of this style, known as the Federal Style in the United States. **St. George's Church**, in Halifax, built between 1800 and 1827, is one of the most original buildings of this period.

In the early 19th century, the region's economic prosperity, accompanied by a demographic and political weight it has since lost, led to the construction of huge public and government buildings with freestone facades.

Province House (see p 127), in Halifax (Nova Scotia) and in Charlottetown (Prince Edward Island) (see p 200) are among the handsomest buildings from this era in Canadian history. These edifices, which would not look out of place in Dublin or Edinburgh, feature a harmonious blend of Georgian, Palladian and neoclassical styles. During this same period, wealthy shipowners and ship's captains built luxurious houses in the countryside (**Prescott House Museum** in Starrs Point, Nova Scotia, see p 151).

Isolated Newfoundland marched to its own beat. Ill-suited to farming, its territory remained largely uninhabited, with only a few fishing villages founded by Irish immigrants punctuating its rocky shores. The first stone houses here, topped by gambrel roofs covered with bluish slate, are reminiscent of those of the Emerald Isle.

In 1830, after a brief period of economic diversification, the Atlantic provinces turned once and for all toward the sea and its resources, leading to the emergence of a **vernacular architecture** that reflected the region's close ties to the Atlantic Ocean. Wooden fishing shacks covered with cedar shingles or clapboard sprang up along the beaches. These buildings often stood on piles made out of tree trunks, which were pounded by the surf at high tide. **Lighthouses** shaped like truncated pyramids were built on the

Province House – Halifax

capes to help cope with the rise in maritime traffic. These high towers covered with white clapboards punctuate the shoreline from the U.S. border to southern Labrador.

Finally, the attics of houses were modified to accommodate bow windows and wide dormer windows shaped like triptychs. The widow's walk—a railed rooftop platform—also became a fairly common feature. These modifications made it easier for local residents to observe the comings and goings of the boats. The lady of the house would thus know if her husband, the captain, would be home for dinner—or ever.

In the second half of the 19th century, Victorian architecture quickly came into fashion in towns inhabited by recent British immigrants. These people's affection for their beloved Albion was reflected in their choice of styles and architects. Gothic Revival was the style *par excellence* for churches, as evidenced so beautifully by the **Christ Church Cathedral** (1853) in Fredericton, New Brunswick (see p 54), with its ogival arches and tall steeple atop its transept. It was designed by **Frank Wills**, a native of Salisbury, England, and is not unlike the cathedral of the same name he designed for the Anglican community of Montréal.

Christ Church Cathedral –Fredericton

The **Anglican Cathedral of St. John the Baptist**, in St. John's, Newfoundland and Labrador, for its part, is in a class of its own, having been designed by the celebrated English architect **Sir George Gilbert Scott**, whose many other credits include the Albert Memorial and the Foreign Office, both in London.

The Renaissance Revival style managed to hold its own in the company of all these impressive Gothic Revival buildings. The projecting cornices, varied rustications and little columns adorning many of the commercial buildings in St. John, New Brunswick and Halifax, Nova Scotia (the **Historic Properties**, see p 128) are all characteristic of this style. The Second Empire style, for its part, was used to lend a certain Parisian chic to the mansions of wealthy neighbourhoods. Their mansard roofs, topped with wrought- or cast-iron ornamentation, are visible between the stately trees lining the peaceful streets of Fredericton, New Brunswick and Charlottetown, Prince Edward Island.

The influence of the late 19th-century institutional architecture of Québec is clearly evident in those areas inhabited by Acadians – mainly in the northern part of New Brunswick. The rusticated limestone facing of the colleges, the silvery steeples of the churches and the wraparound porches of the presbyteries are the major distinguishing fea

Algonquin Hotel – St. Andrews by-the-Sea

tures of this kind of architecture. Around the same time, the Nova Scotians of Cape Breton Island were importing a style of architecture with a strong Scottish flavour, characterized by red and beige sandstone facing, stepped gables and fanciful gargoyles.

As the 19th century marched on, American architecture gained more and more ground in the Atlantic provinces. The designs of Downing and Davis, published in the middle of the century, inspired more than one builder. These catalogues prompted homeowners to adopt the tastes of Midwestern Americans, adorning their cornices and verandas with charming, lacy woodwork of medieval or Italian inspiration.

It should be noted that the Maritime provinces (New Brunswick, Nova Scotia and Prince Edward Island) were attracting more and more summer visitors from both the United States and from the other Canadian provinces. Starting in 1880, the region saw the emergence of an architecture modelled onthe seaside resorts

found along the east coast of the United States. **St. Andrews by-the-Sea** (New Brunswick) and **Summerside** (Prince Edward Island) boast the finest examples. These villages suddenly found themselves graced with huge wooden summer homes in the Queen Anne, Shingle or Stick styles, designed by Montréal architects like brothers **Edward** and **William S. Maxwell** or local architects like **William Crithlow Harris**. These houses had multiple gables and wide, wraparound porches that served as additional rooms during warm weather.

The harsh climate of Newfoundland, however, did not attract summer vacationers. Furthermore, the islanders had to be quite creative in their efforts to protect themselves from the wind and cold. They designed easy-to-build, cube-shaped houses which were covered with multicoloured clapboards.

Most of these houses were built right up against the sidewalk. Some have bow windows, lending the winding, sloping streets of St. John's a friendly air.

The first half of the 20th century was a difficult period for all the Atlantic provinces, which no longer saw the sort of large-scale development that was taking place elsewhere in Canada. Still, a few significant Tudor Revival (the **Algonquin Hotel** in St. Andrews-by-the-Sea, New Brunswick), Arts and Crafts (the **Hydrostone** quarter in Halifax, Nova Scotia), and Art Deco (**John M. Lyle**'s **Bank of Nova Scotia** in Halifax) buildings were erected during this time.

Between 1960 and 1980, a massive investment of provincial and federal funds, combined with a profound malaise induced by the success of big Canadian cities like Montréal and Toronto, led the region to squander its precious architectural heritage.

Many old buildings were replaced by nondescript modern structures designed to house regional branches of companies whose real interests lay elsewhere. Fortunately, this trend started to reverse itself in 1980, as residents of the Atlantic provinces started to become aware of the treasure they possessed in their old architecture. Since then, the focus has been on smaller-scale projects that can be integrated into the existing framework. Some of the finest examples of this new approach are **Market Square** in St. John, New Brunswick, and the Historic Properties in Halifax, Nova Scotia.

Arts and Culture

Visual Arts

Over the years, the three Maritime provinces have established prestigious institutions in order to encourage local artistic expression and promote greater public awareness of the arts. Thanks to the patronage of **Lord Beaverbrook** in 1958, Fredericton was endowed with the remarkable **Beaverbrook Art Gallery**, which houses the works of some of the greatest artists from the Maritimes, as well as from elsewhere in Canada and abroad. Particularly noteworthy is an impressive painting by Salvador Dalí.

In Moncton, the excellent **art gallery of the Université de Moncton** showcases the works of contemporary Acadian artists.

The **art gallery** of Sackville's **Mount Allison University** in Southern New Brunswick presents several works by **Alex Colville**, an internationally renowned painter from the area.

In 1964, the **Confederation Centre of the Arts**, a large arts complex that includes theatres, an art gallery and a public library, was inaugurated in Charlottetown, Prince Edward Island. Concerts, plays and dance productions are presented here, and a number of works by local and national artists, including portrait artist **Robert Harris**, are exhibited in the gallery.

In 1975, the **Nova Scotia Art Gallery**, which houses the most impressive art collection in the Maritimes, was founded in Halifax. Its collection of paintings and sculptures from many different eras is internationally renowned.

Museums and Historic Sites

Visitors can relive some of the major chapters in the history of the Atlantic provinces thanks to a wide array of great museums and historic sites. Some of the most impressive sites include in a rebuilt Viking settlement from the year 1000 in Anse aux Meadows, Newfoundland; the reconstruction of Nova Scotia's Abitation de Port-Royal, the first permanent French settlement in North America, founded in 1605; the reconstructed Fortress of Louisbourg in Cape Breton, Nova Scotia, which, from 1719 to 1758, was the largest fortified town in New France; the village of **King's Landing**, New Brunswick, an amazing reconstruction of a 19th-

century Loyalist village located on the shores of the St. John River; the **Village Historique acadien** in New Brunswick, where visitors can learn about 19th-century Acadian life by visiting some 20 period buildings; and the **Halifax Citadel**, in Nova Scotia, which best demonstrates the strategic importance of this town during the last two centuries.

In addition, several interesting museums are dedicated to the history of the region's fishing and marine industries. The two major museums of this kind are the **Maritime Museum of the Atlantic** in Halifax, and the **Fisheries Museum of the Atlantic** in Lunenburg, Nova Scotia.

What is also surprising in the Atlantic provinces is the number of small museums devoted to local history; you can find some in the smallest of villages.

Theatre

Throughout the years, several high-calibre professional theatre companies have been founded in this region. Since 1969, the **New Brunswick Theatre Company**, the only English-language theatre company in the province, has produced modern and classical plays at the Playhouse, in Fredericton. Plays are mostly presented during the winter months.

The Halifax-based **Neptune Theatre**, the oldest professional theatre company in Canada, also produces classical and modern plays from both Canadian and international repertoires.

In Wolfville, Nova Scotia, theatre-lovers can enjoy great plays during the summer at the **Atlantic Theatre Festival**, which has gained a solid reputation in the past few years.

Plays are also presented during the summer months in other small towns, such as Chester, Nova Scotia, and Victoria and Georgetown, Prince Edward Island. While in Charlottetown, many visitors attend a performance of *Anne of Green Gables*, a play based on the famous novel by **Lucy Maud Montgomery**. For more than three decades now, it has been featured at the **Confederation Centre of the Arts** during the summer.

Music

A number of music festivals are held during the summer months throughout the Atlantic provinces, allowing music-lovers to enjoy great shows. In May and June, the **Scotia Music Festival**, held at various sites in Halifax, is the place to be for fans of classical music.

The **International Baroque Music Festival**, for its part, takes place during the third week of July in the enchanting setting of St. Cécile Church, on Lamèque Island, New Brunswick, and offers very interesting programs.

Major jazz festivals are held in Moncton in early July and in Halifax during the second week of the same month. The **By The Sea** festival, held in August in Saint John, New Brunswick, is a fantastic way to discover Canadian music, both contemporary and traditional.

Film

Halifax's film industry is in full growth, and every year, the city hosts the **Atlantic Film Festival**, the largest event of its kind in Atlantic Canada. This festival features Canadian and foreign films.

Literature

Lucy Maud Montgomery, author of *Anne of Green Gables*, is undoubtedly the most widely renowned local English-language writer. Most of her stories take place on Prince Edward Island, where she was born.

Acadian Culture

Over the last 30 years, New Brunswick's Acadian culture has developed at an unprecedented speed, not only in the fields of music and literature, but also in visual arts and cinema. Since the 1960s, artistic expressions of all kinds have been the greatest Acadian ambassador to the world.

Some of the artists that have made their mark

include musicians **Donat Lacroix**, **Calixte Duguay**, **Édith Butler**, **Angèle Arsenault** and **Roch Voisine** (from the Madawaska region), the musical group **1755**, author **Antonine Maillet**, who won the prestigious Goncourt prize in 1979 for *Pélagie la Charette*, sculptor **Marie-Hélène Allain**, filmmaker **Phil Comeau**, and **Hermé-négilde Chiasson**, a remarkable artist whose works include everything from movies and theatre to poetry, novels and paintings.

Among other things, the cultural vitality of Acadians has resulted in the appearance of several art galleries, publishing houses that represent Acadian authors, the **Théâtre Populaire d'Acadie**, in Caraquet, and the **Théâtre l'Escaouette**, in Moncton.

In the summer of 2004, Nova Scotia hosted the third **World Acadian Congress**. This great gathering, which changes venues every five years, showcases and highlights the various aspects of modern Acadian culture. The 2004 congress coincided with celebrations marking the 400th anniversary of Acadia; the Acadian people's odyssey having begun in 1604 with a small settlement on the shores of the present-day Bay of Fundy.

Table of Distances (km)
Via the Shortest Route

©ULYSSES

From \ To	Augusta (Maine)	Charlottetown (P.E.I.)	Corner Brook (Nfld.)	Edmundston (N.B.)	Fredericton (N.B.)	Halifax (N.S.)	Labrador City (Nfld.)	Moncton (N.B.)	Montréal (Que.)	Québec City (Que.)	St. Anthony (Nfld.)	Saint John (N.B.)	St. John's (Nfld.)	Souris (P.E.I.)	Summerside (P.E.I.)	Sydney (N.S.)
Charlottetown (P.E.I.)	820															
Corner Brook (Nfld.)	1530	772														
Edmundston (N.B.)	520	676	1389													
Fredericton (N.B.)	434	373	1095	289												
Halifax (N.S.)	904	280	835	760	415											
Labrador City (Nfld.)	1454	1345	2055	944	12234	2240										
Moncton (N.B.)	622	175	901	475	200	275	1153									
Montréal (Que.)	484	1200	1916	540	835	1250	1284	1025								
Québec City (Que.)	352	960	1694	313	585	982	1062	785	270							
St. Anthony (Nfld.)	1989	1231	468	1850	1554	629	2513	1359	2375	2153						
Saint John (N.B.)	402	344	1054	400	111	315	1334	146	931	709	1512					
St. John's (Nfld.)	1715	957	687	1572	1281	1020	2240	1086	2101	1879	629	1239				
Souris (P.E.I.)	898	77	795	755	463	288	1422	268	1284	1062	1253	421	980			
Summerside (P.E.I.)	785	78	849	639	350	325	1310	156	1171	949	1308	308	1034	154		
Sydney (N.S.)	1152	367	429	1008	695	422	1676	497	1520	1280	888	675	614	416	476	
Yarmouth (N.S.)	363	574	1144	577	288	344	1511	323	711	606	1602	177	1329	597	486	766

Example: the distance between Halifax (N.S.) and St. John (N.B.) is 315km.

Practical Information

The information

in this chapter will help visitors plan their trip to Canada's Atlantic provinces.

Entrance Formalities

Passport and Visa

A valid passport is usually sufficient for most visitors planning to stay less than three months in Canada. U.S. citizens do not need a passport, but it is, however, a good form of identification. U.S. citizens and citizens of Western Europe do not need a visa. For a complete list of countries whose citizens require a visa, see the **Canadian Citizenship and Immigration** Web site *(www.cic.gc.ca)* or contact the Canadian embassy or consulate nearest you.

Extended Visits

Visitors must submit a request **in writing** to extend their visit **before** the expiration of the first three months of their visit or of their visa (the date is usually written on your passport) to an Immigration Canada office. To make a request you must have a valid passport, a return ticket, proof of sufficient funds to cover your stay, as well as a $75 non-refundable filing fee. In some cases (work, study), however, the request must be made **before** arriving in Canada. Contact **Canadian Citizenship and Immigration**'s Web site *(www.cic.gc.ca)*.

Customs

If you are bringing gifts into Atlantic Canada, remember that certain restrictions apply:

Smokers (the minimum age is 19 in each of the Atlantic provinces) can bring a maximum of 200 cigarettes, 50 cigars, 400 g of tobacco, or 200 tobacco sticks.

For **wine,** the limit is 1.5 litres; for **liquor**, 1.14 litres. The limit for **beer** is 24 355ml cans or 341ml bottles. Remember that you must be of legal drinking age (19) to bring these items into the Atlantic provinces.

There are very strict rules regarding the importation of **plants, flowers,** and other **vegetation**; it is therefore not advisable to bring any of these types of products into the country.

If you are travelling with your **pet,** you will need a rabies vaccination certificate. For more information on travelling with animals, plants or food, contact the

Canadian Food Inspection Agency (*www.cfia-acia. agr.ca*) or the Canadian embassy or consulate nearest you before your departure for Canada.

Finally, visitors from out of the country may be reimbursed for certain taxes paid on purchases in Canada (see p 32).

Embassies and Consulates

Canadian Embassies and Consulates Abroad

Denmark

Canadian Embassy
Kr. Bernikowsgade,
1105 Copenhagen K, DK
☎(45) 33.48.32.00
↝(45) 33.48.32.20

Germany

Canadian Consulate General
Internationales Handelzentrum
Friedrichstrasse 95, 12th floor
10117 Berlin
☎(30) 20.312-0
↝(30) 20.312-121

Great Britain

Canada High Commission
Macdonald House,
One Grosvenor Square,
London, W1X 0AB
☎(207) 258-6600
↝(207) 258-6333

Netherlands

Canadian Embassy
Sophialaan 7, 2514 JP
La Haye, NL
☎(70) 311-1600
↝(70) 311-1620

Sweden

Canadian Embassy
Tegelbacken 4, 7th floor,
Stockholm
☎(8) 453-3000
↝(8) 453-3016

United States

Canadian Embassy
501 Pennsylvania Ave. NW
Washington, DC, 20001
☎(202) 682-1740
↝(202) 682-7726

Canadian Consulates General
1175 Peachtree St. NE
100 Colony Square, Suite 1700,
Atlanta, Georgia, 30361-6205
☎(404) 532-2000
↝(404) 532-2050

Three Copley Place, Suite 400
Boston, Massachusetts, 02116
☎(617) 262-3760
↝(617) 262-3415

Two Prudential Plaza, 180 N
Stetson Ave., Suite 2400,
Chicago, Illinois, 60601
☎(312) 616-1860
↝(312) 616-1877

St. Paul Place, Suite 1700,
750 N. St. Paul St., Dallas,
Texas, 75201-3247
☎(214) 922-9806
↝(214) 922-9815

600 Renaissance Center, Suite
1100, Detroit, Michigan,
48234-1798
☎(313) 567-2340
↝(313) 567-2164

550 South Hope St., 9th floor
Los Angeles, California,
90071-2627
☎(213) 346-2700
↝(213) 346-2767

701 Fourth Ave. S., 9th floor,
Minneapolis, Minnesota,
55415-1899
☎(612) 333-7486
↝(612) 332-4061

1251 Avenue of the Americas,
Concourse Level, New York, NY
10020-1175
☎(212) 596-1628
↝(212) 596-1790

3000 HSBC Center, Buffalo, NY
14203-2884.
☎(716) 858-9500
↝(716) 852-4340

412 Plaza 600, Sixth and
Stewart Sts., Seattle, Washington
98101-1286
☎(206) 442-1777
↝(206) 443-9662

Foreign Consulates Closest to Atlantic Canada

None of the following countries are represented in Atlantic Canada. Following are the closest consulates, in Montréal, Québec.

Denmark

Consulate General
One Pl.-Ville-Marie, 35th floor,
Montréal, Québec, H3B 4M4
☎(514) 877-3060

Germany

1250 Boul. René-Lévesque
Ouest, Suite 4315, Montréal,
Québec H3B 4X1
☎(514) 931-2277
↝(514) 931-7239

Great Britain

1000 de la Gauchetière Ouest
Suite 4200, Montréal, Québec
H3B 3A7
☎*(514) 866-5863*
⇋*(514) 866-0202*

Netherlands

1002 Rue Sherbrooke Ouest,
Suite 2201, Montréal, Québec
H3A 3L6
☎*(514) 849-4247*
⇋*(514) 849-8260*

Sweden

1170 rue Peel, Montréal,
Québec, H3B 4S8
☎*(514) 397-4444*

United States

Place Félix-Martin
1155 Rue Saint-Alexandre,
Montréal, Québec
☎*(514) 398-9695*
⇋*(514) 398-9748*
Mailing address:
C.P. 65, Station Desjardins,
Montréal, Québec, H5B 1G1

Tourist Information

This guide covers four
provinces: New Brunswick
(N.B.), Nova Scotia (N.S.),
Prince Edward Island
(P.E.I.), and Newfound-
land and Labrador (Nfld.).
Within each province
you will find tourist information offices that can
provide brochures con-
cerning attractions, res-
taurants and hotels. You
can also pick up listings of
bed and breakfasts in the
area.

Tourist Information on the Internet

New Brunswick:
   www.tourismnewbrunswick.ca
   www.gnb.ca

Nova Scotia:
   www.gov.ns.ca
   www.explorens.com
   www.tians.org
   www.novascotia.com

Prince Edward Island:
   www.gov.pe.ca
   www.peiplay.com

Newfoundland and Labrador:
   www.gov.nf.ca

National Parks of Canada:
   www.parkscanada.ca

New Brunswick

**Department of Tourism
and Parks**
PO Box 12345, Campbellton,
New Brunswick, E3N 3T6
☎*(506) 789-2044 or
800-561-0123*
*www.tourismnbcanada.
com*

Nova Scotia

**Nova Scotia Information
& Reservations**
PO Box 130, Halifax, B3J 2M7
☎*(902) 425-5781 or
800-565-0000*
⇋*(902) 453-8401*
www.novascotia.com

Prince Edward Island

Visitors Centre
PO Box 940, Charlottetown,
C1A 7M5
☎*(902) 368-4444 or
888-734-7529*
⇋*(902) 368-4438*
*www.gov.pe.ca/visitors
guide/*

Newfoundland and Labrador

**Newfoundland and
Labrador Tourism**
PO Box 8730, St. John's, A1B 4J6
☎*(709) 729-2830 or
800-563-6353*
⇋*(709) 729-0057*
www.gov.nf.ca

Practical Information

Finding Your Way Around

By Plane

European visitors will arrive in the Atlantic provinces in Halifax, since it is the only airport that regularly receives international flights; airports in New Brunswick, Prince Edward Island, and Newfoundland and Labrador occasionally receive flights from the United States.

From Montréal, **Air Canada** and **WestJet** offer direct flights to Halifax (N.S.), Fredericton (N.B.), Moncton (N.B.) and Saint John (N.B.), as well as a flight with a stop-over for Charlottetown (P.E.I.).

For more information:

Air Canada
☎888-247-2262
www.aircanada.ca

Air Canada Tango
☎800-315-1390
www.flytango.com

Canjet
☎800-809-7777
www.canjet.com

WestJet
☎888-937-8538
www.westjet.com

Inter-Provincial Flights

Flying within the Atlantic provinces is by far the most expensive mode of transportation; however, some airline companies, especially the regional ones, regularly offer special rates (off season, short

stays). It is always wise to shop around and compare prices.

Airports

Following are the main airports in Atlantic Canada. All are mainly served by Air Canada and WestJet, though a few are served by some of the other airlines listed above.

Nova Scotia

Halifax International Airport
40km north of the city, Rte. 102, Exit 6
☎(902) 873-4422
⇒(902) 873-4750
www.halifaxairport.com
Halifax International Airport is the largest airport in the Atlantic provinces. There is a currency exchange office open everyday from 7am to 9pm. Car-rental companies have offices in the airport. Taxis and limousines offer transportation to downtown for about $30. A shuttle bus makes the trip from the airport to downtown about every hour (*$11*).

Sydney Airport
280 Airport Rd.
☎(902) 564-7720
www.sydneyairportauthor ity. com

New Brunswick

Fredericton Airport
16km from the city, Lincoln Rd.
☎(506) 460-0920
www.frederictonairport.ca
Fredericton's airport does not have an exchange office. Four car-rental companies have offices here. Taxis offer transportation to downtown.

Greater Moncton International Airport
12km east of the city, 777 Aviation Dr., Dieppe
☎(506) 856-5444
⇒(506) 856-5431
www.gma.ca
Moncton's airport does not have an exchange office. Four car rental companies have offices here. Taxis and a shuttle bus offer transportation to downtown.

Saint John Airport
4180 Loch Lemond
☎(506) 638-5555
www.saintjohnairport. com
Saint John's airport does not have an exchange office. Five car-rental companies have offices here. Taxis offer transportation to downtown for around $10.

Prince Edward Island

Charlottetown Airport
250 Maple Hills Ave.
☎(902) 566-7997
⇒(902) 566-7929
www.flypei.com
Charlottetown's Airport does not have an exchange office. Four car-rental companies have offices here. Taxis offer transportation to downtown for about $10.

Newfoundland and Labrador

St. John's International Airport
38 Pearson St.
☎(709) 758-8510 or 866-758-8581
www.stjohnsairport.com
St. John's has the largest airport in the province, located 6km from downtown. There are regular direct flights between

St. John's and some of the major Canadian cities, such as Halifax, Montréal and Toronto, among others.

By Car

Considering the large distances to be covered and the lack of good public transportation systems, the easiest way to tour the Atlantic provinces is by car. Furthermore, the roads are generally in good condition.

Things to Consider

Driver's License: As a general rule, foreign driver's licenses are valid for six months from the arrival date in Canada.

Pedestrians: Drivers in the Atlantic provinces are very respectful of pedestrians, and willingly stop to give them the right of way, even in big cities. Crosswalks are usually indicated with a yellow sign. When driving, pay special attention that there is no one about to cross near these signs.

Turning **right on a red light** when the way is clear is permitted in the Atlantic provinces.

When a **school bus** (usually yellow in colour) has stopped and has its signals flashing, you must come to a complete stop, no matter what direction you are travelling in. Failing to stop at the flashing signals is considered a serious offense and carries a heavy penalty.

Wearing of **seatbelts** in the front and back seats is mandatory at all times.

There are no **tolls** on highways in Atlantic Canada. There is an occasional toll for bridges; note that there is a major toll to cross the Confederation Bridge to P.E.I. (see p 196).

The **speed limit** on highways is 100km/h. The speed limit on secondary highways is 90km/h, and 50km/h in urban areas.

Winter Driving: Though roads are generally well plowed, particular caution is recommended. Watch for violent winds and snow drifts and banks. In some regions, gravel is used to increase traction, so drive carefully. Remember to keep a brush and ice scraper in your car at all times.

Gas Stations: Gasoline prices are less expensive than in Europe. However, due to hidden taxes, gas prices are considerably higher than those in the United States and in Western Canada. Some gas stations (especially in the downtown areas) might ask for payment in advance as a security measure, especially after 11pm.

Car Rentals

The best way to get a good price for car a rental is to reserve well in advance. Many travel agencies have agreements with the major car rental companies (Avis, Budget, Hertz, National) and offer good values; contracts often include added bonuses (reduced ticket prices for shows, etc.).

When renting a car, find out if the contract includes unlimited kilometres, and check that the insurance provides full coverage (accident, property damage, medical costs for you and your passengers, theft).

Note: To rent a car you must be at least 21 years of age and have had a driver's license for **at least** one year. If you are between the age of 21 and 25, certain companies (for example Avis, Thrifty and Budget) will ask for a $500 deposit, and in some cases will also charge an extra sum for each day you rent the car. These conditions do not apply for those over 25 years of age.

A credit card is extremely useful for the deposit to avoid tying up large sums of money, and can in some cases (gold cards) cover the collision and theft insurance.

Most rental cars come with an automatic transmission, however you can request a car with a manual shift.

Child safety seats cost extra.

Accidents and Emergencies

If you run into trouble on the highway, pull onto the shoulder of the road and turn the hazard lights on. If it is a rental car, contact the rental company as soon as possible. Always

Practical Information

file an accident report. If a disagreement arises over who was at fault in an accident, ask for police help (**☎911**).

By Bus

Besides the car, travelling by bus is the best way to get around. Buses cover most of the major routes and highways of the Atlantic provinces and are relatively inexpensive. Several companies serve the region.

Smoking is forbidden on all lines. Pets are not allowed. Generally, children five years old or younger travel for free and seniors and students are eligible for discounts.

By Train

Travelling by train is not always the cheapest way to get around, however it is a comfortable alternative for long distances. **VIA Rail Canada** offers trips east to New Brunswick and Nova Scotia.

Via Rail
☎888-842-7245
www.viarail.ca

The **Canrailpass** *(☎888-842-7245, www.via.ca)* allows unlimited travel in economy class over 12 days within a one-month period. It is a great and inexpensive way to experience the Canadian landscape.

The Bras d'Or Train

From May to October, VIA Rail offers a land cruise across Nova Scotia aboard the new *Bras d'Or* train, which runs between Sydney, on Cape Breton Island, and Halifax. The Bras d'Or leaves Halifax Tuesdays at 7:30am and arrives at the station in Sydney at 6:15pm. The return trip runs on Wednesdays (departure from Sydney at 7:30am and arrival in Halifax at 6:15pm).

Travel Times
Montreal – Halifax
20 hours

Moncton – Halifax
5 hours

Ferries

The biggest ferry company in the Atlantic provinces is **Marine Atlantic** *(☎800-341-7981, www.marine-atlantic.ca)*. Information on the ferries' schedules can be found at *www.gov. nl.ca/ferryservices*. **The Cat** *(☎888-249-7249, www. catferry.com)* also provides ferry service between several spots in Atlantic Canada. To reach **Newfoundland and Labrador** *(www.gov.nl.ca/ferry services)*, many crossings are possible: North-Sydney (Cape Breton Island, N.S.) to Port-aux-Basques (Nfld.); North-Sydney to Argentia (Nfld.); Goose Bay (Labrador) to Lewisporte (Nfld.). For **Nova Scotia**, certain crossings greatly cut down on driving time: Saint John (N.B.) to Digby (N.S.); Bar Harbour *(Maine, U.S.A.; The Cat; ☎888-249-7249, www.catferry.com)* to Yarmouth (N.S.); Portland (Maine, U.S.A.) to Yarmouth (N.S.).

Since the construction of the Confederation Bridge in 1997, there is no more ferry service between Cape Tourmentine (N.B.) and Borden (P.E.I.); however, there is service to the Wood Islands (P.E.I.) from Pictou (N.S.).

Cycling

Cycling is very popular and a great way to see the countryside. Tranquil backroads are numerous in each province but caution is always advised, even on these quiet roads.

Hitchhiking

Hitchhiking is common, especially in the summer, and much easier outside the big centres. Nevertheless do not forget that hitchhiking is actually illegal on highways. And remember that the usual risks apply, here as anywhere else.

Money and Banking

Currency

The monetary unit is the Canadian dollar ($), which is divided into cents (¢). One dollar=100 cents.

Bills come in 5-, 10-, 20-, 50-, 100-, 500- and 1000-dollar denominations; coins come in 1- (pennies), 5- (nickels), 10- (dimes), 25- (quarters) cent pieces and in 1- (loonies) and 2- (twoonies) dollar coins.

Exchange Rates*

$1 CAN = $0.82 US $1 US   = $1.21 CAN
$1 CAN = £0.43   £1   = $2.30 CAN
$1 CAN = €0.63   €1   = $1.59 CAN

*Samples only—rates may fluctuate

Exchange

Most banks readily exchange U.S. and European currencies, but almost all will charge commission. There are, however, exchange offices that do not charge commissions and have longer hours. Just remember to ask about fees and compare rates.

Traveller's Cheques

Traveller's cheques are accepted in most large stores and hotels; however, it is easier and to your advantage to cash your cheques at an exchange office. For a better exchange rate, buy your traveller's cheques in Canadian dollars before leaving home.

Credit Cards

Most major credit cards are accepted in stores, restaurants and hotels. While the main advantage of credit cards is that they allow visitors to avoid carrying large sums of money, using a credit card also makes leaving a deposit for car rental much easier; some cards, gold cards for example, automatically insure you when you rent a car (check with your credit card company to see what coverage it provides). In addition, the exchange rate on a credit card is generally better. The most commonly accepted credit cards are Visa, MasterCard, and American Express.

Banks

Most bank services are available to tourists. Those travellers who are planning extended stays should note however that non residents cannot open a bank account. The best way to get money in this case is to carry travellers' cheques. Withdrawing money from your overseas account can be costly, as commission costs are high. However, some automatic teller machines accept foreign bank cards, thus allowing you to make withdrawals. The other choice is a postal money order, for which no com- mission is charged; however they can be time consuming to process. Those travellers who have gained resident status, permanent or not (such as immigrants or students), can open a bank account. To do so, be sure to bring your passport and proof of residence status with you to the bank.

Automated Teller Machines (ATMs)

Most banks have ATMs that allow you to make cash withdrawals. You can use your card as you normally would—you'll be given Canadian dollars with a receipt, and the equivalent amount will be debited from your account. All this will take no more time than it would at your own bank! That said, the network can sometimes experience communication problems that will prevent you from obtaining money. If your transaction is refused by the ATM at one bank, try another bank where you might have better luck. In any case, take precautions so that you do not find yourself empty-handed.

Taxes and Tipping

Taxes

The ticket price on items usually does not include tax. In the Atlantic provinces, an 8% provincial sales tax (PST) is applicable, as well as the federal 7% goods and services tax

(GST). These taxes must be added to the price of most goods and services, including restaurant-bought meals and accommodations.

Some exceptions to this taxation system are books, which are only taxed 7%, and food (except for ready-made meals), which is not taxed at all.

Tax Refunds for Non-Residents

Non-residents can be refunded for taxes paid on their purchases made while in Canada. To obtain a refund, it is important to keep your receipts. A separate form for each tax (federal and provincial) must be filled out to obtain a refund. Conditions for refunds are different for the GST and the PST. It is important to note that to be eligible, your purchases must total at least $200. For further information, call ☎800-668-4748 or visit *www.ccra-adrc.gc.ca/visitors* (for GST).

Tipping

In general, tipping applies to all table service in restaurants and to both table and bar service in bars and nightclubs (no tipping in fast-food restaurants). The tip is usually about 15% of the bill before taxes, but varies, of course, according to the quality of service.

Tipping is also standard in taxis (approximately 10% of the fare) and hair salons (10-15%). A $1 to $3 tip is usually given for valet parking, regardless of

whether or not you pay a parking fee. In deluxe hotels, housekeeping staff should be tipped approximately $5 or more per day, although $2 to $3 per day is fine in a less swanky hotel. As for bell hops, the tip is sometimes included in the hotel rate, (particularly for large groups travelling together), but if it is not, $3 to $5 per bag is appropriate.

Business Hours and Public Holidays

Business Hours

Stores

The law on business hours allows stores to be open the following hours:

Mon to Wed
10am to 6pm
Thu and Fri
10am to 9pm
Sat
9am or 10am to 5pm
Sun
noon to 5pm

Well-stocked convenience stores that sell food are found throughout the Atlantic provinces and may be open later, sometimes 24hrs a day.

Banks

Banks are generally open Monday to Friday from 10am to 3pm. ATMs operate 24hrs a day.

Post Offices

Large post offices are open from 9am to 5pm. There

are several smaller post offices throughout eastern Canada located in shopping malls, convenience stores, and even pharmacies; these post offices may open much later than the larger ones.

Holidays and Public Holidays

The following are public holidays in Atlantic Canada. Most administrative offices and banks are closed on these days.

New Year's Day
January 1 and 2

Good Friday or Easter Monday

Victoria Day
3rd Monday of May

Canada Day
July 1

Labour Day
1st Monday of September

Thanksgiving
2nd Monday of October

Remembrance Day
November 11; only banks and federal government services are closed

Christmas
December 25

Time Difference

Atlantic Canada spans two time zones: Atlantic Standard Time, which is four hours behind Greenwich Mean Time, and Newfoundland Time, which is three and a half hours behind GMT and is only observed on the island of

Newfoundland. When it is noon in Montreal and New York City it is 1pm in Halifax, Moncton and Charlottetown and 1:30pm in St. John's.

Climate and Clothing

Climate

The sea air makes for milder temperatures, especially close to the Bay of Fundy, which is warmed by the Gulf Stream. Temperature ranges are however quite significant. Summer temperatures hover around 25°C, and in the winter around -2°C. Temperatures vary on the coasts, where it is colder in summer and winter. The coasts are also often shrouded in a thick fog, especially along the Bay of Fundy and on the island of Newfoundland.

Winter

December to March is the best season for skiing, snowmobiling, skating, snowshoeing and other winter sports. Temperatures remain low, and warm clothing (coats, scarves, hats, gloves or mittens, wool sweaters and boots) is a necessity. On the coast, it remains quite humid in winter.

Spring and Fall

Spring is short, lasting roughly from the end of March to the end of May. Everything thaws and streets are often slushy. In fall, it's time to watch the colours change. It can get quite cool during both these seasons, so be sure to pack a sweater, scarf, gloves, wind-breaker and umbrella.

Summer

From the end of May to the end of August it can get very hot. Pack some T-shirts, lightweight shirts and pants, shorts and sunglasses. A jacket or sweater can still come in handy in the evening. In certain regions of Atlantic Canada, notably near the Bay of Fundy, on the Atlantic coast of Nova Scotia and on the island of Newfoundland, rain and fog are frequent; an umbrella and raincoat are a good idea.

Health

Vaccinations are not necessary for people coming from Europe, the United States, Australia or New Zealand. Bring along all medication, especially prescription medicine. Unless otherwise stated, the water is drinkable throughout Atlantic Canada.

In the winter, moisturizing lotion and lip balm are useful for people with sensitive skin, since the air in many buildings can be very dry.

The Sun

Despite its benefits, the sun can also cause numerous problems. It is needless to say that the rising occurrence of skin cancer is due in part to overexposure to the sun's harmful rays. It is thus important to keep yourself well protected; always use sunscreen (with a minimum SPF of 15 for adults and 25 for children), which should be applied 20 to 30min before exposure. Many of the sunscreens on the market do not provide adequate protection, so before setting off on your trip, ask your pharmacist which ones are truly effective against UVA and UVB rays.

Remember to use sunscreen whenever you go outdoors, not just when lying on the beach or lounging by the pool, even when the sky is overcast. Also take note that having a tan offers no protection against the sun's harmful rays—you'll still need to apply cream regularly. Even with adequate protection, avoid prolonged exposure, especially during the first few days of your trip, as overexposure can cause sunstroke, symptoms of which include dizziness, vomiting and fever.

A parasol, a hat and a good pair of sunglasses are indispensable accessories to help you avoid harmful exposure while still enjoying a day at the beach. However, remember that the sand and water will reflect the sun's rays, which will still reach you, even in the shade!

It's best to wear light clothing and avoid synthetic fabrics–cotton and linen are ideal. Taking several cold showers per day (if possible) is a great way to keep the heat at bay, and don't go rushing around during the peak hours of the afternoon. But above all, remember to drink water, water and more water!

Emergencies

The ☎*911* emergency number is available throughout the Atlantic provinces.

Security

By taking the usual precautions, there is no need to worry about your personal security in Atlantic Canada. In the event that trouble should arise, remember that ☎*911* is the emergency telephone number.

Insurance

Cancellation

Your travel agent will usually offer you cancellation insurance when you buy your airline ticket or vacation package. This insurance allows you to be reimbursed for the ticket or package deal if your trip must be cancelled due to serious illness or death.

Theft

Most residential insurance policies protect some of your goods from theft, even if the theft occurs in a foreign country. To make a claim, you must fill out a police report. It may not be necessary to take out further insurance, depending on the amount covered by your current home policy. As policies vary considerably, you are advised to check with your insurance company.

Health

This is the most useful kind of insurance for travellers, and should be purchased before departure. Your insurance plan should be as complete as possible because health care costs add up quickly. When buying insurance, make sure it covers all types of medical costs, such as hospitalization, nursing services and doctor's fees. Make sure your limit is high enough, as these expenses can be costly. A repatriation clause is also vital in case the required care is not available on site. Furthermore, since you may have to pay immediately, check your policy to see what provisions it includes for such situations. To avoid any problems during your vacation, always keep proof of your insurance policy on you.

Mail and Telecommunications

Mail

Mail service in Canada is the responsibility of Canada Post. Sending a letter within Canada costs $0.50, to the United States $0.85, and internationally $1.45. Stamps can be purchased at the post office as well as at some pharmacies and grocery stores.

Telephone

Local area codes are clearly indicated in the "Practical Information" section at the start of each chapter. You do not have to dial this code for local calls. For long distance calls, dial *1* for the United States and Canada, followed by the appropriate area code and the number. Phone numbers preceded by *800*, *888*, *866*, or *877* allow you to call without charge from Canada, and often from the United States as well. Dial *1* first. If you wish to contact an operator, dial *0*.

When calling abroad you can use a local operator and pay local phone rates. First dial *011*; then the international country code followed by the phone number.

Country Codes

United Kingdom	*44*
Ireland	*353*
Australia	*61*
New Zealand	*64*
Netherlands	*31*
Germany	*49*

For example, to call the U.K., dial *011-44*, followed by the area code and the subscriber's number.

Another way to call abroad is by using the direct access numbers below to contact an operator in your home country.

**United States
AT&T
☎800-CALL ATT
MCI
☎800-888-8000**

**British Telecom Direct
☎800-408-6420**

**Australia Telstra Direct
☎800-663-0683**

**New Zealand Telecom Direct
☎800-663-0684**

Considerably less expensive than in Europe, public phones are scattered throughout most cities and are easy to use. Local calls cost $0.25 for unlimited time. For long distance calls, equip yourself with quarters ($0.25 coins). It is now possible to pay by credit card or with a pre-paid calling card; take note, however, that these methods are usually more expensive.

Internet

Thanks to the Internet, keeping in touch with the folks back home has never been so easy. In fact, this increasingly popular means of communication is in the process of relegating the good old postcard to the wastepaper basket. All you have to do is obtain the e-mail addresses of the people you wish to contact before you leave.

In addition to Internet cafés, some large hotels, inns, and bed and breakfasts provide their guests

with Internet access. Inquire about any fees, as they can be higher than those of Internet cafés.

Senior Citizens

Reduced transportation fares and entertainment tickets are often made available to seniors. Do not hesitate to ask.

Children

Facilities for children are available almost everywhere you go. Generally, children under five travel for free, and those under 12 are eligible for fare reductions. The same rules apply for various leisure activities and shows. Find out before you purchase tickets. High chairs and children's menus are available in most family restaurants, while some larger stores and malls provide a baby-sitting service while parents shop.

Pets

The restrictions on animal companions vary from one province to another. Pets are not allowed in restaurants and are frequently barred from beaches. Inquire, to be sure. Note that in this guide, the following pictograph, 🐾, appears in the description of accommodations in which pets are permitted. In some cases, there is a small extra charge or restrictions may apply according to the size of the animal. For the safety of

your pet and of those who will follow you, make sure that your pet is treated for fleas with a reliable product (available from your veterinarian) before bringing it to any commercial lodging.

Gay and Lesbian Life

In general, Canadians have an open and tolerant attitude towards homosexuality. Over the years, federal legislation has updated laws concerning gay rights, reflecting a favourable public opinion.

However, in the Atlantic provinces, structured gay communities exist only in Halifax.

Exploring

Each chapter in this guide-book leads you through a province or region of Atlantic Canada, detailing major tourist attractions with a historical and cultural description. Note that major cities (Halifax and Fredericton) and tours are star rated. Attractions are also rated according to a star system, allowing you to quickly determine what are the must-sees.

★	Interesting
★★	Worth a visit
★★★	Not to be missed

The name of each attraction is followed by its address and phone number in parentheses. The price of admission for one adult is also provided. Most establishments offer discounts for children, students, senior citizens and families. Opening hours are also given within these same parentheses. Note that attractions in tourist areas may open only during tourist season. Even in the off-season, however, some of these places welcome visitors, particularly groups, upon request.

Accommodations

A wide choice of types of accommodation to fit every budget is available in most regions of Atlantic Canada. Most places are very comfortable and can offer a number of extra services. Prices vary according to the type of accommodation and the value is generally good, but remember to add the taxes (see p 31). When reserving in advance, which is strongly recommended during the summer months, a credit card is indispensable for the deposit, as payment for the first night is often required.

Nova Scotia, New Brunswick, Prince Edward Island, and Newfoundland and Labrador all graciously offer visitors a hotel-reservation service.

New Brunswick
☎*800-561-0123*
www.tourismnbcanada.com

Nova Scotia
☎*800-565-0000*
www.novascotia.com

Prince Edward Island
☎*888-734-7529*
www.gov.pe.ca

Newfoundland and Labrador
☎*800-563-6353*
www.gov.nl.ca

Prices and Symbols

All the prices mentioned in this guide apply to a **standard room for two people in peak season**. Prices are indicated with the following symbols:

$	less than $60
$$	$61 to $100
$$$	$101 to $150
$$$$	$151 to $225
$$$$$	mor than $225

The actual cost to guests is often lower than the prices quoted here, particularly for travel during the off-peak season. Also, many hotels and inns offer considerable discounts to employees of corporations or members of automobile clubs (CAA, AAA). Be sure to ask about corporate and other discounts, as they are often very easy to obtain.

The various services offered by each establishment are indicated with a small symbol, which is explained in the legend in the opening pages of this guidebook. By no means is this an exhaustive list of what the establishment offers, but rather the services we consider to be the most important.

Please note that the presence of a symbol does not

mean that all the rooms offer this service; you sometimes have to pay extra to get, for example, a whirlpool tub. And likewise, if the symbol is not attached to an establishment, it means that the establishment cannot offer you this service. Please note that unless otherwise indicated, all lodgings in this guide offer private bathrooms.

The Ulysses Boat

The Ulysses boat pictogram is awarded to our favourite accommodations and restaurants. While every establishment recommended in this guide was included because of its high quality and/or uniqueness, as well as its high value, every once In a while we come across an establishment that absolutely wows us. These, our favourite establishments, are awarded a Ulysses boat. You'll find boats in all price categories: next to exclusive, high-price establishments, as well as budget ones. Regardless of the price, each of these establishments offers the most for your money. Look for them first!

Hotels

There are countless hotels across Atlantic Canada, and they range from the modest to the luxurious. Most hotel rooms are equipped with a private bathroom. The prices we have listed are rack rates in high season. In the majority of establishments, however, a whole slew of

discounts, up to 50% in some cases, are possible, particularly during off-peak season (peak is generally considered to be July and August). Weekend rates are often lower when a hotel's clientele is mostly business people.

Inns

Often set up in beautiful historic houses, inns offer quality lodging. They are often more charming and usually more picturesque than hotels. Many are furnished with beautiful period pieces. Breakfast is often included. Remember that in B&Bs and inns, individual room rates vary widely; we have provided the rate for the least expensive room.

Bed and Breakfasts

Bed and breakfasts are well distributed throughout Atlantic Canada, in the country as well as in the city. Besides the price advantage, they offer a uniquely welcoming atmosphere. They can be a wonderful option for those

who want to get to know local people and enjoy personalized service. Credit cards are not always accepted in bed and breakfasts. Unlike hotels or inns, rooms in private homes do not always have a private bathroom.

If you need assistance, the following associations can arrange accommodation in a bed and breakfast:

New Brunswick

N.B. Bed & Breakfast Association
☎*(506) 363-2759*
⇆*(506) 363-2799*

Nova Scotia

N.S. Bed & Breakfast Association
1099 Marginal Rd., Suite 200, Halifax, B3H 4P7
☎*(902) 423-4480 or 800-948-4267*
⇆*(902) 422-0184*

Prince Edward Island

Tourism P.E.I.
PO Box 940, Charlottetown, C1A 7M5
☎*(902) 368-4444 or 800-565-0267*

Bed & Breakfast/Country Inns of PEI
PO Box 2551, Charlottetown, C1A 8C2

Newfoundland and Labrador

Bed & Breakfast/Country Inns Association of Newfoundland & Labrador
PO Box 8730, St. John's, A1B 4K2
☎*(709) 729-2830*
⇆*(709) 729-0057*
www.bbinn-nfld.org

Motels

There are many motels throughout the provinces, and though they tend to be inexpensive, they offer little in the way of ambiance. These are useful, however, when time or budgetary constraints arise.

University Residences

Due to certain restrictions, this can be a complicated alternative. Residences are only available during the summer (mid-May to mid-August); reservations must be made several months in advance, usually by paying the first night with a credit card.

However, this type of accommodation is less costly than the "traditional" alternatives, and making the effort to reserve early can be worthwhile. Visitors with valid student cards can expect to pay approximately $25 plus tax. Bedding is included in the price, and there is usually a cafeteria in the building (though meals are not included in the price).

Practical Information

Camping

Next to staying with friends, camping is the most inexpensive form of accommodation. Unfortunately, unless you have winter camping gear, camping is limited to a short period of the year, from June to August. Services provided and prices vary considerably, from $10 to $30 or more per night, depending on whether the site is private or public. Reservations are recommended.

Restaurants

There are several excellent restaurants in Atlantic Canada. The big specialty is without a doubt fish and seafood, notably lobster.

Prices in this guide are for a meal (appetizer, main course and dessert) for one person, **before taxes and tip** (See "Taxes and Tipping," p 31).

$	less than $10
$$	$11 to $20
$$$	$21 to $30
$$$$	more than $30

These prices are often based on the cost of set dinner menus, but remember that lunchtime meals are often considerably less expensive.

For information on Ulysses's favourite establishments, see "The Ulysses Boat," p 36.

Bars and Dance Clubs

Most pub-style bars do not demand a cover charge (although in winter there is usually a mandatory coat-check). Expect to pay a few dollars to get into nightclubs on weekends. Most provinces stop the sale of alcohol at 2am. Some bars remain open past these hours, but serve only soft drinks. Drinking establishments that only have a liquor license must close at midnight. In small towns, restaurants also frequently serve as bars. For entertainment come nightfall consult the "Restaurant" and "Entertainment" sections of every chapter.

Wine, Beer and Alcohol

The legal drinking age in Atlantic Canada is 19. Beer, wine and alcohol can only be purchased in liquor stores run by the provincial governments. Very little wine-producing goes on in Atlantic Canada. Several good beers are brewed, however, including Moosehead.

Advice for Smokers

As in the United States, cigarette smoking is considered taboo, and is prohibited in more and more public places, including shopping centres, buses and all government offices.

Most public places (restaurants, cafés) have smoking and non-smoking sections. Cigarettes are sold in bars, grocery stores and news-paper and magazine shops. You must be 19 years of age to purchase them in Atlantic Canada.

Shopping

What to Buy

Lobster and salmon: you'll find these products for sale at good price on piers and docks. Most merchants can also sell you a hermetically sealed container for transporting your catch on a plane.

Books: books by local authors are widely available.

Local crafts: paintings, sculptures, woodwork, ceramics, copper-based enamels and weaving, among other crafts, are readily available in all the Atlantic provinces.

Miscellaneous

Drugs

Recreational drugs are against the law and not tolerated (even "soft" drugs). Drug users and dealers caught with drugs in their possession risk severe consequences.

Electricity

Voltage is 110 volts throughout Canada, the same as in the United

States. Electricity plugs have three prongs and adaptors are available here.

Laundromats

Laundromats are found almost everywhere in urban areas. In most cases, detergent is sold on site. Although change machines are sometimes provided, it is best to bring plenty of quarters ($0.25) with you.

Museums

In most cases, admission is charged for museums, though it is rarely more than a few dollars. Reduced rates are charged for those over 60 and for children. Be sure to ask.

Newspapers

Each big city has its own local newspaper.

Fredericton (N.B.)
The Gleaner

Saint John (N.B.)
Telegraph Journal and *Times-Globe*

Moncton (N.B.)
Times-Transcript

Halifax (N.S.)
Chronicle Herald and *The Daily News*

Charlottetown (P.E.I)
The Guardian and *Evening Patriot*

St. John's (Nfld.)
Evening Telegram

The larger national newspapers, for example *The Globe and Mail*, are widely available. Many international newspapers are also for sale in Halifax.

Pharmacies

The classic chemist of old is harder and harder to find. Most pharmacies are superstores of sorts, selling everything from cough syrup and headache medicine to laundry soap, boxes of chocolates and magazines.

Restrooms

Public restrooms can be found in most shopping centres. If you cannot find one, it usually is not a problem to use one in a bar or a restaurant.

Cape Bonavista Lighthouse – Newfoundland and Labrador

Respect the Forest!

As a hiker, it is important to realize your role in preserving and respecting the fragile ecosystem and to understand your impact on your sur-roundings. Here are a few guidelines:

• First of all, stay on the trails, even if they are covered in snow or mud, in order to protect the ground vege-tation and to avoid widening the trail.

• Unless you're heading off on a long trek, wear lightweight hiking boots; they will do less damage to the vegetation. When hiking as a group in alpine regions, spread out and walk on rocks as much as possible to avoid damaging the vegetation.

• It is just as important to protect the waterways, bodies of water and ground water of the mountainous regions. When digging back-country latrines, place them at least 30m from all water sources, and cover everything (paper included) with soil

• Never wash yourself in lakes or streams.

• At campsites, only dispose of waste water in designated areas.

• The water in lakes, rivers and streams is not always potable and therefore should be boiled for at least 10min before drinking.

• Never leave any garbage behind. Garbage bags are usually provided at park offices.

• Certain plants are endangered, so do not pick any.

• Leave everything as you find it, so that those who follow will enjoy the beauty of nature as you did.

• For safety reasons, always keep your dog on a leash or leave it at home. Dogs that roam free have a tendency to wander off and chase wild animals. They have even been known to chase down bears before taking refuge with their masters.

Outdoors

Nova Scotia,
New Brunswick, Prince Edward Island and Newfoundland and Labrador all boast vast, untouched stretches of wilderness protected by national and provincial parks that visitors can explore on foot or by bicycle.

Red-sand beaches and cliffs overhanging the sea (Prince Edward Island National Park), shorelines with tides as high as 18m (Fundy National Park, N.B.), mountains that tower over the rough waters of the Atlantic Ocean (Cape Breton Highlands National Park, N.S.) and rugged, rocky terrain (Gros Morne National Park, N.F.) all await discovery. The following pages contain a description of the various outdoor activities that can be enjoyed in these parks.

Parks

In Atlantic Canada, there are both national parks, run by the federal government, and provincial parks, each administered by their province's government. Most national parks offer services such as information centres, nature programs, guides, accommodation (loges, inns, equipped and wilderness camping sites) and dining facilities. Not all of these services are available in every park (and some vary by season) so it is best to contact park authorities before setting off on a trip. Provincial parks are usually smaller and generally offer fewer services.

A number of parks are crisscrossed by marked trails several kilometres long, perfect for hiking, cycling and cross-country skiing. Wilderness camp-sites or shelters can be found along some of these paths. Some of these camp-sites are very rudimentary, and a few don't even have water; it is therefore essential to be well equipped. Since some of the trails lead deep into the forest, far from human habitation, visitors are strongly advised to heed all signs. Useful maps showing trails, camp-sites and shelters are available for most parks.

Anyone deciding to spend more than a day in a park should remember that the nights are cool (often even in July and August) and that long-sleeved shirts or sweaters can be very practical in some regions. In June, an effective insect repellent is almost indispensable for an outing in the forest.

National Parks

There are seven national parks in Atlantic Canada: Fundy National Park (Alma, N.B.), Kouchibouguac National Park (along the Acadian coast of New Brunswick), Prince Edward Island National Park (Cavendish, P.E.I.), Cape Breton Highlands National Park (Baddeck, N.S.), Kejimkujik National Park (Maitland Bridge, N.S.), Terra Nova National Park (in the centre of Newfoundland) and Gros Morne National Park (in western Newfoundland). In addition to these parks, Parks Canada also operates a number of national historic sites, which are described in the "Exploring" section of each chapter.

For more information on national parks, contact:

**Parks Canada
Atlantic Service Center**
1869 Upper Water St., Halifax, Nova Scotia, B3J 1S9
☎(902) 426-3436
=(902) 426-6881
www.pc.gc.ca

Provincial Parks

Each of the four Atlantic provinces manages a wide variety of parks. Some of these are small and open only during the day, while the larger ones offer a broader scope of activities. There are more than 20 provincial parks in New Brunswick, about thirty on Prince Edward Island, over 100 in Nova Scotia and more than 20 in Newfoundland and Labrador.

These parks provide visitors with access to beaches, campgrounds, golf courses and hiking trails. Throughout this guide, the most important parks are described in the "Exploring" section of each chapter.

For more information on provincial parks, write to:

New Brunswick

Department of Tourism
PO Box 12345, Campbelton, N.B., E3N 3T6
*www.tourismnew
brunswick.ca*

Nova Scotia

**Department of Natural
Resources**
RR1, Belmont, N.S., B0M 1C0
☎*(902) 662-3030*
www.gov.ns.ca/natr

Prince Edward Island

**Department of Economic
Development and Tourism**
www.gov.pe.ca

Newfoundland
and Labrador

**Provincial Parks and
Natural Areas**
Confederation building, 4th floor, West Block, PO Box 8700, St. John's, NFLD, A1B 4J6
☎*800-563-6181*
*www.gov.nf.ca/parks&
reserves*

Beaches

White- and red- sand beaches, shores washed by 18m tides, sand dunes

teeming with fascinating animal life, endless beaches with no sign of human life and others located near charming villages... Without question, these are some of Atlantic Canada's most precious natural treasures. Each province takes care to offer visitors clean, well maintained beaches that are perfect for swimming. A visit to Atlantic Canada would not be complete without a stop at one of the region's many beaches.

Its beaches alone merit a trip to New Brunswick. Particularly popular are the beautiful white-sand beaches of the Acadian coast, especially in the southeast of the province, near Shediac. Aside from their beauty, their waters are the warmest north of Virginia, perfect for swimming and other aquatic activities.

Summer
Activities

In mild weather, visitors can enjoy the activities listed below.

Hiking

Hiking is an activity open to everyone, and can be enjoyed in all national and most provincial parks. Before setting out, plan your excursion by checking the length and level of difficulty of each trail. Some parks have long trails that require more than a day of hiking and lead deep into the wilderness. When taking one of these trails, which can stretch tens of kilometres, it is crucial to respect all signs.

To make the most of a hike, make sure to bring along the right equipment. Remember to wear a good pair of walking shoes and to bring maps, sufficient food and water and a small first-aid kit containing a pocket knife and bandages.

Visitors to Nova Scotia can enjoy the use of many trails leading into the heart of superb natural settings or offering lovely views of the coast. The government publishes a book on these trails entitled *Hiking Trails of Nova Scotia*, which is available by contacting:

Nova Scotia Government Bookstore
PO Box 367, 1700 Granville St., Halifax, N.S., B3J 2T3
☎*(902) 424-7580*

You can also visit the following Internet sites for more information:
www.trails.gov.ns.ca
www.trailtc.ns.ca.

New Brunswick also offers many interesting hiking trails. A web site has been set up to help visitors discover the trails that crisscross its territory: *www.sentiernbtrail.com* supplies a wealth of information for anyone who would like to practice this activity. A trail guide listing some 1,100km of trails can

also be ordered through this web site.

Cycling

Cycling is practised throughout Atlantic Canada, whether along the usually quiet secondary roads or the trails located within the parks. The roads offer prudent cyclists one of the most enjoyable means of visiting these picturesque regions. Keep in mind, however, that even though these are Canada's smallest provinces, distances here can still seem very long.

If you wish to bring your own bicycle, you are allowed to bring it on any bus; just be sure it is properly protected in an suitable box. Another option is to rent one on site. For bike rental locations, look under "Cycling" in the "Outdoor Activities" section of each chapter, contact a tourist information centre or check under "Bicycles-Rentals" in the *Yellow Pages*. Adequate insurance is a good idea when renting a bicycle. Some places include insurance against theft in the cost of the rental, so inquire before renting.

Canoeing

Many parks are studded with lakes and rivers that offer canoe-trippers a day or more of exploring.

Simple campsites have been laid out to accommodate canoers during long excursions. Canoe rentals and maps of possible routes are usually available at the park's information centre.

If you're heading out for adventure on Nova Scotia's waterways, maps and information are available at:

Canoe Nova Scotia
5516 Spring Garden Rd., PO Box 3010, South Halifax, N.S., B3J 3G6
☎*(902) 425-5450*

Fishing

Fishing is permitted in the Atlantic provinces, but visitors should remember that it is a regulated activity. Fishing laws are complicated, so it is wise to request information from the Ministry of Natural Resources of each province and obtain the brochure stating key fishing regulations.

Keep in mind, however, the following general rules:

- it is necessary to obtain a permit from the provincial government before going fishing;

- a special permit is usually required for salmon fishing;

- fishing seasons are established by the ministry and must be respected at all times; the season varies depending on the species;

- fishing is permitted in parks, but it is necessary to obtain a permit from park officials beforehand.

Bird-Watching

The shores of the Atlantic provinces attract all sorts of birds, which can easily be observed with a pair of binoculars. Among the species frequenting this region are cormorants, kingfishers, a wide variety of ducks (including the mallard) and great blue herons. If you're lucky, you might catch a glimpse of an Atlantic puffin, a piping plover or a bald eagle. For help identifying the various species of birds, get a copy of *Peterson's Field Guide: All the Birds of Eastern and Central North America*, published by Houghton Mifflin. Although parks are often the best places to observe certain species,

bird-watching is an activity that can be enjoyed all over Atlantic Canada.

Whale-Watching

Whales swim near the coasts of Atlantic Canada in the Gulf of St. Lawrence, the Bay of Fundy and in the Strait of Belle Isle.

Visitors who wish to get a closer view of these impressive and harmless sea mammals can take part in a whale-watching cruise. The most commonly seen whales are the humpback whale, the finback whale, the minke whale, the blue rorqual and, occasionally, the bowhead whale. These excursions usually start near St. Andrews in New Brunswick, Digby and Cape Breton in Nova Scotia and in many places along Newfoundland's coast.

Atlantic puffin

Seal-Watching

Seals also swim off the coasts of Nova Scotia, New Brunswick and Prince Edward Island, and anyone wishing to observe them up close can take part in seal-watching. Attracted by the boats, these curious mammals will occasionally pop their heads out of the water to gaze at the passengers with their big black eyes. Other times, they can be spotted sunning on a deserted beach. The best place for seal-watching is along the eastern shore of Prince Edward Island.

Golf

All over Atlantic Canada there are magnificent golf courses, renowned for their remarkable natural settings. Stretched out along the seashore, they offer stunning views. Golf lovers can enjoy unforgettable vacations here, as some courses lie in the heart of provincial parks, in the most tranquil surroundings imaginable, with luxurious hotels just a short distance away.

Winter Activities

In winter, the Atlantic provinces are covered with a blanket of snow.

Most parks with summer
hiking trails adapt for the
season, welcoming cross-
country skiers. New
Brunswick also features an
extensive network of
snowmobile trails. Finally,
although there are only a
few mountains in this
region, visitors can downhill ski in New Brunswick,
Nova Scotia and New-
foundland.

Cross-Country Skiing

Some parks, such as Ke-
jimkujik and the Cape
Breton Highlands in
Nova Scotia, as well as
Mount Sugarloaf and
Kouchibouguac in New
Brunswick, are renowned
for their long cross-country ski trails. Daily ski
rentals are available at a
number of resorts.

Downhill Skiing

Although Atlantic Canada is
not really known for
downhill skiing, there are a
few noteworthy moun-
tains. New Brunswick has
some lovely ski resorts,
most importantly Mount
Sugarloaf and Mount
Crabbe. Though the
mountains in Nova Scotia
are lower, Keltic Cape
Smokey is also worth
mentioning.

The best place for down-
hill skiing in the region,
however, is in Newfound-
land and Labrador: Marble
Mountain, near Corner
Brook, in the western part
of the island, has excellent
runs and enjoys a lengthy
ski season.

Snowmobiling

Snowmobiling is gaining
popularity in the Atlantic
provinces. Visitors can
explore the region by
snowmobile, but should
take care to heed all regulations. Don't forget,
though, that a permit is
required. It is also advisable to take out liability
insurance.

The following rules should
always be obeyed:

- **stay on the snowmobile trails;**
- **always drive on the right side of the trail;**
- **wear a helmet;**
- **all snowmobiles must have headlights.**

To help you plan a snow-
mobile excursion, contact:

New Brunswick

**New Brunswick Federa-
tion of Snowmobile Clubs**
147 Houlton Rd., Woodstock,
N.B., E7M 1Y4
☎*(506) 325-2625*
⇒*(506) 325-2627*
www.nbfsc.com

Nova Scotia

**Snowmobilers Association
of Nova Scotia**
5516 Spring Garden Rd., 4th
floor, Halifax, N.S., B3J 1G6
☎*(902) 425-5606*
www.snowmobilersns.com

Outdoors

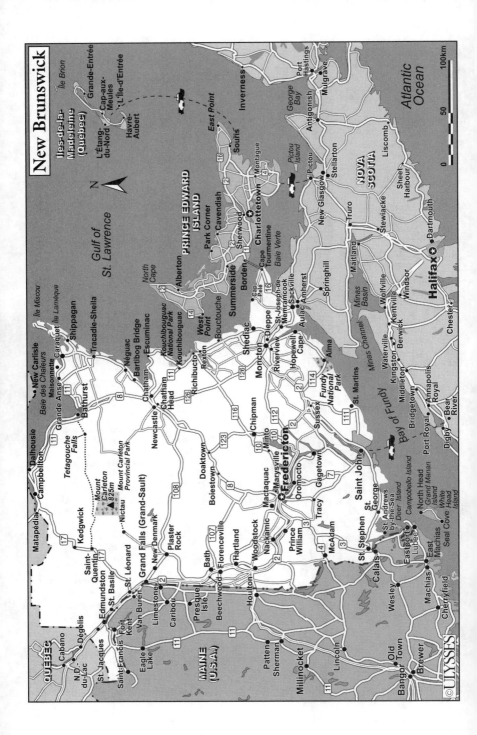

New Brunswick

E nchanting in its diversity,
New Brunswick is the gateway to Atlantic Canada.
Geographically, it is remarkably varied, combining more than

a thousand kilometres of shoreline and seascapes with picturesque farmlands and endless stretches of often mountainous wilderness.

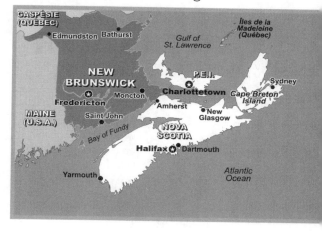

Forests cover a full 85% of New Brunswick's territory, which is traversed from north to south by the majestic St. John River, whose source lies in the Appalachian foothills. This river has always been essential to the province's development, and charming towns and villages have sprung up along its richly fertile banks.

Among these are Fredericton, New Brunswick's pretty capital, with its old-fashioned feel, and Saint John, the province's chief port city and industrial centre.

After winding its way through a pastoral landscape, the St. John River empties into the Bay of Fundy, whose often

spectacularly steep shores mark the southern border of New Brunswick. An amazing natural phenomenon occurs in this bay twice a day when the highest, most powerful tides in the world surge up onto the shores, reshaping the landscape in sometimes unusual ways, and actually reversing the current of the rivers! Without question, the Bay of Fundy's giant tides constitute one of the greatest natural attractions in the eastern part of the continent.

The bay's shoreline, furthermore, is of incomparable beauty. Be that as it may, New Brunswick's other coast, on the Atlantic Ocean, has charms of its own. It is here, from the border of Nova Scotia to that of Québec, that visitors will find the province's most beautiful sandy beaches, washed by uncommonly warm waters that are perfect for swimming. Most importantly, however, this is the Acadian coast. It is here, in towns and villages like Caraquet, Shippagan and Shediac, that visitors can learn about Acadia and its warm, hospitable inhabitants.

In addition to its varied scenery, New Brunswick offers a rich medley of strong, distinct cultures. In fact, despite a past scarred by the rivalry between the French and the British for control of the continent during the 18th century, New Brunswick is now Canada's only officially bilingual province.

Originally inhabited by the Mi'kmaq and Malecite nations, the territory corresponding to present-day New Brunswick was first visited by envoys of the King of France. In 1604, a trading post was established on Île Sainte-Croix, right near the city of St. Stephen, marking the birth of Acadia. The following year, the French moved the

trading post to the opposite shore of the Bay of Fundy, founding Port-Royal in what is now Nova Scotia.

For a century and a half, Acadia developed mainly along the shores of the Bay of Fundy. In 1755, however, a tragic event took place: the Deportation of the Acadians by the British. Approximately half of the 14,000 Acadians were put on boats and deported, while the others hid or escaped into the woods. Many of these eventually took up residence on the Atlantic coast of New Brunswick.

A little more than two decades later, another event, the end of the American Revolution, would have a tremendous influence on the course of history in this region. From 1783 on, when American

revolutionary forces finally defeated the British, thousands of soldiers and civilians wishing to remain loyal to Great Britain sought refuge in Atlantic Canada; many settled on the banks of the St. John River.

Later, a heavy flow of immigrants from the British Isles added to the province's population. Today, English is the mother tongue of the majority of New Brunswick's inhabitants, although French-speakers still make up a third of the population. The Acadians still live, for the most part, on the Atlantic coast, while another group of French-speakers, known as the *Brayons*, can be found along the St. John and Madawaska Rivers, in the northwestern part of the province.

Hopewell Cape

A typical little fishing harbour in one of Prince Edward Island's many pretty coastal villages. - *John Sylvester*

The 13km-long Confederation Bridge spans the Strait of Northumberland,
linking Prince Edward Island to the mainland in New Brunswick. - *P. Quittemelle*

Fredericton

Fredericton ★★ is
definitely one of the most precious jewels in the province's crown.

Capital of New Brunswick, Fredericton has managed to preserve the remarkable historical legacy and architectural harmony handed down to it from the 19th century, giving it a subtle elegance and old-fashioned character. Adorned with magnificent churches and government buildings, as well as large green spaces, some of which lie alongside the St. John River, Fredericton is one of those cities that charms visitors at first sight. Its quiet streets, lined with stately elms, are graced with vast, magnificent Victorian residences. These pretty houses, with their invariably well-tended front gardens, abound in Fredericton, contributing greatly to the city's charm.

The site now occupied by the city originally was an Acadian trading post named "Sainte-Anne" that was founded in the late 17th century. Acadians lived here until 1783,

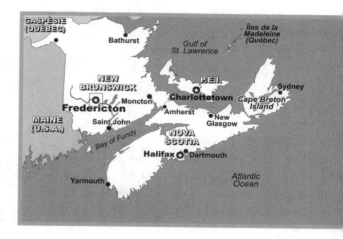

when they were driven away by arriving Loyalists. The city of Fredericton was founded the following year. It became the provincial capital and was named Fredericton in honour of the second son of George III, Great Britain's king at the time. Over the years, very few industries have set up shop here, opting instead for Saint John. Today, Fredericton's chief employers are the provincial government, the universities and the service sector.

Finding Your Way Around

The city of Fredericton (over 80,000 inhabitants) grew up on either side of the St. John River, but the downtown area and most tourist attractions lie on the west bank. Visitors will have no difficulty finding their way around the small city centre, which can be explored on foot. The two main downtown arteries are Queen and King streets, both of which run parallel to the river.

Most attractions, as well as many restaurants and businesses, lie on one or the other of these streets.

By Plane

Fredericton Airport is located about 16km southeast of the city, on Lincoln Road (☎506-460-0920); it is mainly served by **Air Canada** (☎888-247-2262). Visitors can take a taxi to the downtown area.

Bus Station

The bus station (☎506-458-6000) is located at the corner of Brunswick and Regent streets.

Practical Information

Area Code: **506**

Tourist Information Offices

Frederiction Tourism
PO Box 130, Fredericton, N.B., E3B 4Y7
☎**460-2041 or 888-888-4768**
≈**460-2474**
www.fredericton.ca

on the Trans-Canada Hwy.
☎**460-2191**

city hall, Queen St.
☎**460-2129**

Exploring

The best place to begin a tour of downtown Fredericton is at the excellent tourist office located inside the city hall (*at the corner of Queen and York Sts.*, ☎452-9616), which also offers very good guided bus tours of the city. The oldest part of the **city hall** ★ (*free admission; mid-May to Aug, every day 8am to 8pm; Sep to mid-May, by appointment; corner of Queen and York Sts.*, ☎460-2129) was built in 1876, at which time it included not only the municipal offices and council rooms, but also an opera house, a farmer's market and a number of prison cells. The fountain in front of city hall dates from 1885; the building's second wing was erected between 1975 to 1977. The Council Chamber, open to the public during summer, makes for an interesting visit.

On the other side of York Street, visitors will see the **courthouse** (*no visits; at the corner of Queen and York Sts.*), a large stone building erected in the late 1930s. The edifice was used as a high school before adopting its present purpose in 1970. Right next to the courthouse stands the **New Brunswick College of Craft and Design** (*no visits*), the only post-secondary school in Canada to offer a program entirely devoted to training artisans.

A little farther, visitors will come upon the **Military Compound and Guard House** ★★ (*free admission; early Jun to early Sep, every day 10am to 6pm; at the corner of Queen and Carleton Sts.*, ☎453-2324). These stone buildings, erected in 1827 as replacements for the city's original wooden military buildings, served as barracks for British troops until 1869. One room has been restored to illustrate the building's initial use, and a soldier in period dress serves as a guide. A sundial was reconstructed on the barracks' wall. Up until the beginning of the 20th century, residents of Fredericton could check the time by referring to devices such as this one.

Head up Carleton Street to the corner of King Street, where **Wilnot United Church** ★★ is located. Its rather austere facade conceals a superb, exceptionally colourful interior abounding in hand-carved woodwork.

This church was built in 1852, although the Fredericton Methodist Society, which joined the United Church of Canada 1925, was founded back in 1791.

A beautiful Second-Empire–style building erected in 1881 houses the **New Brunswick Sports Hall of Fame** (*free admission; early Jun to early Sep, every day 10am to 6pm; early Sep to Jun, Mon-Fri noon to 4pm; 503 Queen St.*, ☎453-3747), dedicated to New Brunswick's finest athletes.

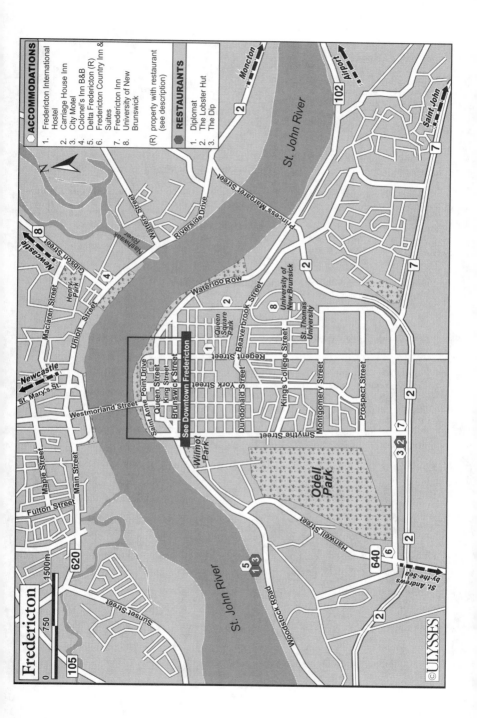

Fredericton

ACCOMMODATIONS

1. Fredericton International Hostel
2. Carriage House Inn
3. City Motel
4. Colonel's Inn B&B
5. Delta Fredericton (R)
6. Fredericton Country Inn & Suites
7. Fredericton Inn
8. University of New Brunswick

(R) property with restaurant (see description)

RESTAURANTS

1. Diplomat
2. The Lobster Hut
3. The Dip

N

0   750   1500m

St. John River

Sunset Street

105

620

Fulton Street

Main Street

Maple Street

St. Mary's St.

Newcastle

Westmorland Street

Union Street

Maclaren Street

Henry Park

Gibson Street

Newcastle

8

Nashwaak River

Waters Street

4

Riverside Drive

Waterloo Row

Princess Margaret Street

St. John River

Moncton

2

102

Airport

Saint John

7

Saint-Anne Point Drive

Queen Street

King Street

Brunswick Street

See Downtown Fredericton

Wilmot Park

Queen Square Park

1

2

Regent Street

York Street

Dundonald Street

Kings College Street

Beaverbrook Street

University of New Brunswick

8

St. Thomas University

2

Montgomery Street

Prospect Street

Smythe Street

Odell Park

Hanwell Street

Woodstock Road

5

1 3

St. Andrews by-the-Sea

640

6

2

3 2

7

2

7

Also on Queen Street, **Officer's Square ★★** is an attractive park. Facing it is the building that was once used as officers' quarters and was erected in two stages, from 1839 to 1840 and in 1851. Its bow-shaped stone columns, railings and iron stairs are typical of architecture designed by royal engineers during the colonial era. The former quarters now house the **York-Sunbury Museum** *($3; mid-Jun to Aug, every day 10am to 5pm; Sep to Dec and Apr to mid-Jun, Tue-Sat 1pm to 4pm; Dec to Apr by appointment; ☎455-6041)*, which is devoted to the province's military and civilian history.

Continue along Queen Street to the pretty **York County Courthouse ★** *(no visits; Queen St., after Regent St.)*, erected in 1855. In those years, there was a market on the ground floor. Today, the building houses the services of the Ministry of Justice, as well as a courtroom.

A little farther along Queen Street, on the opposite side of the street, stands the **Playhouse** *(686 Queen St., at the corner of Saint John St., ticket sales: ☎458-8344)*, built in 1964. Since 1969, it has served as home base for the only English-speaking theatre company in the province, the **New Brunswick Theatre**. Construction of the Playhouse was financed by Lord Beaverbrook, a British newspaper tycoon who lived in New Brunswick as a child.

Not far from the Playhouse, visitors will see the **New Brunswick Legislature ★★** *(free admission; Jun to Aug, every day 8am to 7pm; late Aug to early Jun, Mon-Fri 9am to 4pm; Queen St., at the corner of Saint John St., ☎453-2527)*.

This legislature has been the seat of the provincial government since 1882. Inside, an impressive spiral wooden staircase leads to the library, which contains over 35,000 volumes,

some of which are very rare. Of particular interest are the Assembly Chamber, where the members of Parliament gather and the portraits of King George III and Queen Charlotte, by British painter Joshua Reynolds, hang.

Across from the Legislative Assembly Building stands the **Beaverbrook Art Gallery ★★★** *($5; Jun to Sep, Mon-Fri 9am to 6pm, Sat-Sun 10am to 5pm; Oct to May, Tue-Fri 9am to 5pm, Sat 10am to 5pm, Sun noon to 5pm; guided tours at 11am; 703 Queen St., ☎458-8545, www.beaverbrookartgallery.org)*, another of Lord Beaverbrook's gifts to the city of Fredericton. The gallery houses, among other things, a superb collection of works by highly renowned British painters, as well as a number of other lovely canvases by Canadian artists such as Cornelius Krieghoff and James Wilson Morrice.

Without question, however, the most impressive piece on display is Catalan artist Salvador Dali's *Santiago el Grande*.

After touring the fascinating Beaverbrook Art Gallery, summer visitors can enjoy a delightful stroll on Fredericton's splendid **Green ★** (see p 55, in "Hiking"), which stretches 4kms alongside the St. John River, enabling both walkers and cyclists to explore the banks of the river. The Green contributes greatly to the quality of life in the city. Visitors can stop at the

Provincial Legislature

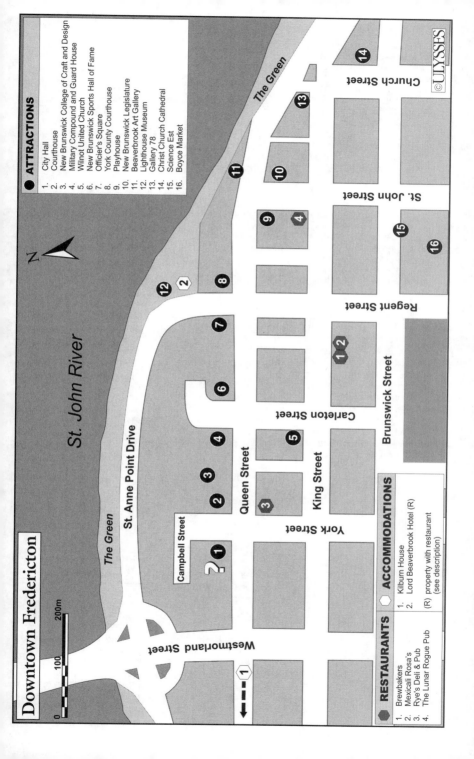

Downtown Fredericton

St. John River

The Green

St. Anne Point Drive

The Green

Campbell Street
York Street
Queen Street
King Street
Carleton Street
Regent Street
Brunswick Street
St. John Street
Church Street

Westmorland Street

N

0   100   200m

● ATTRACTIONS

1. City Hall
2. Courthouse
3. New Brunswick College of Craft and Design
4. Military Compound and Guard House
5. Wilmot United Church
6. New Brunswick Sports Hall of Fame
7. Officer's Square
8. York County Courthouse
9. Playhouse
10. New Brunswick Legislature
11. Beaverbrook Art Gallery
12. Lighthouse Museum
13. Gallery 78
14. Christ Church Cathedral
15. Science Est
16. Boyce Market

⬡ ACCOMMODATIONS

1. Kilburn House
2. Lord Beaverbrook Hotel (R)

(R) property with restaurant (see description)

⬢ RESTAURANTS

1. Brewbakers
2. Mexicali Rosa's
3. Rye's Deli & Pub
4. The Lunar Rogue Pub

© ULYSSES

Lighthouse Museum *($2; May, Jun and Sep, Mon-Fri 10am to 4pm, Sat-Sun noon to 4pm; Jul and Aug, every day 10am to 9pm; ☎459-2515)*, which presents a historical exhibit.

Back on Queen Street, the pretty silhouette of Crocket House, which now houses **Gallery 78** *(796 Queen St., ☎454-5192)*, is visible. Built at the end of the 19th century, Croquet House is a magnificent three-storey Queen Anne–style home. It was named after the Crocket family who lived here from the 1930s; in 1963, it was given to New Brunswick Heritage. Since 1989, it has been home to Gallery 78, one of the best galleries in the province, which features works by renowned Canadian artists. In addition to viewing the works in the gallery, visitors can admire the beautiful interior of the home.

Take Queen Street to Church Street to visit the Gothic-style **Christ Church Cathedral ★ ★** *(☎450-8500)*, whose construction, completed in 1853, was largely due to the efforts of Fredericton's first Anglican bishop, John Medley.

Christ Church Cathedral

From the cathedral, **Science East** *($5; Mon-Sat 10am to 5pm, Sun 1pm to 4pm; 668 Brunswick St., ☎457-2340)* can be reached by taking Brunswick Street. The fundamentals of scientific principles become child's play in a sense through the more than 100 interactive displays of Science East. Visitors can enter a giant kaleidoscope, play with lasers, project gigantic shadows on the wall and participate in countless other amusing activities. There is also an outdoor playground with more than 20 additional exhibits, a gallery on climactic change to better understand global warming and a scientific workshop with an array of entertaining scientific toys. This makes for an interesting family outing.

Not far from Science East is **Boyce Market** *(Sat 6am to 1pm; 665 George St., ☎451-1815)*, a public market where farmers, artisans and artists sell their products every Saturday morning. Right next door, on the left side of Brunswick Street, lies Fredericton's **Old Loyalist Cemetery**. It was here that the most notable figures in Fredericton's early history were buried from 1787 to 1878.

Beyond Downtown

Situated beyond the downtown area, the **Old Government House** *(free admission; end of May to early Sep, every day 10am to 6pm; 51 Woodstock Rd., ☎453-2505)* once served as the official residence of

the lieutenant-governor of the province

The **University of New Brunswick** *(at the end of University St.)*, founded in 1785 by newly arrived Loyalists, is made up of several different edifices. Its arts building is the oldest university facility still in use in Canada.

On the same site, visitors will also find **St. Thomas University**, a Catholic institution originally located in Chatham, on the Miramichi River. This is a wonderful spot from which to view the city below.

Odell Park ★ *(Rockwood Ave., northwest of the city)* covers over 175ha and includes 16km of trails. This beautifully preserved, peaceful natural area has been enhanced by the addition of an enclosure for deer, duck ponds, picnic tables and a play area for children.

Outdoor Activities

Cycling

Cycling is not only a great sport, but also a fantastic means of exploring New Brunswick, which abounds in peaceful roads and bike paths. Fredericton is a marvellous city to tour by bicycle. In addition to its often quiet streets, Fredericton has a magnificent bike path that runs 4km along the river.

Bicycle Rental

Key Cycle
28 Main St.
☎*458-8985*

Radical Edge
386 Queen St.
☎*459-3478*

Hiking

A good way to explore Fredericton's beauty is on foot: it has 12 trails that meander through the outskirts of town. The longest trail, the **North Side**, follows the north shore of the St. John River for about 10km. The **Green**, which snakes through the southwest shore for 4km through the prettiest areas of town, is probably the most scenic trail. It links up with other shorter trails, which are also beautiful. All of the trails offer interesting hiking. You can obtain a copy of the *Trail Guide* by contacting the **New Brunswick Trails Council** (*235 Main St.,* ☎*459-1931, www.sentiernbtrail.com*).

Cruises

River Routes
$2
☎*447-4794*
River Routes offers a ferry service that connects different areas in Fredericton.

The boat ride is inexpensive and enjoyable, offering a good chance to see several bird species up close. Several departures daily until sunset from Regent Street pier, the Delta hotel and Carleton Park.

Canoeing and Kayaking

After strolling along the streets of Fredericton, there's nothing like a guided river tour aboard a canoe or kayak. You say you don't know how to paddle? Not to worry: this business offers short training sessions on handling these crafts and trips that offer a chance to explore the river and see its beautiful flora and fauna up close.

Small Craft Aquatic Centre
Woodstock Rd.
☎*460-2260*

Accommodations

Fredericton International Hostel
$
K
621 Churchill Row, E3B 1M3
☎*450-4417*
Located in a gigantic house, this youth hostel is undoubtedly one of the best choices for those on a tight budget. It offers a perfect location, only 5min on foot from the centre of town. What's more, unlike

most facilities of its kind which have dormitories, it offers rooms of different sizes. Guests have access to a kitchenette and a game room. Fewer rooms are available in winter, since a part of the building serves as a students' residence.

University of New Brunswick
200 beds
Jun to mid-Aug
$
20 Bailey Dr., at the end of University Ave., E3B 5A3
☎*453-4891*
⇄*453-3585*
During the summer, the rooms of the student residence can be rented at the University of New Brunswick.

Kilburn House
$$ bkfst incl.
3 rooms
80 Northumberland St., E3B 3H8
☎*455-7078 or 866-365-5500*
⇄*455-8192*
Located close to the centre of town, this reasonably priced facility offers a few simply decorated but clean rooms. The downside, however, is that Kilburn House is situated on a busy street.

Carriage House Inn
$$
≡
11 rooms
230 University Ave., E3B 4H7
☎*452-9024 or 800-267-6068*
⇄*458-0799*
www.carriagehouse-inn.net
The many opulent Victorian residences lining the streets of Fredericton provide much of the

town's charm. The Carriage House Inn is one of these magnificent houses, built in 1875 and transformed into an inn with a unique atmosphere that transports guests to another era. There are several large rooms, including a ballroom, a library and a solarium, as well as 11 guest rooms furnished with antiques. The inn looks out onto a quiet, well-to-do street shaded by large elm trees, and lies just a few minutes' walk from downtown. It is best to reserve in advance, regardless of the season.

City Motel
$$
ℜ, ≡
55 rooms
1216 Regent St., E3B 3Z4
☎*450-9900 or*
800-268-2858
⇄*452-1915*
It would be difficult to find a more boring decor than that of the rooms at the City Motel, located next to the Trans-Canada Highway. For visitors aiming to see the main sights of Fredericton, this hotel is a little out of the way. Nevertheless, it is clean, not too expensive and there is a good seafood restaurant next door.

Colonel's Inn B&B
$$$ bkfst incl.
≡, ⊛, ℜ̃
3 rooms
843 Union St., E3A 3P6
☎*452-2802 or*
877-455-3303
⇄*457-2939*
A charming B&B with only a few rooms, the Colonel's Inn is a beautiful century-old home. Its welcoming hosts, who gladly offer information

about the region, ensure an enjoyable stay. To get here from the town centre, you can take a scenic drive on the north shore of the St. John River, near Carleton Park.

Fredericton Country Inn & Suites
$$$ bkfst incl.
K, ≡, ✗
99 rooms
665 Prospect St. W., E3B 6B8
☎*459-0035 or*
800-456-4000
⇄*458-1011*
Located outside of town, this hotel offers decent rooms. Guests enjoy many little extras, such as free newspapers and all-day coffee, which make the stay quite enjoyable. For longer stays in Fredericton, travellers can rent a room with a kitchenette and living room.

Fredericton Inn
$$$
ℜ, ≈, K, ☺, ≡
199 rooms
1315 Regent St., E3B 1A1
☎*455-1430 or*
800-561-8777
⇄*458-5448*
Located just outside the downtown area and close to several shopping malls along the Trans-Canada Highway, the Fredericton Inn offers a large choice of rooms, from suites to motel-style accommodation. The latter offer good value.

Lord Beaverbrook Hotel
$$$
ℜ, ≡, △, ✿, ☺, ≈
168 rooms
659 Queen St., E3B 5A6
☎*455-3371 or*
866-444-1946
⇄*455-1441*
You won't find a hotel more centrally located

than the Lord Beaverbrook, which has been a landmark of downtown Fredericton for half a century. With its back to the St. John River, it faces the New Brunswick Legislature. The hotel's prestigious history is evident in its richly decorated entrance hall and the aristocratic air about the **Governor's Room** (see p 57), a small dining room tucked away. Nevertheless, despite renovations, the rooms are comfortable without being overly luxurious.

✦ Delta Fredericton
$$$$
△, ☺, ℜ, ≈, ≡, ✗, &, ⊛
222 rooms
225 Woodstock Rd., E3B 2H8
☎*457-7000 or*
800-462-8800
⇄*457-4000*
The elegant Delta Fredericton is beautifully located on the shore of the St. John River, just outside downtown Fredericton. It is by far the most luxurious hotel in the capital and one of the nicest in the province. The architects made the most of the location, including a superb terrace looking out over the river, the ideal spot for cocktails, a dip in the pool or a relaxed meal while taking in the scenery. The rooms are very comfortable, pretty and functional, and several offer great views. The Delta is equipped with an indoor pool and exercise facilities, a very good restaurant (**Bruno's Seafood Cafe**, see p 57), a bar and conference rooms. It has clearly been designed to please both business and leisure travellers.

Restaurants

The Lunar Rogue Pub
$-$$
625 King St.
☎450-2065
This is a great place to be on beautiful sunny days, when guests can enjoy the terrace. Although fairly predictable, the food here is worth the trip. Enjoy generous portions of hamburgers, sandwiches or steak.

Rye's Deli & Pub
$-$$
73 Carleton St.
☎472-7937
Rye's Deli & Pub is a favourite with lovers of smoked-meat, and according to their advertisements, they follow the original Montréal recipe. What the decor lacks in atmosphere is more than made up for by the terrace when the warm weather arrives. Rye's is particularly popular among the employees of the neighbouring offices and shops.

Diplomat
$$
251 Woodstock Rd., next to the Delta Fredericton
☎454-2400
Open 24hrs a day, seven days a week, the Diplomat is a favourite perch for night owls. The menu is varied but simple, consisting essentially of typical delicatessen fare. Chinese food is also one of its specialties. The Diplomat serves copious breakfasts at very good prices.

The Lobster Hut
$$
1216 Regent St., City Motel
☎455-4413
The Lobster Hut could almost be listed as a Fredericton attraction, due to its bizarre, almost psychedelic decor, made up of an eclectic collection of photos, posters and gadgets all having to do with maritime life. The restaurant is as friendly as can be, and, as you may have guessed, it specializes in fish and seafood. The food is good and relatively inexpensive.

Mexicali Rosa's
$$
546 King St.
☎451-0686
Mexicali Rosa's is a good spot for fans of Mexican food. Servings are usually quite large, and a small terrace allows for outdoor dining.

Brewbakers
$$-$$$
546 King St.
☎450-0067
Brewbakers has something for everyone. Those who like to chat over a scrumptious dessert and coffee will enjoy its main floor. The second floor is a pleasant mezzanine and the third floor has a dining room and a terrace, where guests can enjoy hearty portions of delicious pasta, pizza, steak, chicken or seafood. Convivial ambiance.

The Dip
$$-$$$
Delta Fredericton, 225 Woodstock Rd.
☎454-2400
During mild summertime weather, it would be hard to imagine a better spot for a drink, light snack or

meal than The Dip, the Delta's terrace restaurant with a bistro-style menu. Besides the attentive and courteous service, The Dip offers an absolutely unbeatable view of the St. John River.

Bruno's Seafood Cafe
$$$-$$$$
Delta Fredericton, 225 Woodstock Rd.
☎451-7935
If the weather proves prohibitive, you can always take shelter at Bruno's Seafood Cafe, the indoor restaurant at the Delta (see p 56). The cuisine is just as good, the service, impeccable and the ambiance, cozy. The menu offers an array of culinary delights, ranging from steak to seafood. There is also a children's menu. In addition, Bruno's usually offers a seafood buffet on Friday evenings.

Governor's Room
$$$-$$$$
659 Queen St., Lord Beaverbrook Hotel
☎455-3371
The **Lord Beaverbrook Hotel** (see p 56) boasts a dining room and a terrace looking out over the St. John River (see The Terrace, below). For a fancier dinner, however, make reservations at the Governor's Room, two private dining rooms with an antique decor and a slightly aristocratic atmosphere. The chef specializes in French cuisine.

The Terrace
$$$-$$$$
659 Queen St., Lord Beaverbrook Hotel
☎451-1804
The **Lord Beaverbrook Hotel** (see p 56) houses

New Brunswick

two restaurants, the Governor's Room (see above) and The Terrace. The latter has a friendly ambiance and is a good choice for its pleasant dining room and, above all, its terrace overlooking the Saint John River.

Entertainment

Bars and Pubs

Social Club
University of New Brunswick
Student Union Building
The students may come and go, but the Social Club at the University of New Brunswick remains a sure bet year after year. It is packed just about every night in winter, while in the summer, most of the action is limited to weekends.

The Lunar Rogue Pub
625 King St.
☎450-2065
There's nothing like a night out at The Lunar Rogue Pub. It offers a lively terrace which is overflowing on weekend evenings. It also has great beer on tap.

Dolan's Pub
349 King St.
☎450-7474
The 25-plus clientele at this pub is serenaded by live music, mainly courtesy of Maritime musicians.

Festivals and Cultural Activities

The **Playhouse** *(Queen St.)* is a lovely hall that presents the productions of the New Brunswick Theatre, the only professional English-language theatre company in the province. It also regularly hosts other cultural events *(schedule: ☎458-8344).*

During summer months, **outdoor concerts** are presented on Tuesdays and Thursdays at 7:30pm at **Officer's Square** (see p 52), on Queen Street.

The first few days of September are jazz and blues time in Fredericton. The **Harvest Jazz & Blues Festival** *(☎888-622-5837, www.harvestjazzblues.nb. ca)* is a special occasion for those who love these two musical styles. Shows are presented in bars, parks, restaurants and theatres in town.

Film

Empire Theatre
Regent Mall
☎458-9704

Shopping

The **Regent Mall** *(1381 Regent St.)* is the largest shopping centre in town with 95 shops.

No visit to Fredericton would be complete without a stop at **Gallery 78** *(796 Queen St.)*, which exhibits and sells works by some of the best-known New Brunswick artists. It is also a wonderful way to visit a sumptuous Victorian house overlooking the St. John River. With its high ceilings, large rooms, hardwood floors and stately staircase, you'll be wishing it was for sale too!

The **New Brunswick Crafts Council** *(87 Regent St., ☎450-8989)* gallery exhibits and sells a superb collection of high quality products created by the province's artists and craftspeople. It is one of the best craft shops in New Brunswick.

Beaverbrook Gallery Gift Shop
Queen St.
☎458-8545
The Beaverbrook Gallery Gift Shop sells reproductions, art books, decorations and the like. A great place to find a quality souvenir.

Soldiers' Barracks Crafts Shops
458 Queen St.
In summertime, soldiers' barracks are transformed into charming little boutiques. A few of them also have workshops, which offer a great opportunity to see the artists at work.

Cultures
383 Mazzuca's Ln.
☎462-3088
Cultures is an innovative shop selling crafts and products made in developing nations. Several beautiful objects can be found here. The boutique is located at what is probably one of the most difficult corners to find in Fredericton: a small alley off York Street, between King and Queen Streets.

St. John River Valley

From the République
de Madawaska, in the northwestern part of the province, to the industrial city of Saint John, where it empties into the Bay of Fundy, the majestic St. John River is the keystone of New Brunswick's most continental region.

Each bend in the river reveals new scenery and different facets of a land full of contrasts. Around Edmundston and Grand Falls (Grand-Sault), French-speaking areas graced with flamboyant Catholic churches, visitors will discover a lovely, gently rolling landscape, where the local economy centres on lumbering and potato farming. Farther south, as the valley widens, the river runs through an entirely different region, studded with towns and villages boasting a rich architectural heritage.

Among these is Fredericton, the province's capital. Two centuries ago, this entire portion of the St. John valley became a veritable "promised land" for thousands of Loyalists

(American colonists wishing to remain loyal to the British crown after the Revolutionary War). Despite these cultural and social differences, the valley is united by one force: an endless fascination with the mighty St. John, from its source to its estuary.

Finding Your Way Around

This tour of the **St. John River Valley** ★ takes you from Saint-Jacques, on the

Québec border, south to Gagetown, New Brunswick. Note that Fredericton is covered in a separate chapter.

By Car

From the Québec border, visitors can take Highway 2 (the Trans-Canada Highway) or any other parallel road to the province's capital, Fredericton. After passing through Fredericton, take Highway 7, then Route 102 to Gagetown, the last stop on the tour. By continuing south, visitors will soon reach the city of Saint John, on the shores of the Bay of Fundy.

Bus Stations

Edmundston
169 Victoria St., near Hébert Blvd.
☎*(506) 739-8309 or 328-2245*

Practical Information

Area code: **506**

Tourist Information Offices

New Brunswick Tourist Information Centre
☎*800-561-0123*

Saint-Jacques

Trans-Canada Hwy.
☎*735-2747*

Edmundston

7 Canada Rd., E3V 1T7
☎*739-2115 or 866-737-6766*
⇝*737-6820*
www.ville.edmundston. nb.ca

Grand Falls (Grand-Sault)

☎*877-475-7788*
www.grandfalls.com

Exploring

Saint-Jacques

This is the first village that many travellers (or at least those arriving from Québec) will encounter on their tour of New Brunswick. It is therefore no coincidence that Saint-Jacques is home to one of the province's largest tourist-information centres, as well as a provincial park, **Les Jardins de la République**, which has campsites, a pool and play area for children, as well as hiking and cycling trails. There are also two major attractions nearby.

The **New Brunswick Botanical Garden ★★** *($3; Jun to Sep; Hwy. 2, Exit 8,* ☎*737-5383)*, destined to become one of the region's greatest draws, is worth visiting for a number of reasons. Some 75,000 plants have been distributed over a well laid-out 7ha area that offers a lovely panoramic view of the region's gentle, wooded valleys. The garden's designers had the clever idea of installing an unobtrusive sound system, enabling visitors to explore the garden while the music of Bach, Chopin or Mozart plays the background.

The **Antique Automobile Museum ★** *($2.50; late May to mid-Sep; right beside the garden,* ☎*735-2525)* grew up around the private collection of Edmund-ston resident Melvin Louden. It displays a lovely selection of antique cars, some of which are very rare nowadays, including the *Bricklin*—the only automobile made in New Brunswick—and the 1933 Rolls Royce *Phantom*.

Edmundston

The region's largest urban area, Edmundston is also the heart of northwestern New Brunswick's French-speaking community, which refers to it affectionately as the capital of the mystical République de Madawaska. The driving force behind the city's prosperity is immediately evident in its urban landscape. The pulp and paper industry has flourished due to the richness of the neighbouring forests and the city's highly advantageous location at the confluence of the Madawaska and St. John rivers. While Edmundston's industrial character is unmistakable, the city is also very proud of its festive spirit and cultural life, which reaches its peak during the **Foire Brayonne** *(*☎*739-6608)*, the largest French-speaking event in the country to be held outside of Québec. It is during this period, at the end of July each year, that visitors can best discover the richness and generosity of the local population.

The impressive **Cathedral of the Immaculate Conception ★** *(145 Rice St.)* towers over the city of Edmundston. It was built

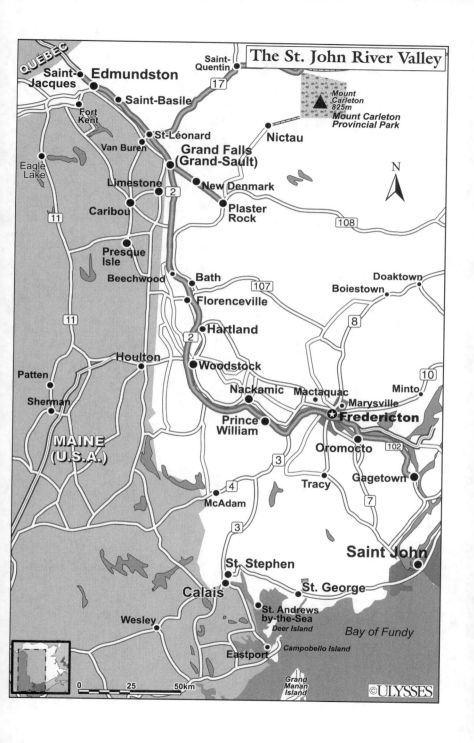

The St. John River Valley

The République de Madawaska

The origins of the mythical "République de Madawaska" date back to the region's early colonization, a time when the British and the Americans were continuously redefining the border between Maine and New Brunswick, after skirmishes and tortuous political negotiations. Tired of being mere pawns in all of this, the people of Madawaska scorned the authorities, deciding to "establish" their own republic, defined by the very vaguest of borders, but more or less encompassing the French-speaking population of this part of the country. Pushing the fantasy even further, they decided that the republic would have its own president in the person of the mayor of Edmundston. Behind this peculiar historical legacy lies a very strong cultural bond between French-speakers on both sides of the border, which can best be appreciated during Edmundston's Foire Brayonne, a festival held each year at the end of July.

during the dark years of the Great Depression with materials from all over the world, including Africa, India, Italy and France. Its stained-glass windows are superb.

Visitors interested in learning about the history of the area and its inhabitants can stop by the **Madawaska Historical Museum** *($3.50; mid-Jun to Sep, every day 9am to 8pm; Sep to mid-Jun, Wed and Thu 7pm to 10pm, Sun 1pm to 5pm; 195 Hébert Blvd., ☎737-5282)*, which houses a permanent collection of artifacts linked to the region's development. The museum also includes a gallery devoted to the work of contemporary Madawaskan artists.

The **Petit-Témis Interprovincial Linear Park** *(☎739-1992)* stretches some 130km and connects Edmundston and Rivière-du-Loup (Québec). This green space includes a network of hiking and cycling trails, some of which offer breathtaking views along the Madawaska River.

Saint-Basile

For many years, colonists from Québec and Acadians who came here seeking refuge formed only a small community, served for more than four decades by a single parish, Saint-Basile. Founded in 1792, the parish originally stretched from the Saint-François River to the present-day city of Grand Falls. Saint-Basile has therefore been dubbed the "Cradle of Madawaska." Saint-Basile has recently become known for an entirely different reason as well: popular singer Roch Voisine was born here.

Saint-Léonard

Without a doubt, Saint-Léonard offers the clearest possible illustration of the arbitrary nature of the Canada-U.S. border, which has separated the town from Van Buren (on the U.S. side) since 1842. In any case, these two communities, linked by both history and language, still bear allegiance to the same republic: Madawaska!

From Saint-Léonard, visitors can either go to Mount Carleton Provincial Park or head to the northeastern part of the province on Rte. 17.

Mount Carleton

Mount Carleton Provincial Park ★ *(take Rte. 180 from St-Quentin, ☎235-0793, ≈235-0795)* is located in the heart of New Brunswick, in the wildest part of the province. At 820m, Mount Carleton is the tallest peak in the

Atlantic provinces. This park is mostly frequented by hikers and offers campsites.

From Saint-Léonard, you can continue on Hwy. 2 along the St. John River up to Grand Falls.

Grand Falls (Grand-Sault)

A charming little town on the banks of the St. John, at the point where the river plunges 23m, Grand Falls is a dynamic, engaging community whose mostly French-speaking population has Québécois and Acadian roots. This pretty spot was known to the Malecite First Nation for many years before becoming a British military post in 1791. The city was finally established in 1896.

In addition to its attractive location, Grand Falls has a charming town centre. Its wide boulevard, flanked by low houses facing right onto the street, gives it a slightly Midwestern character. It is worth noting that Grand Falls is the only town in Canada with an officially bilingual name: Grand Falls-Grand Sault. With its green valleys, perfect for potato farming, Grand Falls makes for a lovely outing.

The magnificent **waterfall ★ ★** that inspired the town's name is the largest and most impressive in Atlantic Canada. The waters of the St. John River plunge 23m, then rush for about 2km

The Brayons

The inhabitants of the "République de Madawaska" are known as the "Brayons," a term whose origins remain obscure. The word might come from brayer, which means "to crush," since crushing flax was a common chore for Madawaskan women.

The Brayons are descendants of both Quebecers and Acadians. The former came to New Brunswick in the 18th and 19th centuries seeking new lands to settle, while the latter were driven here from the lower St. John River area by an influx of Loyalist colonists at the end of the 18th century.

through a gorge whose sides reach as high as 70m.

At the far end of the gorge, the turbulent water has eroded the rock, creating cavities known here as "wells," since water stays in them after the river rises. Visitors can start off their tour by dropping by the **Malobiannah Centre** *(on Chemin Madawaska, alongside the falls),* which is both an interpretive centre and a regional tourist information centre. The spot enjoys a splendid

view of the falls and the hydroelectric dam. A footpath heading out from the centre makes it possible to observe the falls and the gorge from all different angles. At the **Centre La Rochelle** *($1; Centennial Park),* on the opposite bank, right in the centre of town, there is a staircase that leads down to the river bed, offering a better view of the gorge, the wells and the waterfall.

To learn more about Grand Falls and its surrounding area, visitors can head to the little **Grand Falls Museum** *(free admission; Jun to Aug, Mon-Fri 9am to 5pm; 142 Court St., ☎473-5265),* which displays a diverse assortment of objects linked to the region's history.

Rte. 108 leads to New Denmark, Plaster Rock and finally the Miramichi River, which flows into the Atlantic.

New Denmark

New Denmark is a small rural community similar in every way to other towns in the region, except that it also happens to be the hub of the largest Danish colony in North America. Its origins date back to 1872, when the provincial government invited a handful of Danes to settle at the confluence of the Salmon and St. John rivers. These people were promised good, arable land, but instead found themselves on uneven, rocky soil. The provincial authorities apparently chose this precise spot along the river so

New Brunswick

that the Danes would act as a buffer between the French-speakers of the north and the English-speakers of the south. The settlers ended up staying anyway, and their descendants, who now number just under 2,000, hold an annual festival on June 19 to commemorate their ancestors' experience.

Beechwood

Visitors can stop in this tiny hamlet to examine its **hydroelectric power station** or enjoy a picnic in the park by the river.

Bath

The pretty, peaceful village of Bath, located on the east bank of the St. John River, has no particular attractions, per se, but is graced with a few lovely white homes, which are owned by local notables. Visiting Bath is like stepping back into another era, far from the hustle and bustle of modern cities.

Florenceville

This little village witnessed the humble origins of the McCain company, now an international frozen-food empire, known especially for its potatoes and French fries. The McCain family is the second wealthiest in New Brunswick, after the Irvings. At the edge of Florenceville stands an imposing factory, which still processes tonnes of locally grown potatoes each year. In the centre of the village, visitors can stop by the **Andrew & Laura McCain Gallery ★** *(free admission; Wed noon to 5pm, Thu noon to 5pm and 6pm to 8pm, Fri 10am to 5pm, Sat 10am to 3pm; 8 McCain St.,* ☎ *392-6769)*, which displays works by New Brunswick artists, artisans and photographers, and also presents the occasional international exhibit.

Hartland

The home town of Richard Hatfield, the province's eccentric former prime minister, Hartland is an adorable village typical of the St. John River Valley. It is known for its remarkable **covered bridge ★★**, the world's longest. Stretching 390m across the river, the structure was built in 1899, at a time when simply covering a bridge could make its framework last up to seven times longer. Today, there are more covered bridges in New Brunswick than anywhere else on Earth. Visitors who would like to stop for a picnic and admire the local scenery will find an attractive park on the west bank of the river.

Woodstock

After the Revolutionary War, tens of thousands of U.S. citizens who had fought on the British side took refuge in Canada, a territory Great Britain had wrested from France two decades earlier. In 1784, one of these Loyalists, Captain Jacob Smith, sailed up the St. John River to the mouth of the Meduxnekeag River, where British authorities had granted him a piece of land. A few decades later, Woodstock was founded on that spot. Now a medium-size town, it is the seat of Carleton County. Although known for its conservatism, Woodstock takes pride in living up to its nickname, "Hospitality Town." At the end of July, the town holds an annual festival known as **Old Home Week**, which celebrates family and tradition.

Covered bridge

Restaurants

Grand Falls (Grand-Sault)

Hill Top Motel Restaurant
$-$$
131 Madawaska Rd.
☎473-2684
The best thing about this restaurant is its incredible view of the waterfall. It serves up decent family-style cuisine.

La Renaissance
$$
Motel Léo
☎473-2090
The Grand Falls region is a big potato producer, so much so that the house specialty of the **Motel Léo's** (see p 67) restaurant is the "stuffed potato": half a baked potato stuffed with ham, chicken, cheese, etc. Whatever the variation, the "stuffed potato" is quite filling and makes an economical meal. The rest of this family restaurant's menu includes typical home-style cooking. The decor is simple and the service is courteous.

La Violette
$$
Auberge Près du Lac
☎473-1300
La Violette is also a family restaurant, but with a more elaborate menu than its competitor's at La Renaissance (see above). In an open-plan, elegant dining room, you'll choose from a menu that includes meat,

seafood... basically, a bit of everything!

Karl's German Cuisine
$$$
Lakeside Lodge & Resort, Gillespie Rd.
☎473-6252
Grills, sausages, sauerkraut and other German dishes are among the specialties offered at this restaurant, which serves up hearty fare. Situated in the middle of the countryside, the setting is enchanting. The country-style decor, with a fireplace in the dining room and large bay windows, is charming.

Woodstock

Heino's German Cuisine
$$
John Gyles Motor Inn, Rte. 2, 8km south of Woodstock
☎328-6622
Heino's restaurant in the **John Gyles Motor Inn** (see p 68) is famous throughout the region for its excellent German family cuisine. Of course, several varieties of sausage figure on the

menu, as well as the great classics of that country's cuisine.

Down House B&B
$$-$$$
698 Main St.
☎328-1819
The **Down House B&B** (see p 67) has a restaurant that prepares innovative cuisine using fresh, healthy ingredients—something not seen too often in this region. From dawn to dusk, guests file into this place to enjoy delicious dishes in the dining room, which has a cozy fireplace, or on the adjoining terrace.

Gagetown

Steamers Stop Inn
$$-$$$
74 Front St.
☎488-2903
The menu of the **Steamers Stop Inn** (see p 68) is rich in traditional regional specialties, with a focus on fresh ingredients. Diners can enjoy a lovely view of the river from the back veranda.

New Brunswick

Entertainment

Grand Falls (Grand-Sault)

Grits Bar & Grill
456 Broadway
☎473-3311
Grits is one of the favourite meeting places for the youth of the region. Beer on tap as well as typical pub fare is served. Friendly, festive atmosphere.

Woodstock

J.R.
Main St., 500m after the community college
☎328-9326
A well-known local bar, J.R. is somewhat of an institution in Woodstock. This spot is quite popular on weekends, when young college students

and locals come for drinks, dinner and dancing.

Shopping

Saint-Jacques

The Visitor Information Centre Boutique
Hwy. 2
☎735-2747
The Visitor Information Centre Boutique is a great place to pick up a few souvenirs. This shop sells beautiful creations by local artists, as well as CDs and books by Acadian and New Brunswick artists and authors.

King's Landing

Kings Landing Museum Shop
☎363-5805
The Kings Landing Museum Shop offers not only

a good selection of souvenirs of king's Landing, but also a wide selection of books on the history of the region and Atlantic Canada.

Gagetown

Acadia Gallery of Canadian Art
late Jun to late Sep, every day 11am to 4pm
1948 Lakeview Rd.
☎488-1119
The charming contemporary Acadia Gallery of Canadian Art, located on the outskirts of Gagetown, exhibits a particularly interesting selection of works by artists using a variety of media. Since the gallery also serves as a workshop, it is often possible to meet some of the artists that were inspired by this enchanting site along the St. John River.

Southern New Brunswick

All along the coastal road that leads from the U.S. border to Nova Scotia, the landscape, villages and towns are marked by one of the most incredible natural phenomenas on Earth: the tides of the Bay of Fundy.

Twice a day, the highest tides in the world, storm the shores of the Bay of Fundy at lightning speed. In some places, the water can reach as high as 16m (the equivalent of a four-storey building) in just a few hours, transforming the landscape in remarkable ways over the years. The tides are so powerful that they actually reverse the flow of a waterfall in Saint John and create a tidal bore (a small tidal wave) on the Petitcodiac River.

Then, receding just as rapidly, they leave behind endless beaches perfect for clam-digging,

which can be explored until the next massive rise in the water level. Adding to the pleasure of visiting this magnificent coastal region, the shores of the Bay of Fundy are studded with picturesque villages that boast a rich architectural heritage.

Saint John, the province's largest city, and Moncton, its most dynamic, are also located here. Furthermore, the bay is also one of the best places in the world for whale-watching, since more than 20 different

species come here to feed in the summer.

Finding Your Way Around

This tour of **Southern New Brunswick ★ ★** takes you from St. Stephen to Aulac, near the Nova Scotia border.

By Car

From St. Stephen to Saint John, and then on to Sussex, the major road is Highway 1. In Sussex,

Highway I connects with Highway 2, which leads to Moncton and Aulac, at the Nova Scotia border, where the tour ends. To reach Deer Island, take the exit for St. George from Highway 2, then follow the signs to the tiny village of Letete. A ferry crosses from there to Deer Island. It is possible to reach Campobello Island from the state of Maine by taking the road from Calais to Lubec. To reach Grand Manan Island, visitors must take the ferry from Blacks Harbour.

By Plane

Saint John Airport is located about 10km east of the city. A shuttle carries passengers from the large downtown hotels to the airport several times a day. The airport is served mainly by **Air Canada** (*☎888-247-2262*).

Moncton Airport is located at 1575 Champlain Street, in Dieppe. The downtown area may be reached by taxi. The airport is mainly served by **Air Canada** (*☎888-247-2262*).

Great blue heron

Bus Stations

Saint John
300 Union St., at the corner of Carmarthen St.
☎648-3566

Moncton
961 Main St., downtown
☎859-5060

Train Stations

Moncton
1240 Main St., west side of downtown
☎857-9830

By Ferry

Saint John

A ferry makes the crossing from Saint John to Digby, Nova Scotia, all year-round, with up to three daily crossings during the summer. Departures are made from a dock on the west bank of the St. John River.
☎649-7777 or 888-249-7245
www.nfl-bay.com

Grand Manan Island

A ferry makes its way to Grand Manan Island five or six times a day from Blacks Harbour.
☎662-3724

Practical Information

Area code: **506**

Tourist Information Offices

St. Stephen

5 King St.
☎466-7390
www.town.ststephen.nb.ca

St. Andrews by-the-Sea

Hwy. 1
☎466-4858
www.town.standrews.nb.ca

Saint John

Hwy. 1, PO Box 1971, E2L 4L1
☎658-2990, 866-463-8639 or 866-364-4444
⇌632-6118
www.cityofsaintjohn.com
near the Reversing Falls
☎658-2937
downtown, near the market
☎658-2855

Moncton

Main St., near Boreview Park
☎856-4399
City Hall, 665 Main St., E1C 1E8
☎853-3590 or 800-363-4558
⇌859-2629
www.gomoncton.com

Exploring

St. Stephen

The most important border town in Atlantic Canada, St. Stephen is a small, lively community that was founded in 1784 by American colonists wishing to remain loyal to the British crown after the

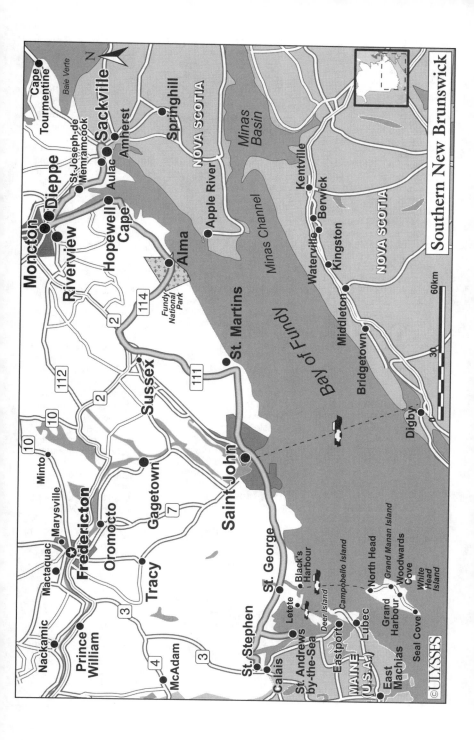

Southern New Brunswick

Revolutionary War. Today, ironically, St. Stephen and Calais, its twin town in the state of Maine, could easily be mistaken for a single town if it weren't for the Saint Croix River, which forms a natural border between the two. This lively community is celebrated on both sides of the border each year during the **International Festival**, which takes place at the end of August. In early August, a festival dedicated to **chocolate** is held in St. Stephen, which holds the distinction of being the birthplace of the chocolate bar, invented here in 1910 by the Ganong company. The ever successful **Ganong Chocolatier** *(73 Milltown Blvd.,* ☎*465-5611)* shop and its **Chocolate Museum** *(same address,* ☎*466-7848)* are a must for anyone with a sweet tooth.

The **Charlotte County Museum** *(free admission; Jun to Aug, Mon-Sat 9:30am to 4:30pm; 443 Milltown Blvd.,* ☎*466-3295)* is set up inside a Second Empire-style residence built in 1864 by a prosperous local businessman. It now houses a collection of objects related to local history, especially the period when St. Stephen and the small neighbouring villages were known for shipbuilding.

Bayside

In Bayside, on the way to St. Andrews, you can visit the Canadian side of the **Saint Croix Island International Historic Site ★** *(free admission; Jun to mid-Oct)*. A self-guided interpretive trail reveals the way of life of the first French colonists to settle in North America. The site provides a superb panoramic view of Saint Croix Island, located in the middle of the Saint Croix River.

Saint Croix Island occupies a symbolic place in the history of the French colonization of the New World as the location of the first attempt at a permanent settlement in North America.

In 1604, Pierre du Gua, sieur de Monts, and his crew arrived in Acadia aboard the flagship *Bonne-Renommée*. Searching for a suitable settlement site, the expedition arrived in Passamaquoddy Bay at the end of June. De Monts chose this island, christened it Saint Croix, and attempted to establish the first permanent French settlement in the Americas. The settlement was short-lived, however; by the summer of 1605, De Monts had transferred his

people to the shores of the Annapolis Basin, on the other side of the Bay of Fundy in present-day Nova Scotia, and founded Port-Royal, which would become the heart of Acadia.

You can also visit the American section of the Saint Croix Island International Historic Site, located 13km south of Calais, in the state of Maine.

St. Andrews by-the-Sea

The most famous vacation spot in southern New Brunswick, St. Andrews by-the-Sea is a lovely village facing the bay. Its popularity is due in large part to its astonishingly rich architectural heritage. Like many other communities in the area, St. Andrews by-the-Sea was founded by Loyalists in 1783, and enjoyed a period of great prosperity during the 19th century as a centre for shipbuilding and the exportation of wood billets. A number of the opulent houses flanking its streets, particularly on **Water Street ★**, date back to that golden era. At the end of the 19th century, St. Andrews by-the-Sea began welcoming affluent visitors who came here to drink in the invigorating sea air.

St. Andrews by-the-Sea's new vocation was clearly established in 1889 with the construction of the magnificent **Algonquin ★★** hotel, on a hill overlooking the village. In

Algonquin hotel

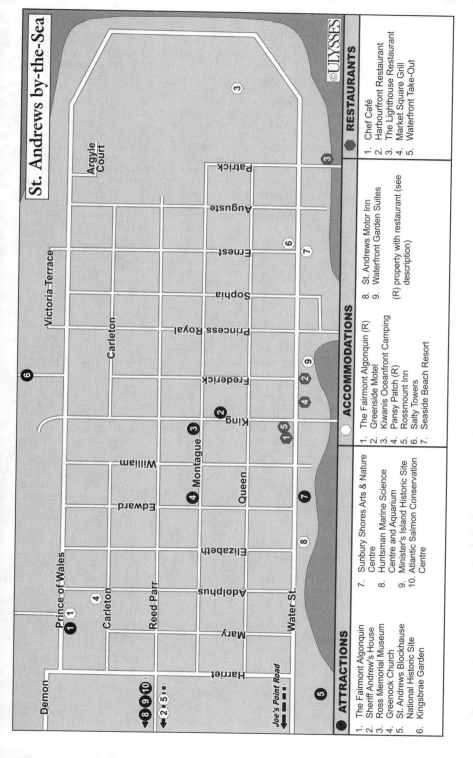

St. Andrews by-the-Sea

© ULYSSES

ATTRACTIONS

1. The Fairmont Algonquin
2. Sheriff Andrew's House
3. Ross Memorial Museum
4. Greenock Church
5. St. Andrews Blockhause National Historic Site
6. Kingsbrae Garden
7. Sunbury Shores Arts & Nature Centre
8. Huntsman Marine Science Centre and Aquarium
9. Minister's Island Historic Site
10. Atlantic Salmon Conservation Centre

ACCOMMODATIONS

1. The Fairmont Algonquin (R)
2. Greenside Motel
3. Kiwanis Oceanfront Camping
4. Pansy Patch (R)
5. Rossmount Inn
6. Salty Towers
7. Seaside Beach Resort
8. St. Andrews Motor Inn
9. Waterfront Garden Suites

(R) property with restaurant (see description)

RESTAURANTS

1. Chef Café
2. Harbourfront Restaurant
3. The Lighthouse Restaurant
4. Market Square Grill
5. Waterfront Take-Out

addition to the picturesque charm of its many historic buildings and its location alongside the bay, St. Andrews by-the-Sea now boasts a wide selection of accommodations and fine restaurants, numerous shops and a renowned golf course. All of this makes St. Andrews by-the-Sea a perfect place to stay during a tour of the region and its islands.

Erected in 1820, **Sheriff Andrews' House ★** *(free admission; late Jun to early Sep, every day 9:30am to 4:30pm; 63 King St., ☎453-2324)* is one of the town's best-preserved homes from that era. It was built by Elusha Shelton Andrews, sheriff of Charlotte County and son of distinguished Loyalist Reverend Samuel Andrews. Since 1986, it has belonged to the provincial government, which turned it into a museum. Guides in period costumes describe the sheriff's life and times.

A sumptuous 19th century neoclassical residence, the **Ross Memorial Museum ★** *(free admission; mid-Jun to early Oct, Tue-Sat 10am to 4:30pm; 188 Montague St., ☎529-5124)* contains an antique collection, which Henry Phipps Ross and Sarah Juliette Ross, an American couple who lived in St. Andrews by-the-Sea from 1902 until they died, had assembled over their lifetime. The Rosses had a passion for travelling and antiques; they acquired some magnificent pieces of Chinese porcelain and other now priceless imported objects, as well as

some lovely furniture made in New Brunswick.

There are several remarkable churches in St. Andrews by-the-Sea. The most flamboyant is **Greenock Church ★ ★** *(at the corner of Montague and Edward Sts.)*, a Presbyterian church that was completed in 1824. Its most interesting feature is its pulpit, a good part of which is made of Honduran mahogany.

Until very recently, the **St. Andrews Blockhouse** *($1; Jun to early Sep, every day 9am to 8pm; early Sep to mid-Sep, 9am to 5pm; 23 Joe's Point Rd., at the west end of Water St., ☎636-4011)*, a national historic site, was the last surviving blockhouse from the War of 1812. Pretty **Centennial Park** lies opposite.

Located in the heart of St. Andrews by-the-Sea, **Kingsbrae Garden ★** *($8.50; mid-May to mid-Oct, every day 9am to 6pm; 220 King St., ☎529-3335 or 866-566-8687, www.kingsbraegarden.com)* is a true horticultural masterpiece covering 10ha and highlighting the rich gardening tradition of the region. Visitors can explore the rosary, a Victorian-inspired garden, a perennial garden, a rock garden and a wild-plant garden, among others. You'll while away the hours in these magnificent gardens overlooking Passamaquoddy Bay. A restaurant located in the garden's historic home serves light meals.

The **Sunbury Shores Arts & Nature Centre** *(139 Water St., ☎529-3386)*

houses a small art gallery where visitors can admire the work of New Brunswick artists. The centre is better known, however, for its summer courses on art, crafts and nature, they are offered to groups of children and adults.

At the **Huntsman Marine Science Centre and Aquarium ★ ★** *($7.50; May and Jun, every day 10am to 4:30pm; Jul and Aug, every day 10am to 6pm; Sep and Oct, Mon-Tue noon to 4:30pm; Wed-Sun 10am to 4:30pm; 1 Lower Campus Rd., ☎529-1200)* visitors can learn about the bay's many natural treasures. Several animal species can be observed here, including seals, who are fed every day at 11am and 4pm. There is also a touch-tank, where visitors can touch various live species of shellfish.

At the beginning of the 19th century, the **Ministers Island Historic Site ★** *($5 per car, includes a tour of the house; Jun to mid-Oct; Mowat Drive Rd., take Bar Rd. until the end, ☎529-5081)* was the property of Reverend Samuel. It was purchased in 1890 by Sir William Van Horne, a Montréal resident famous for building the Canadian Pacific Railway, the first railroad linking Montréal to Vancouver. On this large estate, Van Horne erected an immense 50-room summer home. Ministers Island is only accessible at low tide. To arrange a visit, contact the tourist information office *(☎529-3000 or 529-5081)*.

Salmon

At the **Atlantic Salmon Conservation Centre** *($4; late May to mid-Oct, every day 9am to 5pm; 24 Chamcook Rd., 8km from St. Andrews by-the-Sea on Rte. 127, ☎529-1384)*, visitors can learn about the life cycle of the Atlantic salmon, most notably by viewing the fish in its natural environment, through a window.

St. George

St. George, nicknamed "Granite Town" because of the rich granite deposits found in this area, is a small town with a Loyalist heritage, located alongside a pretty **waterfall ★** on the Magaguadavic River. A small lookout at the town entrance, beside the bridge on Brunswick Street, offers a lovely view of the waterfall, the gorge, the former St. George Pulp & Paper Company dam and the ladder built to help salmon swim upriver in summer.

Like many towns and villages founded on the shores of the bay in the late 18th century, St. George has its share of interesting buildings, such as the **post office** *(Brunswick St.)*, with its red granite facade, and several churches, including the **Kirk Presbyterian** *(on Brunswick St., at the east exit of the village)*, the

oldest church of its denomination in Canada.

From St. George, visitors can head to Letete, where a free ferry service takes passengers to Deer Island between 7am and 10pm every day.

Deer Island

After cruising through a scattering of little islands covered with birds, the free ferry from Letete lands at Deer Island, with its wooded landscape, untouched beaches and tiny fishing villages. Three hours before high tide each day, visitors can view an interesting natural phenomenon from the southern point of the island– one of the largest whirlpools in the world, known locally as the **Old Sow ★**.

In summertime, a private ferry makes the crossing between Deer Island and Campobello Island every hour or so.

Campobello Island

Campobello, the beloved island of former U.S. president Franklin D. Roosevelt (1882-1945), is a good place for history buffs who enjoy the great outdoors. People come here

to enjoy the lovely untouched beaches, cycle on the quiet roads or walk along the well-maintained trails that follow the shoreline.

On the eastern tip of the island, the picturesque lighthouse at **East Quoddy Head ★** occupies a magnificent site on the bay, from which it is sometimes possible to spot whales and other sea mammals. In the early 19th century, Campobello's beauty began to attract the attention of wealthy families living in the northeastern cities of the United States, who built lovely summer homes here. The most famous of these families was that of Franklin D. Roosevelt, whose father James had purchased 1.6ha on the island in 1883. Franklin himself, and then his own family, spent most of his summers here from 1883 to 1921, the year he contracted polio. He returned on several later occasions to visit his friends on the island while serving as President of the United States.

Although Campobello lies within Canada, it is most easily accessible from the U.S. border town of Lubec, Maine. During the summer months, a private ferry also shuttles hourly between Deer Island and Campobello.

Roosevelt-Campobello International Park ★★ *(free admission; late May to early Oct, 10am to 6pm; Rte. 774, ☎752-2922)* is a joint project of the Canadian and U.S. governments, launched in 1964 with the aim of increasing

Roosevelt House

public awareness of Roosevelt's special attachment to Campobello Island and his magnificent property there. The visitor centre shows a short film on Roosevelt's sojourns on the island.

Afterward, visitors can tour the extraordinary **Roosevelt House**, most of whose furnishings belonged to the former U.S. president, then stop at the **Prince House**, the site of the **James Roosevelt House** and the **Hubbard House**. The park also includes a beautiful natural area, south of the visitor centre, where lovely hiking trails have been cleared along the shore.

Located near Roosevelt International Park, **Herring Cove** (☎752-7010) is a lovely nature site with hiking trails, an interpretation centre, a golf course and campsites.

Grand Manan Island

For many years, Grand Manan's 275-odd bird

species and unique rock formations mainly attracted scientists, including the famous James Audubon in the early 19th century. More recently, however, Grand Manan has begun to benefit from the current ecotourism craze, since the island obviously has a lot to offer nature lovers. It is a pleasant place to explore by bicycle, and even better on foot, thanks to the excellent network of trails running alongside the jagged shoreline, with its often spectacular scenery. Without question, one of the most picturesque places on the island is the lighthouse known as **Swallowtail Light** ★, which stands at the tip of a peninsula at North Head. From here, whales can regularly be seen swimming off the shores of the island. Grand Manan also features a **museum** (*Grand Harbour*, ☎662-3524) and serves as the point of departure for numerous whale-watching excursions and expeditions to **Machias Seal Island** ★, a remarkable bird sanctuary.

The island has several lighthouses, beaches and

great bird-watching spots. Travellers have a choice of several B&Bs as well as an excellent **campground** (*The Anchorage*, ☎662-7022).

To reach Grand Manan Island, visitors must take the ferry from Blacks Harbour (☎662-3724), which makes five or six trips every day.

Saint John

Saint John, New Brunswick's largest city, occupies a hilly area on either side of the St. John River, at the point where it flows into the Bay of Fundy. A perfect example of the old industrial port cities in the eastern part of North America, it has a unique, slightly mysterious charm. Lofty cranes and warehouses line the docks, which look strangely like wooden fences rising high out of the river at low tide. To add to its mysterious character, Saint John is often blanketed with a thick fog that can envelop the city at any

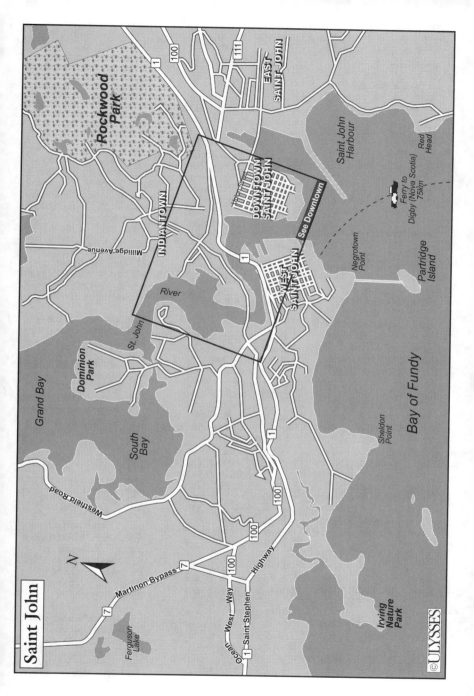

Saint John

Rockwood Park

Millidge Avenue

INDIANTOWN

DOWNTOWN SAINT JOHN

See Downtown

WEST SAINT JOHN

EAST SAINT JOHN

Saint John Harbour

Red Head

River

St. John

Dominion Park

Grand Bay

South Bay

Negrotown Point

Partridge Island

Ferry to Digby (Nova Scotia) 75km

Westfield Road

Sheldon Point

Bay of Fundy

N

Martinon Bypass

Ferguson Lake

Ocean West Way

Saint-Stephen Highway

Irving Nature Park

© ULYSSES

moment, before disappearing just as quickly. The growth of the city's industries is largely due to its port, which is ice-free all year long.

The site itself was scouted out for the first time on June 24, 1604 by explorer Samuel de Champlain, who christened the river St. John (Saint-Jean) in honour of the patron saint of that day. Later, in 1631, Charles de La Tour established a trading post here. The city's history didn't really start, however, until 1783, under the English regime. From May 10 to May 18 of that year, some 2,000 Loyalists landed in Saint John, seeking a fresh start in life after the defeat of British forces by American revolutionaries. More arrived before winter, doubling the population of Saint John.

The city then absorbed a large number of immigrants, mainly from the British Isles. In those years, Partridge Island, in Saint John's port, was Canada's chief point of entry and quarantine station for immigrants. Today, Saint John has a higher concentration of Irish-Canadians than any other city in the country.

It is a pleasant place to visit, particularly in mid-July during the **Loyalist Days**, which commemorate the arrival of Loyalists in 1783. The excellent **By-the-Sea Festival**, held in August, celebrates the performing arts, while the **Franco-Frolic**, held in June, honours Acadian culture and traditions.

★★
Downtown

Downtown Saint John, with its narrow streets lined with historic buildings and houses, lies on a hill on the east side of the river. A tour of the area usually starts at **Market Square**, laid out a little more than a decade ago as part of an effort to revitalize the city centre. The square includes a shopping mall, a convention centre, several restaurants and a hotel that combines modern construction with 19th century buildings. An excellent **tourist information office** is located at the entrance to Market Square.

The **New Brunswick Museum** ★ *($6; Mon-Fri 9am to 9pm, Sat 10am to 6pm, Sun noon to 5pm; Market Sq., ☎643-2300)* was recently moved to Market Square. The oldest museum in Canada, it is devoted not only to the work of New Brunswick artists, but also to the history of the province's various inhabitants—Aboriginals, Acadians, Loyalists, and others. The permanent collection features certain imported objects as well, including pieces of Chinese porcelain.

On the south side of Market Square stands **Barbour's General Store** *($2; mid-May to mid-Oct; ☎658-2939)*, a small brick building displaying consumer goods that were typically available in this type of shop during the 19th century. Guided tours of the city are also offered from here.

Visitors can head up Union Street to the **Loyalist House National Historic Site** ★ *($3; mid-May to mid-Sep; 120 Union St., ☎652-3590)*, a very simple house built in the first decade of the 19th century, which is decorated with elegant period furniture. Union Street later intersects with Charlotte Street, where visitors can turn right to reach **King's Square** ★, a pretty urban park marking the centre of Saint John. The paths in the park are laid out in the pattern of the Union Jack; what better way for the inhabitants of Saint John to express their attachment to their mother country?

Standing opposite the park on Charlotte Street is the **Old City Market** ★ *(free admission; Mon-Thu 7:30am to 6pm, Fri 7:30am to 7pm, Sat 7:30am to 5pm; 47 Charlotte St., ☎658-2820)*, dating back to 1876, where shoppers can still purchase fresh produce from local farmers. Some merchants sell dulse, a type of seaweed that people in Saint John often use as an accompaniment to various dishes.

On another side of the park, visitors will find the sumptuous **Imperial Theatre** ★ *(24 King Sq. S., ☎674-4100)*, built in 1913 and restored in 1994, which is dedicated to the performing arts.

The **Aitken Bicentennial Exhibition Centre** *(free admission; Jun to Sep, every day 10am to 5pm; Sep to Jun, Tue-Sun 11:30am to 4:30pm; 20 Hazen Ave., ☎633-4870)* presents exhibits specifically de

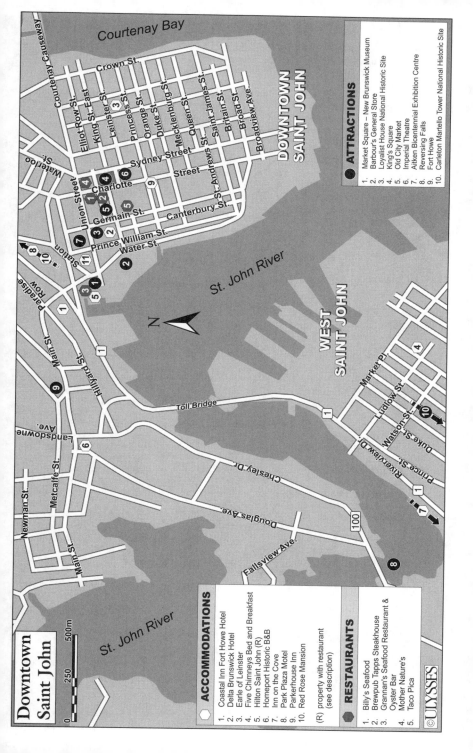

Downtown Saint John

0 250 500m

St. John River

Courtenay Bay

Crown St.

King St. East

Elliot Row St.

Leinster St.

Princess St.

Orange St.

Duke St.

Mecklenburg St.

Queen St.

Saint James St.

Britain St.

Broad St.

Broadview Ave.

Sydney Street

Saint Andrews St.

Street

Canterbury St.

Charlotte

Germain St.

Prince William St.

Water St.

Union Street

Waterloo St.

Station

Paradise Row

Main St.

Hilyard St.

Landsdowne Ave.

Metcalfe St.

Newman St.

Main St.

Douglas Ave.

Fallsview Ave.

Chesley Dr.

Toll Bridge

St. John River

WEST SAINT JOHN

DOWNTOWN SAINT JOHN

Riverview Dr.

Market Pl.

Ludlow St.

Watson St.

Duke St.

Prince St.

N

1

100

● ATTRACTIONS

1. Market Square – New Brunswick Museum
2. Barbour's General Store
3. Loyalist House National Historic Site
4. King's Square
5. Old City Market
6. Imperial Theatre
7. Aitken Bicentennial Exhibition Centre
8. Reversing Falls
9. Fort Howe
10. Carleton Martello Tower National Historic Site

⬡ ACCOMMODATIONS

1. Coastal Inn Fort Howe Hotel
2. Delta Brunswick Hotel
3. Earle of Leinster
4. Five Chimneys Bed and Breakfast
5. Hilton Saint John (R)
6. Homeport Historic B&B
7. Inn on the Cove
8. Park Plaza Motel
9. Parkerhouse Inn
10. Red Rose Mansion

(R) property with restaurant (see description)

⬡ RESTAURANTS

1. Billy's Seafood
   Brewpub Tapps Steakhouse
2. Grannan's Seafood Restaurant &
   Oyster Bar
3. Mother Nature's
4. Taco Pica
5.

© ULYSSES

signed to teach children about the various facets of science in a dynamic fashion.

Outside Downtown

The **Reversing Falls** ★ ★ *(on Rte. 100, at the river)* are a unique natural phenomenon that occurs twice a day at high tide. The current of the river, which at this point drops 4m at low tide, is reversed at high tide when the water level of the bay becomes several metres higher than that of the river. This counter-current can be felt as far up-river as Fredericton.

For an excellent **view** ★ of the city, head to the site of **Fort Howe** *(Main St., ☎658-2090)*. There is a wooden blockhouse on the site, which was built in Halifax and moved here in 1777 to protect the port of Saint John in the event of a U.S. attack.

The **Carleton Martello Tower National Historic Site** ★ ★ *($3.50; Jun to Oct, 10am to 6pm; on the west bank, Whipple St., ☎636-4011)* is a circular tower built during the War of 1812 to protect the port from U.S. attack. It was also used as a command post for the Canadian army during the Second World War. Guides in 19th-century dress present the history of both the tower and the city of Saint John. From the top, visitors can enjoy a magnificent panoramic view of the city, the port and the bay.

If Saint John were a person, 880ha **Rockwood**

Park *(main entry on Mt. Pleasant Ave.)* would be its lungs. All sorts of outdoor activities can be enjoyed here, including hiking, swimming, fishing, canoeing and pedal-boating. A number of other activities are organized for children. In the north section of the park is the **Cherry Brook Zoo** *($6; open year-round, 10am to nightfall; Sandy Point Rd., in the north part of Rockwood Park, ☎634-1440)*, the only zoo in the Maritimes featuring exotic animals. About 100 or so different species may be found here.

For many years, **Partridge Island** was the main point of entry for immigrants coming to Canada from the British Isles and the European continent. Between 1785 and 1942, it was the transition point and quarantine station for some three million immigrants who then settled in Saint John or, more commonly, elsewhere in Canada or the United States.

About 2,000 of these individuals died here; having survived the often difficult journey across the Atlantic, they never had the chance to see anything beyond Partridge Island. They were buried in one of the six cemeteries located here. The island is also the site of New Brunswick's oldest lighthouse. Unfortunately, the island has been closed to visitors for several years now.

Perfectly marvellous **Irving Nature Park** ★ ★ *(free admission; at the end of Sand Cove Rd., ☎653-7367)* has a great deal to offer nature lovers. Loca-

ted just a few kilometres west of the industrial city of Saint John, this magnificent park covers a 225ha peninsula trimmed with untouched beaches. The city seems a million miles away from here. Visitors can also enjoy a pleasant stroll along one of the park's trails, communing with nature and observing the plant and animal life of southern New Brunswick.

St. Martins

St. Martins is one of New Brunswick's best-kept treasures. An idyllic fishing village looking out on the Bay of Fundy, St. Martins is adorned with numerous houses built during the 19th century, when it was known as a major producer of large wooden ships. Today, the village is very picturesque, with local fishing boats moored in its little port. It also has two covered bridges, one of which leads to the famous **echo caves** ★, cavities created in local cliffs by the tides of the Bay of Fundy. Nature lovers will find long, untouched beaches in St. Martins, as well as attractive **Lions Park**, which is a good place to take a walk or go swimming. As home to one of the province's best inns (the **Quaco Inn**, see p 92), the village also has something to offer connoisseurs of fine cuisine. Finally, to enjoy a **spectacular view** ★ of the local red cliffs, head to the **Quaco Head lighthouse**, located several kilometres west of St. Martins.

The **Fundy Trail Parkway** ★★ *(10km east of St. Martins)* is a seasonal, multi-purpose coastal-access network. It comprises a low-speed roadway dotted with lookouts, a walking/cycling trail, footpaths leading to the beaches and estuaries and an interpretive centre at Big Salmon River. The interpretive centre and many of the lookouts are wheelchair-accessible.

Fundy National Park

Fundy National Park *(Rte. 114, near Alma, ☎887-6000, 887-6015 or 888-773-8888, ≈887-6008)* is the ultimate place to explore the shores of the bay, observe its plant and animal life and appreciate the power of its tides. It covers 206km^2 of densely wooded mountainous territory abounding in spectacular scenery, lakes and rivers with nearly 20km of shoreline. All sorts of athletic activities can be enjoyed here.

The park is a hiker's paradise, with its 120km of trails running through the forest, near lakes and alongside the magnificent bay. Visitors can also enjoy fishing, camping on one of the many equipped or back country sites, playing a game on the excellent golf course or swimming in the heated pool (the waters of the bay are too cold for swimming). Travellers pressed for time should make sure at the very least to visit **Pointe Wolfe** ★★, where nearby trails offer spectacular

views of cliffs plunging straight into the waters of the bay. At each entrance to the park, employees offer information on the various activities that are available.

Alma

Alma, a small fishing village located at the entrance to the park, features a variety of accommodations and numerous restaurants. When the tide is at its lowest, vast stretches of the sea bed are exposed, offering an interesting place for a stroll. From Alma, Route 915 leads to a peninsula with the evocative name of **Cape Enrage** ★.

This peninsula offers beautiful views of the bay and is a great place to enjoy several different aquatic sports. It also has a beautiful beach off the beaten track.

The route runs alongside the bay to **Mary's Point** ★, a water-bird sanctuary where hundreds of thousands of semi-palmate sandpipers alight between mid-July and mid-August.

Hopewell Cape

Hopewell Cape's rock formations, the **Hopewell Rocks**, also known as the **Flowerpot Rocks** ★★ *(mid-May to mid-Oct; Rte. 114, ☎734-3429 or 877-734-3429)*, are one of the province's most famous attractions. All by themselves, they symbolize the massive force of the tides in the bay. At high tide, they look like small wooded islands right off the coast. As the waters recede at low tide, they expose lofty rock formations sculpted by the endless coming and going of the tides. When the tide is at its lowest, visitors can explore the sea bed. Numerous water sports are organized from Hopewell Cape.

The **Hopewell Rocks Interpretive Centre** *($7; mid-May to mid-Jun, every day 9am to 5pm; mid-Jun to mid-Aug, every day 8am to 8pm; mid-Aug to early Sep, every day 8am to 7pm; early Sep to mid-Oct, every day 9am to 5pm; 131 Chemin Discovery, ☎734-3429)* features a multimedia exhibit that explains the

Hopewell Cape

New Brunswick

natural phenomenon that is the Bay of Fundy. Other exhibits enable visitors to better understand the Fundy ecosystem, as well as the cultural and human history of Albert County.

Moncton

Due to its location in the heart of Atlantic Canada, as well as its qualified, bilingual workforce, Moncton is New Brunswick's current rising star. Up until the Acadians were expelled from the region, this site on the banks of the Petitcodiac River was a small Acadian trading post. Colonists from the United States then settled here and founded the city, which thrived in the mid-19th century as a ship-building centre before becoming a transportation hub for the Intercolonial Railway. Moncton's economy is now chiefly based on commerce and the service sector.

For the Acadians who constitute 35% of the population, Moncton offers a unique opportunity to face the challenges and savour the pleasures of city living. Despite their minority status, they have made Moncton a base for their most important economic and social institutions and the city is the home of the province's only French-speaking university, the Université de Moncton. Ironically, the city, and by extension the university, were named after officer Robert Monkton, commander of the British

forces who captured of Fort Beauséjour in 1755, an event that heralded the fall of the French Empire in North America.

Moncton is now the centre of Acadian rebirth and the vibrant energy in the air here is due in large part to the entrepreneurial spirit that characterizes today's Acadians. Moncton's immediate surroundings include such varied communities as **Dieppe**, most of whose inhabitants are Acadian, and English-speaking **Riverview**. An excellent time to visit the city is in early July, when the atmosphere is enlivened by the **Moncton Jazz Festival**.

The Petitcodiac River, known locally as the Chocolate River because of the colour of its waters, empties and then fills back up again twice a day, in accordance with the tides in the Bay of Fundy. The rise in the river's water level is always preceded by an interesting phenomenon known as a **tidal bore ★**, a wave up to several dozen centimetres high that flows upriver. The best spot to watch this wave is in **Bore Park** *(downtown on Main St.)*. To find out what time of the day the tidal bore will occur during your stay, contact Moncton's tourist information office *(at the corner of Main St., facing Bore Park, ☎856-4399)*.

The Second Empire–style **Thomas Williams House ★** *(free admission; Jul and Aug, Mon-Sat 9:30am to 4:30pm, Sun 1pm to 5pm; rest of the year by appointment only;*

103 Park St., ☎857-0590) is a 12-room residence built in 1883 for the family of Thomas Williams, who was an accountant for the Intercolonial Railway at the time. His heirs then lived here for nearly a century. Today, the house is a museum where visitors can learn about the lifestyle of the Moncton bourgeoisie during the Victorian era. Back in 1883, Moncton was no more than a tiny village, and the house lay outside its boundaries, in the middle of the countryside.

The **Moncton Museum ★** *(free admission; Mon-Sat 9am to 4:30pm, Sun 1pm to 5pm; 20 Mountain Rd., ☎856-4383)* houses a lovely collection of objects linked to the history of the city and its surrounding area. During the summer, the museum often presents large-scale temporary exhibits. Its sumptuous facade was salvaged from the city's former city hall. Moncton's oldest building, dating back to 1821 and very well preserved, stands right next door.

The **Musée Acadien ★** *($2; Mon-Fri 10am to 5pm, Sat and Sun 1pm to 5pm; Université de Moncton, Clément Cormier Bldg., ☎858-4088)* displays over 35,000 objects, including a permanent collection of Acadian artifacts dating from 1604 up to the 19th century. The museum was founded in Memramcook in 1886 by Père Camille Lefebvre of the Collège Saint-Joseph, before being moved to its present location in 1965. Also in the same building as the museum, visitors will find

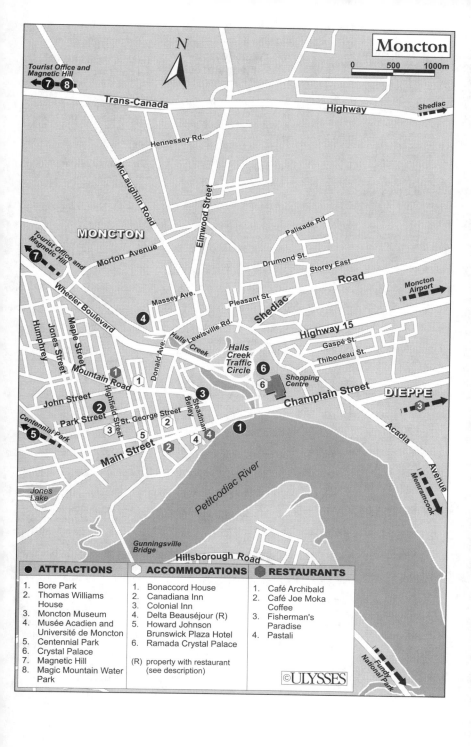

Moncton

0   500   1000m

Tourist Office and Magnetic Hill

Trans-Canada

Highway

Shediac

Hennessey Rd.

McLaughlin Road

Elmwood Street

MONCTON

Palisade Rd.

Morton Avenue

Drumond St.

Storey East

Road

Tourist Office and Magnetic Hill

Wheeler Boulevard

Massey Ave.

Pleasant St.

Shediac

Moncton Airport

Maple Street

Jones Street

Humphrey

Mountain Road

Halls Lewisville Rd.

Halls Creek

Highway 15

Gaspé St.

Thibodeau St.

John Street

Highfield Street

Donald Ave.

Steadman

Belley

Halls Creek Traffic Circle

Shopping Centre

Champlain Street

DIEPPE

Park Street

St. George Street

Centennial Park

Main Street

Jones Lake

Petitcodiac River

Acadia

Avenue

Memramcook

Gunningsville Bridge

Hillsborough Road

Fundy National Park

● ATTRACTIONS	⬡ ACCOMMODATIONS	⬡ RESTAURANTS
1. Bore Park	1. Bonaccord House	1. Café Archibald
2. Thomas Williams House	2. Canadiana Inn	2. Café Joe Moka Coffee
3. Moncton Museum	3. Colonial Inn	3. Fisherman's Paradise
4. Musée Acadien and Université de Moncton	4. Delta Beauséjour (R)	4. Pastali
5. Centennial Park	5. Howard Johnson Brunswick Plaza Hotel	
6. Crystal Palace	6. Ramada Crystal Palace	
7. Magnetic Hill		
8. Magic Mountain Water Park	(R) property with restaurant (see description)	

©ULYSSES

the **Centre d'Art de l'Université de Moncton** ★★, where works by Acadian artists are exhibited. On the west side of the city, **Centennial Park** *(St. George Blvd.)* is a place where the whole family can come to relax any time of the year. The area includes hiking trails, a small beach, tennis courts and a playground. Canoe and pedal-boat rentals are also available.

The **Crystal Palace** *(499 Rue Paul, beside Place Champlain, Dieppe,* ☎*858-8584)* is a family entertainment centre featuring carousels, games, miniature golf, a swimming pool, movie theatres and a science centre intended for children. Located indoors, it is overrun with families on rainy days.

The **Magnetic Hill** ★ *($2 per car; west of Moncton, Exit 88 from the Trans-Canada Hwy.,* ☎*853-3590)* is an intriguing optical illusion that gives people the impression that their car is climbing a slope. The staff ask drivers to stop their engines at what seems to be the bottom of a very steep hill. Then, as if by miracle, the car seems to climb the slope. This remarkable illusion is a must for families. Other family attractions have sprung up around Magnetic Hill, including a park, a zoo, a mini-train, a go-kart track, a miniature golf course, and most notably, the superb **Magic Mountain Water Park** ★ *(Rte. 126 N.,* ☎*857-9283)*. Here you will also find shops, restaurants and a hotel.

Saint-Joseph-de-Memramcook

A small rural town in the pretty Memramcook valley, Saint-Joseph is of great symbolic importance to the Acadian people. This is the only region on the Bay of Fundy where Acadians still live on the farmlands they occupied before the Deportation. It thus serves as a bridge between pre- and post-Deportation Acadia. Collège Saint-Joseph, where the Acadian elite was educated for many years, was founded here in 1864.

The college hosted the first Acadian national convention in 1881. At the **Monument Lefebvre National Historic Site** ★ *($3.50; Jun to mid-Oct, every day 9am to 5pm; 480 Central St.,* ☎*636-4011)*, visitors can learn about Acadian history by viewing an exhibition on the key factors and pivotal moments that led to the survival of the Acadian people.

Sackville

A subtle aura of affluence and a unique awareness of the past emanate from Sackville, whose beautiful homes lie hidden behind the stately trees that flank its streets. The city is home to **Mount Allison University**, a small, highly reputable institution whose lovely buildings stand on beautiful, verdant plots of land in the centre of town.

On campus, visitors will find the **Owens Art Gallery** ★ *(free admission;* ☎*364-2574)*, which displays a large collection of paintings by New Brunswick artists, including several works by master Alex Colville.

Waterfowl Park ★★ *(free admission; every day until nightfall; entrance on E. Main St.,* ☎*364-4930)* is an interpretive centre focussing on the plant and animal life of a salt-water marsh. Thanks to 2km of trails and wooden footbridges, visitors can enter a world of unexpected richness and diversity. In addition to being exceptionally informative, this park is a wonderful place to relax.

Aulac

After British forces captured Fort Beauséjour in 1755, the Deportation, a tragic event in Acadian history, was initiated in Aulac. Built in 1751, Fort Beauséjour occupied a strategic location on Chignecto Bay, on the border of the French and British colonial empires. The **Fort Beauséjour National Historic Site** ★ *($3.50; Jun to mid-Oct, 9am to 5pm; Hwy. 2, Exit 550A,* ☎*364-5080)* includes an interpretive centre that examines Acadian history and the Deportation. Visitors can also stroll around several of the remaining fortifications of the star-shaped structure. The view of the bay and of New Brunswick and Nova Scotia is excellent from here.

Outdoor Activities

Hiking

The **Fundy Trail Parkway** (☎833-2019 or 866-386-3987, www.fundytrailpark way.com) is a network of trails along the Bay of Fundy, 10km east of St. Martins. Accessible by bike or on foot, it offers panoramic viewpoints of the countryside. Some of the trails lead to beaches.

Cycling

The islands in the Bay of Fundy, especially Campobello and Grand Manan, feature some excellent bike paths. It can also be fun to bike around the towns of St. Andrews by-the-Sea, St. John and Moncton. Several businesses offer bike rentals

Bicycle Rentals

Danny's Bike
59 Carleton St., St. Andrews by-the-Sea
☎529-3834

Covered Bridge Bicycle Tour
Saint John
☎849-9028

Gary's Bicycle Rentals
239 Weldon St., Moncton
☎855-8754

Whale-Watching

Because of its rich feeding grounds, the **Bay of Fundy** is one of the best places in the world to observe certain species of whales. Whale-watching excursions are organized throughout the summer in the following places: **St. Andrews by-the-Sea**, **Deer Island**, **Campobello Island** and **Grand Manan Island**, in the southwestern part of the province. Count on spending about $50 for a three-hour excursion. Contact:

Cline Marine
Departures from St. Andrews by-the-Sea, Deer Island and Campobello Island
☎747-0114 or 800-567-5880

Atlantic Marine Wildlife Tours
Departures from St. Andrews by-the-Sea
☎459-7325

St. Andrews by-the-Sea Outdoor Adventure
☎755-6415

Fundy Tide Runners
16 King St., St. Andrews by-the-Sea
☎529-4481

S/V Cory
St. Andrews by-the-Sea Wharf
☎529-8116
Excursions aboard a sailboat that can carry up to 40 passengers.

St. George Interactive Outdoors
15 Adventure Ln., St. Andrews by-the-Sea
☎755-2699 or 800-241-6906

Island Coast Boat Tours
Departures from Grand Manan Island
☎662-8181

Seawatch Tours
Departures from Grand Manan Island
☎662-8552

Starboard Tours
Departures from Grand Manan Island
☎662-8545

Least sandpiper

Bird-Watching

The forests and extensive coastline of New Brunswick are a haven for hundreds of bird species. Mary's Point, on the Bay of Fundy between Moncton and Fundy National Park, is one of the best-known observation sites in the province. Every year from mid-July to mid-August, admirers of winged wildlife and naturalists from the world over meet here to watch the flight of tens of thousands of semi-palmate sandpipers.

The islands of the Bay of Fundy also are much-lauded bird-watching sites. Grand Manan Island and Machias Seal Island are home to close to 275 species, including the Atlantic puffin and the Arctic tern. **Fundy National Park** spans a 206km stretch of coast, a favourite spot for many different species of birds that can easily be seen by following one of the

numerous hiking trails that crisscross the park.

Located near St. John, **Irving Nature Park** protects the peninsula, which is washed by the powerful tides of the Bay of Fundy. There are sandy beaches on one side of the park and salt marshes on the other, both of which provide excellent sources of food for migratory birds. Long, wooden footbridges and trails have been built so that visitors can observe the various species of birds that come here, such as the great blue heron and the sandpiper.

Canoeing and Kayaking

Grand Manan Island

Adventure High Seas Kayaking
☎662-3563
There's nothing like kayaking to appreciate the beauty of the island. Adventure High Seas

Kayaking offers enjoyable trips.

St. Andrews by-the-Sea

Seascape Kayak Tours
☎747-1884
This company offers kayak trips on the Bay of Fundy, an opportunity to enjoy the great outdoors while getting to know the marine life of the bay. Half-day: $55.

St. George

Outdoor Adventure
79 Main St.
☎755-6415 or
800-667-2010
www.havefun.net
The guided kayak and canoe trips organized by Outdoor Adventure ($49) offer adventure-seekers a chance to see the Bay of Fundy's marine life up close. Visitors may be fortunate enough to spot the occasional seal or eagle.

Piskahegan
☎755-6269
Piskahegan is another St. George company that lets visitors discover the natural beauty of the Bay of Fundy from up close. Courses are also offered. Trips start at $49.

Alma

Freshair Adventure
☎887-2249 or
800-545-0020
www.freshairadventure.
com
Freshair Adventure organizes half-day trips along the coast of Fundy National Park, a wonderful opportunity to explore the flora and fauna of this vast wilderness. Half-day: $55.

Scuba Diving

Navy Island Dive Co.
15 William St., St. Andrews by-the-Sea
☎529-4555
If the underwater world fascinates you, go on a diving trip and explore the rich marine life. Courses and equipment rentals are available.

Accommodations

St. Stephen

Blair House Bed & Breakfast
$$ bkfst incl.
≡
5 rooms
38 Prince William St., E3L 1S3
☎466-2233 or 888-972-5247
⇄*466-1699*
www.blairhouseinn.nb.ca
A lovely period house built in the mid-1800s for an eminent Loyalist family, the Blair House Bed & Breakfast stands on a beautifully landscaped lot in the heart of St. Stephen. Comfortable rooms and a copious English breakfast are offered.

Loon Bay Lodge
$$
ℜ, ᴣ
9 rooms
424 Loon Bay Rd., E3L 2W9
☎466-4213 or 888-566-4229
www.loonbaylodge.com
Situated in the middle of the countryside, the Loon Bay Lodge is a good choice

for those who enjoy a peaceful location. Its nine rooms with fireplaces, private bathrooms and breathtaking views of the sea guarantee an enjoyable stay. The rustic charm of the facility will please those who enjoy the great outdoors but like to have comfortable accommodations. A central log cabin has a dining room and a living room where visitors can meet. Fishing and hunting trips are organized.

St. Stephen Inn
$$
K, ≡, ✘, ℜ
51 rooms
99 King St., E3L 2C6
☎466-1814 or 800-565-3088
⇄*466-6148*
In the heart of the community, the St. Stephen Inn is a pleasant spot with typical, inexpensive motel rooms.

St. Andrews by-the-Sea

Kiwanis Oceanfront Camping
$
160 sites
550 Water St., E5B 2R6
☎529-3439 or 877-393-7070
⇄*529-3246*
www.kok.ca
The best thing about this campground is its location, a stone's throw from the sea and the centre of town. It is also nicely landscaped.

Greenside Motel
$$
K, ≡
16 rooms
242 Mowatt Dr., E5B 2P3
☎/⇄529-3039
Even though St. Andrews by-the-Sea is a rather posh vacation spot, visitors can

still find inexpensive motel-style accommodations with clean, simple rooms. One option is the Greenside Motel, located just outside of St. Andrews by-the-Sea, near the golf course. Some rooms have kitchenettes.

Salty Towers
$$
✘, K
15 rooms
340 Water St., E5B 2R3
☎529-4585
This large beautiful Victorian home, where antiques and knick-knacks can be found in every corner, has 15 rooms, a fireplace and two kitchens to prepare meals. Its eclectic decor will please those who appreciate something a little out of the ordinary. Guests will also enjoy its laid-back atmosphere.

Seaside Beach Resort
$$
K, ✘
24 rooms, 4 cottages
339 Water St., E5B 2R2
☎529-3039 or 800-506-8677
⇄*529-4479*
www.seaside.nb.ca
The Seaside Beach Resort consists of 10 wooden cottages ideally located on the shores of the bay. It is not the most luxurious spot, but the rooms are clean and include kitchenettes. Though this is a "resort," the mood is relaxed and ideal for families.

Waterfront Garden Suites
$$-$$$$
K
10 rooms
22 Douglas St., E5B 1A3
☎529-4571
⇄*525-4583*
Equipped with kitchenettes, the Waterfront is a good choice for those who want to stay a while in

New Brunswick

St. Andrews by-the-Sea but want to cut down on restaurant expenses. The property enjoys a wonderful location near the centre of town, facing the bay.

⚓ Rossmount Inn
$$$ bkfst incl.
≈, ℜ, ⊛
18 rooms
4599 Rte. 127, a few km from
St. Andrews by-the-Sea, E5B 2Z3
☎*529-3351 or*
877-529-3351
⇥*529-1920*
www.rossmountinn.com
Set in the middle of a large property overlooking the surrounding countryside, the Rossmount is a magnificent inn with antique furniture in each room. The Rossmount Inn also offers an excellent dining room.

St. Andrews Motor Inn
$$$
ℜ, K, ≈, ≡
37 rooms
111 Water St., E5B 1A3
☎*529-4571*
⇥*529-4583*
www.standrewsmotorinn.com
The St. Andrews Motor Inn, located right on the bay, offers comfortable, modern rooms with balconies or terraces. Some rooms also have a kitchenette. The outdoor pool behind the building looks out over the bay.

⚓ The Fairmont Algonquin
$$$-$$$$$
ℜ, K, ≈, ≡, △, ⅄, ✿, ⊛, 🐎
234 rooms
Hwy. 127, 184 Adolphus St.,
E5B 1T7
☎*529-8823 or*
800-441-1414
⇥*529-7162*
www.fairmont.com
Dominating the quaint setting of St. Andrews by-

the-Sea is the best and most reputed hotel in the Maritimes, the Fairmont Algonquin. A majestic neo-Tudor grouping in the centre of a large property, this dream hotel has withstood the test of time by carefully preserving the aristocratic refinement and British character of an elite resort of the late 1800s.

Built in 1889, the Algonquin was completely devastated by a fire in 1914. Most of it was rebuilt the next year. Then, in 1991, a new convention centre was added, followed by a new wing with 54 rooms and suites in 1993. The Fairmont Algonquin offers superb, modern and very comfortable rooms and suites, excellent food at the **Passamaquoddy Veranda** (see p 95) dining room, flawless service and a whole slew of activities. If the nightly rate is beyond your budget, do at least visit the hotel and treat yourself to Sunday brunch, lunch or supper, a drink in the Library Bar or a stop at the gift shop.

Pansy Patch
$$$$ bkfst incl.
ℜ, ≈, △, K, ⊛
9 rooms
59 Carleton St., E5B 1M8
☎*529-3834 or*
888-726-7972
⇥*529-9042*
www.pansypatch.com
St. Andrews by-the-Sea's excellent reputation is partly due to quality establishments like the Pansy Patch. It offers nine rooms in a wonderful home built in 1912 and an equally charming cot-

tage. Each of its tastefully decorated rooms offers a view of St. Andrews by-the-Sea's harbour. A magnificent garden surrounds the building. Guests can also use the facilities next door at the Fairmont Algonquin, which has a spa and tennis courts.

St. George

Granite Town Hotel
$$$
ℜ, K, ≡
32 rooms
79 Main St. E., E3C 3J4
☎*755-6415 or*
800-667-2010
⇥*755-6009*
www.bavefun.net
The Granite Town Hotel provides a conventional level of comfort. It is a good address to remember mainly because it is clean and ideally located for guests wanting to visit the islands in the bay.

Campobello Island

Lupine Lodge
$$-$$$
ℜ
11 rooms
610 Rte. 774, E5E 1A5
☎*752-2555 or*
888-912-8880
www.lupinelodge.com
Well situated near the park, the Lupine Lodge offers relatively comfortable accommodation. The neighbouring restaurant is busy during the summer season, all day long until evening falls.

Grand Manan Island

Fishermen's Haven Cottages
$$
5 rooms
12 Fishermen's Haven, Grand Harbour, E5G 4G9
☎*662-8919 or*
888-662-8919
≈*662-6246*
www.fishermenhaven.com
Lots of families spend at least a few days of their vacation on Grand Manan Island. A popular option for such vacationers is to rent a cottage like the ones offered at Fishermen's Haven Cottages, which have two or three bedrooms. Weekly rates are available.

Compass Rose
$$-$$$
ℜ
7 rooms
65 Rte. 776, North Head, E5G 1A2
☎*662-8570*
www.compassroseinn.com
Grand Manan has many bed and breakfasts and several little inns. The Compass Rose, one of these friendly inns, offers rooms that are charming and comfortable, but by no means luxurious. The inn's dining room serves up satisfactory fare.

Saint John

Earle of Leinster
$$ bkfst incl.
K
7 rooms
96 Leinster Ave., E2L 1J3
☎*652-3275*
A low-cost option for accommodations is the Earle of Leinster. It offers simply decorated, comfortable rooms, and a few

little extras, such as a pool table and a kitchen.

Five Chimneys Bed and Breakfast
$$ bkfst incl.
3 rooms
238 Charlotte W., E2M 1Y3
☎*635-1888 or*
888-651-9009
≈*672-2534*
www.fivechimneys.ca
In Saint John West, just a short distance from the pier where the ferry for Digby, Nova Scotia docks, is the Five Chimneys Bed and Breakfast. The establishment is set up in an upper-class house dating from the middle of the 19th century and offers quality accommodations for the price.

Homeport Historic B&B
$$ bkfst incl
K, ≡, ʍ
10 rooms
80 Douglas Ave., E2K 1E4
☎*672-7255 or*
888-678-7678
≈*672-7250*
www.homeport.nb.ca
The Homeport is another magnificent house in the area that has been converted into a pleasant B&B. An effort has been made to keep its original charm, and every one of its large rooms is filled with antiques. The rooms are all tastefully decorated and have private bathrooms.

Coastal Inn Fort Howe Hotel
$$
ℜ, ≈, ≡, *K*, △, ⊛
135 rooms
10 Portland St., E2K 4H8
☎*657-7320 or*
800-943-0033
≈*693-1146*
www.coastalinns.com
For an inexpensive hotel with clean but no-non-

sense rooms, located within a short distance from downtown Saint John and the major highways, the Coastal Inn Fort Howe Hotel is your best bet. The staff is courteous, and as an added bonus, there is a bar and restaurant on the top floor.

Park Plaza Motel
$$
ℜ, ʍ, ⑁
79 rooms
607 Rothesay Ave., E2H 2G9
☎*633-4100 or*
800-561-9022
≈*648-9494*
Within the immediate surroundings of Saint John, numerous motels offer reasonably priced accommodation in simple but clean rooms. The Park Plaza Motel is one of these. To get there, take Exit 117 off Route 1.

Inn on the Cove
$$$ bkfst incl.
⊛, ≡, ℜ, *K*
5 rooms
1371 Sand Cove Rd., E2M 4Z9
☎*672-7799 or*
877-257-8080
≈*635-5455*
www.innonthecove.com
If you can't imagine Saint John as an idyllic spot to take a relaxing and revitalizing vacation it must be because you've never come across the Inn on the Cove, probably one of the best inns in the province. Located in a quiet setting with a spectacular view of the Bay of Fundy, the inn is actually only 5min by car from downtown.

Nature-lovers will find beautiful, wild beaches to explore close by and trails leading to the Irving Nature Park. The house is tastefully furnished and a particular attention to detail, and the comfortable rooms are decorated with antiques. All of the rooms are lovely, but the two that are located on the second floor and facing the back of the house are even better: they are larger and offer a stunning view of the bay. The owners are friendly but discreet and prepare excellent breakfasts.

Parkerhouse Inn
$$$ bkfst incl.
ℜ
8 rooms
71 Sydney St., E2L 2L5
☎ *652-5054 or*
888-457-2520
⇒ *636-8076*
www.parkerhouseinn.net
The Parkerhouse Inn occupies a pretty early-19th-century house that has preserved all of its original splendour. A magnificent dining room, richly ornamented with woodwork, occupies almost the entire ground floor. A beautiful staircase leads to the upper floors, where the antique-furnished guestrooms are located. Each room has its own special charm and all have private washrooms. The Parkerhouse Inn is set right in the heart of Saint John, just behind the Imperial Theatre. The inn's restaurant has an outstanding reputation.

Delta Brunswick Hotel
$$$
ℜ, ≈, ≡, ®, ✖, △, ᴕ
255 rooms
39 King St., E2L 4W3
☎ *648-1981 or*
800-268-1133
⇒ *658-0914*
www.deltahotels.com
In the heart of downtown on its busiest street, the Delta Brunswick Hotel is

the largest hotel in Saint John, with 255 deluxe rooms and suites. Attached to a shopping mall, the building itself is not particularly charming. The hotel is best known for the gamut of services it offers vacationers and business people.

Hilton Saint John
$$$-$$$$
ℜ, ≈, ☺, ®, ≡, ✖, △, ᴕ
197 rooms
1 Market Sq., E2L 4Z6
☎ *693-8484 or*
800-561-8282
⇒ *657-6610*
www.hilton.com
The Hilton Saint John offers high quality accommodation in a beautiful setting, at the end of the pier close to the market. It is a great spot to enjoy the singular beauty of this sea port, whose activity is dictated by the continuous ebb and flow of the tides. Its rooms are spacious and decorated with furniture that is both modern and inviting. Obviously, the rooms at the back of the building, which look out over the port of Saint John, are most desirable. The Hilton also has a good restaurant, the **Turn of the Tide** (see p 96) and a pleasant bar, the **Brigantine Lounge** (see p 95), with a view of the piers.

Red Rose Mansion
$$$$ bkfst incl.
≡, *K*, ®
5 rooms
☎ *649-0913 or*
888-711-5151
⇒ *693-3233*
www.redrosemansion.com
Located in the historic district of Saint John, the Red Rose Mansion is a towering red-brick house dating from 1904, which

used to belong to the owner of the Red Rose Tea company. It's now a comfortable inn, and neither its exterior nor its interior has lost any of its original old-world charm. Its five luxurious rooms are gorgeously decorated in the Victorian style. It also has a magnificent garden.

St. Martins

Quaco Inn
$$$
ℜ, ≡, ®, ⅀
12 rooms
16 Beach St., E5R 1C7
☎ *833-4772 or*
888-833-4772
⇒ *833-2531*
www.quacoinn.com
The tiny coastal town of St. Martins offers a wide choice of quality accommodation. One of these is the reputed Quaco Inn, which provides comfortable lodging in the refined atmosphere of a Victorian house. Beautifully furnished and boasting a dining room with a well-established reputation (see p 96), this inn is among the best in the province.

St. Martins Country Inn
$$$
ℜ, ≡, ®
12 rooms
303 Main St., E5R 1C1
☎ *833-4534 or*
800-565-5257
⇒ *833-4725*
www.stmartinscountryinn.com
The divine St. Martins Country Inn is enchantingly situated on a large property overlooking the town. Built in 1857 for the most important shipbuilder in St. Martins, it has maintained the serene and

perhaps slightly snobby atmosphere befitting the residence of a highly visible member of the British upper class of that era. Everything to satisfy the discerning tastes of the epicurean traveller is in place: beautifully decorated rooms filled with period furniture, a highly reputed kitchen, three splendid dining rooms and impeccable service. Reservations recommended.

Fundy National Park

Fundy Park Chalets
$$
K, ℜ, ≈, ℳ
29 chalets
23 Fundy Park Chalet Rd., E4H 4Y8
☎*887-2808 or 888-887-2808*
⇢*887-2282*
www.fundyparkchalets. com
Visitors to Fundy National Park can choose between campsites and the Fundy Park Chalets. These rather rustic-looking cottages are located near the park administration office and the golf course, not far from the coast. Each one is equipped with a room with two beds, a bathroom and a kitchenette. Provisions are available just a few kilometres away in Alma.

Alma

Captain's Inn
$$ bkfst incl.
10 rooms
8602 Main St., E4H 1N5
☎*887-2017*
⇢*887-2074*
www.captainsinn.ca
The Captain's Inn occupies a charming wooden house

in the heart of Alma. This family hotel is not especially luxurious, but the rooms are comfortable, pretty and well laid out. The owners offer an always-friendly welcome.

Alpine Motor Inn
$$
K, ≈, ℳ
34 rooms
Rte. 114, E1C 8R9
☎*887-2052*
⇢*853-8090*
www.alpinemotorinn.ca
The Alpine Motor Inn, located right in the centre of the village, is the largest hotel in Alma. Its motel-style rooms are clean and spacious. Guests enjoy a beautiful view of the Bay of Fundy.

Parkland Village Inn
$$
ℜ, ≡
5 rooms
Rte. 114, E4H 1N6
☎*887-2313 or 866-668-6337*
⇢*887-2315*
www.parklandvillageinn. com
The Parkland Village Inn, situated in the heart of Alma, offers a few modest rooms above the establishment's very busy ground floor restaurant.

Moncton

Bonaccord House
$$ bkfst incl.
≡
4 rooms
250 Bonaccord St., E1C 5M6
☎*388-1535*
⇢*853-7191*
In the heart of Moncton's historic area, the early-20th-century Bonaccord House today functions as a lovely bed and breakfast. The elegantly decorated,

tastefully furnished guestrooms occupy the building's upper floors. Both the ground-floor living room and the veranda are perfect for reading, sipping afternoon tea or just relaxing. The Bonaccord House is ideal for those in search of an especially tranquil atmosphere.

Colonial Inn
$$
ℜ, ≈, ≡, ℳ
61 rooms
42 Highfield St., E1C 8T6
☎*382-3395 or 800-561-4667*
⇢*858-8991*
www.colonial-inns.com
The Colonial Inn offers motel-style accommodation right in the heart of Moncton. The rooms are well-kept, the service is excellent and guests have use of a pool. This is a good spot for families.

Canadiana Inn
$$-$$$
16 rooms
46 Archibald St., E1C 5H9
☎*382-1054*
Set in a quiet neighbourhood not far from the city's liveliest streets, the Canadiana Inn occupies a large, lovely Victorian house built at the end of the 19th century. Its rooms, equipped with comfortable furnishings, are handsomely decorated and inviting. The establishment has a pleasant upstairs terrace, as well as two dining rooms where generous breakfasts are served. Very congenial service.

New Brunswick

Howard Johnson Brunswick Plaza Hotel
$$-$$$$
ℜ, ≈, ⊛, ≡, 🐾
193 rooms
1005 Main St., E1C 1G9
**☎854-6340 or
888-561-7666**
⇄*382-8923*
There are a few good reasons to stay here, namely the affordable price and the central location.

Delta Beauséjour
$$$
ℜ, ≈, ⊘, ≡, 🐾
310 rooms
750 Main St., E1C 1E6
**☎854-4344 or
800-268-1133**
⇄*852-3878*
www.deltahotels.com
For those travellers in search of some pampering, elegance and comfort, there is the Delta Beauséjour, Moncton's finest establishment. The hotel offers quality service, as well as beautifully decorated and spacious rooms, an excellent restaurant (the **Windjammer**, see p 96) and piano bar and a lovely indoor swimming pool, where it is easy to put the bustle of urban life behind you. Right in the heart of Moncton, the hotel could not be more suitably located for business and leisure travellers hoping to take advantage of the nearby restaurants and bars.

Ramada Crystal Palace
$$$
ℜ, ≈, ⊛, ≡, △
115 rooms
499 Paul St., E1A 6S5
☎858-8584
⇄*858-5486*
***www.crystalpalacehotel.
com***
Families are particularly fond of the Ramada Crys-

tal Palace, a comfortable hotel equipped with a lovely swimming pool that is right next door to a large indoor amusement park. Its standard rooms are modern and airy. The Ramada appeals to business travellers as well, with its many meeting and conference rooms.

Sackville

Mount Allison University
$
☎364-2250
⇄*364-2688*
www.mta.ca
During summer, Mount Allison University offers the cheapest accommodations in Sackville. The campus is located right in the heart of this little town.

Borden's Restaurant & Motel
$-$$
ℜ, K, 🐾 ≡
8 rooms
146 Bridge St., at the southern end of town, E4L 3P7
☎364-1066
⇄*364-1306*
Borden's Restaurant & Motel, a small red brick building at the edge of town, has a few inexpensive, clean rooms.

Different Drummer
$$ bkfst incl.
8 rooms
7 Main St., E4L 4A4
**☎536-1291 or
877-547-2788**
⇄*536-8116*
The Different Drummer, an excellent bed and breakfast, is set up in a spacious Victorian house. All of the rooms are comfortable and furnished with real antiques. The healthy breakfast is generous and delicious.

Marshlands Inn
$$-$$$
ℜ, 🐾
20 rooms
55 Bridge St., E4L 3N8
**☎536-0170 or
800-561-1266**
⇄*536-0721*
www.marshlands.nb.ca
The charm of Sackville is due in good part to its multitude of large, beautiful houses from the 1800s. One of these has been converted into the outstanding Marshlands Inn, once a sumptuous residence offered as a wedding gift by William Crane, an important man of that era, to his daughter. The inn has 20 rooms, each one impeccably furnished.

Restaurants

St. Andrews by-the-Sea

Waterfront Take-Out
$
40 King St.
☎529-4228
There's nothing refined about the Waterfront Take-Out, but the place is the perfect spot to have a quick snack of fried clams. There are tables at the back or you can, as the name suggests, take out.

Chef Café
$-$$
180 Water St.
☎529-8888
Imagine the United States during the 1950s and you've got the decor of the Chef Café, a popular restaurant that clashes with the inherent chic of

St. Andrews by-the-Sea. The menu includes simple dishes like fish and chips and lobster rolls, as well as several inexpensive breakfasts. For a more sophisticated menu, pick a spot at the back of the restaurant, in the cozier dining room known as the Captain's Table.

Market Square Grill
$$
211 Water St.
☎**529-8241**
The perfect place for an afternoon snack, the Market Square Grill is a charming café whose menu offers simply prepared but delicious dishes. Among the choice of soups, sandwiches and fish, the chowder is a must. The evening menu, which is a little bit more refined, offers an excellent selection of fish and seafood dishes. Relaxed ambiance.

The Lighthouse Restaurant
$$-$$$
Patrick St.
☎**529-3082**
For many visitors, fresh lobster at a reasonable price is in itself enough of a reason to visit Atlantic Canada. When passing through St. Andrews by-the-Sea, these seafood fanatics converge on The Lighthouse Restaurant. This pretty spot, overlooking Passamaquoddy Bay, is located on the last street at the eastern edge of town.

Harbourfront Restaurant
$$-$$$
225 Water St.
☎**529-4887**
The Harbourfront has a wonderful location facing the bay, offering a beautiful

view of the waves. A terrace, which faces the sea, is the perfect place to enjoy this picturesque setting. The attractively decorated interior makes you feel like you're inside an old boat. Its fish and seafood specialties, such as the lobster, are all deliciously prepared.

Pansy Patch
$$-$$$
59 Carleton St.
☎**529-3834**
Those who enjoy the pleasant setting of a restaurant as much as its food will love the Pansy Patch. The tastefully decorated dining room opens onto the garden and offers a wonderful view. While enjoying this country-style atmosphere, guests can sample some delicious fish dishes, such as the *coulibiac de saumon*, as well as seafood specialties, like paella. A reasonably priced lunch menu is also offered.

Passamaquoddy Veranda
$$$-$$$$
The Fairmont Algonquin
☎**529-8823**
The Passamaquoddy Veranda offers an outstanding dining experience, as much for the elegance of its decor as for the exceptional quality of its international and regional cuisine. A meal at the Veranda is not within everyone's budget, but fortunately there is a much less expensive lunch and Sunday menu.

Saint John

Mother Nature's
$
Brunswick Sq.
☎**634-0955**
For a change from the traditional bacon and eggs

served in most of Saint John's breakfast joints, take a morning stroll over to Mother Nature's. Muffins, pastries and rich coffees are the essential elements of its morning menu. The rest of the day, they prepare salads, sandwiches and other light dishes.

Brigantine Lounge
$-$$
Hilton Saint John
At noontime or in late afternoon, the **Hilton Saint John**'s (see p 92) friendly Brigantine Lounge is the place to go, thanks to its breathtaking view of the port and its lunch special.

Brewpub Tapps
Steakhouse
$$
78 King St.
☎**634-1957**
The Brewpub is particularly well known for its home-brew and convivial atmosphere. It also has a menu that offers hearty dishes, such as hamburgers and grilled chicken, for those with an insatiable appetite.

Taco Pica
$$
96 Germain St.
☎**633-8492**
Mexican and Guatemalan family cooking is featured at Taco Pica, a friendly little neighbourhood restaurant. Simple, nourishing dishes, such as enchiladas, tacos and burritos, are the mainstays of the menu.

Billy's Seafood
$$-$$$
49-51 Charlotte St.
☎**672-3474**
Billy's Seafood, located just next to the Saint John

market, facing King Square, offers a splendid menu of fresh fish, seafood and steaks. The very well-prepared Atlantic salmon and the lobster are especially recommended. The catch of the day is served as part of a full meal. All of these ocean delights are offered up in a warm, understated atmosphere.

Grannan's Seafood Restaurant & Oyster Bar
$$-$$$
Market Sq.
☎634-1555
Grannan's Seafood Restaurant & Oyster Bar has become an institution in Saint John. The restaurant, whose decor presents a hodgepodge of eccentric maritime-related relics and photos—a real fishmonger's paradise—opens onto an outdoor terrace, perfect for warm summer evenings. The menu of this restaurant, which can get very crowded in the evening, is predictably mainly composed of fish and seafood dishes.

🌴 Turn of the Tide
$$$-$$$$
Hilton Saint John, 1 Market Sq.
☎632-8564
The Turn of the Tide offers a varied menu typical of a hotel of the calibre of the **Hilton Saint John** (see p 92), with a vast choice of meat, game, and of course the requisite fresh seafood and fish. The menu is a bit pricey, but the food is sure to please, and the view of the port makes it all the more worthwhile. The decor is classic, airy and tasteful.

St. Martins

Quaco Inn
$$-$$$
16 Beach St.
☎833-4772
To top off a romantic stay in the quiet village of St. Martins, the delicious pleasure of a candlelit supper in the dining room of the **Quaco Inn** (see p 92), one of the best restaurants on the coast, is a must. International and local specialties figure on the menu, the staples of which are, of course, fish and seafood.

Moncton

Café Joe Moka Coffee
$
837 Main St.
☎852-3070
At the corner of Main Street and Robinson Street, Moncton's only pedestrian thoroughfare, stands Café Joe Moka Coffee. This small, unpretentious establishment is a pleasant spot for a light meal, a good cup of coffee or breakfast.

Café Archibald
$-$$
221 Mountain Rd.
☎853-8819
A little set back from the Main, Café Archibald is worth the trip for its well-prepared, inexpensive light meals. Salads, sandwiches, pizzas and succulent crepes are offered. The establishment has an especially pleasant terrace for summertime dining.

Pastali
$$
611 Main St.
☎383-1050
Pastali is a good place to keep in mind if you enjoy Italian food. Patrons enjoy the restaurant's inviting decor, warm atmosphere and delicious pasta dishes.

Fisherman's Paradise
$$-$$$
330 Dieppe Blvd.
☎859-4388
The Fisherman's Paradise, where seafood and fish dishes share the menu with steaks, is a contender for the title of best seafood restaurant in the area.

🌴 Windjammer
$$$
750 Main St., Hôtel Beauséjour
☎854-4344
Moncton's gourmets meet at the Windjammer, one of the best restaurants in the province. Its dining room has the seductive elegance of a 19th-century trans-Atlantic liner. The menu has a few pleasant surprises in store, including caribou *tournedos* and many other game dishes, although obviously fish and seafood are its main highlights. In addition, the Windjammer offers a reasonably priced set menu.

Sackville

Marshlands Inn
$$$
55 Bridge St.
☎536-0170
The Marshlands Inn offers fine dining that will satisfy the most discerning of palates. The menu is quite extensive and features

mostly continental specialties, as well as several regional dishes. The atmosphere is quite formal, but also very friendly.

Entertainment

Saint John

Bars and Pubs

O'Leary's
46 Princess St.
☎634-7135
The Irish influence is known to be very strong in Saint John. It is therefore no surprise to find O'Leary's, an excellent Irish pub. The clientele is generally young, and live music is often presented.

Brigantine Lounge
Hilton Saint John
The Brigantine Lounge is charming, with its unimpeded view of the port and its busy piers across the St. John River. Guests of the rather chic **Hilton Saint John** (see p 92) make up most of the clientele of this quiet bar, which has an interesting selection of liqueurs. Evenings are usually enhanced by a pianist.

Cultural Activities

Imperial Theatre
King Sq.
☎683-9494
The spectacular auditorium of the Imperial Theatre, which was renovated in 1994, has been the home of the performing arts in Saint John for a

century. Concerts, plays and dance performances are presented here year-round.

Moncton

Bars and Pubs

Lobby Bar
Delta Beauséjour, 750 Main St.
☎854-4344
Bar-hopping and pub-crawling does not appeal to everyone. Luckily there is an alternative, the Lobby Bar, which serves excellent liqueurs in a relaxing, soothing atmosphere that is actually conducive to conversation.

Student bar
Université de Moncton
The student bar at the Université de Moncton presents concerts in the summer, providing visitors an excellent opportunity to experience the culture and music of modern-day Acadians.

Triangles
234 St. George St.
☎857-8779
Triangles is the main gathering place of the Moncton area's gay community, and although its atmosphere is rather low-key, it does have a dance floor.

Cultural Activities and Festivals

Capitol Theatre
811 Main St.
☎856-4377
The sumptuous Capitol Theatre is the main performing arts centre in Moncton. Since its reopening in 1993, after renovations restored the

panache of days gone by, the theatre has presented a variety of quality productions.

July is jazz-time in the city during the **Moncton Jazz Festival**.

Shopping

St. Stephen

Ganong Chocolatier
73 Milltown Blvd.
☎465-5611
The oldest candy maker in Canada (1873), Ganong Chocolatier was also the first to produce the chocolate bar. Today, the shop sells about 75 different varieties of chocolate; just try to choose...

St. Andrews by-the-Sea

North of Sixty Art
238 Water St.
☎529-4148
North of Sixty Art is an Inuit art gallery that can be visited like a museum. Works exhibited include some uniquely diverse and beautiful sculptures. Among the dozens of boutiques along Water Street, this one is probably the most interesting.

Boutique La Baleine
173 Water St.
☎529-3926
Boutique La Baleine is known mostly for its quality crafts; however, it also sells books, trinkets and some clothing. There is

New Brunswick

another Boutique La Baleine inside **The Fairmont Algonquin** (see p 90).

Cottage Craft
209 Water St.
☎529-3190
Cottage Craft is worth visiting for its interesting selection of tweed clothing and items knitted with 100% pure wool, as well as the array of coloured yarn it has for sale.

Garden By the Sea
17 Walter St.
☎529-8905
To stock up on essential-oil soaps made on the premises, stop by this pretty boutique.

Saint John

Saint John Market
47 Charlotte St.
☎658-2820
There's nothing like a walk in the market, where stalls overflow with fresh produce from the region's farms. There is also a lovely selection of local crafts.

Handworks
12 King St.
☎652-9787
Art lovers will enjoy this gallery, where a variety of works by Atlantic artists are on display.

Moncton

Librairie Acadienne
Taillon Bldg., Université de Moncton
☎858-4140
Located on the Université de Moncton campus, Librairie Acadienne offers an excellent selection of works by Acadian authors as well as books on Acadian history and culture. Acadia numbers many talented writers, among whom Herménégilde Chiasson and Antonine Maillet are two of the best known.

Chapters
499 Paul St.
☎855-8075
If you love to read, go to the huge Chapters bookstore situated in the Crystal Palace. In addition to a vast selection of books on a range of topics, there is also a café and a restaurant.

La Différence
881A Main St.
☎861-1800
This shop sells a variety of crafts from the Atlantic provinces.

Wharf Village
Hwy. 2
☎868-8841
This reconstructed fishing village is a pleasant spot for a stroll. You can also stumble upon some great finds in the shops that sell crafts, a variety of souvenirs, antiques and other decorative objects.

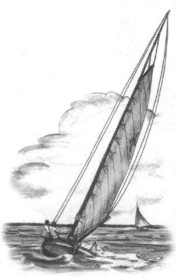

Acadian Coast

Modern Acadia mainly lies along the east coast of New Brunswick, which is studded with a string of villages and towns whose inhabitants are mostly of Acadian descent.

It was here that the majority of Acadians fleeing deportation or returning from exile sought refuge over two centuries ago, to build a new Acadia. This lovely region is chiefly known for the simple beauty of its landscape and the candid hospitality of its inhabitants, but also evokes all sorts of other images–long white-sand beaches washed by incredibly warm waters, fresh lobster to be enjoyed at any time of the day, fishing ports bustling with activity and a population with an inherently festive spirit.

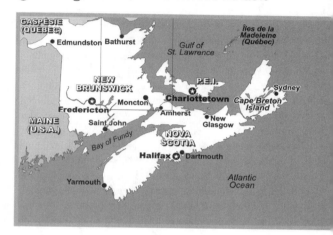

In short, the Acadian coast offers visitors a wealth of delightful activities, as well as an opportunity to discover not only the legacy of 18th- and 19th-century Acadia, but also modern Acadia, which is marching resolutely forward, more confident than ever.

Thanks to its beaches, which are blessed with surprisingly warm water, Shediac has been the main vacation spot on the coast for a long time. Over the past few years, however, a few other places have

sprung up, so it is now possible to explore all of the diversity that the Acadian coast has to offer.

Finding Your Way Around

This tour of the Acadian Coast ★★ takes you from Cap-Pelé to Campbellton.

By Car

Except for a small section between Cape Tourmentine and Shediac, Highway

11 is the main road used on this tour. The highway passes through most of the towns and villages on the coast, skirts around the peninsula, then runs alongside the Baie des Chaleurs to the Québec border. From Newcastle, visitors can cross New Brunswick from east to west via Highway 8, which runs through the Miramichi River valley.

Highway 180 leads from Bathurst to Saint-Quentin, passing near Mount Carleton, while Highway 17 heads from Campbellton to Saint-Leonard (on the St. John River). These two highways also cross the mountainous Appalachian countryside.

Practical Information

Area code: **506**

Tourist Information Offices

New Brunswick Tourist Information Centre
☎**800-561-0123**

Caraquet
Hwy. 11
☎**726-2676**

Shediac
229 Main St.
☎**532-7788**
www.shediac.org

Shippagan
near the Marine Centre in the lighthouse
☎**336-3907**

Bouctouche
☎**744-8811 or
866-444-2411**
www.bouctouche.org

Exploring

Bayfield

A string of little villages unfurls along the Atlantic coast in the southern part of the province, near the bridge to Prince Edward Island and the Nova Scotia border. One of these is Bayfield, and nearby is the **Cape Jourimain Nature Centre** *($4; early May to mid-Oct, every day 9am to 6pm; 5039 Rte. 106,* ☎*538-2220 or 866-538-2220, www.capejourimain.ca).* This nature centre highlights the flora and fauna particular to this portion of the province's coastline. The exhibit is dynamic and interesting. Walking trails reveal the beauty of the forests, fields, salt marshes and beaches of the site. Watch out for the mosquitoes, however, as they can be rather irritating. Cape Jourimain offers great views of the Confederation Bridge.

Cap-Pelé

Cap-Pelé offers visitors a wonderful opportunity to discover the fascinating world of fishing. Founded at the end of the 18th century, this Acadian community still depends on the riches of the sea for its sur-

vival. The village is also home to *boucanières* (smokehouses), barn-like buildings where the fish is smoked before being exported. The 30-odd *boucanières* in the Cap-Pelé region provide 95% of the world's smoked herring.

Beautiful **Plage de l'Aboiteau** ★★ (Aboiteau Beach) is not far from Cap-Pelé. This splendid beach is ideal for swimming and much less crowded than Parlee Beach Provincial Park (see below). The beach is hidden from the road by an embankment of boulder and rock for which it was named. The **Cap-Pelé fishing harbour** is located about 500m from Aboiteau Beach, along the same road. (*Aboiteau*, a term primarily used in Acadia, refers to a type of sluice gate used in a system of dikes to protect coastal farmland.) Some twenty fishing boats tie up here when they aren't at sea. This genuine place comes complete with a fish market and small snack bar. There are also two other beautiful beaches in the Cap-Pelé area: Gagnon Beach and Sandy Beach.

The region occupies a little plateau that is almost completely devoid of vegetation and offers lovely views of the ocean. Farther along the same road, visitors will reach **Barachois**. In the centre of the village stands the oldest wooden Acadian church in the Maritimes, the **historic church of Saint-Henri-de-Barachois** ★ *(free admission; Jul and Aug, 11am to 5pm; Hwy. 133,* ☎*532-2976),* built in 1824.

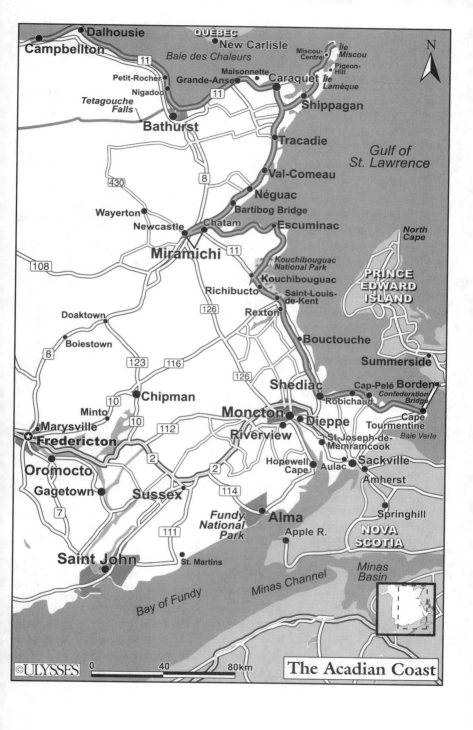

The Acadian Coast

Shediac

The town of Shediac is the best-known vacation spot on the east coast of New Brunswick. Its popularity is largely due to the magnificent beach in **Parlee Beach Provincial Park ★** (Hwy. 15), whose surprisingly warm waters are perfect for swimming. Because of this popularity, a number of recreational facilities have sprung up in and around Shediac, including a lovely golf course and some amusement parks.

The town's reputation, however, is also due in good measure to the abundance of lobster found off its shores, which can be savoured fresh at any time. The town has even proclaimed itself the lobster capital of the world and holds an annual **lobster festival** in early July. Right next to the tourist information centre, there's a gigantic reproduction of a lobster that's 11m long and 5m wide and weighs 90 tonnes, meant to remind visitors of the regional importance of this crustacean.

Shediac was founded as a fishing port in the 19th century. A handful of lovely buildings have endured from that era and contrast sharply with the chaotic atmosphere that characterizes the town during the busy summer season. Heading northward along the coast, visitors will pass through several tiny Acadian communities which survive mainly on fishing.

Bouctouche

A pleasant little town looking out on a large, peaceful bay, Bouctouche was founded at the end of the 18th century by Acadians driven from the Memramcook valley. It has the distinction of being the birthplace of two celebrated New Brunswickers, Antonine Maillet and K.C. Irving. Winner of the 1979 Prix Goncourt for her novel *Pélagie la Charrette*, Antonine Maillet has gained more international recognition than any other Acadian author. She first came into the public eye in the 1960s with *La Sagouine*, a remarkable play

that evokes the lives and spirit of Acadians at the turn of the 20th century.

K.C. Irving, who died in 1992, built a colossal financial empire involved in widely diversified operations, most importantly the oil industry. He started out with nothing and died one of the wealthiest individuals in the world.

The **Pays de la Sagouine ★** ($14; mid-Jun to early Sep, every day 10am to 6pm; at the southern entrance of the village, on Hwy. 134, ☎743-1400, www.sagouine.com), a recreation of early 20th-century Acadia, draws inspiration from Antonine Maillet's highly successful play, *La Sagouine*. Its creators cleverly decided to enliven the atmosphere with characters from the famous play, who perform theatrical and musical pieces.

The highlight is Île-aux-Puces, in the centre of the bay. It is here that the Pays de la Sagouine is the liveliest, and visitors can learn about the lifestyle of early 20th-century Acadians by talking with the characters on site. The restaurant **L'Ordre du Bon Temps** (see p 116), located at the entrance, serves tasty traditional Acadian cuisine. In the evenings, guests can enjoy theatre productions and musical performances.

The **Kent County Museum ★** ($3; late Jun to early Sep, Mon-Sat 9am to 5:30pm, Sun noon to 6pm; on the east side of the village, 150 Convent St., ☎743-5005) is one of the most

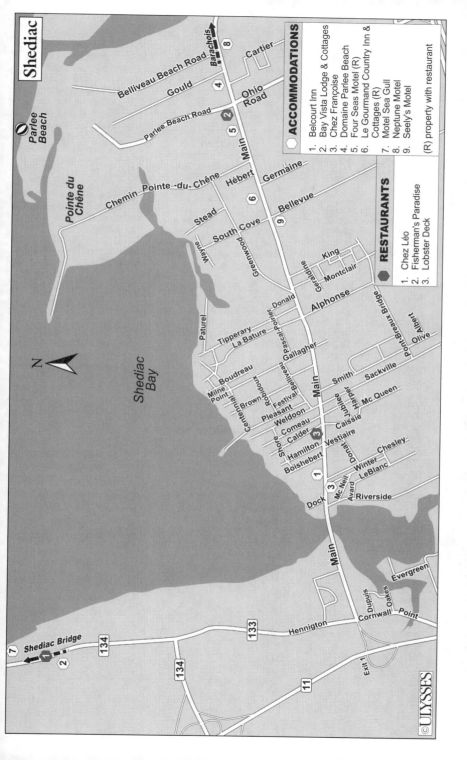

Shediac

ACCOMMODATIONS

1. Belcourt Inn
2. Bay Vista Lodge & Cottages
3. Chez Françoise
4. Domaine Parlee Beach
5. Four Seas Motel (R)
6. Le Gourmand Country Inn & Cottages (R)
7. Motel Sea Gull
8. Neptune Motel
9. Seely's Motel

(R) property with restaurant

RESTAURANTS

1. Chez Léo
2. Fisherman's Paradise
3. Lobster Deck

© ULYSSES

interesting regional museums in the province. The building itself was used as a convent until 1969. Its various rooms contain period furniture and pieces of sacred art that evoke the history of the convent and the daily life of the nuns and their students. The museum's friendly guides offer interesting tours.

The **Irving Eco-Centre, La Dune de Bouctouche** ★ ★ *(Hwy. 475, about 5km north of Bouctouche, ☎ 743-2600 or 888-640-3300, www.irvingecocentre.com)*, which features a dune that extends over 12km into Bouctouche harbour, is the habitat of a great variety of aquatic plants and animals, as well as migratory birds and waterfowl, including great blue herons, piping plovers and long-winged terns. The dune, which protects the calm waters and salt marshes of the bay, was formed over the course of centuries by the ceaseless action of winds, tides and ocean currents.

The twofold goal of the Irving Eco-Centre is to preserve this fragile ecosystem and to educate the public about it. A 2km-long boardwalk has been built to facilitate wildlife viewing, and guides give interpretive tours of the dune. For many years now, the spectacular fine-sand beach that borders the entire perimeter of the dune has been a very popular destination for summer outings; surrounded by particularly warm waters, this is one of the best spots for swimming on the coast. The dune is located a few kilometres north of Bouctouche and can be reached by bicycle or on foot via a forest trail.

Rexton

The English-speaking village of Rexton is the birthplace of Bonar Law (1858-1923), the only prime minister of Great Britain born outside of the United Kingdom. The **Bonar Law Historic Site** *(free admission; late Jun to early Sep, every day 9:30am to 4:30pm; Hwy. 11 or 116, in the centre of Rexton, ☎ 523-7615)* pays homage to that famous New Brunswicker, while offering visitors an idea of how people lived at the time of his birth. The site includes the farm and house where Bonar Law spent his early years.

Kouchibouguac

Blanketed by a forest of cedars and other conifers and studded with peat bogs, magnificent **Kouchibouguac National Park** ★ ★ ★ *($5; Hwy. 11 or 134, ☎ 876-2443)*, boasts over 26km of spectacular coastline made up of saltwater marshes, lagoons, dunes and golden sandy beaches. It is the natural habitat of several hundred animal and bird species, including the extremely rare piping plover.

This national park is the ideal place for various sporting activities. Hiking and especially cycling enthusiasts will revel in the multitude of trails criss-crossing several dozen kilometres of the park. Canoeing and kayaking are also popular in the summer on the river that crosses the park. These, along with bicycles, can be rented on site. Above all, however, this park has some of the most spectacular beaches of this part of the province. Washed by warm waters and generally uncrowded, they are perfect for swimming. Kouchibouguac Park is definitely worth a few days of your time. The campsites are well maintained.

Escuminac

Visitors with a taste for pretty, isolated beaches will find several in **Escuminac Provincial Park** *(5km east of Escuminac)*. Those who stop in the village will see a **monument** dedicated to 35 fishers who lost their lives at sea during a storm in 1959.

Miramichi

Situated at the mouth of the river of the same name, Miramichi is the largest town in the region, and, unlike other coastal communities, its population is mostly English-speaking. Each year at the beginning of July, this community celebrates the annual **Irish Festival of Canada** *(☎ 778-8810)*. This region owes its existence to the forest industry, which has been the main economic activity in the region for decades.

The town has few attractions, but the **Ritchie Wharf Park**, which runs along the Miramichi River, is a fun place for the entire family, as a variety of activities are offered.

The 200km-long **Miramichi River ★** is renowned for its exceptional Atlantic salmon fishing. From Miramichi, you can follow the river right up to Fredericton, via Highway 8. This highway offers scenic views of a countryside dominated by majestic evergreens. Also along Highway 8 is the **Miramichi Salmon Museum** (see below).

The Miramichi flows through a lovely landscape whose dense vegetation consists mainly of conifers. On the way to Fredericton, visitors can stop at the **Miramichi Salmon Museum ★** *($5; Jun to mid-Oct, every day 9am to 5pm; Hwy. 8, in Doaktown, ☎365-7787)*, which showcases both fishing and the life cycle of the salmon itself. Farther along in the same direction, visitors will reach the **Central New Brunswick Woodmen's Museum** *($5; mid-May to mid-Oct, every day 9am to 5:30pm; Hwy. 8, in Boiestown, ☎369-7214)*, which stands on the site of a lumber camp and examines the lives of its inhabitants and the arduous line of work they pursued.

Neguac

A small town located at the start of the Acadian peninsula, Neguac is located at the crossroads of the Francophone, Anglophone and Mi'kmaq cultures of New Brunswick. Travellers come here to enjoy the beaches. There is also an information centre for visitors *(1190 Rue Principale, ☎776-3950)*, as well as several lodging establishments.

Bartibog Bridge

From Miramichi, Highway 11 West leads to the Acadian Peninsula. Bartibog Bridge is the first town on this highway.

In addition to offering an excellent view at the mouth of the Miramichi River, this tiny community is home to the very interesting **MacDonald Farm Historic Site** *($2.50; end of Jun to early Sep, every day 9:30am to 4:30pm; Hwy. 11, ☎778-6085)*. Born in Scotland in 1762, Alexander MacDonald served as a private in the British army during the American Revolution. In 1784, after the war had ended, MacDonald took up residence on the banks of the Miramichi River.

Salmon

MacDonald Farm, now open to the public, includes a lovely Georgian-style stone house and several other buildings dating back to the early 19th century.

Tracadie-Sheila

After passing through the villages of Neguac and **Val-Comeau**, each of which has beaches and a provincial park, Highway 11 leads to Tracadie-Sheila, a little town with numerous restaurants and hotels, as well as an attractive wharf. As the institutional buildings attest, the town's history was marked for many years by the presence of the Religieuses Hospitalières de Saint-Joseph (Sisters of Mercy), who nursed the sick—especially lepers—here from 1868 to 1965.

The **Tracadie Historical Museum ★** *($2; Jun to Aug, Mon-Fri 10am to 6pm, Sat and Sun noon to 6pm; on the 3rd floor of the Académie Sainte-Famille, Rue du Couvent, ☎395-6366)* houses an exhibit on the various stages in the history of Tracadie and its surroundings. Visitors will find a selection of Mi'kmaq artifacts, religious objects and 19th-century tools. Not far from the museum lies the **leper cemetery**, where about 60 identical crosses stand in rows.

Shippagan

Protected by the strait that separates it from Île Lamèque, the site now occupied by Shippagan was originally a trading post, which gave way to a sea port at the end of the 18th century. Now a bustling little community, Shippagan boasts several industries and, more importantly, a port that accommodates one of the largest fishing fleets on the Acadian peninsula.

Its charm lies not only in its seaside location, but also in the unique atmosphere created by its port. Anyone interested in learning more about the fishing industry–the mainspring of Acadian economy for over 200 years now–should stop in Shippagan, explore the town, stroll along the wharf and visit the marine centre. In addition, each year around mid-July, the town holds a **Fishing and Aquatic Culture Festival** (*☎336-8726*), made up of a number of fishing related activities, including the blessing of boats.

Most Acadians who succeeded in avoiding deportation fled from the fertile shores of the Bay of Fundy through the woods to the province's east coast. Since the soil there was much poorer, they turned to the sea for survival, taking up fishing, an economic activity that has long been an integral part of Acadian culture.

To discover the fascinating world of modern fishing in Acadia and the Gulf of St. Lawrence, especially the rich animal life inhabiting the sea bed in this region, visitors can head to the **Marine Centre and Aquarium** ★★ (*$6.25; mid-May to Sep, every day*

10am to 6pm; near the Shippagan wharf, ☎336-3013). A visit to the aquarium offers a chance to view tanks containing a variety of fish species from the Gulf of St. Lawrence and the lakes and rivers of the province, as well as lobster and notably, blue lobster. The fish and crustaceans swim about the viewing tanks which recreate their natural environment. This makes the visit particularly interesting. But the most fascinating exhibit has to be the seal tank, especially during feeding time (11am and 4pm).

A documentary is shown for those who would like to learn more about the history of fishing in the region. The complex is also a scientific research centre.

Île Lamèque

A ramp connects Shippagan to Île Lamèque. With its flat landscape and handful of tiny hamlets made up of pretty white or coloured houses, this island is a haven of peace where time seems to stand still. A visit to the **Église Sainte-Cécile** ★ in Petite-Rivière-de-l'Île is a must. This charming, colourful wooden church provides an enchanting setting for the **International Baroque Music Festival** (*☎344-5846*), a wonderful event held each year during the last week of July.

Those who wish to learn more about the fauna and flora of the Acadian penin-

sula should definitely visit the **Acadian Peninsula Ecological Park** (*$4; May to Oct, every day 9am to 9pm; 65 Chemin du Ruisseau, ☎344-3222*). The park features an interpretation centre, a 0.5km footbridge and an observation tower, allowing visitors to discover different aspects of the region's plant and animal life.

Île Miscou

Just a short ferry ride from Île Lamèque lies Île Miscou, another sparsely populated, peaceful place renowned for its lovely, often deserted beaches. At the far end of the island stands the **Île Miscou Lighthouse** ★ (*at the end of Hwy. 113*), one of the oldest in New Brunswick and a marvellous spot from which to view the ocean.

A few kilometres before the lighthouse, on the same road, visitors will find an **interpretive site** ★ (*Hwy. 113*) with a path and footbridges leading through a peat bog.

Caraquet

Caraquet's charm lies mainly in the warmth and vitality of its inhabitants. The largest town on the peninsula, it has a number of hotels and restaurants. Caraquet is also considered the cultural hub of Acadia, and with good reason. It is probably this town and its residents' lifestyle that best illustrate modern Acadian culture, which draws on a variety of influences without, however, renouncing its rich past.

August is by far the best time to visit Caraquet, since August 15 is the Acadian national holiday. The Tintamarre and the Frolic (August 15) alone make for a memorable experience. The **Acadian Festival** (☎ 727-2787) also takes place in August. At other times, visitors can attend performances by the excellent theatre company of the **Théâtre Populaire d'Acadie** (276 Blvd. Saint-Pierre Ouest, ☎ 727-0920), relax on one of the town's little beaches or set off on a cruise from the **Carrefour de la Mer** (51 Blvd. Saint-Pierre Est).

The **Acadian Museum** ★ ($3; mid-Jun to mid-Sep, Mon-Sat 10am to 8pm, Sun 1pm to 6pm; 15 Blvd. Saint-Pierre Est, ☎ 726-2682) houses a small collection of everyday objects from the past 200 years.

An important place of pilgrimage in a lovely natural setting, the **Sanctuaire Sainte-Anne-du-Bocage** ★ (free admission; everyday, year-round; Blvd. Saint-Pierre Ouest) includes a small wooden chapel, the Stations of the Cross and a monument to Alexis Landry, ancestor of most of the Landrys in Acadia.

No history book on Acadia could ever be as effective an educational tool as the **Village Historique Acadien** ★ ★ ★ ($15; mid-Jun to Oct; on Hwy. 11,

about 10km west of Caraquet, ☎ 726-2600). Here, on a vast piece of land, visitors will find a reconstructed village including about 40 houses and other buildings, most of which are authentic, dating from 1770 to the beginning of the 20th century. The atmosphere is enlivened by performers in period costumes who carry out everyday tasks using traditional methods and gladly inform visitors about the customs of the past. A film at the interpretive centre presents a brief history of the Acadian people. You can now stay in town at the Hôtel Château Albert, a replica of an establishment from the early 1900s.

The **Musée de Cire d'Acadie** ★ ($7; Jun and Sep, every day 9am to 6pm; Jul and Aug, every day 9am to 7pm; Hwy. 11, near the Village Historique Acadien, ☎ 727-6424) is a wax museum that recreates the main historical events that marked Acadia, from its foundation to the Deportation, and illustrates the daily life activities of Acadians of that era. In all, 23 scenes, eight of which are animated, present 86 characters. The reconstructions are skilfully accomplished and the tour is instructive. Each visitor is allotted a personal audiocassette guide.

Caraquet has been the oyster capital for ages. As far back as 1758, the first Acadians fished for the oysters which grow in the Bay of Caraquet. Oyster harvesting eventually became oyster farming, thanks to the creation of

ostreicultural farms. You can now find out more about oyster farming by visiting the **Ferme Ostréicole Dugas** (free admission; early May to mid-Nov, Mon-Sat 9:30am to 5:30pm; 675 Blvd. Saint-Pierre Ouest, ☎ 727-3226), which has been converted into an economuseum.

The Dugas family presents their traditional know-how, which they have developed over many years. Visitors can take in a variety of exhibits, such as the oysters themselves and old oyster-farming implements. Workshops on oyster-box making are also offered. The visit ends with an oyster-tasting session.

Maisonnette

This hamlet, also known for its oysters, is graced with one of the most beautiful beaches on the Acadian peninsula: the beach at **Maisonnette Provincial Park** (take Hwy. 11 to Hwy. 303).

Grande-Anse

At Grande-Anse, another tiny coastal village, visitors will find pretty **Ferguson Beach**, which lies at the foot of a cliff, and the unique **Pope Museum** ★ ($5; mid-Jun to early Sep, every day 10am to 6pm; 184 Rue Acadie, ☎ 732-3003). The museum's exhibit includes a model of Saint Peter's in Rome, clothing and pieces of sacred art, as well as a collection of papal iconography. A number of these objects are both rare and interesting. The museum

New Brunswick

serves as a reminder of the important role religion has played in Acadian history.

Paquetville

A few kilometres past Grande-Anse, Highway 135 heads south to Paquetville, the hometown of famous singer Édith Butler. Paquetville is a quaint, peaceful community that has one of the largest churches in the province, the **Église Saint-Augustin** *(Parc St.)*.

Bathurst

An industrial town situated at the mouth of the Nepisiquit River, Bathurst is the largest urban centre in the northeastern part of the province. Accordingly, all sorts of services are available here. For visitors, however, Bathurst's interest lies mainly in the numerous natural sites located nearby. Right after the port, northeast of town, visitors can observe plant and animal life in the salt marshes, wooded areas and fields encompassed by the **Pointe Daly Reserve** *(Hwy. 11, toward the Acadian peninsula)*, a haven of peace stretching 40ha. Nature lovers can also admire nearby **Papineau Falls** *(several kilometres from town on Hwy. 430)*.

Sugarloaf Provincial Park *(off Hwy. 11, ☎ 789-2366)*, a vast garden stretching more than 1,200ha, welcomes outdoor sports enthusiasts all year round. In winter it's popular for downhill skiing, since the park has a 305m mountain

with eight runs. It also has snowmobile trails and 30km of cross-country ski trails that become hiking paths in the summer. Many people also come here during the summer to climb the mountain and enjoy the panoramic view. There is also a campground.

Dalhousie

Dalhousie, like Campbellton, was founded by Scottish settlers at the beginning of the 19th century, although a large segment of the present population of both towns is of Acadian descent. A pleasant little community, Dalhousie has a beach and a pretty marina that serves as the boarding point for cruises on the Baie des Chaleurs. A visit here also offers an interesting opportunity to learn more about local history, from the pre-European-contact period to the present day, at the **Restigouche Regional Museum** *(free admission; Mon-Fri 9am to 5pm, Sat 9am to 1pm, Sun 1pm to 5pm; 115 George St., ☎684-7490)*. During the summer, a ferry makes a daily crossing between Dalhousie and Misquasha, in Québec.

Campbellton

Located alongside the estuary of the Restigouche River, Campbellton is the largest town in this lovely region. It is renowned for fishing, especially salmon. In fact, salmon fishing is so closely linked to Campbellton's history that a

giant salmon was erected here. Furthermore, the town holds a **Salmon Festival** *(late Jun and early Jul; ☎ 759-7997)* each year. Visitors can discover another side of the area at the **Restigouche Gallery** *(39 Andrew St.)*. Because of its proximity to the Québec border, Campbellton is also home to a provincial tourist information centre.

From Campbellton, visitors can head to Mount Carleton Provincial Park by taking Hwy. 17 to Saint-Quentin, and then picking up Hwy. 180.

Beaches

Murray Corner

Murray Beach Provincial Park ★ *(Hwy. 955)* has a lovely beach, a campground and various activities.

Cap-Pelé

Aboiteau Beach ★ *(Hwy. 15)* stretches 2.5km and features lovely sand dunes. The beach is not only an excellent place to swim but is also enchanting. Between Cap-Pelé and Shediac, there are three more pretty beaches along the coast.

Shediac

Parlee Beach Provincial Park ★★ *(near Exit 17 off Hwy. 15)* is probably New Brunswick's most famous beach. It is patrol-led by lifeguards and stretches several kilometres.

Saint-Louis-de-Kent

Some of the most beautiful beaches in the province can be found in **Kouchibouguac National Park** *(Hwy. 134 and 11)*. Visitors can also rent a canoe or rowboat, go hiking or cycling and, in winter, enjoy cross-country skiing here. There are campsites as well.

Escuminac

Escuminac Provincial Park *(Hwy. 117)* has a lovely beach with magnificent sand dunes. There are campgrounds in the neighbouring villages.

Île Miscou

Île Miscou Beach *(Hwy. 113, 14km from the crossing)* is well laid-out and equipped with a campground and cottages.

Caraquet

At **Frolex Beach**, the **Downtown Beach** *(Hwy. 11, downtown)* and the **Caraquet Park Beach** *(Hwy. 11, west of Caraquet)*, visitors can go swimming or enjoy other water sports. There are no lifeguards.

Maisonnette

Maisonnette Provincial Park *(8km east of Hwy. 11, on Hwy. 303)* has a beauti-

ful beach with shallow waters.

Grande-Anse

Peaceful **Ferguson Beach** *(Hwy. 11)* lies tucked away in a pretty spot at the foot of a cliff.

Outdoor Activities

Cycling

Since the creation of the **Sentiers Péninsule Acadienne** (Acadian Peninsula Trails), you can now travel along the peninsula on two wheels. Connecting the towns of Grande-Anse, Caraquet, Shippagan and Lamèque, a distance of about 100km, the trails mostly use former railway lines, which have been filled in with crushed stone. The network of

trails is easy to cover and is accessible to all. The *Sentiers Péninsule Acadienne* cycling map is on sale *($1)* in the province.

For those who want to explore the region by bike, Kouchibouguac National Park also has some pleasant trails. Bike rentals are available on-site.

Ryan's Rental Centre
mid-Jun to early Sep, every day 8am to 9pm
☎*876-2571*

Bird-Watching

Bouctouche

The **Irving Éco-Centre, La Dune de Bouctouche** protects a 12km-long dune, a wonderful location that attracts flocks of birds, especially the great blue heron, the piping plover and the roseate tern. To allow visitors to see these winged creatures without disturbing their fragile habitat, long footbridges have been built under-

Piping plover

neath the dune. You can now come and go as you please by bike or on foot.

Kouchibouguac National Park

In addition to its gorgeous beaches, Kouchibouguac National Park also has marshes and dunes that attract thousands of birds every year, especially the piping plover. Long, wooden footbridges have been built so visitors can bird-watch.

Tabusintac

With an area of 4,100ha, the **bassin et l'estuaire de Tabusintac** (Tabusintac Basin and Estuary) *(Hwy. 11 N. and Hwy. 460,* ☎*779-8304)* is the centre of the action during the summer, when thousands of birds are attracted here by the wetlands. The area is the home of the common eider, osprey and great blue heron, as well as the rare piping plover.

Canoeing and Kayaking

The Acadian coast is a great place for canoeing and kayaking. Several companies offer boat rentals and guided tours.

Bouctouche

Expédition Sud-Acadie Bouctouche
☎*743-1999*
You can explore the rivers of the Bouctouche region by kayak with the help of Expédition Sud-Acadie,

which organizes a variety of tours.

KayaBécano
RR1
☎*743-6265 or 888-529-2232*
In addition to guided tours, KayaBécano also offers kayak rentals.

Saint-Louis-de-Kent

Kayakouch
10617 Rue Principale
☎*876-1199*
⇌*876-1918*
To explore the natural beauty of Kouchibouguac National Park, take a guided tour on the sea with Kayakouch.

Kouchibouguac National Park

Ryan's Rental Centre
mid-Jun to early Sep, every day 8am to 9pm
☎*876-2571*
Canoe rentals are also available in Kouchibouguac National Park at Ryan's Rental Centre.

Miramichi

The Miramichi River also offers some spectacular panoramic views that can be reached by paddling a short distance.

Eastern Scenic Adventure
☎*778-8573*
⇌*778-8222*

Kedgwick River

Centre Echo Restigouche
1397 Hwy. 265
☎*284-2022*
⇌*284-2927*
Centre Echo Restigouche offers trips of one or more days, allowing you to enjoy the magnificent natural

beauty of the Restigouche River.

Downhill Skiing

When **Sugarloaf Provincial Park** is covered with snow, Mount Sugarloaf becomes a haven for downhill skiing enthusiasts. With eight runs, it's one of the most popular ski centres in the province.

Accommodations

Cap-Pelé

Les Chalets de L'Aboiteau
$$-$$$$
K, ℜ
40 cottages
55 Allée des Chalets, E4N 3B3
☎*577-2005 or 888-366-5555*
⇌*577-2083*
If you are one of those people who never get tired of looking at the sea, then L'Aboiteau is the place for you. Its 40 wooden chalets, recently built within walking distance from mag-nificent L'Aboiteau Beach, are an idyllic getaway for those who want to relax. In addition to its wonderful location, all of the cottages are luxurious, with fire-places, large bay windows and fully equipped kitch-ens. Each cottage can accommodate between four and eight people. Reservations are strongly recommended.

Robichaud

Alouette Motel
$$ bkfst incl.
K
21 rooms
149 Promenade Riverside,
E4P 2N8
☎*532-5378*
⇌*386-4053*
The Alouette Motel, located next to a very busy campground, offers clean, basic rooms within walking distance of a sandy beach that is ideal for swimming.

Shediac

The Shediac region attracts a good number of visitors in the summer months, thanks to magnificent Parlee Beach. Various accommodation options are available to vacationers, some of them located near the park entrance, but there is no motel, inn or bed and breakfast directly on Parlee Beach.

For longer stays it is possible to rent one of the many cottages in the area; some of these look out over the ocean. The **Planning Plus** *(RR1, Shediac, E0A 3G0,* ☎*532-3896,* ⇌*532-8914)* rental agency is quite efficient at selecting and reserving cottages in the area that meet visitors' specific needs.

Neptune Motel
$-$$
34 rooms
691 E. Main St., E4P 8W5
☎*532-4299*
Though the rooms at the Neptune Motel are furnished and decorated very simply, they are among the least expensive in the

area. Located near the provincial park entrance.

Chez Françoise
$$ bkfst incl.
10 rooms
293 Main St., E4P 2A8
☎*532-4233*
⇌*532-8422*
Located on a beautifully maintained property in the heart of Shediac, Chez Françoise is a wonderful inn. Built a century ago, it was originally the residence of a wealthy family. The elegant interior, with its wood trim, sumptuous staircase and large front porch, ideal for coffee or a cocktail, make for a charming little spot.

Bay Vista Lodge & Cottages
$$
☇, K
12 rooms
3521 Rte. 134 N., E4P 8T9
☎*532-1265*
At Shediac Cape, a few kilometres north of Shediac, the Bay Vista Lodge & Cottages comprises some 10 chalets spread out over a beautifully landscaped property in a peaceful setting. An undeveloped beach, located nearby, makes for wonderful walks. Each cottage has a small front porch that is perfect for lounging and relaxing. The Bay Vista also rents rooms.

Motel Sea Gull
$$
ℜ, K
21 rooms
Shediac Bridge, Hwy. 134,
E4R 1T5
☎*532-2530*
As previously indicated, there are no accommodations directly on Parlee Beach, but just a few kilometres north of Shediac, at

Shediac Bridge, there is the Motel Sea Gull which looks out over a pretty, placid bay. This is a very relaxing spot: lawn chairs have been set out here and there on the grassy grounds, from which guests can admire the beautiful panorama in complete, undisturbed tranquillity. Though not luxurious, the Sea Gull's rooms are clean and relatively inexpensive and they are very much in demand; reservations are a good idea. A few cottages are also available.

Seely's Motel
$$
K, ≡
34 rooms
21 Bellevue Heights, E4P 1G9
☎*532-6193 or*
800-449-4141
⇌*533-8089*
Close to the entrance to the Parlee Beach Provincial Park, Seely's Motel offers plainly decorated rooms that are nonetheless comfortable and clean.

Four Seas Motel
$$-$$$
ℜ, K, ≡
42 rooms
634 Main St., E4P 2H3
☎*532-2585 or*
877-532-2585
⇌*532-1025*
Near the entrance to Parlee Beach Provincial Park, the Four Seas Motel is a good choice for families. The service is efficient and friendly, the restaurant (see p 115) is very good and the rooms are clean and well furnished, mostly with modern pieces. During the summer season, it is best to reserve early in the morning if you want one of the less expensive rooms, since they go fast.

New Brunswick

Belcourt Inn
$$$

≡

7 rooms
310 Main St., E4P 2E3
☎*532-6098*
A member of the *Association des Auberges du Patrimoine du Nouveau-Brunswick*, the Belcourt Inn occupies a sumptuous patrician house that has belonged to such notables as former premier of New Brunswick Judge Allison Dysart. Erected in 1912, this three-storey Victorian building has preserved all of its olden-day splendour and charm, both inside and out. The common rooms are spacious, furnished with antiques and richly ornamented with wood-work. The inn's seven individually decorated guestrooms are also decked out in period furniture. A very inviting porch provides an ideal setting for reading and relaxing. The Belcourt Inn is situated in the heart of Shediac, just across from Chez Françoise (see above).

Le Gourmand Country Inn & Cottages
$$$
ℜ, K, ℑ
9 cottages
562 Main St., E4P 2H1
☎*532-2885 or 877-532-2585*
⇄*532-1025*
In the summertime, Le Gourmand, located near the entrance to Parlee Beach Provincial Park, rents nine cottages spread out on a small wooded lot just behind the establishment's main building. Each of them has a modern wash-room and kitchenette, two bedrooms and a living room that can be trans-formed into a third bed-

room, all of which are appealingly laid out. In addition, Le Gourmand offers a few very well-kept rooms in the main building, which also houses an excellent restaurant (see p 115).

Domaine Parlee Beach
$$$$
K
20 cottages
642 Main St., E4P 2H3
☎*532-5339 or 800-786-5550*
⇄*532-3399*
www.domaineparleebeach.ca
The Domaine Parlee Beach rents out some 20 cottages near the entrance to Parlee Beach Provincial Park, about 10min on foot from the beach. Each two-storey cottage can accommodate up to six people and includes two bed-rooms, a small living room with a convertible sofa, a very clean bathroom and a kitchen. The cottages' natural-wood interiors are very appealing. Domaine Parlee Beach also offers six rooms in a main building.

Bouctouche

Old Presbytery of Bouctouche
$$ bkfst incl.
ℜ, ≡
22 rooms
157 Chemin du Couvent, E4S 3B8
☎*743-5568 or 866-743-1880*
⇄*743-5566*
www.vieuxpresbytere.nb.ca
The Old Presbytery of Bouctouche occupies a presbytery constructed at the end of the 19th century. Today it is a superb family inn located just outside the centre of Bouc-

touche, with beautiful views of the bay. The atmosphere is first-rate, ideal for relaxation, and the building, which has been renovated several times, is full of charm. An old chapel has been converted into a reception hall. Its restaurant (**Tire-Bouchon**, see p 116) has an excellent reputation as well.

Bouctouche Bay Inn
$$
ℜ, ≡
27 rooms
206 Acadie St., E4S 2T5
☎*743-2726*
⇄*743-2387*
Besides a terrific view of the bay, the Bouctouche Bay Inn offers clean motel-style rooms, some of which are very competitively priced. It is not far from the entrance to the Pays de la Sagouine (see p 102).

Bouctouche Bay Chalet
$$$
🛶
2 cottages
Hwy. 475, E4S 4W4
☎*743-8883 or 888-530-8883*
Not far from the beach and the dune, Bouctouche Bay Chalet consists of two cottages of different sizes, all set in a shady glen near a campground.

Richibucto

Motel Habitant
$$-$$$
⌂, ⊛, ≈, ≡
28 rooms
9600 Main St., E4W 4E6
☎*523-4421 or 888-442-7222*
⇄*523-0155*
www.habitant.nb.ca
The Motel Habitant is situated just over 10km south of the entrance to

Kouchibouguac National Park (see p 104). It is a nice-looking motel with clean rooms and a pool. This is the most comfortable motel near the park.

Les Chalets du Havre
$$-$$$$
℠, K, ≈, ®
24 chalets
79 York St., E4W 4K1
☎*523-1570 or*
800-277-9037
⇄*523-9770*
www.chaletduhavre.nb.ca
Les Chalets du Havre, a holiday resort that includes 24 cottages, occupies a large peninsula near the village of Richibucto. The site is lovely, although the ground is practically bare here. The cottages can accommodate up to six people, and each has two bedrooms, an all-equipped kitchenette, a bathroom and a den that can be converted into an extra bedroom if necessary. The cottages' interior decor is standard and modern. The entire peninsula is bordered by a long beach that is great for swimming but especially pleasant for sea-side strolls. Many outdoor activities can be enjoyed here. In summer, a ferry shuttles passengers to the splendid sand beaches of Kouchibouguac National Park.

Tracadie-Sheila

Complexe Hôtelier Le Boudreau
$$
℠, ≈
66 rooms
3068 Main St., E1X 1G5
☎*395-2244 or*
800-563-2242
⇄*395-6868*
The Boudreau is a fine establishment that rents

very comfortable, modern rooms. Business travellers make up the majority of its clientele.

Shippagan

Camping Shippagan
$
⚓
99 campsites
4km west of Shippagan
☎*336-3960*
⇄*336-3961*
In Shippagan, campers can pitch their tent a short distance from the beach at Camping Shippagan, which is definitely one of the most pleasant campgrounds in the region.

Motel Brise Marine
$$
℠, ≡
35 rooms
172 1st St., E8S 1T1
☎*336-2276*
Among the other accommodation possibilities in town, the clean, comfortable rooms of the Motel Brise Marine are worth mentioning.

Île Lamèque

⚓ **Auberge des Compagnons**
$$$-$$$$ bkfst incl.
℠, ♿
16 rooms
11 Main St., E8T 1M9
☎*344-7762*
⇄*344-0813*
www.aubergedes compagnons.ca
You will definitely have a pleasant stay at this inn—it's both comfortable and ideally located facing the bay. Each of its 16 thematic rooms has a different decor (the circus, the Edwardian Era, fruit and

the like), and each is well kept. The lounge-bar, which has a fireplace, is the ideal spot to end the day.

Caraquet

Gîte Le Poirier B&B
$$ bkfst incl.
≡
5 rooms
98 Blvd. St-Pierre Ouest, E1W 1B6
☎*727-4359 or*
888-748-9311
⇄*726-6084*
www.gitelepoirier.com
Caraquet has a pleasant inn, the Gîte Le Poirier B&B, which was originally built in 1928 and has managed to keep its old-world charm. Its five simply decorated rooms are all cozy.

Maison Touristique Dugas
$$ bkfst incl.
K
16 rooms
683 Blvd. St-Pierre Ouest, E1W 1A1
☎*727-3195 or*
866-727-3195
⇄*722-3193*
www.maisontouristique dugas.ca
There truly is something for all tastes and all budgets at the Maison Touristique Dugas. The main building, a beautiful, massive house built in 1926, numbers over 10 impeccable, pretty rooms of varying sizes. In addition to these rooms, campsites and fully equipped rental cottages are also available on the grounds. The Maison Touristique Dugas offers a very friendly welcome and excellent breakfasts in the morning. From the house, located a little bit west of Caraquet, a trail

New Brunswick

winds through the woods to the Dugas's private beach, just a 10min walk away.

Auberge de la Baie
$$-$$$
ℜ
54 rooms
139 Blvd. St-Pierre Ouest,
E1W 1B7
☎727-3485
⇄727-3634
The Auberge de la Baie provides comfortable, modern, motel-style accommodation. Strangely enough, most of the rooms open onto an interior hallway instead of outdoors. There is a good restaurant (see p 116) with polite, friendly and attentive service. Finally, the ample grounds offer access to a small deserted beach located behind the inn.

Hôtel Paulin
$$$
ℜ, ≡
8 rooms
May to Oct
143 Blvd. St-Pierre Ouest,
E1W 1B6
☎727-9981
⇄727-4808
www.hotelpaulin.com
Also part of the Caraquet skyline for many years, the Hôtel Paulin is actually a pleasant inn that has been run by the Paulin family for the last three generations. The rooms vary in quality: some have been nicely renovated while others are quite out of date but are still very clean; in all cases, however, the rooms are of good value. There is a very pretty suite at the back of the building with a view of the ocean. Guests can relax in the sitting

room and enjoy the restaurant's (see p 117) excellent food.

Bathurst

Le Château Bathurst
$$
ℜ, ≈, ◯, ≡, ®, ✖, ઙ
134 rooms
80 Main St., E2A 1A3
☎546-6691 or
800-561-7666
⇄546-0015
www.lechateaubathurst.ca
Situated in downtown Bathurst, Le Château Bathurst is the largest hotel in the area. Its rooms are comfortable, but without any particular charm.

Danny's Inn
$$
ℜ, ≈, ≡, K, ✖
40 rooms
80 Main St., E2A 2Y9
☎546-6621 or
800-200-1350
⇄548-3266
www.dannys.nb.ca
Slightly on the outskirts of downtown Bathurst, Danny's Inn offers spotless, modern rooms.

Lakeview Inn & Suites
$$
≡, ✖, ઙ
78 rooms
777 St. Peter Ave., E2A 2Y9
☎548-4949 or
877-355-3500
⇄548-8595
www.countryinns.com
With its spacious rooms and suites, the Lakeview Inn & Suites is another Bathurst establishment that offers the comfort of a modern hotel. The little added touches, such as the fireplace in the hall, give this place a charming atmosphere.

Petit-Rocher

Auberge d'Anjou
$$
ℜ, ≡
6 rooms
587 Main St., E8J 1H6
☎783-0587 or
866-783-0587
⇄783-5587
Auberge d'Anjou is considered one of the best places to stay in this part of the Acadian coast. It occupies a beautiful 1917 house that was actually the first hotel in Petit-Rocher.

In those days, in addition to welcoming travellers, it served as the principal meeting place for villagers. The Auberge d'Anjou closed down in the 1960s and did not resume its vocation until 1994. The very successfully renovated main building is embellished by a large porch that greatly enhances its charm. Its rooms are inviting and tastefully decorated. To top it all off, the Auberge also has an excellent restaurant (see p 117).

Dalhousie

Best Western Manoir Adelaide
$$-$$$
ℜ, K, ☺, ≡, ઙ
46 rooms
385 Adelaide St., E8C 1B4
☎684-5681 or
800-934-5444
⇄684-3433
The Best Western Manoir Adelaide offers adequate comfort in its modern rooms, as well as conference facilities, a fitness centre and a pool with slides. Some rooms are equipped with kitchenettes.

Restaurants

Cap-Pelé

Chez Camille
$
2385 Chemin Acadie, Hwy. 15
☎577-4710
A great place to eat in Cap-Pelé is the reasonably priced Chez Camille, which has become very popular for its fried chicken. Patrons claim that it's one of the best restaurants of its kind in the province.

Restaurant de la Plage de L'Aboiteau
$
L'Aboiteau Beach
☎577-2005
If you want to have a bite to eat but don't want to leave the beach, you can have lunch at the Restaurant de la Plage de L'Aboiteau. It offers basic fare at reasonable prices and has a magnificent view of the sea.

Aboiteau Fisheries
$-$$
77 Quai Aboiteau Rd.
☎577-2950
Located right on the docks in Cap-Pelé, Aboiteau Fisheries is a true local institution. It is above all a fish market, probably the best in this part of the province, that sells fresh and cooked lobster and various types of fish (salmon, sole and trout, among others), but also cockles, mussels, clams, scallops and crab. The goods are all fished locally and thus always fresh. You

can also enjoy any of these on site. Simple, but friendly and delicious.

Shediac

Chez Léo
$-$$
Shediac Bridge
☎532-4543
Chez Léo's menu offers several simply prepared seafood dishes, sandwiches and fries. The lunch menu is always delicious—especially the fried chicken.

Four Seas Restaurant
$$
634 Main St.
☎532-2585
The Four Seas, located in the motel of the same name (see p 111), is another family restaurant. This one offers a rather varied menu that includes seafood. Patrons surely don't come for the relatively boring decor, but rather for the reasonable prices and the quality of the food.

Le Gourmand Country Inn & Cottages
$$
562 Rue Main
☎532-2585
The lovely dining room at the **Le Gourmand Country Inn & Cottages** (see p 112) is a pleasant setting for a hearty meal. Grilled scallops, shrimp, lobster in various preparations, filets of salmon and cod, steaks and poultry constitute the main elements on the menu. For starters, both the succulent seafood *chaudrée* (chowder) and the grilled escargots are excellent choices.

Fisherman's Paradise
$$-$$$
640 Main St.
☎532-6811
There are no surprises at the Fisherman's Paradise, which, as its name suggests, is devoted to the treasures of the sea. A special place is reserved on the menu for the king of seafood: lobster. With its exquisite interior decor that displays numerous model ships, this place is among the most chic in Shediac. For those who are not seafood aficionados, Fisherman's Paradise also offers a good variety of steaks.

Lobster Deck
$$$
312 Main St.
☎532-8737
Located in the centre of town, the Lobster Deck has delicious, fresh fish and seafood specialties prepared in a variety of ways: grilled, fried, *au gratin* or coated with sauce. The dining room has an amusing decor: the tables are shaped like lobster pots and the walls are adorned with stuffed lobsters, one of which weighs 20kg. On beautiful sunny days, guests can dine outdoors on the adjoining terrace.

Bouctouche

Restaurant du Gîte de la Sagouine
$$
45 Blvd. Irving
☎743-5554
"*Chu bin fière de vous ouère*" ("I'm really proud to see you"). These are the first words of welcome at the Restaurant du Gîte de la Sagouine—a sure sign of the good things to

come. The menu at this family restaurant offers Acadian dishes, such as *fricot de poulet* (chicken stew) and *poutine râpée*, as well as expertly prepared seafood.

Tire-Bouchon
$$-$$$
Old Presbytery, 157 Chemin du Couvent
☎743-5568
Acadian hospitality is at its best at Tire-Bouchon, the excellent dining room in the **Old Presbytery** (see p 112), where chef Marcelle Albert introduces diners to the most refined regional specialties. The name, which means "corkscrew" in French, is quite fitting considering the fine bottles that stock its wine cellar.

L'Ordre du Bon Temps
$$$$
at the entrance to the Pays de la Sagouine
☎743-1400
L'Ordre du Bon Temps, the restaurant at the **Pays de la Sagouine** (see p 102), offers visitors dinner shows and a chance to sample traditional Acadian specialties like *fricot de poulet*, *poutine râpée*, *poutine à trou*, *pâté à la râpure* or *pâté aux palourdes*. The menu probably has the most extensive selection of Acadian dishes in all of Acadia, so take advantage of it.

St. Thomas

St. Thomas Fish Market
$
Hwy. 535
☎743-5965
Sometimes it's nice to have some simply pre-

pared seafood in a plain-looking restaurant. St. Thomas Fish Market is such a place. The seafood here is prepared on the premises, and the freshness is guaranteed!

Shippagan

Bistro Pirate Maboule
$$
121 16th St.
☎336-0004
The creative menu at Bistro Pirate Maboule is the first thing you notice about this establishment. The dishes have evocative names like "Captain Haddock's Haddock," the "Seven Seas Salad" and the "Captain's Feast." Everything here is scrumptious. The decor, which looks like an old pirate ship, is also quite attractive. The atmosphere is delightful and will please everyone, especially families.

Pavillon Aquatique
$$-$$$
next to the Aquarium
☎336-3013
Very elegant and enjoying a splendid view of the port, the Pavillon Aquatique is, as one might expect, an excellent fish and seafood restaurant. Lunchtime, when lobster rolls and other light meals are available at relatively reasonable prices, is a good time to stop in for a bite. During the evening, gourmets benefit from a wide choice. Those with a big appetite can attempt to discover all the wonders of the sea in one meal with the "Sea in Your Plate" dish.

Île Lamèque

Auberge des Compagnons
$
11 Main St., E8T 1M9
☎344-7762
The Auberge des Compagnons serves delicious meals and is considered one of the best restaurants in the region.

Caraquet

Café Phare
$-$$
186 Blvd. St-Pierre Ouest
☎727-9460
Café Phare, an adorable café that already has a great number of devotees, is a good spot for breakfast or a light meal. It is welcoming and has a pleasant front patio that is very crowded when the weather is nice. Café Phare mainly serves salads, quiches, sandwiches and pastries. The daily menu also offers a few more elaborate dishes.

Le Caraquette
$-$$
89 Blvd. St-Pierre Ouest
☎727-6009
For dining in a friendly family atmosphere, check out Le Caraquette. The reasonably priced menu is varied and includes steaks, pasta, chicken and sandwiches, as well as lots of fish and seafood.

Auberge de la Baie
$$
139 Blvd. St-Pierre Ouest
☎727-3485
Airy and modern, but at the same time friendly and inviting, the **Auberge de la Baie**'s (see p 114) dining room offers a good variety

of dishes, including seafood and steaks. The service is very attentive. Some of this restaurant's specialties are baked scallops, *coquilles St. Jacques au gratin* and Provençale frogs' legs.

Hôtel Paulin
$$
143 Blvd. St-Pierre Ouest
☎*727-9981*
The **Hôtel Paulin**'s (see p 114) dining room offers what has become something of a rarity in the region, a table d'hôte or set menu, instead of the usual à la carte service. Regional and French specialties make up the menu. On nice summer days, there is service on a beautiful terrace.

Poisson d'Or
$$-$$$
Carrefour de la Mer
☎*727-0004*
Come nightfall, Poisson d'Or, a pretty restaurant with the atmosphere of a French bistro, becomes a popular meeting place for locals and visitors alike. The menu offers seafood

and fish, in addition to succulent charbroiled steaks.

Paquetville

La Crêpe Bretonne
$-$$
1085 Rue du Parc
☎*764-5344*
If your tummy starts to grumble as you pass through the little town of Paquetville, silence it with a stop at La Crêpe Bretonne, a small restaurant whose specialties are crepes and seafood. These two are sometimes combined in scallop and béchamel crepes, lobster and béchamel crepes, crab and béchamel crepes, etc. A good place for an inexpensive lunch or a good evening meal.

Nigadoo

Fine Grobe-sur-mer
$$-$$$
289 Main St.
☎*783-3138*
A short side trip from Bathurst or Caraquet to

Fine Grobe-sur-mer in Nigadoo is a must for aficionados of fine cuisine. This little restaurant offers an original menu that includes local and international specialties prepared with ingredients that are always fresh. The bread that accompanies the meals is baked fresh on the premises.

Petit-Rocher

Auberge d'Anjou
$$
587 Rue Principale
☎*783-0587*
Auberge d'Anjou (see p 114) has a pretty dining room and a splendid terrace that is very enjoyable on sunny summer days. The menu lists a great variety of seafood, fish and meat dishes. Auberge d'Anjou is reputed to be one of the best restaurants on the coast.

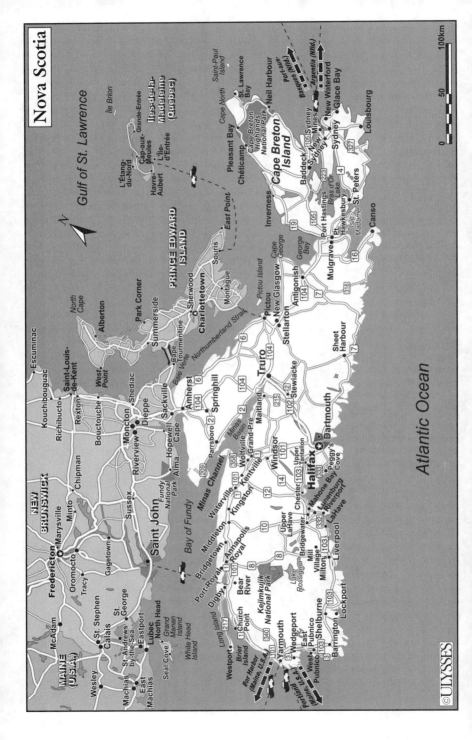

Nova Scotia

Gulf of St. Lawrence

Atlantic Ocean

100km

50

0   50

© ULYSSES

Nova Scotia

The magnificent province
of Nova Scotia is a long peninsula, connected to the continent by nothing more than a narrow strip of land known as the Chignecto Isthmus.

In "Canada's Ocean Playground," the sea is never far away. In fact, no part of the territory of Nova Scotia is more than 50km from water, be it the Atlantic Ocean, the Northumberland Strait or the Bay of Fundy. The proximity of the coast has shaped the character and lives of Nova Scotians as much as it has the splendid maritime landscape.

The hundreds of kilometres of coastline, are punctuated with harbours and bays, their shores dotted with fishing villages and towns. What is most striking about Nova Scotia is the way its architectural heritage blends so harmoniously with the natural setting.

From the tiniest fishing village to the capital of Halifax, there are few places where the architecture of the houses and buildings, often dating back to the 19th century, does

not fit in beautifully with the surrounding landscape.

Beautiful Nova Scotia was long fought over by the French and British empires. First inhabited by the Mi'kmaq, it became the first European colony in North America north of Florida.

In 1605, a year after its failed attempt to settle St. Croix Island (now a part of the state of Maine), a French expedition party led by the sieur de Monts established the settlement of Port Royal, at the

mouth of the present-day Annapolis River.

The foundation of this permanent settlement gave rise to Acadia. In the following decades, Port Royal flourished and the Acadians went on to found new settlements around the Bay of Fundy.

The many wars between the French and the British would prove to be Acadia's undoing, however. In 1713, the French-ruled colony of Acadia was ceded to Great Britain under the Treaty of

Utrecht and renamed Nova Scotia ("New Scotland" in Latin).

As British citizens of French ancestry, the Acadians pledged neutrality in the ongoing war between France and Great Britain. Unfortunately, this failed to appease the British authorities.

In 1755, with another war looming, the British opted to take radical measures: the mass deportation of the Acadians. Between 1755 and 1763, roughly half of the 14,000 Acadians living on the shores of the Bay of Fundy were literally shipped off, with the remaining population fleeing to the woods.

In the following decades, Nova Scotia welcomed a spate of immigrants, notably "Planters" from New England in search of new lands to cultivate, Loyalists fleeing the Unites States in the wake of the American Revolution and citizens of the British Isles, particularly Scots.

In 1867, Nova Scotia joined the Dominion of Canada, which then included three other provinces: New Brunswick, Ontario and Québec. At the time, Nova Scotia was a prosperous colony, thanks mainly to the shipbuilding, fishing and lumber industries. A few years later, in 1874, the province was linked to the rest

of Canada by the Intercolonial Railway.

Halifax prospered from Nova Scotia's union with Canada, becoming the country's leading Atlantic seaport. Its geographical location led it to play a major commercial and military role, the city serving as a launchpad for virtually all Europe-bound convoys and Canadian troops during both the First and Second World Wars.

Today, Nova Scotia is the most populated of Canada's Atlantic provinces.

The American Lobster
(Homarus Americanus)

The American lobster, also known as the "northern lobster," lives along the eastern coast of North America, from Nova Scotia to North Carolina. Long before the arrival of Europeans in the Americas, Aboriginal people knew this crustacean well, mainly using it as fertilizer. It is said that in those days, lobster was so abundant that you could handpick it along the coast.

Things have changed quite a bit, and lobster is now considered to be one of the most delicious and sought-after dishes. It is in high demand in markets all over the world. Its popularity has spawned local fishing industries in many coastal communities in Canada and the United States. To avoid overexploitation, both the Canadian and U.S. governments have imposed norms detailing the minimal length of the lobsters that are caught.

The renewal of the lobster supply is a long and perilous process. Of the 10,000 eggs that are laid by the female, only 1% survives past four weeks and even fewer reach maturity. It takes approximately five years for a lobster to reach its adult size and, to do so, it must moult at least 25 times. As it ages, it con-tinues to grow slowly, moulting less and less frequently. Although necrophagous, lobsters nevertheless prefer live food and feed on cock-les, mussels, sea urchins, crabs and, occasionally, aquatic plants.

Their characteristic colour is due to the presence of three pigments in their shell: blue, red and yellow. Sometimes, one or more of these pigments may be missing at birth, resulting in a shell that can be either red, blue, white (albinos) or black with yellow spots. It is estimated that one in 3 to 4 million lobsters has a blue carapace and one in 10 million has a red one.

Moreover, they can grow to an impressive size. Apparently, it was in Nova Scotia that the largest lobster was spotted; it measured 1.5m, weighed 20kg and had lived to the ripe old age of 100.

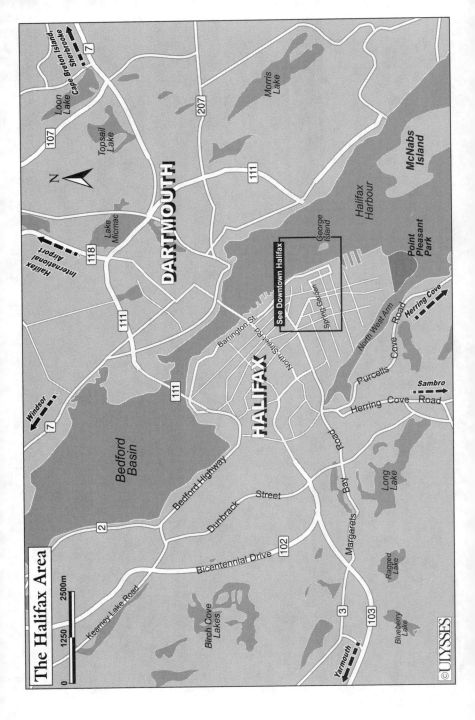

The Halifax Area

0   1250   2500m

© ULYSSES

Kearney Lake Road

Birch Cove Lakes

Bicentennial Drive

Dunbrack   Street

Bedford Highway

Bedford Basin

2

102

3

103

Yarmouth

Blueberry Lake

Ragged Lake

Margarets   Bay   Road

Long Lake

HALIFAX

North Street Rd.

Barrington St.

111

7   Windsor

DARTMOUTH

Lake Micmac

118

Halifax International Airport

107

Loon Lake

Topsail Lake

N

207

Morris Lake

7   Cape Breton Island, Sherbrooke

111

Halifax Harbour

George Island

Spring Garden

See Downtown Halifax

McNabs Island

Point Pleasant Park

North West Arm

Purcells   Cove

Herring   Cove

Sambro   Road

Herring Cove

The beautiful, vibrant

and delightful capital of Nova Scotia, **Halifax** ★★★ is also the largest city in the Atlantic provinces.

A city with a rich architectural heritage, built at the foot of a fortified hill overlooking one of the longest natural harbours in the world, Halifax is a delightful place to visit. The city's location, outstanding from both a navigational and a strategic point of view, has been the deciding factor in its growth.

In 1749, the British began developing the site, which had long been frequented by the Mi'kmaq First Nation. That year, 2,500 British soldiers and colonists led by Governor Edward Cornwallis settled here with the aim of securing Britain's claim to the territory of Nova Scotia.

At the time, France and its North American colonies were the enemy. Over the following decades, Halifax served as a stronghold for British troops during the American Revolution and the War of 1812 against the United States. The city's military past is evident in its present-day urban landscape, its most striking legacy being, of course, the Citadel, whose silhouette looms over the downtown area.

Not just a military city, Halifax has always been a commercial centre as well. Its access to the Atlantic, its excellent port and, starting in the late 19th century, its connection to the Canadian rail network have all favoured trade. The Historic Properties, made up of warehouses built on the pier, is the oldest architectural grouping of its kind in the country, bearing witness to the city's long-established commercial tradition.

On April 14, 1912, a terrible tragedy occurred near the Canadian coast: the wreck of the *Titanic*, which claimed the lives of hundreds of people. Called on for help, several ships set out from Halifax harbour, returning with the remains of the victims, some 150 of whom were buried in the city's cemeteries.

But the most tragic event in the history of the city occurred a few years later. With World War I raging in Europe, Halifax played a major role in the transport of troops and merchandise. On December 6, 1917, a Belgian vessel, the *Imo*, struck the *Mont Blanc*, a French ship laden with explosives. Twenty minutes later came a devastating explosion, laying waste to part of the city, killing 2,000 people instantly and injuring thousands more.

Halifax is now the largest urban centre in the Atlantic provinces, with a population of over 370,000 (including the inhabitants of its twin city, Dartmouth). It has a more varied, even cosmopolitan appearance than the rest of Atlantic Canada, and boasts several superb museums and a whole slew of other attractions. Visitors are sure to enjoy strolling around Halifax and scouting out its restaurants, bustling streets and wide assortment of shops.

Finding Your Way Around

By Car

Entering Halifax and reaching the downtown area is generally very easy by car; many road signs clearly indicate the way. If in doubt, remember that Halifax lies on the southwest side of the harbour (Dartmouth is on the other side), and the downtown area faces right onto the port. Visitors will have little trouble finding their bearings downtown, where Citadel Hill and the port serve as reference points. The most important downtown artery is Barrington Street.

By Plane

Halifax International Airport is served by planes from Canada, Europe and the United States. Air Canada offers flights from major Canadian cities. For more information, please refer to the "Practical Information" chapter, see p 28. There is shuttle service from the airport to the major downtown hotels.

By Train

VIA, Canada's railway network, ends in Halifax. The station is near downtown. To find out the passenger train's schedule, contact ☎*888-842-7245* or *www.viarail.com*.

Practical Information

Area code: *902*

Tourist Information

International Visitor Centre
1595 Barrington St., B3J 1Z7
☎*490-5946*
⇒*490-5973*

Historic Properties
1869 Upper Water St.
☎*424-4248*

www.halifax.ca
www.halifaxinfo.com

Exploring

The Citadel and its Surrounding Area

The **Halifax Citadel National Historic Site** ★★★ (*$9; early May to late Oct, 9am to 5pm, Jul and Aug until 6pm; Citadel Hill,* ☎*426-5080*) is the most striking legacy of the military history of Halifax, a city that has played an important strategic role in the defence of the East Coast ever since it was founded in 1749. The fourth British fort to occupy this site, this imposing star-shaped structure overlooking the city was built between 1828 and 1856. It was the heart of an impressive network of defences intended to protect the port in the event of an attack.

Visitors can explore the Citadel on their own, or take part in an interesting guided tour which traces the history of the various fortifications that have marked the city's land

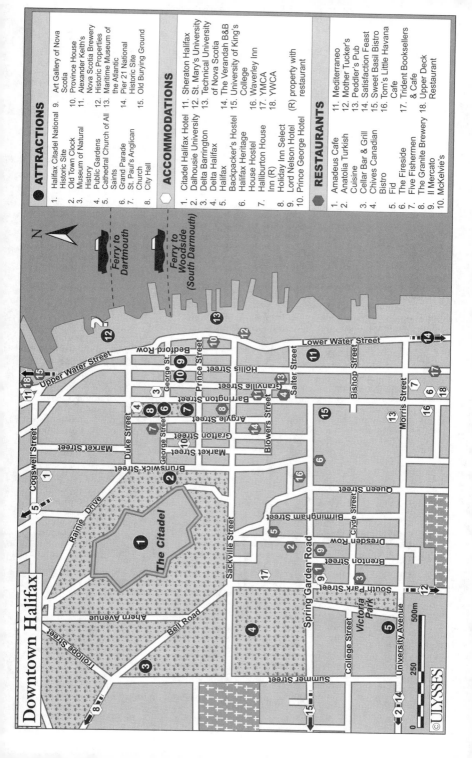

Downtown Halifax

● ATTRACTIONS

1. Halifax Citadel National Historic Site
2. Old Town Clock
3. Museum of Natural History
4. Public Gardens
5. Cathedral Church of All Saints
6. Grand Parade
7. St. Paul's Anglican Church
8. City Hall
9. Art Gallery of Nova Scotia
10. Province House
11. Alexander Keith's Nova Scotia Brewery
12. Historic Properties
13. Maritime Museum of the Atlantic
14. Pier 21 National Historic Site
15. Old Burying Ground

⬡ ACCOMMODATIONS

1. Citadel Halifax Hotel
2. Dalhousie University
3. Delta Barrington
4. Delta Halifax
5. Halifax Backpacker's Hostel
6. Halifax Heritage House Hostel
7. Halliburton House Inn (R)
8. Holiday Inn Select
9. Lord Nelson Hotel
10. Prince George Hotel
11. Sheraton Halifax
12. St. Mary's University
13. Technical University of Nova Scotia
14. The Verandah B&B
15. University of King's College
16. Waverley Inn
17. YMCA
18. YWCA

(R) property with restaurant

⬣ RESTAURANTS

1. Amadeus Cafe
2. Anatolia Turkish Cuisine
3. Cellar Bar & Grill
4. Chives Canadian Bistro
5. Fid
6. The Fireside
7. Five Fishermen
8. The Granite Brewery
9. Il Mercato
10. McKelvie's
11. Mediterraneo
12. Mother Tucker's
13. Peddler's Pub
14. Satisfaction Feast
15. Sweet Basil Bistro
16. Tom's Little Havana Cafe
17. Trident Booksellers & Cafe
18. Upper Deck Restaurant

© ULYSSES

N

Ferry to Dartmouth

Ferry to Woodside (South Dartmouth)

scape since 1749 and explains their strategic value. All of the rooms that were used to accommodate soldiers and store arms and munitions are open to the public, and visitors can move through the corridors leading from one room or level to another. It is also possible to walk along the ramparts, which offer an incomparable view of the city and its port. In summer, students dressed and armed like the soldiers of the 78th Highlanders and the Royal Artillery perform manoeuvres within these walls. The site also includes the **Army Museum** *(free admission; early May to end of Oct; ☎424-5979),* which houses an extensive collection of British and Nova Scotian arms and uniforms. A fascinating 15min audio-visual presentation on the history of Halifax can be viewed here as well.

Right in front of the Citadel, towards the port, stands one of the most famous symbols of Halifax, the **Old Town Clock** ★ *(Citadel Hill, opposite the main entrance of the Citadel).* The clock was presented to the city in 1803 by Prince Edward, son of George III of Britain, who served as Commander in Chief of the Halifax garrison from 1794 to 1800. The clock and its four dials serve as a reminder that the prince was a great believer in punctuality.

Northwest of the Citadel, visitors will find the **Museum of Natural History** ★ *($3; Tue-Sun 9am to 5:30pm; 1747 Summer St., ☎424-6099, www.museum. gov.ns.ca),* whose mission is to collect, preserve and study the objects and specimens most representative of Nova Scotia's geology, plant and animal life and archaeology.

The museum features exhibits on subjects such as botany, fossils, insects, reptiles and marine life. One of the most noteworthy items on display is a whale skeleton.

Visitors can also view a film on the birds that live along the province's coast. The archaeology exhibit is particularly interesting, presenting the lifestyle and material possessions of the various peoples who have inhabited the province's territory over the centuries. The exhibit is organized in chronological order, starting with the Palaeolithic age, then moving on to the Mi'kmaqs, the Acadians and, finally, the British.

Stretching southwest of the Citadel are the lovely, verdant **Public Gardens** ★ ★ *(main entrance on South Park St.),* a Victorian garden that covers an area of 7ha and dates back to 1753. Originally a private garden, it was purchased by the Nova Scotia Horticultural Society in 1836. The garden's present layout, completed in 1875, is the work of Richard Power. A fine example of British know-how, the Public Gardens are adorned with stately trees concealing fountains, statues, charming flowerbeds, a pavilion and little lakes where ducks and swans swim about.

This is an absolutely perfect place for a stroll, far from the occasionally turbulent atmosphere of downtown Halifax.

South of the Public Gardens, near Victoria Park,

Old Town Clock

stands the **Cathedral Church of All Saints ★** *(free admission; Jun to Aug, Mon-Fri 9am to 5pm, Sat 1pm to 4pm, Sun 1:30pm to 4:30pm; 1320 Tower Rd., ☎423-6002)*, whose remarkable stained-glass windows and exquisite woodwork will take your breath away.

The structure was completed in 1910, two centuries after the first Anglican service was held in Canada. It is located in a pretty part of the city, where the streets are flanked by stately trees. Some of Halifax's most prominent educational establishments can be found nearby.

Province House

Downtown Halifax and the Port

As early as a decade after Halifax was founded, **Grand Parade** *(between Harrington and Argyle Sts.)* had become a trading and gathering place for city residents. It is now a garden in the heart of the downtown area, flanked by tall buildings on all sides.

At the south end of Grand Parade, visitors will find **St. Paul's Anglican Church ★** *(free admission; Mon-Fri 9am to 4:30pm; 1749 Argyle St., Grand Parade, ☎429-2240)*, the oldest Protestant church in Canada, built in 1750 after the model of St. Peter's Church in London, England. Despite the wearing effects of time and the addition of several extensions, the original structure has been preserved.

Inside, visitors can examine a piece of metal from the *Mont Blanc*, one of the ships that caused a terrible explosion in Halifax in 1917. On the north side of Grand Parade stands **City Hall** *(free admission)*, an elegant Victorian-style building dating back more than a century.

Children of all ages can come face-to-face with scientific phenomena at the **Discovery Centre** *($6; Mon-Sat 10am to 5pm, Sun 1pm to 5pm; 1593 Barrington St., ☎492-4422, www. discoverycentre.ns.ca)*, where several interactive exhibits aim to teach through hands-on scientific experiments.

The Dominion Building, a fine example of the city's rich architectural heritage erected at the end of the 19th century, houses the **Art Gallery of Nova Scotia ★★★** *($10; every day 10am to 5pm, Thu until 9pm; 1741 Hollis St., opposite Province House, ☎424-7542, www.agns.gov. ns.ca)*. The gallery offers four flours of modern exhibition space containing the most remarkable art collection in Nova Scotia.

The permanent collection, consisting of nearly 3,000 pieces, is devoted to both popular and contemporary art. Although many works are by painters and sculptors from Nova Scotia and the Atlantic provinces in general, artists from other Canadian provinces, the United States and Europe are also represented. The Art Gallery presents the occasional touring exhibition as well. Finally, there is a wonderful boutique that sells local crafts.

Seat of the government of Nova Scotia, **Province House ★** *(free admission; Jul and Aug, Mon-Fri 9am to 5pm, Sat and Sun 10am to 4pm; Sep to Jun, Mon-Fri 9am to 4pm; 1726 Hollis St., ☎424-4661)*, an elegant Georgian-style edifice dating from 1819, is the oldest provincial legislature building in Canada. Visitors can take a guided tour through the Red Chamber, the library and the legislative assembly chamber.

Alexander Keith's Nova Scotia Brewery ★ *($9.50; 1496 Lower Water St., ☎455-1474, www.keiths.ca)* is the most famous in the province, and has been in operation in Nova Scotia since 1820. An animated and very interesting guided tour of the facilities lasts about one hour and ends, of course, with a beer tasting. Next door is Alexander's Pub, a popular two-storey outfit with a rooftop terrace. It goes without saying that Alexander Keith's beer is served here.

The buildings and old warehouses that line the Halifax pier, the oldest of their kind in Canada, have been renovated and now form an attractive and harmonious architectural grouping known as the **Historic Properties ★★★** *(bordered by Duke and Lower Water Sts., ☎429-0530).* Numerous shops, restaurants and cafés have set up business here, along with an excellent provincial tourist information office.

This is a very popular, pleasant place, whose narrow streets lead to a promenade along the pier. The ***Bluenose II*** *($20; Jun to Sep, departures at 9:30am and 1pm; ☎634-1963 or 800-763-1963)* is often moored here during the summer. Built in Lunenberg in 1963, the *Bluenose II* is a replica of the most beloved ship in Canadian history, the *Bluenose*, which sailed the seas from 1921 to 1946 and is depicted on the Canadian ten-cent coin. When it is moored here,

the *Bluenose II* offers two-hour cruises around the Halifax harbour. A tour of Halifax's impressive port aboard this or any other ship offering similar excursions is a marvellous way to get to know the city.

Looking right out onto the harbour, the **Maritime Museum of the Atlantic ★★** *($6; May to Oct, Mon-Sat 9:30am to 5:30pm, Tue until 8pm, Sun 1pm to 5:30pm; Nov to Apr, Tue-Sat 9:30am to 5pm, Tue until 8pm, Sun 1pm to 5pm; 1675 Lower Water St., near the port, ☎424-7490)* presents a wonderful exhibition that offers a comprehensive overview of the city's naval history.

On the ground floor, there is a reconstruction of William Robertson and Son, a store that furnished ship owners, shipbuilders and captains with materials for

a century. On the same floor, visitors will find an assortment of historical artifacts related to Halifax's military arsenal and a varied collection of small craft, particularly lifeboats. The second floor features an absolutely extraordinary assortment of boat models, from sailboats to steamships.

Visitors can also tour the *Acadia*, which is moored at the pier behind the museum. This ship first sailed out of Newcastle-on-Tyne, England back in 1913 and spent most of the following 57 years gathering information for charts of the Atlantic coast and the shores of Hudson Bay. Close to the museum is the *HMCS Sackville*, a convoy ship that was used in World War II and has now been converted into a museum dedicated to the sailors who served in that war. At the **interpretive centre**, located in an

Historic Properties

adjacent building, visitors can view a 15-min film on the Battle of the Atlantic.

Canada has given refuge to thousands of people over the years. For more than 40 years, from 1928 to 1971, many of the men and women who came to the country stopped in Halifax at **Pier 21 National Historic Site** *($7.75; 9:30am to 5pm; 1055 Marginal Rd., ☎425-7770)*. The pier also welcomed thousands of refugees during the Second World War and was the departure point for Canadian soldiers heading off to battle in foreign lands.

A former transit point, this pier has since been transformed into a museum in memory of these people. Interactive exhibits bring these memorable moments back to life, and a slide show tells about the lives of the people in transit. There's also a café, a tourist information centre and a store on the premises.

Farther south, on Barrington Street at the corner of Spring Garden Road, lies the **Old Burying Ground** ★ *(free admission; Jun to Sep, 9am to 5pm, ☎429-2240)*, Halifax's first cemetery, which is now considered a national historic site. Some of the old tombstones are veritable works of art. The oldest, marking the grave of John Connor, was erected in 1754. A map containing information on the cemetery is available at St. Paul's Anglican Church *(Grand Parade)*.

While visiting Halifax, make sure to stroll along **Spring Garden Road** ★, the busiest and most pleasant commercial street in Atlantic Canada. Lined with all sorts of interesting shops, restaurants and cafés, it feels like the local Latin Quarter. Parallel to Spring Garden Road, but farther north, **Blowers Street** is another attractive artery, flanked by somewhat less conventional shops and businesses.

Hydrostone

Bounded by Young, Agricola, Duffus and Gottingen streets, the Hydrostone area is well worth a short visit. This district, today considered a national historic site, was developed following the great explosion of 1917. It includes several hundred stone houses, as well as a pretty public market and shops. Hydrostone is one of the most sought-after residential areas in Halifax.

On the Outskirts of Halifax

Point Pleasant Park ★ *(at the end of Young Ave.)* covers an area of 75ha on Halifax's south point. Here, visitors will find kilometres of hiking trails along the coast, offering lovely views through the forest.

Due to its location at the entrance to the harbour, Point Pleasant was of great strategic importance to the city for many years. The first Martello tower in North America, now the

Prince of Wales Tower National Historic Site ★ *(free admission; Jul to Sep, 10am to 6pm; Point Pleasant Park, ☎426-5080)*, was erected here in 1796-97. Drawing inspiration from a supposedly impregnable tower on Corsica's Martello Point, the British built this type of structure in many places along the shores of their Empire. The Prince of Wales Tower was part of Halifax's extensive network of defences. It now houses a museum on its history.

McNabs Island, measuring 4.8km by 1.2km and located right at the entrance of the harbour, was also part of the city's defences. The British erected Fort McNab here between 1888 and 1892, equipping it with what were then the most powerful batteries in all of the city's fortifications.

Visitors can examine the vestiges of the structure at the **Fort McNab Historic Site** ★ *(☎426-5080)* while enjoying a stroll around this peaceful, pretty island, which features a number of hiking trails. The ferry to McNabs Island leaves from Cable Wharf. For the ferry's schedule, contact the tourist information office *(Historic Properties, ☎424-4248)*.

Located just outside town (about 12km), another attraction is worth a visit: **York Redoubt National Historic Site** *(free admission; mid-Jun to end of Oct, 9am until nightfall; Purcell's Cove Rd., ☎426-5080)*. The redoubt was built in 1793 on a site from which the military could easily watch the comings

Blockhouses and Martello Towers

Besides the fortifications that were built in strategic spots throughout the colony, notably in Halifax and Kingston (Ontario), the English defense system consisted of blockhouses and Martello towers that were dispersed in various parts of the territory.

A "blockhouse" is a two-storey square tower made with squared wooden beams laid horizontally. It is topped with a shingle roof to protect the structure during severe weather. During attacks, soldiers would settle on the second floor from where they could look down on their assailants. The landing was built wider than the base so that the soldiers could shoot their muskets from holes strategically pierced in the floor, thus preventing the enemy from approaching the tower. These autonomous little defensive outposts could also be used as barracks or warehouses. The Fort Edward Blockhouse, in Windsor, Nova Scotia is a good example.

The Martello tower, on the other hand, is made of stone and can reach a height of 10m. The ground floor was used primarily as a storehouse and the one above it, as barracks. Its thick walls were intended to ensure the protection of the soldiers; its round shape allowed soldiers to fire cannons full circle.

Sixteen of these towers were built in Canada: five in Halifax, one in Saint John (New Brunswick), four in Québec City, and six in Kingston. They were popular because of their low construction costs and their robust appearance. None of these towers was ever attacked, however, so we do not know how effective they might have been.

the Second World War. A visit to this historic site also offers a unique view of Halifax harbour.

The road continues to **Sir Sandford Fleming Park**, a vast 95ha garden, which was bequeathed to the town by Sir Fleming. This scientist developed the idea of standard time zones, today in use throughout the world.

Farther south is Sambro, a fishing town where you can take a boat to Sambro Island to see the **Sambro Lighthouse**. Built between 1758 and 1760, it's the oldest operating lighthouse in North America.

Dartmouth

From the pier in front of Historic Properties in Halifax, visitors can take a **ferry** *(about $1)* to Dartmouth, on the opposite shore, which offers a splendid view of both the port and McNabs Island. The town of Dartmouth boasts an attractive waterfront, beautiful residences, a variety of shops and restaurants and several tourist attractions, including the **Historic Quaker House** ★ *(free admission; Jun to Sep, Tue-Sun 10am to 1pm and 2pm to 5pm; 57-59 Ochterloney St., ☎464-2300)*. This is the only remaining example among some 22 similar houses that were built around 1785 by Quakers who came to Dartmouth from New England. Guides in period dress tell visitors about the Quaker lifestyle.

and goings of boats in the town harbour, thereby ensuring adequate defence. It also included a battery, a Martello tower and a stockade. It was used throughout the 19th century and even during

Outdoor Activities

Cycling

Several roads in the Halifax area are wonderful for bike trips. Among these, the trails that meander through Point Pleasant Park (39km in total) are perfect for those who enjoy rides in the forest and along the ocean. However, note that the paths are not open to cyclists on weekends and holidays. The following outfit rents bicycles:

Atlantic Canada Cycling
PO Box 1555, Halifax, B3J 2Y3
☎*423-2453*

Hiking

Tours of the towns of Halifax (Historic Downtown Walk–duration 2hrs) and Dartmouth (Dartmouth Heritage Walk–duration 1hr 30min) have been planned out so visitors can explore the main attractions of these towns on foot. Another pleasant trail to walk on during beautiful summer days is the Halifax Boardwalk, situated by the seaside along the town's piers.

Point Pleasant Park is another great getaway, with 39km of hiking trails, some of which lead into the forest, while others run along the seashore, offering magnificent views.

Cruises

Harbour Hopper Tours
Cable Wharf
☎*490-8687*
www.harbourhopper.com
Harbour Hopper Tours offers exceptional trips. Comfortably seated in an unusual amphibious vehicle, you first ride through the streets of town to discover its historic buildings. Then you head to Halifax harbour for a boat ride–still aboard the same vehicle–which offers a different view of the Nova Scotian capital.

Accommodations

Halifax Heritage House Hostel
$
15 rooms
K
1253 Barrington St., B3J 1Y3
☎*422-3863*
Located a few hundred metres from the train station and about 15min on foot from the city's main attractions, the Halifax Heritage House Hostel is part of the International Youth Hostel Federation. Housed in an attractive, historic building, it can accommodate about 72

people and is equipped with a kitchenette.

A number of other institutions offer inexpensive accommodation. Students are usually offered a discount. During summer, rooms are available at:

University of King's College
$
May to Aug
6350 Coburg Rd., B3H 2A1
☎*423-1756*
⇌*423-3357*

Technical University of Nova Scotia
$
527 Morris St.
☎*491-6722*
⇌*494-3119*

St. Mary's University
$
mid-May to mid-Aug
5860 Gorsebrook Ave., B3H 3C3
☎*420-5049*
⇌*496-8107*
www.smu.ca

Dalhousie University
$
May to Aug
front desk Howe Hall, 6136 University Ave., B3H 4J2
☎*494-8840*
⇌*496-1219*
www.dal.ca/confserv

Inexpensive rooms are also available at:

YMCA
$
1565 South Park St.
☎*423-9622*
⇌*425-0155*

YWCA
$-$$
women only
1239 Barrington St.
☎*423-6162*
⇌*423-7761*

Halifax Backpacker's Hostel

2193 Gottingen St.

$

sb, K

24 beds

☎*431-3170*

www.halifaxbackpackers. com

After extensive travels abroad, two young Haligonians decided to set up this friendly inn aimed at the backpacking set. The project has been a success, as the hostel is very popular with young travellers. Not far away, and espousing the same state of mind, is Alteregos Cafe, a colourful and welcoming place that serves fair-trade coffee and organic food.

The Verandah B&B

$$-$$$ bkfst incl.

3 rooms

1394 Edwards St.

☎*494-9500*

www.theverandahbb.com

Located in a residential neighbourhood not far the universities and downtown, the Verandah B&B occupies a charming Victorian house happily painted in blue and yellow. There are two rooms with private bathrooms and one studio. You'll feel right at home here.

Waverley Inn

$$-$$$ bkfst incl.

ℜ, ⊛

32 rooms

1266 Barrington St., B3J 1Y5

☎*423-9346 or*

800-565-9346

⇒*425-0167*

The Waverley Inn boasts a rich tradition of hospitality dating back more than a century. This sumptuous house, built in 1865-66, was the personal residence of wealthy Halifax

merchant Edward W. Chipman until 1870, when a reversal of fortune plunged him into bankruptcy. A few years later, sisters Sarah and Jane Romans purchased the house for $14,200. In October 1876, the Waverley Inn threw open its doors and was considered the most prestigious hotel in the city for several decades to follow. It has welcomed many famous individuals, including Oscar Wilde, who stayed here in 1882.

Despite the passing of time, the Waverley Inn has managed to preserve most of its original grandeur. Of course, it is no longer as luxurious, since its rooms, decorated in a rather heavy style, are now outmoded according to modern standards of comfort. However, this inn is sure to be of interest to visitors seeking a truly authentic Victorian atmosphere. The Waverley Inn is located near the train station, about 15min walk from the city's major attractions.

Holiday Inn Select

$$-$$$

ℜ, ≈, ⊛, △, ☺, ≡, 🐕

232 rooms

1980 Robie St., B3H 3G5

☎*423-1161 or*

888-810-7288

⇒*423-9069*

www.holiday-inn.com

The Holiday Inn Select offers comfortable, spacious and functional rooms in addition to an excellent dining room. A common room on the executive floor lets guests prepare their own breakfast, which, for frequent travellers, makes for a pleasant change of atmosphere

from hotel restaurants. The only inconvenience of the Holiday Inn Select is its location, at least 15min on foot from downtown and the main activities of interest there, but this drawback is compensated by the hotel's relatively reasonable rates.

🏆 Halliburton House Inn

$$$ bkfst incl.

ℜ, ≡

29 rooms

5184 Morris St., B3J 1B3

☎*420-0658*

⇒*423-2324*

www.halliburton.ns.ca

The Halliburton House Inn lies tucked away on a quiet residential street near the train station, just a short distance from Halifax's main attractions. A pleasant, elegant place, it offers an interesting alternative to the large downtown hotels. In terms of comfort, Halliburton House Inn has all angles covered. The pleasant rooms are well-decorated and adorned with period furniture, giving them a lot of character. There are also several lovely common rooms, including a small living room to the left of the entrance, a library and an elegant dining room where guests can enjoy excellent cuisine (see p 136).

The inn's three buildings look out on a peaceful, pretty garden full of flowers, where guests can sit at a table beneath a parasol. Halliburton House Inn, erected in 1809, was originally the home of Sir Brenton Halliburton, chief justice of the Supreme Court of Nova Scotia.

Citadel Halifax Hotel
$$$
ℜ, ≈, ⊘, ≡, 🐕
264 rooms
1960 Brunswick St., B3J 2G7
☎*422-1391 or*
800-565-7162
⇄*429-6672*
Comfortable but somewhat lacking in charm, the Citadel Halifax Hotel is attractively located just a stone's throw away from the Citadel. Guests have access to an indoor pool and a gym, as well as to a dining room and a bar. Furthermore, parking is free, which is a real bonus in Halifax.

Delta Barrington
$$$
△, ℜ, ≈, ≡, 🐕, ⊘
200 rooms
1875 Barrington St., B3J 3L6
☎*429-7410 or*
800-268-1133
⇄*420-6524*
www.deltabarrington.com
An elegant building located just steps away from the Historic Properties, the Delta Barrington looks out on a lively neighbourhood full of shops, restaurants and outdoor terraces. The rooms are a bit old-fashioned but nevertheless decently furnished and comfortable.

Delta Halifax
$$$
ℜ, △, ⊛, ≈, ≡, 🐕, ⊘
296 rooms
1990 Barrington St., B3J 1P2
☎*425-6700 or*
800-268-1133
⇄*425-6214*
www.deltahalifax.com
The Delta Halifax offers superior accommodation in spacious, and very comfortably furnished rooms. The friendly, pleasant hotel bar, Sam Slick's Lounge, is a perfect spot to enjoy a drink with friends or hold

an informal meeting. The hotel features an indoor pool and numerous sports facilities. It provides access to a shopping centre with stores and restaurants, and lies just minutes away from the city's main sights and the World Trade and Convention Centre.

Lord Nelson Hotel
$$$
ℜ, ≡, ⊘, 🐕
244 rooms
1515 South Park St., B3J 2L2
☎*423-6331 or*
800-565-2020
⇄*491-6148*
www.lordnelsonhotel.com
The Lord Nelson Hotel offers many advantages. Located in an extremely lively section of Halifax, it stands opposite the magnificent Public Gardens, just steps away from Spring Garden Road, the city's busiest commercial artery, and a short distance from several colleges and universities. The smallest rooms rank among the least expensive in Halifax. Although modestly furnished and a bit outdated in appearance, they nevertheless offer an acceptable level of comfort. The Lord Nelson's impressive entrance hall, with its coffered ceiling, is a vestige of the *belle époque*. This is a good option for travellers on a limited budget.

Prince George Hotel
$$$
ℜ, ≈, ⊘, ⊛, △, ≡, 🐕
207 rooms
1725 Market St., B3J 3N9
☎*425-1986 or*
800-565-1567
⇄*429-6048*
www.princegeorgehotel. com
The Prince George Hotel offers excellent accommodation in rooms that are

quite attractively furnished and luxurious. Located right near the World Trade and Convention Centre, this place is particularly popular among business people, and features a conference room that can accommodate up to 200 people. The hotel terrace offers a splendid view of the city.

Sheraton Halifax
$$$$-$$$$$
ℜ, △, ≈, ≡, ⊘
350 rooms
1919 Upper Water St., B3J 3J5
☎*421-1700 or*
800-325-3535
⇄*422-5805*
Halifax is home to a good number of luxury hotels. None of these, however, boasts a more spectacular or enchanting site than the Sheraton Halifax, located right on the pier, next to the Historic Properties. Furthermore, particular care was taken to ensure that the building would blend harmoniously into its surroundings, which make up the oldest part of the city. The rooms are spacious, well-decorated and inviting. The hotel has two restaurants as well as conference rooms, an indoor pool and several other athletic facilities. In addition to all this, the Sheraton is home to the only casino in Halifax, which is very busy evenings and weekends.

Restaurants

The largest city in the Atlantic provinces, Halifax is also the most cosmopolitan; its restaurants' diversity bears witness to its status as the region's number one city. A bit of everything may be found in Halifax, including some great restaurants, the quality and refinement of which rival the best dining rooms of larger North American cities.

Fish and seafood, of course, are favoured on local menus. Nonetheless, to many delights of French, Italian, Chinese and Indian cuisines to mention but a few, can also be enjoyed in Halifax. This being said, what is most surprising is the number of cafés and terraces that line arteries like Spring Garden Road, Blowers Street and Argyle Street and which, in the summertime, lend Halifax an almost European air.

Amadeus Cafe
$
5675 Spring Garden Rd.
☎423-0032
The Amadeus Cafe has a selection of coffees, teas, hot chocolates and cold drinks during the summer, as well as a small assortment of pastries, including mouth-watering cinnamon rolls. It has a beautiful street-front terrace.

The Granite Brewery
$
1662 Barrington St.
☎422-4954
There is no better spot to take the pulse of daily life of Halifax than the Granite Brewery. A little off from the main tourist attractions of the city and, more remarkably, miles away in attitude from the fashionable atmosphere of trendier restaurants, this pub offers simple fare that is inexpensive and always

generously dished out. Checkered tablecloths and an interior decor dominated by wood tones and a few subtle lamps create a convivial, unpretentious atmosphere. The kitchen closes at 12:30am every night.

Mediterraneo
$
1571 Barrington St.
☎423-4403
If you're hankering for some Lebanese cuisine, head to Mediterraneo for excellent food at reasonable prices. With its relaxed atmosphere, the restaurant is popular with students who come here to satiate their appetite while respecting their budget. The place is also renowned for its breakfasts.

Tom's Little Havana Cafe
$
5428 Doyle St.
☎423-8667
Tom's Little Havana Cafe is an unpretentious bar and restaurant in a pleasant neighbourhood where anyone just seems to fit right in. The regulars come for drinks, to read their newspapers or for a bite to eat. The menu lists a hodgepodge of varied dishes, from hummus to clam chowder. Cigars and pipes are welcome here, of course, and there is even a fine selection of cigars available for purchase.

Peddler's Pub
$
Granville St., Barrington Place
☎423-5033
Sunny late afternoons are very enjoyable here; a glass of wine in hand, seated at a table on the patio near the historic district of town. The rather

limited menu offers appetizers and simple dishes. Popular music shows are sometimes presented here at night.

Satisfaction Feast
$
1581 Grafton St.
☎422-3540
Vegetarians and others who enjoy vegetarian cuisine will be in their element at the Satisfaction Feast, where the aromas wafting through the air will make your mouth water with expectation. And you won't be disappointed by the food, since the chef seems to have an unlimited imagination when it comes to preparing meals, including breakfast, that are well-balanced, appetizing and inexpensive. The interior is bright and airy.

Trident Booksellers & Cafe
$
1256 Hollis St.
☎423-7100
What a pleasure it is to enjoy an excellent cup of coffee while poring over a book! That's the concept behind the extremely friendly Trident Booksellers & Cafe. The menu is similar to that of the Amadeus Cafe (see above). Newspapers are always available for customers, and books (often second-hand), are sold at modest prices.

The Fireside
$-$$
1500 Brunswick St.
☎423-5995
The Fireside is a typical pub with cozy wood panelling and a warm atmosphere. People usually come here for drinks (especially martinis), but light

fare, such as the classic salmon sandwich, shrimp dishes and quesadillas are also served.

Anatolia Turkish Cuisine
$-$$
1518 Dresden Row
☎492-4568
This adorable restaurant, done up in tiles and tapestries from Turkey, is popular with locals in search of a bit of exoticism. The wood-burning stove takes centre stage here, infusing the air with the smell of grilled meats. Of course, kebabs of all kinds figure prominently on the menu. You can also choose from a variety of other typical Turkish and Middle-Eastern dishes. A great place to discover some new flavours.

Mother Tucker's
$$
1668 Lower Water St.
☎422-4436
A well-known Canadian institution, Mother Tucker's restaurant has a branch in Halifax, right near the Historic Properties. Mother Tucker's is mainly known for its excellent roast beef, but the menu also lists steak and, on rare occasions, lobster. Brunch is served on Sundays.

Il Mercato
$$
5650 Spring Garden Rd.
☎422-2866
For inspired Italian cuisine, Il Mercato—a little bistro with a modern, inviting decor, located on the liveliest street in the city—is the place. Fresh pasta, pizza and some original meat dishes are featured on the menu, as are Italian ices and other delectable desserts. In just a short

time, Il Mercato has become one of the most popular spots in Halifax.

McKelvie's
$$
1680 Lower Water St.
☎421-6161
Here the name of the game is clearly fish and seafood. A veritable institution in Halifax since 1930, McKelvie's has a vast choice of fish and seafood dishes, each more original than the last and based on local and international recipes. The menu also lists a few pasta, chicken and meat dishes, as well as salads and sandwiches. The large dining room, with its exposed brick walls and large windows, occupies a beautiful building that once was a fire station. McKelvie's is a pleasant, airy and always hopping place.

Fid
$$-$$$
1569 Dresden Row
☎422-9122
Fid intrigues and attracts at the same time. This restaurant, with its small refined dining room, is dedicated to creative cuisine. The friendly chef, Dennis Johnston, offers a menu of simple yet innovative dishes that emphasizes the freshest market goods. The menu changes every day, but is generally French-or Asian-inspired. A fine wine cellar and impeccable service round out the dining experience here.

Chives Canadian Bistro
$$-$$$
1537 Barrington St.
☎422-2825
With a reputation based on a cosy décor, typical relaxed bistro ambiance and,

above all, good food, Chives is one of the darlings of Halifax restaurant-goers. The menu changes with the seasons and features an astounding marriage of traditional and contemporary dishes. Local goods purchased directly from the fishers and growers are favoured here. Nevertheless, chef Craig Flinn, who has travelled the world over, likes to surprise with exotic flavourings. The wine list includes a fine selection of local and international offerings.

Sweet Basil Bistro
$$-$$$
1866 Upper Water St.
☎425-2133
Just a few steps away from the Historic Properties, the Sweet Basil Bistro is a good restaurant that serves bistro-style cuisine. The chef outdoes himself, concocting delicious dishes prepared and presented in an original manner. Top billing goes to the pasta, which is served with fresh, quality ingredients. Both the cuisine and the decor evoke a subtle blend of Latin and modern styles. There is seating outside on the little terrace at the back. This place offers good value.

Upper Deck Restaurant
$$-$$$
1869 Upper Water St.
Privateer's Warehouse,
Historic Properties
☎422-1289
A Halifax classic, the Upper Deck Restaurant occupies the top floor of the Privateer's Warehouse. The dining room's pretty maritime decor, accented by miniature models of great old sailing vessels, leaves no doubt as to the

Nova Scotia

specialties of the house: fish and seafood. Always fresh, these delights from the deep are particularly well prepared and attractively presented here. Poultry and meat are also served. In addition to its excellent cuisine, courteous service and a pleasant ambiance make the Upper Deck one of the best options in the Historic Properties' neighbourhood.

Cellar Bar & Grill
$$$
5677 Brenton Pl.
☎*492-4412*
Located downstairs in an inviting cellar, this lovely establishment offers two dining rooms decorated in brick, stone and wood. The cuisine here is equally delightful. The menu includes *gazpacho* and lobster bisque, calamari, *tzatziki* and mussels, pasta with wild mushrooms and grilled Atlantic salmon—there's something here for everyone. Excellent wine list.

Five Fishermen
$$$
1740 Argyle St.
☎*422-4421*
Set up inside one of the oldest buildings in town, a renovated old school, the Five Fishermen is a great favourite with fish and seafood lovers. Lobster obviously gets top billing on the menu. Other dishes include Atlantic salmon and trout, as well as a variety of steaks. It is worth noting that the restaurant's kitchen closes later than most others in town, around 11pm every night. The wine list, furthermore, is very extensive.

Halliburton House Inn
$$$
5184 Morris St.
☎*420-0658*
The dining room at the elegant **Halliburton House Inn** (see p 132) is a perfect place to enjoy a long, intimate dinner for two, or to linger over a meal among friends. Furnished in a tasteful, elegant manner, the place has a lot of style and emanates an atmosphere of opulence. Aside from a few exceptions, like the alligator appetizer, the menu is made up of classics that include seafood, an excellent *steak au poivre* flambéd with brandy, lamb *à la Provençale*, Atlantic salmon and *coquilles Saint-Jacques*.

Entertainment

Bars and Dance Clubs

The city of Halifax is home to an impressive number of pubs, bars and dance clubs, most of them concentrated in the downtown area.

Lower Deck Pub
Privateer's Warehouse, Historic Properties
☎*422-1289*
Located in the historic district, the Lower Deck Pub presents performances of traditional music from Atlantic Canada.

Peddler's Pub
Granville St., Barrington Place
For a drink on a sunny terrace in late afternoon,

opt for the Peddler's Pub, where popular music shows are sometimes presented.

The Fireside
1500 Brunswick St.
☎*423-5995*
The Fireside is a cozy English pub decorated with attractive woodwork. It's renowned in the capital for its martinis—apparently, the best around. For those who prefer hopped beverages, it also offers an excellent selection of local beers.

Granite Brewery
1662 Barrington St.
The Granite Brewery has all the atmosphere of a local pub. It offers a wide selection of tasty home-brewed beer that varies with the season.

Diamond Pub
1663 Argyle St.
☎*423-5503*
A rather eccentric decor and a wide selection of beers make the Diamond Pub the preferred spot of a young, hip clientele.

Velvet Olive
1770 Market St.
☎*492-1646*
Among the many bars that have sprung up in Halifax, the Velvet Olive is famous because of its Art Deco decor, its martinis and its pool tables—not to mention the fact that it serves food until midnight on Fridays and Saturdays.

Bearly's
1265 Barrington St.
☎*423-2526*
Bearly's hosts live blues from Thursday to Sunday. The atmosphere is friendly and lively.

Reflexions Cabaret
5184 Sackville St.
☎**422-2957**
More sophisticated music sets the rhythm at Reflexions Cabaret, a nightclub that caters primarily to the Halifax region's gay and lesbian communities, although it welcomes a mixed clientele.

Marquee Club
2037 Gottingen St.
☎**429-3020**
Don't be put off by the exterior of the Marquee, or by its location outside the city centre. The Marquee Club is actually one of the hotspots of Halifax's alternative music scene. Local groups perform here and the party lasts well into the wee hours. Attracts the 20 to 30 crowd.

Ginger's Tavern
1662 Barrington St.
☎**422-4954**
Located just above the Granite Brewery (see above), Ginger's Tavern is a micro-brewery where folk-music shows are presented.

Theatres

Halifax's most renowned theatre company, the **Neptune Theatre** *(1593 Argyle St., ☎429-7070)* presents plays from the classic repertoire.

The latest American movies are presented at **Famous Players Cinemas** *(5657 Spring Garden Rd., ☎423-5866)*. Other theatres also show popular films, but they are all located outside the downtown area. To find out what's playing and when,

check the listings in the local newspaper. For less recent movies, head to **Wormwood's Dog & Monkey Cinema** *(2015 Gottingen St., ☎422-3700)*, a repertory theatre.

When artists of international renown come to the Maritimes, they usually choose to play in Halifax. Large-scale rock concerts are held at the **Halifax Metro Centre** *(1284 Duke St., ☎451-1221)*.

Fans of classical music can attend concerts given by the **Symphony Nova Scotia** *(5657 Spring Garden Rd., ☎421-1300)*.

Casinos

A recent addition, the **Nova Scotia Casino** *(1983 Upper Water St., ☎425-7777)* is located near the Historic Properties. This large casino includes a great many slot machines and gaming tables, and is open without interruption from noon on Thursdays to 4am Monday mornings. On Tuesdays and Wednesdays the casino also closes at 4am.

Shopping

Without a doubt, the most pleasant place to shop is the **Historic Properties** *(bordered by Duke and Lower Water Sts.)*, the historic neighbourhood alongside the Halifax wharves. Shops selling crafts and clothing take up a large portion of the

space in this harmonious architectural grouping built in the 19th century.

Another enjoyable place to shop is the **Granville Promenade** and the **Barrington Place Shops** *(on Barrington St., near the Historic Properties)*, located right near one another. Both are renovated historic buildings. Shoppers can stop for a refreshment on one of the many terraces of the nearby cafés and pubs.

For a pleasant stroll in a lively part of town that feels like the local Latin Quarter, take **Spring Garden Road** *(between Barrington and South Park Sts.)*, a large commercial artery lined with cafés, restaurants and numerous shops.

The **Gallery Shop** *(Art Gallery of Nova Scotia, 1723 Hollis St., ☎424-4303)* offers an excellent selection of local crafts, as well as works by painters, sculptors and other artists from Nova Scotia. Pieces by Mi'kmaq artists are also available.

The **Government Bookstore** *(1700 Granville St.)* sells all of the books and publications put out by the government of Nova Scotia. Many of these deal with plant and animal life, geology, history—in short, all the subjects that might interest travellers who would like to know more about Nova Scotia. These publications are also available online at: *www.gov.ns.ca/snsmr/consumer/publications.*

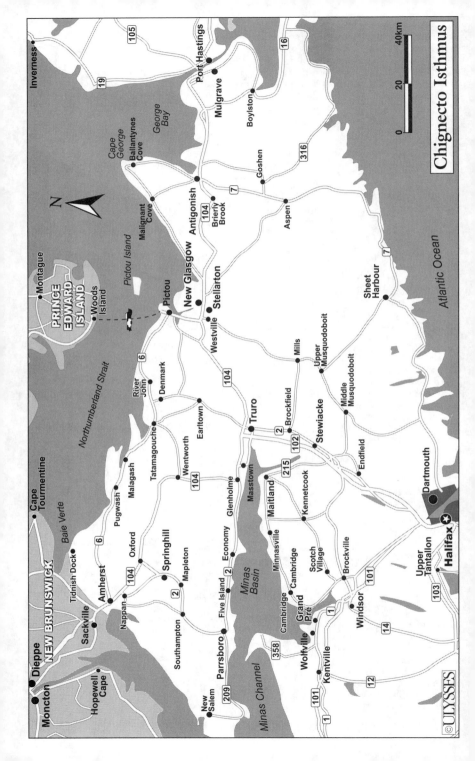

Chignecto Isthmus

Chignecto Isthmus

An narrow strip of land

the Chignecto Isthmus, the narrow strip of land that connects Nova Scotia and New Brunswick, offers a variety of landscapes, bordered by the Northumberland Strait on one side, and the Bay of Fundy on the other.

This region offers a number of spectacular and relatively unexplored areas, especially along the Bay of Fundy. The tides in this bay, which are the highest and most powerful in the world, have carved a unique landscape. The Northumberland Strait side is renowned for its lovely beaches washed by warm water–a great place for a swim. This coast is also famous as the place where the first Scottish colonists settled during the 1770s. Today, a variety of cultural events celebrate this Scottish heritage.

A few average-size towns line the Chignecto Isthmus, such as Amherst, which is the gateway to Nova Scotia.

Finding Your Way Around

The Chignecto Isthmus includes two tours.

Tour A: The Northumberland Strait ★ runs along the strait from Cape Breton Island to the town of Amherst.

Tour B: The Cape Rooute ★, which heads from Amherst to Maitland and Old Acadia (see p 147).

By Bus

Visitors can reach a variety of destinations by bus within Nova Scotia, as there are buses running from Halifax to Yarmouth, Amherst and Sydney (*Acadian Lines*, ☎454-9321) and along the southern coast of the province.

Practical Information

Area code: **902**

Tourist Information

The Northumberland Strait

Antigonish-Eastern Shore Tourist Association
RR1, Musquodoboit Harbour, B0J 2L0
☎*889-2362*
⇒*889-2101*

Pictou
mid-May to mid-Oct
at the intersection of Hwy. 106 and Rte. 6
☎*485-6213*

The Cape Route

Central Nova Tourist Association
575 Prince St., Truro, B2N 5Z5
☎*893-8782*
or 800-895-1177
⇒*897-6641*
www.centralnovascotia.com

Amherst Tourist Bureau
Hwy. 104, on the New Brunswick border
☎*667-0696*

Exploring

Tour A: The Northumberland Strait

A few historic villages and towns lie tucked along the coast of the Northumberland Strait, between Cape Breton and the New Brunswick border. The first Scottish settlers arrived here at the end of the 18th century. There are also several charming beaches here, blessed with the warmest waters in the province. In fact, because of the Gulf Stream, the Northumberland Strait has the warmest waters north of the Carolinas, in the United States.

Antigonish

The small town of Antigonish is home to the lovely buildings of **St. Francis Xavier University**, founded in 1853. Like Pictou, Antigonish welcomed many Scottish colonists from the 1770s onwards. The **Highland Games**, a huge celebration of traditional Scottish music, dance and sports, have been held here since 1861.

Since Antigonish lies at the intersection of several major thoroughfares, it has a few places to spend the night, as well as a number of restaurants and shops.

Melmerby Beach

Near New Glasgow, Route 289 leads to **Melmerby Beach Provincial Park**, which offers some picnic areas and a pleasant beach.

★ Pictou

Pictou holds symbolic importance in Nova Scotia's history. This is where the *Hector*, a ship carrying the first Scottish settlers to Nova Scotia, dropped anchor. Many Scots later followed, seduced by a climate and geography that was reminiscent of home. They colonized other parts of the coast and Cape Breton Island. Pictou's lively downtown streets are lined with handsome buildings dating back to those early years of settlement.

Hector Heritage Quay ★★ *($5; mid-May to mid-Oct, Mon-Sat 9:30am to 5:30pm, Sun 1pm to 5:30pm; downtown, on the port, ☎485-4371)* is an interpretive centre devoted to the history of the *Hector*, the schooner that carried the first Scottish settlers to Pictou in 1773. The exhibition is very thorough. Behind the building, visitors can watch artisans reconstruct an exact replica of the *Hector*.

The **McCulloch House ★** *($1; mid-May to mid-Oct, Wed-Sat 9:30am to 5:30pm, Sun 1pm to 5:30pm; Old Haliburton Rd., ☎485-4563)* is a modest house built in 1806 for Reverend Thomas McCulloch, one of the most influential people in the Pictou area at the time. The house is furnished with original pieces.

Housed in the old railway station, the **Northumberland Fisheries Museum ★** *($4; mid-May to mid-Oct, every day 9am to 6pm; 71 Front St., ☎485-4972)* contains a collection of items related to the history of fishing in this region, and features an authentic fishing hut.

A ferry service runs between Caribou, just beside Pictou, to Wood Islands, on Prince Edward Island. Close by, **Caribou Provincial Park** has a beautiful beach that is perfect for swimming.

Tatamagouche

Less than 2km east of this little community lies **Tatamagouche Provincial Park**, where the inviting waters of the Northumberland Strait are great for swimming.

Malagash

Malagash is home to one of Nova Scotia's two vineyards. Make sure to stop at **Jost Vineyards** *(free admission; mid-Jun to mid-Sep, every day 9am to 6pm; mid-Sep to mid-Jun, Mon-Sat 10am to 5pm; Hwy. 2, ☎257-2636)* for some wine-tasting. The Jost family, originally from the Rhine Valley in Germany, came to Canada in 1970.

Pugwash

Pugwash is a popular vacation spot. It is primarily known for the **Gulf Shore Provincial Park**, located about 5km north of the village, whose long beach is ideal for swimming.

Tour B: The Cape Route

This tour joins Amherst to Maitland by way of the Minas Basin, with many capes jutting out onto the Bay of Fundy and revealing splendid natural landscapes.

In addition to the magnificent coastal landscape, shaped by the largest tides in the world, the Cape Route also covers several quaint towns and picturesque villages.

Amherst

Gateway to Nova Scotia, Amherst is home to several hotels and a large provincial tourist information centre. This site, on the Chignecto Isthmus, first attracted Acadians, who founded a settlement here named Beaubassin in 1672.

Controlled by the British since 1713, Beaubassin was abandoned by the Acadians in 1750 by order of the French army, who erected Fort Beauséjour (N.B.) on French territory, several kilometres to the north, the following year. The British responded by building Fort Lawrence on the former site of Beaubassin.

Fort Lawrence was in turn abandoned in 1755, after the British captured Fort Beauséjour, an event that heralded the deportation of the Acadians. In 1764, one year after the signing of the Treaty of Paris, under which France ceded all its North American possessions to Great Britain, colonists from the British Isles began flooding into the region, where they founded Amherst. This community flourished in the 1880s, when it was integrated into the Canadian rail network. It is now a quiet town with about 10,000 inhabitants.

The centre of Amherst boasts several magnificent public buildings made of stone. Visitors will also find the **Cumberland County Museum** *($3; Mon-Sat 9am to 5pm, except Oct to Apr; closed Mon; 150 Church St., ☎667-2561)*, which exhibits an assortment of objects related to local history.

From Amherst, visitors can take Highway 242 along the banks of Cumberland Basin and Chignecto Bay. Those so inclined can stop at the **Joggins Fossil Centre** *($5; mid-Jun to mid-Sep, 9am to 5:30pm; Main St., ☎251-2727)*, which features the world's largest collection of fossils. Visitors can also take a guided tour of a site containing a large number of fossils.

Hwy. 2 and Hwy. 104 both lead from Amherst to Springhill. You can also take Hwy. 209 to Advocate Harbour, at the tip of the Chignecto Isthmus.

Springhill

Springhill was founded in 1790 by Loyalist colonists who intended to support themselves by farming. The area did not actually develop, however, until 1871, when the Springhill Mining Company coal mine opened. For most of the next century, Springhill was one of the largest coal producers in Nova Scotia.

The difficulties and dangers of coal mining were not without consequence. In 1891, 125 men and boys lost their lives in an accident in one of the galleries. Two more catastrophes, in 1956 and 1958, claimed the lives of 39 and 75 men respectively. After that, several mines remained in operation, but large-scale coal mining came to an end in Springhill. To add to this string of bad luck, the city was also the victim of two devastating fires (in 1957 and 1975).

To find out everything there is to know about popular singer Anne Murray, a Springhill native, head to the **Anne Murray Centre** *($5.50; mid-May to early Oct, 9am to 5pm; 36 Main St., ☎597-8614)*. Her fans will be delighted by the exhaustive collection of objects that either belonged to Murray at one time, or summon up key moments in her life and career. Audiovisual aids complement the presentation. Few details have been neglected; the exhibit starts off with a family tree that traces Murray's family origins back two centuries.

The **Springhill Miners' Museum ★★** *($4.50; mid-May to mid-Oct, every day 9am to 5pm; 145 Black River Rd., via Hwy. 2, ☎597-3449)* offers an excellent opportunity to discover what life was like for Springhill's miners. A visit here starts out with a stop at the museum, which explains the evolution of coal mining techniques and tells the often dramatic history of Springhill's mining industry. Visitors are then invited to tour an old mining gallery.

Continue along Hwy. 2 to Parrsboro.

Parrsboro

Situated at the edge of the Minas Basin, marking the farthest end of the Bay of Fundy, Parrsboro is a small community graced with several handsome buildings dating back to the 19th century. The region's tide-sculpted shoreline is a treasure-trove for geologists. It is therefore no surprise that Parrsboro was chosen as the location for the **Fundy Geological Museum ★** *($5; Jun to mid-Oct, every day 9:30am to 5:30pm; late Oct to end of May, Tue-Sat 9am to 5pm; Two Islands Rd., near the centre of Parrsboro, ☎254-3814)*, a provincial museum devoted to the geological history of Nova Scotia and other regions. Various types of fossils, rocks and stones are on display. The exhibit is lively and interesting, and was created with the lay person in mind. There is also a fun video designed to teach children about geology.

Near Parrsboro is the **Ottawa House Museum By-the-Sea** *($2; early Jun to mid-Sep every day 10am to 6pm; 3km from Parrsboro)*. Built as an inn in the late 18th century, this establishment later became the summer home of Sir Charles Tupper, a former prime minister of Canada, who also was one of the fathers of Confederation. The exhibition includes objects from the beginning of colonisation in the region. Some of the rooms are furnished with antiques.

Also in Parrsboro, dramatic works by Atlantic play-

wrights are staged each summer aboard a restored ferry at the **Ship's Company Theatre** *($13 to $24; 198 Main St., ☎254-3000 or 800-565-7469)*.

Continue along Rte. 2, then Hwy. 104, to Truro. You can also go in the opposite direction, on Rte. 209, to reach Advocate Harbour, at the tip of the Chignecto Isthmus.

Advocate Harbour

Cape Chignecto Provincial Park *($2; Hwy. 209, ☎424-5937)* is a wonderful place for a hike, since it has 20km of trails that provide some breathtaking views of the region. This park also has some campsites.

Also close to Advocate Harbour, **Cape D'Or Lighthouse** *(6km from Hwy. 209)* overlooks the Bay of Fundy at the point where it meets the Minas canal. The buildings that belonged to the former lighthouse keeper now house an interpretation centre, as well as a café.

Truro

Served by the railway since 1858, and now located at the heart of the province's road network, Truro is the region's chief industrial and commercial centre. The town, which has a population of about 12,000, features several historic buildings and numerous shops, restaurants and accommodations. The downtown area lies on either side of the Salmon River, which empties into the Minas Basin further on. The **tidal bore ★**, a wave that flows upriver twice a day, is a rather strange natural phenomenon caused by the Bay of Fundy's powerful tides, which can be observed here.

In the centre of town, visitors can relax or go for a walk in **Victoria Park ★** *(entrance on Brunswick St.)*, a 400ha natural park with a stream running through it. There are several waterfalls along the stream.

To get to know the history of the region, head to the **Colchester Historical Society Museum** *($2; Jul and Aug, every day; Sep to May, Tue-Sat; 29 Young St., ☎895-6284)*. In addition to its exhibits, mostly devoted to history and genealogy, the museum also displays temporary expositions on a range of different themes.

From Truro, continue along Hwy. 2, then take Rte. 215 towards Maitland. Visitors who don't want to go to Maitland can reach Windsor (see p 148) quickly by taking Hwy. 102 and then Hwy. 101.

Maitland

A major shipbuilding centre in the 19th century, Maitland is now a tiny hamlet with a few lovely homes. It was here that a prosperous local entrepreneur by the name of William D. Lawrence built the largest wooden ship in Canadian history. The *William D. Lawrence*, a magnificent vessel with three 80m masts, nearly ruined its creator. Completed in 1874, the boat nevertheless enjoyed a

very successful career, sailing on oceans around the world.

Today, visitors can tour **Lawrence House ★** *($2; Jun to mid-Oct, Mon-Sat 9:30am to 5:30pm, Sun 1pm to 5:30pm; Hwy. 215, ☎261-2628)*, the entrepreneur's main residence, built in 1870 at the top of a dale overlooking the bay. Most of the furniture that adorns this beautiful house belonged to Lawrence. In one of the rooms, visitors will find a 2m model of the *William D. Lawrence*.

Continue along Rte. 215 to reach Windsor (see p 148).

Beaches

Tour A: The Northumberland Strait

There are some beautiful beaches along the Northumberland Strait, including

those in **Amherst Shore** *(Hwy. 366, west of Northport)*, **Gulf Shore** *(5km north of Pugwash)*, **Heather** *(Port Howe)*, **Caribou** *(near Pictou)* and **Pomquet Beach** *(on the road north of Pomquet)* provincial parks.

Outdoor Activities

Hiking

Tour B: The Cape Route

Situated at the tip of the Chignecto Isthmus near Advocate Harbour, **Cape Chignecto Provincial Park** *($2; Hwy. 209, ☎424-5937)* offers some great views of the coastal landscape along its 20km of hiking paths. Some of the trails lead to beaches and spectacular cliffs.

Accommodations

Tour A: The Northumberland Strait

Antigonish

Maritime Inn Antigonish
$$
ℜ, ≡, 🐾
32 rooms
Hwy. 104, Exit 33, 158 Main St., B2G 2B7
☎*863-4001 or*
888-662-7484
⇒*863-2672*
www.maritimeinns.com
Conveniently located in the heart of town, the Maritime Inn Antigonish offers comfortable accommodation in spacious, modern rooms.

Pictou

Auberge Walker Inn
$$ bkfst incl.
ℜ, ⊛
10 rooms
34 Coleraine St., B0K 1H0
☎*485-1433 or*
800-370-5553
Located in the heart of Pictou, Auberge Walker Inn is located in a handsome brick building dating back to 1865. This place is charming, and its rooms have been renovated in order to furnish each with a private bath. The Auberge Walker Inn is kept by a friendly French Canadian couple. By reservation only, evening meals may be enjoyed in the inn's beautiful dining room.

Consulate Inn
$$
⊛, ℜ, ≡, 🦋, ℝ
5 rooms
157 Water St., B0K 1H0
☎*485-4554 or*
800-424-8283
⇒*485-1532*
www.consulateinn.com
Constructed in 1810, this beautiful stone house stands in the heart of Pictou, facing the bay. At different times during the 19th century, it was home to the Bank of British North America and then to the American Consulate in Pictou, from which it drew inspiration for its name. The guestrooms are attractively decorated and comfortable. Some of them have whirlpool baths and balconies overlooking the bay. Behind the house, there is a lovely pavilion that is ideal for reading or simply whiling away the long days of summer.

Pictou Lodge Resort
$$$-$$$$$
K, ℜ, ≈, ☺, ≡, 🦋
51 rooms
Braeshore Rd., B0K 1H0
☎*485-4322 or*
888-662-7484
⇒*485-4945*
www.maritimeinns.com
Just outside the town of Pictou, along a little stretch of beach washed by the Northumberland Strait's pleasant waters, is the Pictou Lodge Resort, a group of cottages built on a large, grassy lawn. The log cottages are very appealing, and each of them includes a bedroom, a modern washroom, a little living room, a kitchen and a porch. The Pictou Lodge Resort restaurant, located

in an elegant and inviting wooden building, serves refined cuisine in a dining room set around a central stone fireplace.

Tatamagouche

Train Station Inn
$$
10 rooms
21 Station Rd., B0K 1V0
☎*657-3222 or*
888-724-5233
⇒*657-0313*
www.trainstation.ns.ca
The pretty Train Station Inn is a former railway station that dates back more than a century. Its four rooms, each with a private bath, are adorned with period furniture. Guests have access to a terrace on the second floor.

Tour B: The Cape Route

Amherst

Victorian Motel
$$
20 rooms
150 E. Victoria St., B4H 1Y3
☎*667-7211*
If you are driving in from New Brunswick, Amherst is the first town you will pass through. It is a good place to stay overnight, since there are several motels here, most situated alongside the big access roads. The inexpensive Victorian Motel is located downtown, and is a good option for travellers on a limited budget. The rooms are clean and quiet, if not particularly charming.

The Cabot Trail provides a colourful tour circling
Cape Breton Island in Nova Scotia. - *Nova Scotia Tourism*

Peggy's Cove's landscape is typical of the Atlantic coast of New Brunswick and lays claim to being one of Canada's most photographed sites. - *Nova Scotia Tourism*

Comfort Inn
$$$
≡, 🐾
61 rooms
143 S. Albion St., B4H 2X2
☎*667-0404 or*
800-228-5150
⇌*667-2522*
The Comfort Inn, located near the downtown area, shopping malls and fast food restaurants, offers a standard level of comfort, and is perfect for travellers stopping for the night.

Springhill

Rollways Motel
$$
ℜ
12 rooms
9 Church St., B0M 1X0
☎*597-3713*
Although Springhill has little to offer in terms of accommodation, visitors can stay at the Rollways Motel, whose rooms are decent, but no more than that.

Truro

Comfort Inn
$$
≡, 🐾
81 rooms
12 Meadow Dr., B2N 5V4
☎*893-0330 or*
800-228-5150
⇌*897-0176*
The Comfort Inn's, whose modern rooms are well-suited to the needs of business travellers.

Stonehouse Motel
$$
K, ℜ, ≡, 🐾
40 rooms
165 Willow St., B2N 4Z9
☎*893-9413 or*
877-660-6638
⇌*897-9937*
www.stonehousemotel.com
Located at the heart of Nova Scotia's road net-

work, Truro has several hotels and motels that provide decent rooms at reasonable rates. One of these is the Stonehouse Motel, which offers comfortable rooms, some of which are equipped with a kitchenette.

Restaurants

Tour A: The Northumberland Strait

Antigonish

Sunshine on Main Cafe & Bistro
$-$$
332 Main St.
☎*863-5851*
The menu at this pleasant restaurant lists a wide selection of dishes, including Italian pasta, excellent pizza, seafood, meat and many vegetarian options. Tasty desserts and various types of coffee are also served. The Sunshine on Main opens early in the morning for breakfast.

Pictou

 **Salt Water Cafe**
$$
on the dock, next to Hector's
☎*485-2558*
The Salt Water Cafe is an enchanting spot for lunch. Its menu consists of a few

light seafood and meat dishes, sandwiches and salads. The café has a pretty patio overlooking the waters of the port.

Stone House Cafe & Pizzeria
$$
11 Water St.
☎*485-6885*
Established in a lovely house in Pictou's historic district, the Stone House Cafe & Pizzeria is a very appealing family restaurant that serves simple, well-prepared food that will please fans of American-style pizza. In nice weather it is possible to sit on the restaurant's terrace facing the port.

Shopping

Tour A: The Northumberland Strait

Pictou

Grohmann Knives
1168 Water St.
☎*485-4224*
Grohmann Knives is a family business that was founded in the 1950s. Their high-quality knives are now sold in many countries around the world.

Green Thumb Farmer's Market
Rte. 104, exit 20
The Green Thumb Farmer's Market is a great place to buy fresh fruits and vegetables, as well as numerous local products.

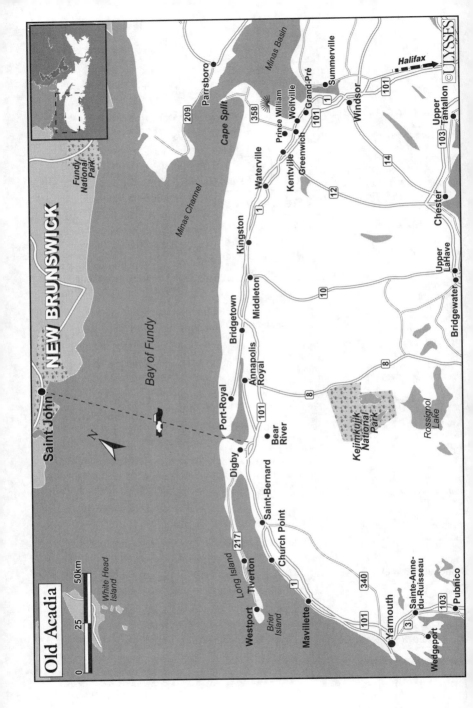

Old Acadia

Old Acadia

Once upon a time,
the magnificent land of Nova Scotia was the focus of a rivalry between the French and British empires.

Originally inhabited by the Mi'kmaq First Nation, it was the site of the first European colony in America north of Florida.

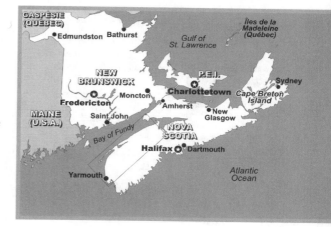

In 1605, one year after a failed attempt to settle Île Sainte-Croix, a French expedition led by de Monts founded Port-Royal at the mouth of what is now known as the Annapolis river. The founding of this permanent settlement marked the birth of Acadia.

Port-Royal continued to grow over the following decades, and the Acadians even founded new settlements on the shores of the Bay of Fundy. The many wars waged between the French and the British proved fatal for Acadia, however.

In 1713, with the signing of the Treaty of Utrecht, France ceded Acadia to Great Britain, who renamed the territory "Nova Scotia". As British citizens of French origin, the Acadians declared themselves neutral in the conflict between France and Great Britain. British authorities, however, were not reassured.

In 1755, when war was imminent, the British took a drastic step by deporting 14,000 Acadians over the next eight years. In the following decades, various immigrants settled in Nova Scotia, including New England Planters seeking new land to farm, Loyalists fleeing the American Revolution, and citizens of the British Isles, especially Scots.

Visitors will discover many fascinating sites that bear witness to Nova Scotia's turbulent history, such as the Fortress of Louisbourg (Cape Breton Island), Citadel Hill (Halifax), the Grand-Pré National Historic Site (Old Acadia), commemorating the deportation of the Acadians, and the Port-Royal National Historic Site (Old Acadia), a replica of the first permanent French settlement in North America (1605).

Finding Your Way Around

This tour of **Old Acadia** ★★ takes you from Windsor, in the centre of Nova Scotia, to Yarmouth, in the south.

By Ferry

Saint John (N.B.) to Digby (N.S.)

MV Princess of Acadia
Departures: three times daily during summer, once daily in the off-season.
☎*(902) 566-3838 or 888-249-7245*
⇸*(902) 566-1550*
www.nfl-bay.com

Portland (Maine) to Yarmouth (N.S.)

M/S Scotia Prince
Departures: daily from May to Oct.
☎*866-412-5270 from Canada and the United-States*
www.scotiaprince.com

From Bar Harbor (Maine) to Yarmouth (N.S.)

The Cat
Departures: every day from late May to mid-Oct.
☎*888-249-7245*
www.catferry.com

Marine Atlantic
Departures: once daily, mid-May to mid-Sep; twice daily, Jul and Aug.
☎*(902) 566-3838 or 888-249-7245*
⇸*(902) 566-1550*
www.nfl-bay.com

By Bus

There are buses running from Halifax to Yarmouth, Amherst and Sydney *(Acadian Lines,* ☎*902-454-9321, www.smtbus.com)* and along the southern coast of the province.

Practical Information

Area code: *902*

Tourist Information Offices

Yarmouth County Tourist Association
PO Box 477, Yarmouth, B5A 4B4
☎*742-5355 or 866-850-9900*
⇸*742-1967*
www.aboutyarmouth.com

On Site

Annapolis Royal
mid-May to mid-Oct
Annapolis Tidal Project, Rte. 1
☎*532-5769*

Digby
mid-May to mid-Oct
237 Shore Rd., towards the ferry landing
☎*245-5714*

Yarmouth
May to Oct
228 Main St.
☎*742-6639*

Exploring

★

Windsor

The site now occupied by the city of Windsor, at the confluence of the Avon and Sainte-Croix rivers, was known to the Mi'kmaq for many years before it was colonized. They referred to it as Pisiquid, meaning "meeting place." Acadians began settling here in 1685 and succeeded in cultivating the land by creating a network of dikes.

Although this part of Acadia was ceded to Great Britain under the terms of the Treaty of Utrecht in 1713, the British presence was not felt in the area until Charles Lawrence erected Fort Edward here in 1750. By building the fort, Lawrence was attempting to strengthen Britain's authority over the territory and protect the British from the Acadians. In 1755, about 1,000 of the region's Acadians were rounded up here before being deported.

During the 19th century, Windsor was an important centre for shipbuilding and the exportation of wood and gypsum. Despite major fires in 1897 and 1924, the town has managed to preserve some lovely homes. It is the starting point of the Evangeline Route.

The **Fort Edward National Historic Site ★** *(free admission; late Jun to early Sep, 9am to 5pm; in the centre of Windsor, ☎798-4706)* consists only of a blockhouse, the oldest fortification of its kind in Canada. This structure is all that remains of Fort Edward, erected in 1750. An interpretive centre provides information on the history of the fort. The site also offers a gorgeous view of the Avon River.

Built in 1835, **Haliburton House ★** *($3; early Jun to mid-Oct, Mon-Sat 9:30am to 5:30pm, Sun 1pm to 5:30pm; 414 Clifton Ave., ☎798-2915)*, also known as **Clifton House**, was the home of Thomas Chandler Haliburton (1796-1865), a judge, politician, businessman, humorist and successful author. This plain-looking wooden house is adorned with magnificent Victorian furniture. It stands on a large, attractively landscaped 10ha property.

Haliburton made a name for himself in Canada and elsewhere by writing novels featuring the character Sam Slick, an American merchant who comes to Nova Scotia to sell clocks. Through this colourful character, Haliburton offered a harsh but humorous critique of his fellow Nova Scotians' lack of enterprise. A number of the expressions Haliburton created for his character, such as "Truth is stranger than fic-

tion", are still commonly used today.

The **Shand House** *($2; Jun to mid-Oct, Mon-Sat 9:30am to 5:30pm, Sun 1pm to 5:30pm; 389 Avon St., ☎798-8213)*, a fine example of Victorian architecture, was built between 1890 and 1891. The furniture that can still be found inside belonged to the family of Clifford Shand, the house's original owner.

Windsor claims to be the birthplace of ice hockey, Canada's national sport. Of course, lots of other cities make this claim; nevertheless, folks have been playing hockey in Windsor for ages. The **Windsor Hockey Heritage Centre** *(free admission; Mon to Sun 9am to 5pm; 128 Gerish St., ☎798-1800)* presents a fine collection of old photographs of the first teams along with original old-fashioned equipment.

From Windsor, Hwy. 1 leads to Grand-Pré, then passes through the communities of the Annapolis valley.

Grand-Pré

Before the Deportation of 1755, Grand Pré was one of the largest Acadian communities on the Bay of Fundy. The dikes built by Acadians in that period, which still protect the region's fertile land, are visible nearby.

The **Grand-Pré National Historic Site ★★** *($5.75; site open year-round, church from May to Oct, 9am to 6pm; Hwy. 1 or Hwy. 101, Exit 10, ☎542-3631)* commemorates the tragic deportation of the Acadians, Here, visitors will find Église Saint-Charles, a replica of the Acadian church that stood on this site before the Deportation, and now houses a museum. The walls are hung with six large and extremely moving paintings by Robert Picard, depicting life in colonial Acadia and during the Deportation.

Grand-Pré National Historic Site

The Deportation

In the 1670s, a small group of Acadians moved from the region of Port-Royal, the first Acadian settlement, founded in 1605, to the fertile lands along the Minas Basin. These industrious farmers managed to free up some excellent grazing land alongside the basin by developing a complex system of dikes and *aboiteaux* (sluice gates). The area became relatively prosperous, and its population grew steadily over the following decades.

Not even the signing of the Treaty of Utrecht in 1713, under which France ceded Acadia to Great Britain, could hinder the region's development. Relations between the Acadian colonists and British authorities remained somewhat ambiguous, however. When France and Great Britain were preparing for their final battle for control of North America, the Acadians declared themselves neutral, refusing to swear allegiance to either country. The British accepted this compromise at first. However, as tensions mounted between the two colonial powers, the British began to find the Acadians' neutrality more and more irritating.

Various events, such as the surprise attack on the British garrison at Grand-Pré by troops from Québec—with the help, it was suspected, of Acadian collaborators—increased British doubts about the Acadians' sincerity. In 1755, Charles Lawrence, then governor of Nova Scotia, took an extraordinary step, ordering the expulsion of all Acadians.

With 5,000 inhabitants, the region along the Minas Basin was the most populated part of Acadia, and Grand-Pré its largest community. That year, British troops hastily rounded up the Acadians, confiscated their land and livestock and burned their houses and churches.

The Acadians were put on boats, often separated from their families, and deported. Of the approximately 14,000 colonists living in Acadia at the time, about half were sent away. Some of the ships went down at sea, while others transported their passengers to various ports in North America, Europe and elsewhere. After years spent wandering, some of these Acadians, ancestors of today's Cajuns, found refuge in Louisiana. Those who escaped deportation had to hide, fleeing through the woods to the northeast coast of present-day New Brunswick, all the way to Québec and elsewhere. One thing is for sure: the deportation order issued by Charles Lawrence succeeded in wiping Acadia from the map. In the following years, their lands were offered to Planters from New England, who were joined by Loyalists at the end of the American Revolution, in 1783.

The stained-glass windows, designed by Halifax artist T.E. Smith-Lamothe, show the Acadians being deported at Grand-Pré. Visitors will also find a bust of American author Henry Wadsworth Longfellow and a statue of Evangeline. In 1847, Longfellow wrote a long poem entitled *Evangeline: A Tale of Acadie*, which told the story of two lovers separated by the Deportation. The site also includes a smithy and a placard explaining the principle behind the dikes and *aboiteaux* (sluice gates) that were developed by the Acadians before they were expelled from the region.

The superb **Domaine de Grand Pré** *(free admission; mid-Mar to end of Dec; 11611 Hwy. 1, Rte. 101, Exit 10, ☎542-1753, www.grandprewines.ns.ca)* is the oldest winery in Nova Scotia and well worth a stop. Guided tours and wine-tastings are offered almost every day from mid-March through to the end of December. The winery also has a good restaurant, only open in the evening. Several of the wines produced here are among the best in the province.

Wolfville

Wolfville is a charming little university town. Its lovely streets are lined with stately elms concealing sumptuous Victorian residences. The city has about 3,500 permanent residents, while the university, **Acadia University**, founded in 1838, welcomes about 4,000 students a year. With its Victorian atmosphere, magnificent inns and excellent cafés and restaurants, this beautiful town is a perfect place to stay during a tour of the region.

Wolfville was founded in 1760, several years after the deportation of the Acadians, by Planters from New England who were attracted by the excellent farmlands available here. The community was known as Upper Horton and then Mud Creek before being christened

Wolfville, in honour of local judge Eilsha DeWolf in 1830. Twice a day, from the shores of the small, natural harbour, visitors can observe the effects of the high tides of the Bay of Fundy.

The *Aboiteaux* that were constructed by the Acadians in the 17th century still mark the landscape. Today, interesting walking trails run along the tops of them for many kilometres; the opportunity to see them up close should not be missed.

While touring the university's pretty campus, take the time to stop in at the **Acadia University Art Gallery** *(free admission; every day 1pm to 4pm; Beveridge Art Centre, at the corner of Main St. and Highland Ave., ☎585-1373)*, which presents interesting exhibitions of contemporary art, as well as works from other periods.

The **Randall House Historical Museum** *(free admission; mid-Jun to mid-Sep, Mon-Sat 10am to 5pm, Sun 2pm to 5pm; 171 Main St., ☎542-9775)* displays objects, furniture, paintings and photographs from the region, dating from 1760 to the present day.

Continue along Hwy. 1 to Greenwich, then take Hwy. 358 to Port Williams. Once there, turn right and continue until you reach Starrs Point.

Starrs Point

This prosperous rural region is home to the

Prescott House Museum ★ *($2; Jun to mid-Oct, Mon-Sat 9:30am to 5:30pm, Sun 1pm to 5:30pm; near Hwy. 358, ☎542-3984)*, a remarkable Georgian style residence erected around 1814. Its first owner was Charles Ramage Prescott, a local businessman and eminent horticulturist, who introduced a variety of new plant species into the province. The interior, decorated with period furniture, is magnificent. Most delightful of all, however, is the little garden, where visitors can enjoy a lovely stroll.

Continue along Hwy. 358 towards Cape Split.

The Route to Cape Split

After passing through some of the region's beautiful rolling landscape and picturesque little villages, take a few moments to stop at the **Lookoff** ★ *(Hwy. 358)*, which offers an extraordinary view of Minas Basin and the Annapolis Valley. Then, go to the end of Highway 358, where a hiking trail (13km return) leads to the rocky points of **Cape Split** ★★.

At Cape Split, get back onto Hwy. 1, heading to the right. This road runs along the Annapolis Valley to Annapolis Royal, passing through a number of lovely communities founded in the late 18th century along the way. Before reaching Annapolis Royal, turn right.

Nova Scotia

Port-Royal

In 1604, one year after the king of France granted him a monopoly on the fur trade in Acadia, Pierre du Gua, sieur de Monts, accompanied by Samuel de Champlain and 80 men, launched the first European attempt to colonize North America north of Florida. In the spring of 1605, after a difficult winter on Île Sainte-Croix, de Monts and his men settled at the mouth of the waterway known today as the Annapolis River, where they founded Port-Royal.

From 1605 to 1613, the settlement of Port-Royal occupied the area now known as the Port-Royal National Historic Site. After efforts to colonize this region were abandoned, the capital of Acadia was moved first to La Have (on the Atlantic coast) for several years, and then to the present site of Annapolis Royal.

The **Port-Royal National Historic Site** ★ ★ (*$3.50; mid-May to mid-Oct, every day 9am to 6pm; from Hwy. 1, take the road leading to Granville Ferry,* ☎*532-2898*) is an excellent reconstruction of the small wooden fortification known as "Abitation" as it appeared in 1605. It was here that fruitful, cordial relations were first established between the French and the Mi'kmaqs.

This site also witnessed the first performance of the Neptune Theatre and the founding of the first social club in North America,

"L'Ordre du Bon Temps." Today, visitors can see the various facilities that enabled the French to survive in North America. Staff in period costumes take visitors back to those long-lost days. One of the guides is of Mi'kmaq origin and can explain the relationship between the French and the Mi'kmaqs, who were always allies.

Annapolis Royal

It was here that Port-Royal, the capital of Acadia, was established in 1635. Because of its advantageous location, the settlement was able to control maritime traffic. In 1710, the British took over the site and renamed the town Annapolis Royal, in honour of Queen Anne. Until Halifax was founded in 1749, Annapolis Royal was the capital of the British colony of Nova Scotia. Today, Annapolis Royal is a peaceful village with a rich architectural heritage, with homes dating back to the early 18th century. Wandering along its streets is a real pleasure. It is also possible to stay in some of the lovely houses here.

At the **Fort Anne National Historic Site** ★ ★ (*$3.50; mid-May to mid-Oct, every day 9am to 6pm; Saint George St.,* ☎*532-2321*), visitors will find an old fort, in the heart of which lie the former officers' quarters, now converted into a historical museum. The exhibition provides a detailed description of all the different stages in the history of the fort, which was French before being taken over by the British. Visitors can enjoy a pleasant stroll around the verdant grounds, which offer lovely views of the surrounding area.

The **Annapolis Tidal Project** (*mid-May to mid-Oct; Upper St. George St., Hwy. 1,* ☎*532-5454*) is an experimental project where visitors can discover how the powerful tides of the Bay of Fundy can be used to produce electricity. There is a tourist information office here as well.

While in the area, make sure to take a walk in the **Annapolis Royal Historic Gardens** ★ ★ (*$6; May to mid-Oct, every day 8am until dark; 441 Saint George St.,* ☎*532-7018*), which have been carefully laid out according to British and Acadian horticultural traditions.

Fort Anne National Historic Site

Digby

A charming town with a picturesque fishing port, Digby lies alongside Annapolis Basin and the Digby Strait, which opens onto the Bay of Fundy. It is known for its scallop-fishing fleet, the world's largest. As a result, its port is a very lively place, where visitors will want to linger, fascinated by the comings and goings of the boats. From Digby, visitors can also head over to Saint John, New Brunswick aboard the ferryboat *MV Princess of Acadia*, which sets out from the port.

From Digby, Hwy. 217 leads to Brier Island.

Long Island and Brier Island

Veritable havens of peace, Long Island and Brier Island attract thousands of visitors each year because the waters off their shores are frequented by sea mammals, especially whales who come to the Bay of Fundy to feed during summertime. Whale-watching cruises set out from Westport (Brier Island) and Tiverton (Long Island) every day during the summer. Many walking trails on Brier Island allow for pleasant strolls along the island's rocky shore and offer very lovely views of the bay.

From Brier Island, visitors have no other option but to head back towards Digby.

Saint-Bernard

Heading out of the very British atmosphere of the Annapolis Valley, visitors will be surprised by the sudden change in the architecture. Case in point, an imposing Catholic church stands in the centre of the little Acadian village of Saint-Bernard.

The **Église Saint-Bernard** is not only a symbol of the fervour of the local Catholics, but also of the courage and perseverance of the Acadian people. It was built over a period of 32 years, from 1910 to 1942, by villagers who volunteered their time and effort. From Saint-Bernard to the outskirts of Yarmouth, the coast is studded with more than a dozen Acadian villages. These communities were founded after the Deportation by Acadians who, upon finding their former lands around Grand-Pré and Port-Royal occupied by Planters, began settling along this barren coast in 1767.

Pointe-de-l'Église (Church Point)

Farther along the coast, the road passes through another little Acadian village, Pointe-de-l'Église (Church Point), which is home to splendid **Église Sainte-Marie ★**. Built between 1903 and 1905,

it is the largest and tallest wooden church in North America. Its interior has a very harmonious appearance.

Right next door stands **Université Sainte-Anne**, Nova Scotia's only French-language university, which plays an important cultural role in the province's Acadian community. The university houses a museum containing objects related to the history of the local Acadians.

A visit to Pointe-de-l'Église and its surroundings would not be complete without taking the time to eat a *pâté de râpure* (an oven-baked dish that includes grated potatoes mixed with pieces of chicken, beef or scallops), a local delicacy available at the university's snack-bar, among other places.

The Acadian flag is flown in front of many residences along the road to Yarmouth. In **Meteghan**, travellers can stop a spell at **La Vieille Maison** (*free admission; Jun and Sep, every day 10am to 6pm; Jul and Aug, every day 9am to 7pm; Meteghan, ☎645-2389*), a 19th-century house in which the lifestyle of Acadians of the period is exhibited.

Yarmouth

Yarmouth was founded in 1761 by colonists from Massachusetts. Life here has always revolved around the town's bustling seaport, the largest in western Nova Scotia. Now a major port of entry

Nova Scotia

for visitors from the United States, Yarmouth has a large selection of hotels and restaurants, as well as an excellent **tourist information office** *(228 Main St.)*. Two ferries link Yarmouth to the state of Maine: *The Cat (☎800-249-7245, www.catferry.com)*, which shuttles between Yarmouth and Bar Harbor all year round, and the *M/S Scotia Prince (☎888-341-7540, www.scotiaprince. com)*, which offers service between Yarmouth and Portland from the beginning of May to the end of October.

A good way to learn about Maritime history and the town's heritage is to view the extraordinarily rich collection on display at the **Yarmouth Country Museum ★** *($3; Jun to mid-Oct, Mon-Sat 9am to 5pm, Sun 2pm to 5pm; mid-Oct to May, Tue-Sat 2pm to 5pm; 22 Collins St., ☎742-5539)*, a small regional museum set up inside a former Presbyterian church. This vast jumble of objects includes miniature replicas of ships, furniture, old paintings and dishes. The museum's most important piece, however, is an octagonal lamp formerly used in the Cape Fourchu lighthouse.

Equally remarkable is the **Firefighters Museum ★** *($2.50; Jun and Sep to mid-Oct, Mon-Sat 9am to 5pm; Jul and Aug, Mon-Sat 9am to 9pm; mid-Oct to May, Mon-Fri 9am to 4pm, Sat 1pm to 4pm; 451 Main St., ☎742-5525)*, which displays two full floors of fire engines. The oldest vehicle, which had to be pulled

by firefighters, dates back to the early 19th century.

Cape Fourchu ★ *(turn left after the hospital and continue for 15km)* is undeniably less spectacular than Peggy's Cove, but much more peaceful. Its lighthouse, erected in 1839, stands on a rocky promontory. Visitors who arrive at the right time will be able to see Yarmouth's impressive fishing fleet pass by just off shore.

From Yarmouth, head east on Hwy. 3 to begin the "Lighthouse Route" (see p 163).

Outdoor Activities

Hiking

Several provincial parks with hiking paths have been created so that visitors can enjoy the natural beauty of the Bay of Fundy. This is a wonderful opportunity to disappear into the woods or walk along the coast and admire the beautiful flora and fauna of this region. **Blomidon Provincial Park** (Canning) offers 16km of hiking paths as well as a picnic area at the summit of Cape Blomidon.

Hiking trails run the length of **Digby Neck**, near Tiverton. Hikers can go to a spot from where they can

see the Balancing Rock, a basalt formation.

Whale-Watching

Every year, whales come to the Gulf of St. Lawrence and the waters south of Nova Scotia, in the Atlantic Ocean. During this period, visitors can take part in one of the whale-watching expeditions organized by various local companies (excursions last about 3hrs).

Brier Island Whale & Seabird Cruises *$40 two to five departures daily, May to mid-Oct* Westport ☎839-2995 or 800-656-3660

Pirate's Cove *$39 three departures daily, Jun to Oct* Tiverton ☎839-2242 or 888-480-0004

Bird-Watching

The Bay of Fundy is a haven for birds, especially during spring and fall when they stop here during their seasonal migration. Brier Island, surrounded by the waters of the Bay of Fundy and St. Mary's Bay, is one of the best bird-watching spots in the province. The rich waters here attract nearly 250 species.

The Whales of the Bay of Fundy

The Bay of Fundy is one of the best places in North America for whale-watching. Every summer, various species travel to the bay, which is rich in plankton and krill, to feed. During the season, four predominant species appear.

The **humpback whale** (Megaptera novaeangliae) can be found in many of the world's waters. There are presently about 10,000 of them. Easily identifiable by their large fins, they can reach a length of 15m and live up to 80 years.

The **fin whale** (Balaenoptera physalus) is distinguished by its large nose. The estimated population of the fin whale is about 123,000, and a small group of them swims in Atlantic waters. With a length that can reach 25m and a weight of 80 tonnes, it is the second-largest mammal after the blue whale.

The **minke whale** (Balaenoptera acutorostrata), with a maximum length of 10m, is a fast swimmer. It prefers shallow coastal waters and estuaries and can therefore frequently be spotted. It can be recognized by a white spot in the middle of its fin and can live up to 50 years.

The **right whale** hasn't been hunted since 1935, but its world-wide population is not more than 2,000, 300 of which are found on the eastern coast of the Americas. They can reach a length of up to 18m and live 40 years. They have whalebones up to 2m long and can be recognized by their particularly large heads.

Boat trips are offered from many ports on the Bay of Fundy, whether they be in New Brunswick or Nova Scotia.

Accommodations

Grand-Pré

Olde Lantern Inn
$$-$$$$ bkfst incl.
🛏, 🐕
4 rooms
11575 Hwy. 1, Rte. 101, Exit 10
☎*542-1389 or*
877-965-3845
www.oldlanterninn.com
In an enchanting setting overlooking the vines and not far from the sea, the Olde Lantern is a splendid inn located next door to the Domaine de Grand Pré. The inn's interior is both subtle and elegant, and really quite lovely. The four spacious and pleasant rooms are beautifully furnished. Gourmet breakfasts are served each morning.

Wolfville

Blomidon Inn
$$
ℜ, ≡, ⊛
21 rooms
195 Main St., B4P 1C3
☎*542-2291 or*
800-565-2291
⇌*542-7461*
www.blomidon.ns.ca
At the elegant Blomidon Inn, visitors can stay in a sumptuous manor built in 1877. At the time, costly materials were used to embellish the residence, which still features marble fireplaces and a superb, carved wooden staircase. This place has all the ingredients of a top-notch establishment: a splendid dining room (see p 160)

where guests can enjoy refined cuisine, impeccable, friendly service and richly decorated sitting rooms. This majestic building stands in the centre of a large property bordered by stately elms. The Blomidon Inn is a veritable symbol of Nova Scotian hospitality. All of the rooms are adorned with antique furniture and include private baths.

Roselawn Lodging
$$
≈, ≡, 🐕
12 cottages, 28 rooms
32 Main St., B4P 1B7
☎*542-3420 or*
866-710-5900
⇌*542-0576*
www.roselawnlodging.ca
Located on the way into Wolfville, Roselawn Lodging offers motel rooms and cottages, all of them very well maintained and of excellent value. It occupies vast grounds that include a swimming pool and a playground. The Roselawn is especially suitable for families. Special rates are available for stays of one week or longer.

Harwood House Bed & Breakfast
$$-$$$ bkfst incl.
⊗
3 rooms
33 Highland Ave.
☎*542-5707 or*
877-897-0156
www.harwoodhouse.com
Set back from the main road on a quiet street close to the university, lovely Harwood House dates back to 1932. Its three rooms are pleasant and welcoming. One of them is equipped to accommodate families. The property is beautifully landscaped.

Hidden Valley Chalets
$$-$$$$
K, ⊗, 🍴
3 chalets
310 Slauter Rd., Gaspereau Valley
☎*542-3034*
The peaceful and quaint Gaspereau Valley is a superb agricultural region of orchards and vineyards that is a pleasure to discover. The Hidden Valley Chalets offer a chance to experience the valley, and this just a short drive from Wolfville. The chalets are modern and well equipped. The vast property is great for enjoying the outdoors and there are walking trails nearby.

Tattingstone Inn
$$$
≡, ≈, ℜ
10 rooms
620 Main St., B4P 1E8
☎*542-7696 or*
800-565-7696
⇌*542-4427*
www.tattingstone.ns.ca
The superb Tattingstone Inn offers tastefully decorated rooms, some containing 18th-century furniture. The accent here is on comfort and elegance. Guests can stay in one of two buildings; the main residence has the most luxurious rooms.

Victoria's Historic Inn
$$$
≡, ⊛
15 rooms
600 Main St., B4P 1E8
☎*542-5744 or*
800-556-5744
www.victoriashistoricinn.com
The charming village of Wolfville boasts several high-quality, luxurious establishments, most of which are located along Main Street. One of these,

Victoria's Historic Inn, harks back to another era. A lovely residence dating from 1893, it has been renovated in order to make the rooms more comfortable and improve the decor. Furthermore, all of the rooms include private baths. The inn is adjoined by a motel with several rooms.

Canning

The Farmhouse Inn
$$ bkfst incl.
⊛, ℑ, ≡
5 rooms
9757 Main St., B0P 1H0
☎*582-7900 or*
800-928-4346
⇋*582-7480*
www.farmhouseinn.ns.ca
The Farmhouse Inn goes a little overboard with the country-style ambiance in each of its rooms, which are decorated with wallpaper, flowery quilts, dolls, artificial fireplaces (in some rooms) and wood furniture. Nevertheless, this kitschy decor makes the rooms cozy enough. Guests appreciate the little added touches, such as coffee and tea served in the rooms every morning. Located in town, this establishment also boasts a lovely garden with maple

trees, which gives the property a certain charm.

Annapolis Royal

Annapolis Royal Inn
$$
⌂, ⊛, ≡, 🐾
30 rooms
Rte. 1, B0S 1A0
☎*532-2323 or*
888-857-8889
⇋*532-7277*
www.portroyalinn.com
Located slightly west of Annapolis Royal, on the road to Digby, this motel rents about 30 well-tended, functional rooms. The inn is particularly appropriate for families.

Hillsdale House
$$-$$$
13 rooms
519 Saint George St.
☎*532-2345 or*
877-839-2821
www.hillsdalehouse.ns.ca
St. George Street boasts a succession of beautiful Victorian houses that are a sight for sore eyes. One of these is lovely Hillsdale House, a stately residence that was built in the mid-19th century. Its rooms are well equipped and elegant. Several common areas, including a veranda off the back of the house, offer guests the opportunity to enjoy the space.

Queen Anne Inn
$$-$$$$ bkfst incl.
⊛, &
12 rooms
393 Upper St.
☎*532-7850 or*
877-536-0403
⇋*532-2078*
www.queenanneinn.com
Occupying a majestic manor built at the end of the 19th century, this impressive inn offers accommodation of an exceptional quality amid splendid surroundings. The large high-ceilinged rooms of the inn are all furnished with antiques. The house originally belonged to Norman Ritchie, who received it as a wedding gift from his father. The Ritchie family has been an important part of Nova Scotia's political scene since 1820. Normand Ritchie held a seat on the Supreme Court of the province at the end of the 19th century and his brother, politician John William Ritchie, is considered one of the fathers of the Confederation. The home converted into an inn more that 80 years ago. The pretty rooms are cosy and some have whirlpool baths. An excellent breakfast is served each morning.

🌴 Garrison House Inn
$$$
ℜ
Apr to Dec
7 rooms
350 Saint George St., B0S 1A0
☎*532-5730 or*
866-532-5750
⇋*532-5501*
Several excellent bed and breakfasts and inns offer visitors the pleasure of staying in the heart of Annapolis Royal, one of the oldest towns in North America. One of these is the magnificent Garrison

Nova Scotia

House Inn, located in the heart of Annapolis Royal, facing Fort Anne. Its antique-filled rooms are simply gorgeous. The room on the top floor with a view out the back is definitely the most stunning with its large windows and many skylights; reservations are a good idea for this room in particular. Very inviting common areas, including a delightful library and a restaurant on the ground floor, contribute to the pleasure of a stay here.

Smith's Cove

🏨 **Mountain Gap Inn**
$$$
ℜ, ≈, ≡, 🐾, ⊛, ℑ
May to Oct
107 rooms
Rte. 101, B0V 1A0
☎245-5841 or
800-565-5020
⇄245-2277
www.mountaingap.ns.ca
The Mountain Gap Inn is the oldest resort in the province (1915) and has an irresistible old-fashioned charm reminiscent of 19th-century New England. Its wooden cottages and other buildings occupy expansive grounds strewn with wildflowers on the shores of Digby Bay. Rooms, suites and cottages, not overly luxurious but always comfortable, are available. Each cottage has a porch–the perfect place for gazing out at sunsets over the bay; cottage number 23 is especially well situated. There is a staircase that leads down to the beach at low tide, and the grounds also include a swimming pool, a playground for children, a tennis court and a pleasant restaurant.

Digby

Digby is a sizeable vacation spot with a number of impressive resorts. Visitors can, however, also find inexpensive rooms here. Two options are the **Siesta Motel** *($$; 15 rooms; 81 Montague Row, B0V 1A0, ☎245-2568, ⇄245-2560)* and the nearby **Seawind Motel** *($$; 10 rooms; 90 Montague Row, B0V 1A0, ☎245-2573)*. Both are well located alongside Digby's natural harbour, just a few minutes' walk from most of the local restaurants.

Admiral Digby Inn
$$$ bkfst incl.
≈, ℜ, ≡
May to Oct
44 rooms
Shore Rd., B0V 1A0
☎245-2531 or
800-465-6262
⇄245-2533
www.digbyns.com
Lodging is also available at the Admiral Digby Inn, a very well-maintained two-storey motel near the home port of the ferry to Saint John, New Brunswick.

Pines Resort
$$$
≈, ☺, ℜ, K, ℑ, ♿
78 rooms, 30 cottages
Shore Rd., B0V 1A0
☎245-2511 or
800-667-4637
⇄245-6133
www.signatureresorts.com
The impressive Pines Resort stands on a hill overlooking the bay in a lovely natural setting. Every part of this hotel was conceived to ensure an excellent stay, from the superb interior design and pretty, comfortable rooms

to the excellent restaurant and inviting bar. Guests also have access to a wide range of athletic facilities, including tennis courts, a swimming pool and a gym; there is also a golf course nearby.

Westport

Brier Island Lodge
$$$
⊛, ℜ, ♿
40 rooms
PO Box 1197, B0V 1H0
☎839-2300 or
800-662-8355
⇄839-2006
www.brierisland.com
The most comfortable place to stay on Brier Island is the Brier Island Lodge. This two-storey motel occupies an auspicious site at the top of a small valley and overlooks the village of Westport and St. Mary's Bay. The rooms are modern and spacious; most of them are enhanced by large windows facing the bay. The restaurant (see p 161), which serves tasty local cuisine, also contributes to the quality of a stay here.

Mavilette Beach Park

Cape View Motel & Cottages
$$
K, ℜ, 🐾
May to Oct
10 rooms, 5 cottages
Salmon River, B0W 2Y0
☎645-2258 or
800-876-1960
⇄645-3999
Driving along the coast between Digby and Yarmouth, visitors will pass through several Acadian communities. The Cape View Motel & Cot-

tages lie alongside a beach near one of these villages. This is not a very luxurious place, but the rooms are well-kept and decently furnished. The region itself is conducive to relaxation, and visitors can enjoy pleasant strolls along the beach.

Yarmouth

Harbour's Edge B&B
$$ bkfst incl.
3 rooms
12 Vancouver St., B5A 2N8
☎742-2387
⇄742-4471
www.harboursedge.ns.ca
This B&B is a great choice for those who love old houses. Meticulously renovated, it successfully recaptures the charm of yesteryear. It offers three cozy rooms, all of which are attractively decorated and include private bathrooms. In addition to the beauty of this home, guests can enjoy the veranda, which opens onto a large garden facing the town harbour. The garden is an ideal spot for bird-watching.

Best Western Mermaid Hotel
$$
ℜ, ≈ , 🐾
45 rooms
545 Main St., B5A 1J6
☎742-7821 or
800-772-2774
⇄742-2966
www.bwmermaid.com
The Best Western Mermaid Hotel occupies a two-storey building at the west entrance to Yarmouth. Its rooms are modern and immaculate. There is no dining room on the premises, but coffee is served in the

morning and **Captain Kelly's Restaurant** (see p 162), located nearby, is reputed to be among the best restaurants in Yarmouth.

Rodd Colony Harbour Inn
$$
ℜ, ℝ, 🐾
65 rooms
6 Forest St., B5A 3K8
☎742-9194 or
800-565-7633
⇄742-6291
www.rodd-hotels.ca
The Rodd Colony Harbour Inn lies directly opposite the boarding point for the ferry to Maine. Since it is located on the side of a hill, there is a lovely view from the back. The rooms are spacious and well-designed. The bar is a pleasant place for a drink.

Manor Inn Lakeside
$$$
≈, ℜ, ℑ, ≡, ◉, ♿
53 rooms
PO Box 56, B0W 1X0
☎742-2487 or
888-626-6746
⇄742-8094
www.manorinn.com
The Manor Inn stands isolated a few kilometres east of Yarmouth, on a large lot on Doctors Lake. This four-building establishment includes 53 rooms with varying levels of comfort. There are some attractively decorated rooms occupying the main building, a house that dates to the middle of the 19th century, and the old coach house just next to it. A few of these are adorned with fireplaces. Most of the rooms located in the other two buildings, set back a little from the main one, are modern and motel-style, equipped with porches or patios. The

fare in the dining room is more than adequate.

Restaurants

Windsor

Spitfire Arms Ale House
$-$$
29 Water St.
☎792-1460
When passing through Windsor, stop in at the Spitfire Arms, a charming and authentic little English pub with a friendly staff. The varied yet typical pub fare is very popular with the locals and inexpensive to boot. There is also a great selection of beers. A real find!

Wolfville

Coffee Merchant
$
corner of Main and Elm Sts.
☎542-4315
If you're craving a good cup of coffee, head over to the Coffee Merchant, which serves good cappuccino and espresso. This is a pleasant place, where it is tempting to linger, read a newspaper or gaze out the window at the comings and goings of the people on the street. The menu is fairly limited, but nevertheless lists a few sandwiches and muffins.

Library Pub & Study Dining Room
$
472 Main St.
☎542-4315
The Library Pub is a quiet and peaceful spot that

offers hamburgers, thin-crust pizzas, quesadillas, kebabs and other simple, inexpensive dishes. This is also a good spot to enjoy a drink and some smooth music. The Library Pub is located just above the Coffee Merchant.

Acton's Grill & Cafe
$$
268 Main St.
☎542-7525
Despite its small size, Wolfville numbers many impressive dining rooms, Acton's Grill & Cafe being a case in point. This little restaurant, with its rather subdued ambiance, offers regional nouvelle cuisine that is both savoury and original. In addition, the menu posts a fine wine list.

Blomidon Inn
$$$$
159 Main St.
☎542-229
The **Blomidon Inn** (see p 156) has two dining rooms—a small, very cozy one in the library and a larger one richly decorated with mahogany chairs. The latter is embellished by a picture window that looks out onto a beautiful landscape. The menu is equally exceptional, featuring such delicious dishes as poached salmon and scallops and salmon Florentine.

Kentville

Paddy's Brew Pub & Rosie's Restaurant
$-$$
42 Aberdeen St.
☎678-3199
One of the friendliest places in Kentville, Paddy

& Rosie's is both a pub, where you can sample home-brewed beer while nibbling on nachos or chicken wings, and a restaurant that offers refined dishes, such as mussels, shrimp and other seafood. Relaxed atmosphere and courteous service.

Annapolis Royal

Cafe Compose
$-$$
235 Saint George St.
☎532-1251
An inviting dining room done up in warm tones and boasting picture windows and a superb patio with an exceptional view of the bay make this restaurant one of the most popular in Annapolis Royal. The menu includes several Eastern European specialties, including beef Stroganoff, schnitzel and Hungarian goulash. You can also choose from a good selection of sandwiches, soups and, above all, salads. Top it all off with a fine choice of coffees and a few desserts, including some Austrian specialties.

Ivy Deck Garden & Bistro Restaurant
$-$$
8 Elm Ave.
☎542-1868
There's nothing fancy about the Ivy Deck, just a popular student hangout that serves quiches, salads and other simple dishes, plus a variety of home-made desserts.

Leo's
$$
222 Saint George St.
☎532-7464
Leo's occupies the oldest house in the Maritimes

(1712). It is the place to keep in mind for breakfast, a light lunch or a more elaborate evening meal. A friendly, unpretentious spot, it offers a menu of seafood, meat and pasta.

Ye Olde Towne Pub
$$
9-11 Church St.
☎522-2244
Ye Olde Towne Pub's ambiance and décor put it in the true English tradition. Set in a historic building (1884) that was once a bank, the place oozes charm. Many people come here for the typical pub fare: steaks, pasta and seafood. The outdoor patio is particularly popular on summer days.

Tempest Restaurant
$$$$
117 Front St.
☎542-0588 or 866-542-0588
The new darling of Wolfville's gourmet set, the Tempest offers a choice of dishes inspired by local, European and Asian cuisines. The menu is rather pricey in the evening; at lunchtime, however, the prices are more reasonable. The Tempest is a real charm with its refined décor and warm colours.

Digby

Boardwalk Cafe
$-$$
40 Water St.
☎245-5497
The initial appeal of the Boardwalk Cafe is its patio's excellent view of the bay. As for its menu, it comprises a nice selection of light lunch fare: salads, soup and sandwiches,

among other things. In the evening, however, the menu becomes a little more sophisticated. Dishes change from one day to the next, depending on what's fresh and the chef's mood.

Fundy Dockside Restaurant
$-$$

34 Water St.
☎245-4950

Digby's famous scallops are of course *the* local specialty; most of the town's restaurants are located near the port. The Fundy Dockside Restaurant presents a varied menu, though scallops remain, of course, the star.

Royal Fundy Seafood Market and Eatery
$-$$

141 Prince William
☎245-6528

The Royal Fundy is above all an excellent fish market with fresh pickings from the sea. But it is also a small restaurant with just a few tables. Several seafood and fish dishes are available for $10 and less. There is a children's menu as well.

Annapolis Dining Room
$$$

Pines Resort, Shore Rd.
☎245-2511

At the dining room in the **Pines Resort** (see p 158) visitors will find classic cuisine served in a refined atmosphere. The menu features an excellent Bras d'Or Lake salmon. In addition, an excellent wine list and an interesting selection of desserts are offered. This dining room is the undisputed favourite of local gourmets.

Westport (Brier Island)

Brier Island Lodge
$$-$$$
☎839-2300

For an intimate dinner or a light lunch, the best place on the island is the dining room at the **Brier Island Lodge** (see p 158), where a beautiful, large window provides a splendid view of the bay. The restaurant's menu lists a great variety of seafood and meat dishes.

Belliveau Cove

Roadside Grill
$
☎837-5047

Just west of Church Point, travellers can break bread at the local Roadside Grill. French Canadians gather at this unpretentious little restaurant to share the latest local news. The menu offers a few Acadian specialties, including beef, chicken or shellfish *râpures*.

Mavilette Beach Park

Cape View Motel
$-$$

Salmon River
☎645-2258

The restaurant at the **Cape View Motel** (see p 158) offers a lovely view over St. Mary's Bay. Some Acadian specialties are featured on the menu, including *râpure*, as are many seafood, chicken and meat dishes. Very friendly service.

Yarmouth

Harris' Quick-N-Tasty
$-$$

490 Route 1, Dayton
☎742-3467

Harris' has made the lobster roll its specialty. And while it might look like a snack bar, this little restaurant offers a surprising variety of options, from hamburgers to seafood dishes. The mood is unpretentious and family friendly. You can also get your meal to go.

Ceilidh Desserts Plus & Café / Bruno's After Five
$-$$$

278 Main St.
☎742-0031

Two restaurants in one! During the day, the Ceilidh Desserts Plus & Café serves the typical lunchtime fare you'd expect to find in a café. From 5pm on, the place changes into Bruno's After Five, and the ambiance becomes more chic and the menu more refined: salmon with maple syrup and haddock in *provençale* sauce are two examples. The wine list includes some fine local and imported selections. The atmosphere is elegant but not stuffy.

Joshua's Restaurant & Café
$$

95 Water St.
☎742-6566

Joshua's is well-located on the waterfront and is great for lunch. It offers a good choice of salads, soups and sandwiches, as well as a handful of tasty homemade desserts and several different ice creams.

Nova Scotia

Joshua's sundaes are actually one of its biggest draws. In the evening, patrons are invited upstairs to the more formal dining room, where the menu becomes more elaborate.

Rudder's Seafood Restaurant & Brew Pub
$$
96 Water St.
☎742-7050
Very popular and always hopping, Rudder's serves simple pub food at reasonable prices. People come for the food but also for the house beer brewed on site. In summer, when the weather is fine, the large outdoor terrace is particularly popular.

Captain Kelly's Restaurant
$$-$$$
577 Main St.
☎742-9191
This beautiful dining room is decorated with woodwork and laid out in a

large, century-old home that also houses an English pub. The captain's cuisine varies greatly, from hamburgers to seafood by way of Acadian *râpure* and beef stew. Dishes are generally well prepared.

Entertainment

Wolfville

Atlantic Theatre Festival
504 Main St.
☎542-4242 or 800-337-6661
www.atf.ns.ca
Excellent classic plays are presented from mid-June to early September in the city's 500-seat amphitheatre. Ticket prices vary between $10 and $37 per person.

Paddy's Brew Pub
42 Aberdeen St.
☎678-3199
Paddy's is a pleasant surprise: not only is it the favourite hangout of university students, but it is also one of the funnest pubs in Wolfville. There are live shows regularly, and several beers sold here are brewed on site.

Yarmouth

Rudder's Brew Pub
96 Water St.
☎742-7050
Rudder's is *the* place for a drink in Yarmouth. The beer is brewed on site, live music is a regular occurrence and the mood is always festive, especially as the evening wears on. The large terrace is the place to be when the sun shines during the summer months.

Lighthouse Route

This route, which runs along the southwest coast of Nova Scotia, boasts some of the most picturesque landscapes in the province.

Here, a string of charming villages blends harmoniously into the beautiful, unspoiled natural setting.

While exploring the area, visitors will pass through hamlets and fishing ports with wooden houses dating back to the 19th century, when the region enjoyed an era of prosperity due to the local construction of fishing schooners. The tips of the rocky capes all along the coast are crowned by the silhouettes of lighthouses, the most famous being the one at Peggy's Cove.

Practical Information

Area code: **902**

Tourist Information

Tourism Bureau
11 Blockhouse Hill Rd.,
Lunenberg
☎*634-8100*
⇥*634-3194*

South Shore Tourism Association
PO Box 1390, Lunenburg,
B0J 2C0
☎*634-8844*
⇥*634-8056*
www.ssta.com

Exploring

The **Lighthouse Route ★** leads eastward from Wedgeport, south of Yarmouth, along the coast to Peggy's Cove.

Wedgeport and Surroundings

Wedgeport is still a very active fishing harbour; it's home to the **Wedgeport Sport Tuna Fishing Museum** (*$2; Jun to Sep; Rte. 344,* ☎*663-4345*), a little museum dedicated to sport tuna fishing.

The road from Wedgeport to Pubnico West links a series of little Acadian fishing villages. The Acadian presence in this part of the province has persisted since 1653, a rare feat of continuity in Nova Scotia. Many people in the area bear the surname "Entremont" and are direct descendants of the sieur d'Entremont, the first French colonist to settle the region. Interestingly, Acadians from this part of the province have preserved various old terms and expressions that are no longer current among other French Canadians. A nice example is that instead of saying *soixante-dix*, *quatre-vingt* and *quatre-vingt-dix* ("seventy," "eighty" and "ninety," respectively), people here say *septante*, *octante* and *nonante*.

Tusket

A stop at the **Argyle Township Court House & Goal** ★ *($2; Jun to Oct, Mon-Fri 9am to 5pm; Jul and Aug, every day 9am to 5pm; Hwy. 3,* ☎*648-2493)* is an absolute must when in Tusket, a pretty village bordered by expanses of calm water. Erected in 1805, this is the oldest building of its kind in Canada. The courtroom, the cells and the jailor's quarters are all open to the public.

Continuing along Highway 3, **Sainte-Anne-du-Ruisseau Church** ★ *(Hwy. 3; Sainte-Anne-du-Ruisseau)*, exquisite with its splendid ceilings and stained-glass windows, is impossible to miss. It was built in 1900 and is located in the oldest Catholic parish in the region (1699).

Continue westward; Hwy. 3 intersects Hwy. 335, which leads to West Pubnico.

West Pubnico

West Pubnico is an Acadian fishing village that offers picturesque seascapes. **Le Musée Acadien** *($2; mid-Jun to mid-Sep, Mon-Sat 9am to 5pm, Sun 12:30pm to 4:30pm; Hwy. 355,* ☎*762-3380)* exhibits antique objects, some of which date back as far as the 18th century. There is a gift shop on the premises.

Continue heading east on Hwy. 3.

Barrington

Barrington was founded in 1761 by a dozen Quaker families from Cape Cod, in the United States. Four years later, the community began building what is now the **Old Meeting House Museum** ★ *($2; early Jun to end of Sep, Mon-Sat 9:30am to 5:30pm, Sun 1pm to 5:30pm; Hwy. 3,* ☎*637-2185)*, today a national historic site.

In addition to its obvious function as a meeting place, the Meeting House also served as a place of worship for the various religious denominations. This New England–style building is the oldest Nonconformist site in Canada,

and the only remaining building among the five that were built during this period of Nova Scotia's history. The museum recounts the history of the building and the region.

Barrington features another interesting historic site, the **Barrington Woolen Mill Museum** ★ *($1; Jun to Sep, Mon-Sat 9:30am to 5:30pm, Sun 1pm to 5:30pm; Hwy. 3,* ☎*637-2185)*, a mill built in 1884 and originally powered by a waterfall. The Woolen Mill is an interpretive centre where visitors can learn how mills revolutionized the process of weaving wool.

Cape Sable Island

From Barrington Passage, Route 330 leads across a one-kilometre-long causeway to Cape Sable Island, a peaceful little island whose landscape has been fashioned by the sea. Cape Sable Island, which lies off the tourist track and so does not get very much tourist traffic, remains true to itself with its handful of fishing hamlets, lighthouses, magnificent wild white-sand beaches and protected nesting grounds. Local history buffs can visit the **museum** *(Centreville, Route 330)* dedicated to the life of Archelaus Smith, the first British colonist to settle the island. There are also a few lodging establishments and two restaurants on Cape Sable Island.

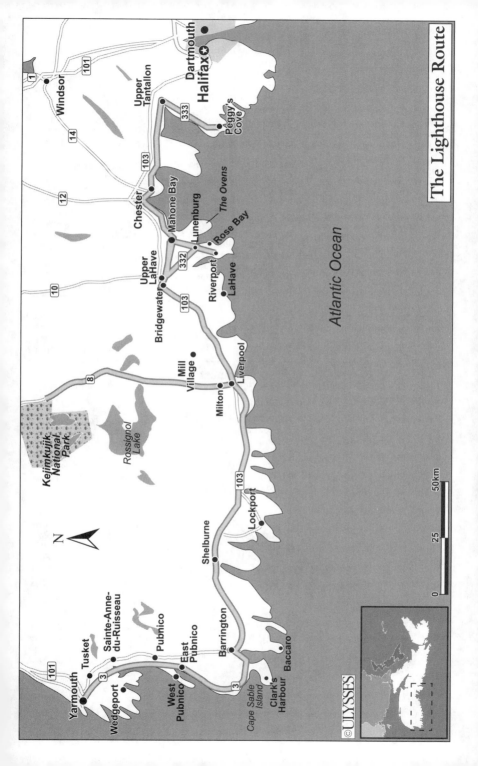

The Lighthouse Route

Shelburne

Shelburne was founded in 1783, the final year of the American Revolution, when about 30 ships carrying thousands of Loyalists arrived in Nova Scotia. By the following year, the town already had over 10,000 inhabitants, making it one of the most densely populated communities in North America. Today, Shelburne is a peaceful village. **Dock Street ★**, which runs alongside the natural harbour, is flanked by lovely old buildings that form a harmonious architectural ensemble.

This historic section features several points of interest, including the **Ross-Thomson House & Store Museum ★** *($3; Jun to mid-Oct, every day 9:30am to 5:30pm; 9 Charlotte Ln., ☎875-3141)*, whose general store dates back to the late 19th century. It is furnished in a manner typical of that type of business in 1820.

In the same neighbourhood, visitors can stop in at the **Dory Shop Museum ★** *($3; Jun to mid-Oct, every day 9:30am to 5:30pm; Dock St., ☎875-3219)*, a workshop where fishing vessels were built in the 19th century.

Also noteworthy is the **Shelburne County Museum** *($2; Jun to mid-Oct, every day 9:30am to 5:30pm; mid-Oct to May, Tue-Sat 2pm to 5pm; 8 Maiden Ln., ☎875-3219)*, whose collection deals with the arrival of the Loyalists and the history of shipbuilding in this area, among other subjects.

A $4 pass grants admission to all three of these museums.

Lockeport

This pretty town, located a few kilometres past Shelburne, has some of the most beautiful white-sand beaches in the province. There are five of these in the immediate vicinity of Lockeport, including spec-

tacular **Crescent Beach ★**, which extends over 1.5km and was once depicted on the Canadian 50-dollar bill.

It is possible to stay in Lockeport, at bed and breakfasts or in cottages along the beach. On the way to Liverpool, a few other exquisite sand beaches make up part of the landscape, notably in **Summerville Centre**, **Hunts Point** and **White Point**. Accommodation is also available near these beaches.

Liverpool

In the late 19th and early 20th centuries, the port of Liverpool was regularly frequented by privateers recruited by Great Britain. Privateers differed from pirates in that they were working in the name of a government, which gave them an official status of some sort, thereby protecting them. After pillaging villages or attacking enemy ships, they had to hand over a part of their booty to their protector.

The **Perkins House Museum ★** *(free admission; Jun to mid-Oct, Mon-Sat 9:30am to 5:30pm, Sun 1pm to 5:30pm; 105 Main St., ☎354-4058)* was the home of writer Simeon Perkins, famous for his journal describing life in the colony between 1766 and 1812. The Perkins House, now open to the public, is an example of the Connecticut style and dates back to 1876.

Ross-Thomson House

The multifunctional **Rossignol Cultural Centre** ★ *(Mon-Sat 10am to 5:30pm, Sun noon to 5:30pm; 205 Church St., ☎354-3067)* opened its doors in July of 2002. It encompasses a variety of cultural attractions: museums, art galleries, libraries and exhibits on flora and fauna. There are a dozen distinct spaces under one roof, including the Apothecary Museum, the Folk Art Museum, the Hunting & Mikmaq Museum and the Wildlife Museum. The quality of the exhibits is particularly remarkable, as is the originality used to highlight the various themes of the displays. This is an excellent family stop.

From Liverpool, visitors can set off on an excursion to **Kejimkujik National Park** ★★ *(see p 170)* by taking Route 8.

Those who don't wish to go to Kejimkujik National Park can take Hwy. 3 east to Exit 17, near Mill Village, to get back onto Hwy. 331.

LaHave

Christened LaHave by Champlain and de Monts, who stayed here for a while in 1604, this little cape was chosen by Isaac de Razilly to be the site of the capital of Acadia from 1632 to 1636. Visitors will now find a monument marking the location of the former Fort Sainte-Marie-de-Grâce, built to protect the little colony. Right nearby, the **Fort Point Museum** *(free admission; Jun to Aug, every day 10am to 6pm; Hwy. 331, ☎688-2696)* presents an exhibition on local history and the early days of the colony.

Bridgewater

Located on either side of the LaHave River, Bridgewater is a bustling little town with several restaurants and hotels. Visitors can stop at the **DesBrisay Museum** *($2; mid-May to Sep, Mon-Sat 9am to 5pm, Sun 1pm to 5pm; Oct to mid-May, Tue-Sun 1pm to 5pm; 130 Jubilee Rd., ☎543-4033)*, which houses a collection of objects related to local history and regularly hosts touring exhibitions in a modern space.

To learn all there is to know about how the mill revolutionized the wool-weaving industry, head to the **Wile Carding Mill Museum** ★ *(free admission; Jun to Sep, Mon-Sat 9:30am to 5:30pm, Sun 1pm to 5:30pm; corner of Pearl St. and Victoria Rd., ☎543-8233)*. Guides in period dress offer interesting tours of the mill and explain the various steps involved in weaving wool.

At Upper LaHave, take Hwy. 332 towards Riverport and Rose Bay.

Rose Bay

In 1861, gold diggers came to try their luck at **The Ovens Natural Park** ★ *($5; mid-May to mid-Oct, 9am to sunset; Hwy. 332, ☎766-4621)*. Little by little, these prospectors abandoned the area, only to be replaced by other inquisitive individuals who were

attracted by the beauty of the setting. For many years, the sea has been sculpting the rock of the cliffs here, hollowing out caves that the water surges into with great force. Paths have been cleared alongside the precipices, affording some magnificent views. Boating excursions make it possible to view the cliffs from the water as well.

Get back on Hwy. 3 near Lunenberg.

Lunenburg

Lunenburg is definitely one of the most picturesque fishing ports in the Maritimes. Founded in 1753, it was the second British settlement in Nova Scotia, Halifax being the first. Its original population consisted mainly of "foreign Protestants" from Germany, Montbelliard and Switzerland. German was commonly spoken in Lunenburg up until the end of the 19th century, and various culinary traditions have survived to the present day. The village occupies a magnificent site on the steep shores of a peninsula with a natural harbour. A number of the colourful houses and buildings here date back to the late 18th and early 19th centuries. In fact, because of the architecture, parts of Lunenburg are somewhat reminiscent of the Old World. Lunenburg was recently named a UNESCO World Heritage Site, due to its historic architecture.

The Bluenose

The *Bluenose* holds a special place in Canadian maritime history. Built in Lunenburg in 1921, this extraordinary schooner won every race it participated in throughout its career.

In October 1921, after a summer of fishing, to everyone's surprise, the *Bluenose* received the International Fisherman's Trophy for winning a race involving Canadian and American sailors. From then on until 1938, the *Bluenose* did not lose a race, despite the many Canadians and Americans who built ships in the sole purpose of defeating it.

Equipped with eight sails, the *Bluenose* was a superb 49m schooner. Its hull was made of red oak, spruce and pinewood, its deck of Douglas fir, and its structure of mahogany. The *Bluenose* needed an 18-man crew and could reach speeds of up to 16 knots.

The glorious era of the *Bluenose* and other fishing schooners ended in the early 1940s with the arrival of massive modern trawlers with steel hulls. In 1942, despite the efforts of its captain Angus Walters, the *Bluenose* was sold in the West Indies.

The *Bluenose* was immortalized, however, and its image now appears on the Canadian 10-cent coin. In addition, a copy of the *Bluenose* was built in Lunenburg in 1963, the *Bluenose II*, which now travels the seas. In summer, the *Bluenose II* is moored at Lunenburg or Halifax harbour, and offers pleasant cruises. More about the *Bluenose* and its history can be found on the Internet at: ***www.bluenose2.ns.ca***

A very busy fishing port, Lunenburg also has a long tradition of shipbuilding. The celebrated *Bluenose*, a remarkable schooner that was never defeated in 18 years of racing, was built here in 1921.

Lunenburg is an extremely pleasant place to visit in the summertime. Its streets are lined with shops selling quality products. The art galleries are particularly interesting.

The atmosphere here is also enlivened by all sorts of activities, including the **Nova Scotia Fisheries Exhibition and Fisherman Reunion**, a celebration of the world of fishing, which has been held each year at the end of August since 1916.

The **Fisheries Museum of the Atlantic ★★** *($9; May to Oct, every day 9:30am to 5:30pm, mid-Oct to mid-May, Mon-Fri 8:30am to 4:30pm; on the waterfront, ☎634-4794)*, set up inside an old fish-processing plant, commemorates the heritage of the fishers of the Atlantic provinces. Visitors will find an exhaustive introduction to the world of fishing, including an aquarium, an exhibit on the 400-year history of fishing on the Grand Banks of Newfoundland, a workshop where an artisan can be observed building a small fishing boat, an exhibit on whaling and another on the history of the *Bluenose*, and more.

Three ships are tied to the pier behind the building, including the *Theresa E. Connor*, a schooner built in Lunenburg in 1938 and used for fishing on the Banks for a quarter of a century. Expect to spend at least 3hrs for a full tour of this three-storey museum.

The ***Bluenose II*** *($20; Jun to Sep, departures every day at 9:30am and 1pm; ☎641-1963, www.bluenose2.ns.ca)* is moored in Lunenburg harbour when it is not in Halifax. Built in 1963, it's a 43.5m schooner, a replica of the famous *Bluenose* that is portrayed on the Canadian 10-cent coin. Enjoy cruises on this historic ship.

Wandering the streets of Lunenburg, visitors are invariably seduced by the town's pretty houses and beautiful buildings, especially **St. John's Anglican Church** and **St. Andrew's Presbyterian Church**.

Make sure to take the opportunity to visit the little fishing hamlet of **Blue Rock** ★, located a short distance from Lunenburg. Peaceful and picturesque, this handful of houses lies on a rocky cape overlooking the ocean.

Continue heading east on Hwy. 3.

Mahone Bay

Mahone Bay is easily recognizable by its three churches, each more than a century old, built side by side facing the bay. Like Lunenburg, Mahone Bay was first settled by "Protestant foreigners" in 1754, and like a number of other communities on the Atlantic coast, its port served as a refuge for privateers.

Until 1812, these individuals pillaged enemy ships and villages, while paying British authorities to protect them. Later, until the end of the 19th century, Mahone Bay enjoyed a period of great prosperity, thanks to its fishing and shipbuilding industries. The lovely old houses lining the streets of the village bear witness to this golden era. Mahone Bay has an attractive sailing harbour and several good inns and bed and breakfasts.

Visitors can also go to the **Settlers Museum** *(free admission; Jun to Sep, Tue-Sat 10am to 5pm, Sun 1pm to 5pm; 578 Main St., ☎624-6263),* which features a collection of antique furniture, dishes and other vintage objects from the area. The house itself dates back to 1850.

Continue along Hwy. 3.

Chester

Chester was founded in the 1760s by New England families. It has been a popular vacation spot since the beginning of the 19th century. Many well-

heeled residents of Halifax have second homes here, and visitors will find a number of quality hotels and restaurants, an 18-hole golf course, three sailing harbours, several craft shops and a theatre, the **Chester Playhouse** *(22 Pleasant St., ☎275-3933 or 800-363-7529, www.chesterplayhouse. ns.ca).* Perched atop a promontory overlooking Monroe Bay, Chester cuts a fine figure with its lovely homes and magnificent trees.

From Chester, Highway 12 leads to the **Ross Farm Living Museum of Agriculture** ★ *($5; May to Oct, every day 9:30am to 5:30pm; Nov to Apr, Wed-Sun 9:30am to 4:30pm; New Ross, ☎689-2210),* a 23ha farm inhabited by five successive generations of the Ross family from 1916 onwards. Guides in period dress liven up the museum, which has about 10 buildings typical of those found on large farms in the 19th century.

At Upper Tantallon, take Hwy. 333.

Peggy's Cove

The picturesque appearance of the tiny coastal village of Peggy's Cove has charmed many a painter and photographer. The little port, protected from turbulent waters, is lined with warehouses standing on piles.

Farther along, visitors can stroll across the blocks of granite that serve as a base

Mahone Bay

for the famous lighthouse of Peggy's Cove, which houses a post office during the summer. It is best to be careful when walking here, especially when the water is rough. On the way out of Peggy's Cove, visitors can stop at the **William E. deGarthe Memorial Provincial Park ★** to see a sculpture of 32 fishers, along with their wives and children, carved into a 30m-long rock face. William deGarthe, who spent five years creating this sculpture, was fascinated by the beauty of Peggy's Cove, where he lived from 1955 until his death in 1983, and by the lifestyle and courage of the local fishers.

Parks

Kejimkujik National Park ★ ★ *($4.50 per day; PO Box 236, Maitland Bridge, B0T 1B0;* ☎*682-2772),* which covers 381km² in the heart of Nova Scotia, can be accessed via Highway 8. Crisscrossed by peaceful rivers teeming with fish, this territory was once inhabited by Mi'kmaqs, who established their hunting and fishing camp here. It is still considered a prime canoeing location. The park also features camping sites, a pleasant beach (Merrymakedge) and various trails leading into the forest.

A portion of the park, **Kejimkujik Seaside Adjunct National Park ★**, stretches 22km along the shoreline, near Port Mouton. The landscape here is more rugged than in the rest of the park. Although the area is bordered by steep, glacier-sculpted cliffs, there are a few coves nestled here and there, with sandy beaches tucked inside. Trails have been cleared to enable visitors to explore the park and observe the local plant and animal life; seals can sometimes be seen along the shore.

Beaches

Along the Atlantic coast of this route there are gorgeous beaches of fine sand in the area of Lockeport, close to **Shelburne** and near Liverpool at **Summerville Centre**, **Hunts Point** and **White Point**. Spectacular **Crescent Beach ★**, in Lockeport, is 1.5km long and is but one of five beautiful beaches in that area.

Outdoor Activities

Whale-Watching

The southwest coast is home to a variety of marine animal life. Seals, humpback whales and Atlantic puffins are just a few of the numerous species that you can see by taking one of the boat trips departing from different towns in the region.

Lunenburg Whale Watching Tour
mid-May to Oct
4 excursions per day
PO Box 11, Lunenburg, B0J 2C0
☎**527-7175**

Peggy's Cove Whale & Puffin Tours
Jun to mid-Oct
Rte. 333, Peggy's Cove, B0J 2N0
☎**823-1818**

Diving

There have been many shipwrecks along the southwest coast of Nova Scotia because of the heavy sea traffic through these waters over the years. A few of these wrecks have turned into incredible artificial reefs for marine life that attract divers. Along Port Mouton, **Spectacle Marine Park** has 16 dive sites, some of which abound with marine fauna, while others are shipwrecks. Among these, Matthew Atlantic is one of the artificial reefs that can be explored by divers of all levels.

Queens County Marine Park Society
Port Mouton
☎**683-2188**

Lunenburg offers a unique dive site. In 1994, the *HMCS Saguenay*, a Canadian destroyer, was intentionally sunk off Lunenburg to become the figurehead of **Lunenburg Marine Park**. This wreck has also become a unique refuge for thousands of marine animals, making this spot a magnificent place to go diving in Nova Scotia.

Hiking

Kejimkujik National Park has lovely trails for those who enjoy hiking in the forest. 14 paths cover several kilometres, offering breathtaking natural beauty. Whether you choose to hike along Roger's Creek, Mill Falls or Merrymakedge beach, or prefer to bird-watch at Peter's Peak, each trip is a chance to discover some of the many treasures of this vast wilderness.

Canoeing and Kayaking

The southwest coast is sprinkled with many little islands and coves, which makes it the perfect spot for canoeing and sea-kayaking. For those who get excited about the idea of paddling on the waves, several companies rent boats and organize trips.

Seaclusion Kayak Adventures
1270 Argyle Sound Rd., West Pubnico
☎648-8339
www.seaclusion.ca

Mahone Bay Kayak Adventures
618 Main St., Mahone Bay
☎624-0334

Rossignol Surf Shop
600 St. Catherine's River Rd., Liverpool
☎354-3733 or 877-990-3733
www.surfnovascotia.com

The best place to go canoeing in Nova Scotia is undoubtedly **Kejimkujik National Park** (☎682-2772), which is crisscrossed by scores of rivers that are easily accessible aboard these vessels. From amateurs interested in short excursions to more experienced canoeists, everyone can enjoy this thrilling activity here. Canoes may be rented in **Jakes Landing**.

Accommodations

Barrington Passage

Old School House Inn & Cottages
$$
ℜ
14 rooms
Hwy. 3, B0W 1G0
☎637-3770
≈637-3867
This old village school, which served its original function from 1889 to 1969, was transformed a few years ago into a lodging establishment. Its rather modestly decorated rooms occupy the two upper floors of the building. On the ground floor, a restaurant and a bar attract local clientele.

A little set back from the school are some adequately comfortable rental cottages.

Cape Sable Island

Cape Sable Cottages
$$$$
K
5 cottages
37 Long Point
☎745-0168
www.capesablecottages. com
Far from the usual tourist track, Cape Sable Island attracts vacationers in search of peace and quiet, authenticity and a healthy lack of pretension. There are a few places to stay, including the Cape Sable Cottages, whose five units all offer views of the sea. Canoes, kayaks and pedalboats are available to guests and swimming is possible nearby. This is a great place for a family vacation.

Sable River

Sable River View Cottages
$$
K, ℜ, △, ⊕, ⊘
4 cottages
Cottage Dr., RR 2
☎656-3071 or 875-7087
These four cottages have stood for some time now on this enchanting and peaceful property overlooking the Sable River. Each of the well-equipped cottages has two rooms. The interior décor is simple but clean and comfortable. You can swim nearby as well as enjoy several outdoor activities. Bicycles and canoes are available for guests to use. This spot is

particularly popular with families.

Shelburne

Cooper's Inn
$$ bkfst incl.
ℜ, ♿
7 rooms
875 Dock St., B0T 1W0
☎/≈875-4656
☎800-688-2011
Located in the very heart of Shelburne's historic section, over-looking the harbour, lovely Cooper's Inn is one of the best hotels in the province. It occupies a magnificently renovated old house that was built for a wealthy Loyalist merchant in 1785.

The decor of each room and the choice of furniture for the house were carried out with such minute attention to detail that a simple visit to Cooper's Inn is a pleasure in itself. All of the rooms are comfortable and equipped with private bathrooms. A splendid, very bright suite has been laid out on the top floor. In addition, one of the rooms is easily accessible to travellers with disabilities. Each room is named for one of the house's former owners. To top it all off, the inn's dining room serves up cuisine that pleases the most distinguishing palates.

Cape Cod Colony Motel
$$
🐕
23 rooms
234 Water St., B0T 1W0
☎875-3411
≈875-1575
www.capecodmotel.ns.ca
For inexpensive accommodation, opt for the peaceful Cape Cod Colony Motel, which has clean, modern rooms and lies just a short walk from Dock Street.

Shady Pines Farm and Country Inn
$$ bkfst incl.
4 rooms
12 Falls Lane
☎875-3495
At the end of a gravel road, a few minutes from Shelburne, you'll come upon a pretty log building surrounded by pine forest. The setting couldn't be more charming. Twenty-one acres along the shores of the Roseway River surround this pretty and peaceful country inn, which stands out from the usual seaside lodging options so common in this part of the province. The three rooms are large and comfortable and the sitting room has a lovely patio overlooking the river. Of note here: llamas and alpacas are bread at the farm. To get there, take Exit 26 off of Route 103, turn left on Roger Lane and then right at the end of Roger Lane.

Millstones Bed & Breakfast
$$-$$$ bkfst incl.
4 rooms
2 Falls Lane
☎875-4525 or
866-240-9110
≈875-3692
www.millstonesbedand
breakfast.com
This welcoming B&B occupies a quaint house built in the mid-19th century on the way into Shelburne. There are three pleasant rooms, each with a private bathroom, plus one more luxurious suite. The Mill stones boasts a beautiful setting alongside the Roseway River.

Lockeport

To fully profit from the fine-sand beach in Lockeport, visitors can stay a **Ocean Mist Cottages** (*$$$$*; ℜ; *6 rooms; Crescent Beach, B0T 1L0,* ☎656-3200, ≈656-2203) or at **Seaside Cottages** (*$$$; 8 rooms; Rte. 3, Crescent Beach, B0T 1L0,* ☎/≈656-2089, *www.seasidecottages. ns.ca*). These closely built, comfortable two-bedroom houses offer a direct view of Crescent Beach.

Summerville Beach

Quarterdeck Beachside Villas & Cabins
$$$
ℜ, ℜ, K, ⊛
16 rooms
Rte. 3, B0T 1T0
☎683-2998 or
800-565-1119
≈683-2457
www.quarterdeck.ns.ca
Cottages equipped with all the comforts, a long fine-sand beach, a relaxed atmosphere and an excellent restaurant are the foundations of the Quarterdeck's reputation. Its villas, built directly on the beach, each have two bedrooms, a living room with a fireplace, a very well-equipped kitchenette and a modern bathroom. The largest room in each house is on the second floor and is splendidly laid out with a whirlpool bath and a superb terrace overlooking the ocean. The Quarterdeck leaves nothing to be desired, either as the

setting for a restful family vacation or as an intimate lovers' retreat.

White Point

White Point Beach Resort
$$$$$
ℜ, ≈, ⊛
74 rooms, 44 cottages
Rte. 3, Exit 20A or 21 off
Hwy. 103, B0T 1G0
☎*354-2711 or*
800-565-5068
⇌*354-7278*
www.whitepoint.com
The White Point Beach Resort offers luxurious modern accommodation in small cottages or in a large building facing directly onto a beach that stretches 1.5km.

This attractive resort has been carefully and tastefully laid out in order to make the most of its beautiful surroundings. In addition to swimming at the beach or in the pool, visitors can play golf or tennis or go fishing. The bar, which offers a magnificent view of the ocean, is particularly pleasant.

Liverpool

Lanes Privateer Inn
$$ bkfst incl.
ℜ, ≡
27 rooms
27 Bristol Ave., B0T 1K0
☎*354-3456 or*
800-794-3332
⇌*354-7220*
www.lanesprivateerinn.com
Lanes Privateer Inn offers clean, modestly decorated rooms at reasonable rates. It is well located alongside the Mersey River, on the shore oppo-

site the centre of town. This is one of the least expensive places to stay in the area.

Bridgewater

Auberge Wandlyn Inn
$$$
ℜ, ≈, △, ≡, 🐎
70 rooms
50 North St., B4V 2V6
☎*543-7131 or*
800-561-0000
⇌*543-7170*
www.wandlyninns.com
Bridgewater has several modern motels, including the Auberge Wandlyn Inn, whose rooms have little charm but are clean and well laid-out. The Wandlyn Inn, like other establishments in Bridgewater, has the advantage of being a only half-hour drive from Lunenburg, where the choice of accommodations is sometimes limited during the summer.

Lunenburg

1826 Maplebird House B&B
$$ bkfst incl.
≈, pb/sb
4 rooms
36 Pelham St., B0J 2C0
☎/⇌*634-3863*
☎*888-395-3863*
www.maplebirdhouse.ca
Built more than 150 years ago, this home witnessed the first years of Lunenburg's history. All these years left their mark on the house, so it was completely renovated to restore some of its original charm. It now exudes the atmosphere of a bygone era and offers comfortable accommodation.

Its many amenities include a pool in the garden as well as a veranda facing the harbour.

Hillcroft Cafe & Guest House
$$ bkfst incl.
ℜ, sb
3 rooms
53 Montague St., B0J 2C0
☎/⇌*634-8031*
Hillcroft, which is also home to a restaurant, is a pretty little house dating from the 1850s. The establishment offers three decent rooms with sloping ceilings and shared bathrooms.

Brigantine Inn
$$ bkfst incl.
ℜ
7 rooms
82 Montague St., B0J 2C0
☎*634-3300 or*
800-360-1181
www.brigantineinn.com
The Brigantine Inn is advantageously located facing the port. Most of the spotless, attractively decorated rooms feature large windows and balconies with splendid views.

🦞 Mariner King Inn
$$ bkfst incl.
5 rooms
15 King St., B0J 2C0
☎*634-8509 or*
800-565-8509
www.marinerking.com
A visit to Lunenburg offers an opportunity to discover the old-fashioned charm of the town's numerous 19th-century homes, many of which have been converted into pleasant inns. One good, relatively inexpensive option is the Mariner King Inn, a lovely Victorian house built around 1825. The decor remains quite typical of

that era, when tastes leaned towards heavily furnished rooms. In the evening, guests can enjoy a delicious meal in the dining room.

Arbor View Inn
$$ bkfst incl.
ℜ
6 rooms
216 Dufferin, B0J 2C0
☎/⇆634-3658
☎800-890-6650
www.arborviewinn.ns.ca

The magnificent view on the harbour distinguishes this establishment from the others in town. Situated on a hill close to the centre of town, it enjoys a peaceful location and a large, lovely, well-tended garden. The interior decor is also attractive: each room has beautiful antiques, wallpaper, paintings and a cozy ambiance. There's also one other draw: it offers some of the best cuisine in the region (see p 178).

Boscawen Inn
$$ bkfst incl.
ℜ
20 rooms
Mar to Dec
150 Cumberland, B0J 2C0
☎634-3325 or
800-354-5009
⇆634-9293
www.boscawen.ca

A superb Victorian house dating from 1888, the Boscawen Inn lies in the heart of Lunenburg, on the side of the hill overlooking the port. The location is spectacular, and a pleasant terrace offers an unimpeded view of the town's historic section. Guests can also relax in one of three sitting rooms, which, like all the other rooms in the house, are adorned with period furniture.

Pelham House B&B
$$ bkfst incl.
4 rooms
224 Pelham St., B0J 2C0
☎634-7113 or
800-508-0446
⇆634-7114
www.pelhamhouse.ca

For those who appreciate impeccably run B&Bs, Pelham House is the place to stay. The four bedrooms are creatively decorated and offer some little extras (one of them has access to a veranda that faces the harbour). Guests are pampered here and nothing is left to chance: the breakfast is delectable, the dining room is gorgeous and the living room, where you can read or watch television, is large and cozy. However, the place is not suitable for young children.

Rum Runner Inn
$$
ℜ, ℝ
13 rooms
66 Montague St., B0J 2C0
☎634-9200 or
888-778-6786
⇆634-4822
www.rumrunnerinn.com

Located right near the Brigantine Inn (see above), the Rum Runner Inn offers similar lodgings: motel rooms with views of the port.

The Artisans Bed & Breakfast
$$-$$$ bkfst incl.
4 rooms
141 Pelhan
☎634-4935 or
866-450-9010
www.theartisans.ca

In the heart of Lunenburg's historic district and not too far from the town's main attractions is this three-storey residence that has been transformed into a lovely and welcoming bed & breakfast. The rooms on the top floor are pretty and airy and all are decorated with antiques and more modern art pieces. Each has a private bathroom. Guests also enjoy some lovely common areas.

Lamplighter Bed & Breakfast
$$-$$$ bkfst incl.
3 rooms
108 York St.
☎634-8401
⇆634-8732

The Lamplighter lies on the other side of Lunenburg, on a pretty street in a quiet neighbourhood. A short distance from the historic district, this B&B allows you to discover a less touristy side of the town. The big old house has been well renovated and you are sure to feel right at home in its comfortable private and common areas.

Daniel Rudolf House Bed & Breakfast
$$-$$$ bkfst incl.
4 rooms
325 Lincoln St.
☎634-8668 or
877-858-1883
www.rudolfhouse.ns.ca

Set in a gaily-painted old house, the Daniel Rudolf House Bed & Breakfast has four large, pleasant and well-furnished rooms, some of which can accommodate families. The B&B is named for the house's most famous owner, Daniel Rudolf, who was once mayor of Lunenburg.

Lunenburg Inn
$$-$$$$ bkfst incl.
⊛
7 rooms
26 Dufferin St.
**☎634-3963 or
800-565-3963**
⇌634-9419
www.lunenburginn.com
This inn is without question one of the most pleasant places to stay in Lunenburg. Located in a sumptuous Victorian house on the edge of the city's historic district, the Lunenburg Inn offers quality accommodations. Guests enjoy several beautiful common areas as well as two covered verandas. The five rooms are comfortable and modern, as are the suites which feature whirlpool baths. Come morning, breakfast is always copious and tasty. The owner Dan is passionate about Lunenburg's history and likes to regale visitors with its stories.

1775 Solomon House Bed and Breakfast
$$$ bkfst incl.
ʒ
3 rooms
69 Townsend St.
☎634-3477
⇌634-3298
This lovely house dates from around 1775 and is located away from, but still within walking distance of, Lunenburg's touristy area. The place oozes charm, with its creaky wood floors and its ambiance which hearkens back to Lunenburg's early days. The rooms are comfortable and elegant.

Mahone Bay

Ocean Trail Retreat
$$
cottages $700/week
≈, K, ʒ
17 rooms, 2 cottages, 1 penthouse
Apr to Nov
RR1, B0J 2E0
**☎624-8824 or
888-624-8824**
⇌624-8899
www.oceantrailretreat. com
The recently built Ocean Trail Retreat presents different accommodation options to meet the varying needs of travellers: guest rooms, a penthouse and cottages. All of them have modern, but rather drab interiors. Nevertheless, they offer several advantages, such as kitchenettes in the cottages and balconies with barbecues.

Fisherman's Daughter Bed & Breakfast
$$$ bkfst incl.
4 rooms
97 Edgewater St.
☎634-0483
www.fishermans-daughter.com
This lovely historic house, built in the 1840s, boasts a superb location overlooking Mahone Bay and nextto three picturesque churches. Its four rooms, each with its own private bathroom, are cosily equipped. This is a peaceful and truly pleasant spot.

Manse at Mahone Bay Country Inn
$$$ bkfst incl.
4 rooms
88 Orchard St., B0J 2E0
☎624-1121
⇌624-1182
This magnificent inn stands on a hillside just off the main road, behind the three churches of Mahone Bay. This house was originally the residence of the United Church pastor. The Manse at Mahone Bay Country Inn offers four superb rooms, all of them decorated and furnished with flawless taste. The common rooms, including a living room with a fireplace, are all equally ravishing and offer breathtaking views of the bay. The guest rooms, each of which has a private bathroom, are located in the main building and in the adjoining carriage house; one of them has a pleasant balcony. In Mahone Bay, more charming lodgings than these are hard to find indeed!

Amber Rose Inn
$$$ bkfst incl.
ℝ
3 rooms
319 W. Main St., B0J 2E0
☎624-2060
⇌624-1060
www.amberroseinn.com
Built as a general store in 1875, the Amber Rose Inn is now a well-kept inn, adorned with antique furniture that gives it an old-world charm. Guests have access to a living room where they can relax and read a book.

Chester

Windjammer Motel
$$
ℜ
18 rooms
Hwy. 3, B0J 1J0
☎275-3567
Chester has always been a favourite with wealthy families. However, the relatively low prices of the rooms at the Windjammer

Motel help make the local tourist industry a bit more diversified. The rooms are fairly standard for this type of accommodation. The Windjammer lies at the entrance to town on Highway 3, on the way in from Mahone Bay.

🏠 Mecklenburgh Inn
$$$ bkfst incl.
ℜ, pb/sb
4 rooms
Jun to Oct
78 Queen St., B0J 1J0
☎275-4638
www.mecklenburghinn.ca
A charming residence built at the end of the 19th century, the Mecklenburgh Inn has adorable rooms, a terrace and a charming, relaxing sitting room. The dining room is open in the evening.

Haddon Hall Inn
$$$$$
ℜ, ≈, ≡, ⊛, ℑ, ℝ
11 rooms
Apr to Oct
67 Haddon Hill Rd., B0J 1J0
☎275-3577
⊷275-5159
www.haddonhallinn.com
Chester is home to numerous excellent hotel establishments. The Haddon Hall Inn is slightly set back from the centre of town and perched on a hill. Built in 1905, this magnificent house belonged to a number of important personalities in the province's history, before being transformed into an inn a few years ago. Nothing was overlooked in the process of making Haddon Hall the most luxurious hotel in the area: each of its uniquely decorated rooms is splendid; exquisite cuisine is served in its elegant, ground-floor dining room;

a lounge area has been set up around a pleasant swimming pool and the grounds are resplendent with flowers, just to mention a few examples.

Blandford

🏠 Century House B&B
$$ bkfst incl.
3 rooms
Apr to Oct
5206 Hwy. 329, B0J 1C0
☎228-2041 or
888-680-8808
⊷228-2827
Located on the road between Chester and Peggy's Cove, this charming B&B is nestled by the sea in a 19th-century home. The lovely Century House B&B is adorned with works by local artists—a great way to get to know the regional art. Guests receive royal treatment here, with well-kept rooms and a courteous welcome.

Hubbards

🏠 Dauphinee Inn
$$$ bkfst incl.
ℜ, ⊛
May to Oct
6 rooms
167 Shore Club Rd., B0J 1T0
☎857-1790 or
800-567-1790
⊷857-9555
www.duaphineeinn.com
Built high up on the shores of Hubbards' Cove, the Dauphinee Inn is an extremely peaceful place that offers an opportunity to relax in an enchanting setting. Each room has a wide balcony where guests can sit comfortably and gaze at the boats sailing in and out of the bay. Equipped with a

whirlpool, the suites, located on the top floor, are particularly beautiful. In the evening, guests can savour excellent cuisine in the dining room or on the terrace, which is very pleasant at sunset.

Restaurants

West Pubnico

Red Cap Restaurant
$-$$
☎762-2112
Travelling through the Acadian villages of this part of the province, the urge is strong to stop a spell and chat with the area's friendly residents. Lunch at the Red Cap presents an excellent opportunity for just such an encounter. This unpretentious restaurant proposes a menu that includes a few Acadian dishes, regional specialties and affordable seafood dishes.

Shelburne

Loyalist Inn
$-$$
160 Water St.
☎975-2343
For family-style cuisine with a Maritime flavour, head to the Loyalist Inn, which, in spite of its nondescript dining room, features a good menu. The food is simple—seafood chowders, lobster rolls, poached fish and all sorts of other dishes, especially meat and chicken. This is a good

place to enjoy a satisfying meal with the family.

Sea Dog Saloon
$-$$
1 Dock St.
☎875-2862
The Sea Dog Saloon's menu may not be original, but the food is good. Its main attractions though are its late closing time and the beautiful view of the seafront that can be enjoyed from here.

Charlotte Lane Cafe
$$
13 Charlotte Ln.
☎875-3314
The very charming Charlotte Lane Cafe prepares original, refreshing cuisine that includes such diverse items as Gorgonzola spaghetti, filet of Atlantic salmon, Camembert chicken, cutlets in port, vegetable curry, in addition to the 20 or so other delicious, always beautifully presented dishes. The appetizers are just as mouth-watering. Behind the establishment there is a small patio with just a few tables, which, in good weather, is the most delightful spot in all of Shelburne.

Nellie Bly's Cafe
$$-$$$
149 Water St.
☎875-1220
Crowds of locals meet at Nelly Bly's, a simple spot decorated with all manner of seagoing paraphernalia. The menu is fairly typical of this type of establishment and includes various fish and seafood dishes as well as meat and chicken. A good choice of desserts, including home-made pies, rounds out the offerings.

LaHave

LaHave Bakery
$
If you happen to be passing through LaHave, take the time to stop in at this traditional bakery. The smell of fresh-baked bread fills the air, and the mismatched chairs and tables do just fine for savouring a sandwich or pizza.

Summerville Beach

Quarterdeck Beachside Villas & Grill
$$
Rte. 3, Exit 20 off of Hwy. 103
☎683-2998
The Quarterdeck Beachside Villas & Grill, located almost right on Summerville Beach, is an excellent spot for fish and seafood. The restaurant, whose large rear deck stands on piles, looks out on the ocean. It is particularly pleasant to sit outside for breakfast. In the evening, guests can eat either on the deck or in the warm, inviting dining room. The food is succulent and the service is friendly and attentive. The Quarterdeck also rents out rooms and cottages that look out onto the beach (see p 172).

Lunenburg

Historic Grounds Coffee House
$
100 Montague St.
☎634-9995
For a muffin or a sandwich, a quick stop at this little café and its patio overlooking the docks will hit the

spot. This modest-looking establishment serves good cappuccino, espresso and café au lait, as well as a variety of teas.

Knot Pub
$
4 Dufferin St.
☎634-3334
A traditional pub, the Knot Pub has darts, a selection of beer and a menu that offers typical fare, such as hamburgers, steak, fried fish and chicken wings–and a friendly, unpretentious ambiance to boot.

Laughing Whale Cafe
$-$$
263 Lincoln St.
☎640-2233
It is easy to while away a whole afternoon in this small and popular café-bistro, whose owners left Montréal some time ago. With its big windows and walls adorned with the work of local artists, it is an inviting space. The menu lists a fine variety of dishes: soups, salads, pasta, pizzas, meat and seafood, all prepared with originality. This café also serves breakfast.

Magnolia's Grill
$-$$
128 Montague St.
☎634-3287
With walls covered in photographs from different eras, high booths and bouquets of fresh flowers adorning its tables, this restaurant is very attractive indeed. Simple but delicious cuisine, perfect for lunch, is served here. The menu revolves around excellent soups, sandwiches and salads, as well as a few more elaborate dishes. The fish cake, a

local recipe, is one of the better selections. Desserts, black and herbal teas, and a nice variety of coffees complete the menu.

Boscawen Inn
$$
150 Cumberland St.
☎*634-3325*
Lunenburg boasts a magnificent location overlooking a natural harbour. The **Boscawen Inn** (see p 174), a Victorian house standing on the side of a hill, is a good place to appreciate the natural beauty of the surroundings and the harmony of the local architecture. The dining room menu consists mainly of excellent fish and seafood dishes.

Grand Banker Seafood Grill
$$
82 Montague St.
☎*634-3300*
On some evenings it can be difficult to find a free table at the Grand Banker Seafood Grill. It has become this popular thanks to its location and its very inviting dining room. The menu is composed mainly of simple, well-prepared dishes, including grilled scallops or shrimp, crab cakes, seafood, pasta dishes and steaks. There is a small patio.

Fleur de Sel
$$-$$$
53 Montague St.
☎*640-2121*
Fleur de Sel is run by a young couple from Halifax who purchased this lovely house and converted it into a restaurant a few years ago. The dining room décor and furnishings are refined, elegant

and inviting. One of the key reasons behind the success of this restaurant is the freshness of the ingredients, so much so that the menu changes with the seasons and according to the availability of these ingredients. As of the summer of 2005, Fleur de Sel will also have two rooms for rent on the second floor.

The Old Fish Factory
$$-$$$
68 Bluenose Dr.
☎*634-3333*
This restaurant is part of the Fisheries Museum, and without question, the fish and seafood make its reputation. The reasonable prices are another big drawing card, as is the beautiful view over the docks, probably one of the best in Lunenburg. The dining room, with its big picture windows and high ceilings, is pleasant. This is a good choice for families. The Old Fish Factory also serves its own beer, Ice House Ale.

⚓ Arbor View Inn
$$$
216 Dufferin St.
☎*634-3658*
Outside of town, but with a beautiful view of the harbour, the Arbor View Inn will delight those who enjoy a good meal in a peaceful setting. Although you have to walk a ways from town to get there, it's well worth the trip. The artistically inspired original dishes–including steamed fillet of salmon in a banana leaf, fresh seafood linguini with curry sauce and steak with Cape Breton Island chanterelle mushrooms–are all delicious.

Mahone Bay

The Cheesecake Gallery
$-$$
533 Main St.
☎*624-0579*
The countless works of local artists adorning the walls are a bit of a surprise at this engaging little café. The menu is simple and includes many local dishes. Of course, the selection of desserts and cakes is superb. In good weather, you can enjoy the outdoor seating.

Innlet Cafe Seafood House & Grill
$$
east end of the bay, 249 Edgewater St.
☎*624-6363*
This pleasant, pretty restaurant is equipped with a small terrace and presents an astonishing variety of meat, poultry, seafood and fish dishes. Some lighter meals such as quiches, pasta, salads and sandwiches, also figure on the menu and are just right for lunch.

⚓ Mimi's Ocean Grill
$$-$$$
662 Main St.
☎*624-1342*
A small restaurant with a very attractive interior, Mimi's is a top choice for either lunch or dinner. Lamb chops, excellent grilled fish, Cajun shrimp and sauteed scallops are some of the dishes on the evening menu. At lunchtime, tasty light meals may be savoured for under $10. The menu also lists a variety of desserts, including Italian ices, lemon pie and cheesecake.

Chester

Foc'sle
$
42 Queen St., corner of Pleasant St.
A well-known local institution, Foc'sle serves family-style cuisine that is hardly original, but nonetheless satisfying and inexpensive. Since this is one of the oldest taverns in Nova Scotia, people also come here to enjoy a night out.

The Rope Loft
$$
36 Water St.
☎*275-3430*
With its interior decked out like a warm Irish pub and its terrace facing the marina, this restaurant has everything going for it, morning, noon and night, fair weather or foul. Its menu is reliable, although not especially original. It mainly features fish and seafood dishes, steak and poultry, all of it well prepared.

Entertainment

Chester

Chester Playhouse
about $20
22 Pleasant St.
☎*275-3933 or*
800-363-7529
www.chesterplayhouse.ns.ca
During July and August, Chester Playhouse presents plays and concerts in the evening.

Shopping

Shelburne

Charlotte Lane Cafe & Craft
13 Charlotte Ln.
☎*875-3314*
Not only is this one of the best places to eat in town, but Charlotte Lane Cafe also sells a variety of beautiful crafts created by Nova Scotian artists.

Lunenburg

Houston North Gallery
110 Montague St.
☎*634-8869*
Visitors interested in First Nations and Inuit art should make sure to stop in at the Houston North Gallery, which displays a remarkable assortment of sculptures and paintings.

Bluenose II Company Store
121 Bluenose Dr.
☎*634-1963*
The famous *Bluenose* is honoured at the Bluenose II Company Store. Those looking for a memento of this schooner will have an endless selection to choose from. The profits go to a good cause: keeping the *Bluenose II* in operation.

Carriage House Gallery
290 Lincoln St.
☎*634-4010*
The Carriage House Gallery exhibits and sells works by a variety of Nova Scotian artists.

Chester

The Warp & Woof Gifts & Gallery
81 Water St.
☎*275-4795*
The Warp & Woof Gifts & Gallery sells carvings, pottery, woolen sweaters and other beautiful crafts made by Maritime artists.

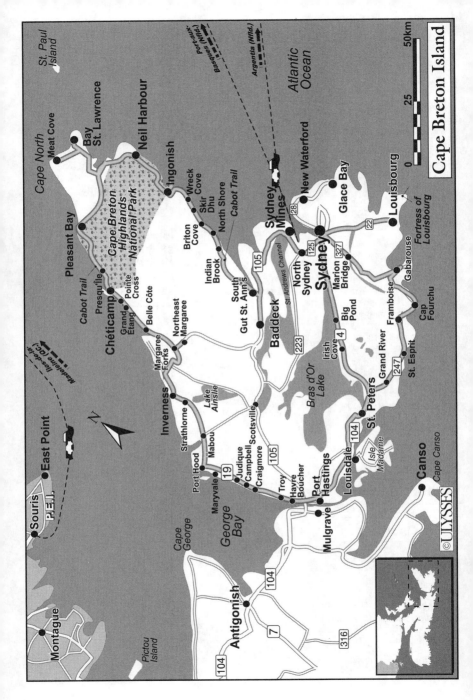

Cape Breton Island

The charming villages,

untouched forests and rugged cliffs of Cape Breton Island lie in the northeastern part of nova Scotia. The meeting of land and sea will take your breath away.

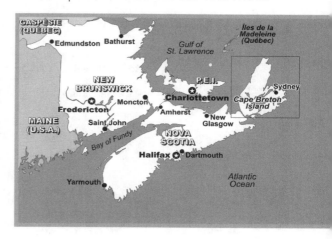

The island, it seems, was discovered in 1497 by John Cabot, and colonized quite early by the French, who settled here in the 17th century. They called the island "Île Royale." In 1713, Acadia was ceded to Great Britain under the Treaty of Utrecht. France compensated for this loss by accelerating the development of Île Royale, most notably by building the Fortress of Louisbourg in 1719. Acadian villages therefore also sprang up along the north shore of Île Royale.

The island did not remain under French rule, however, and finally ended up in the hands of the English in 1758. Louisbourg was destroyed two years later, in 1760. Since rebuilt, the fortress ranks among the most impressive historic sites in eastern Canada.

In addition to its vivid history, Cape Breton boasts marvellous stretches of wilderness, to the delight of countless nature lovers each year. Cape Breton Highlands National Park is a perfect example, with its hiking trails and spectacular views.

The Cabot Trail is the best way to enjoy and appreciate the beauty of Cape Breton Island. This steep, winding road makes a full circle around the island, passing through dense forests and charm-

ing villages along the way. No visit to Nova Scotia would be complete without seeing Cape Breton Island.

Finding Your Way Around

This tour of **Cape Breton Island** ★ ★ ★ covers all of the island.

By Plane

Yarmouth Airport
☎ *(902) 742-6484*
🖷 *(902) 742-6881*

The city of Yarmouth is located on Cape Breton Island. Once there, you can either goto Sydney, Louisbourg or near Baddeck, which marks the beginning of the Cabot Trail.

By Car

The quickest way to get to Cape Breton Island from Halifax is via Highway 102, and then the Trans-Canada Highway to Port Hastings. The island is also accessible via Highway 7, which follows the Atlantic Ocean.

The route passes through peaceful rural communities and a few fishing ports, such as Musquodoboit Harbour, with its superb stretches of sand at **Martinique Beach**.

By Bus

From Halifax, visitors can take the bus as far as Sydney. It is worth noting, however, that no bus goes all the way around the island (aside from private tour buses). There is no way to get around easily, except in Sydney, so it is best either to rent a car or rely on your own resources, such as hitchhiking or, if you are fit, cycling.

Transit Cap Breton
around Sydney
☎*(902) 539-8124*

By Ferry

Caribou (N.S.) to Wood Islands (P.E.I.)

Northumberland Ferry
PO Box 634, Charlottetown, P.E.I., C1A 7L3
☎*(902) 566-3838 or 800-565-0201 (N.S. or P.E.I.)*
Departures: once daily, from May to December.

Port-aux-Basques (Nfld.) to North Sydney (N.S.)

Marine Atlantic
Box 355 Purvers St.
North Sydney, B2A 3V2
☎*800-341-7981*
Departures: once daily year-round.

Practical Information

Area code: *902*

Tourist Information

By Mail

Destination Cape Breton Association
PO Box 1448, Sydney, B1P 6R7
☎*563-4636*
⇄*564-5422*
www.cbisland.com

On Site

Port Hastings
on the way onto the island, along the Canso Causeway
☎*625-4201*
Mar to mid-Dec

There are also tourist information booths in Louisbourg, Baddeck and Margaree Forks.

Exploring

Sherbrooke

A handful of quaint little houses make up this tiny hamlet of about 400 people. What attracts most travellers, however, is the fishing in St. Mary's River, which flows nearby. Take time as well to visit **Sherbrooke Village** *($9; early Jun to mid-Oct, every day 9:30am to 5:30pm; ☎522-2400, ⇄522-2974)*, a reconstruction of an 1860-1880 village. Guides in period costumes lead tours of the 30 buildings.

Continue on Hwy. 211, then Hwy. 316 until it intersects with Hwy. 16. Continue towards Canso.

Canso

The post of Canso was established on this site in 1605 because it was protected from strong ocean currents by Grassy Island, and because of its location at the entrance to Chedabucto Bay. The town is a departure point for visits to the **Grassy Island National Historic Site** *(free admission, donations are welcome; Jun to mid-Sep; free ferry leaves at 11am, second departure in Jul and Aug at 2pm; 0.5km from Canso pier, PO Box 159, Baddeck, B0E 1B0, ☎295-2069).*

An integral part of the fishing industry during the 18th century, the Canso region was coveted by many and was the object of dispute between the English and the French. At the Canso **Visitor information Centre** *(Jun to mid-Sep, every day 10am to 6pm; on the pier near Union St.,* ☎*366-2170),* you can view a short film on the colonization of Grassy Island and its eventual destruction in 1744. Visitors can then take a boat to the island, where an interpretive trail leads to some interesting attractions.

Get back onto the Trans-Canada Highway via Hwy. 16.

Port Hastings

The small town of Port Hastings is the gateway to Cape Breton Island. Although not a particularly pretty town, it is a major crossroads for travellers, with highways leading to both Baddeck and Sydney.

Port Hastings does offer many practical facilities, including restaurants, service stations and most importantly, a tourist information office (see p 182).

Head towards Sydney via Hwy. 4. At Louisdale, you can take Hwy. 320 to get to Isle Madame.

Isle Madame

This tranquil peninsula covers an area of 42.5km^2 and has several pleasant picnic areas. Isle Madame was settled by the Acadians and retains a significant French-speaking community.

From Isle Madame, go back to Hwy. 4 and continue towards Sydney.

St. Peters

St. Peters is situated on the narrow strip of land that separates the Atlantic Ocean from Bras d'Or Lake. Colonists settled here in 1630 and built Fort Saint-Pierre. About 20 years later, Nicolas Denys took over the fort and turned it into a trading and fishing post. To learn more about this French pioneer, visit the **Nicolas Denys Museum** *($0.50; Jun to Sep, every day 9am to 5pm; 46 Denys St.,* ☎*535-2379).*

The trading post developed gradually, but really took off 140 years ago, when a canal was dug between Bras d'Or Lake and the ocean to provide passage for boats. Every year, from the park located on either side of the canal, many ships can be observed passing through the canal. An outdoor display shows how the locks work.

Bras d'Or Lake

Bras d'Or Lake is an inland sea with 960km of shoreline. It thus occupies a good part of the island, dividing it into two areas, the Cape Breton Lowlands and Highlands. This vast salt-water expanse attracts many animal species, including the magnificent bald eagle. For those who like to fish, trout and salmon abound in the lake and its many channels (St. Andrews Channel, St. Patrick Channel).

Aboriginal peoples have long been attracted to the shores of this lake with its abundance of fish. The Mi'kmaqs established themselves here permanently. Their presence remains constant to this day on four reserves: Whycocomagh, Eskasoni, Wagmatcook and Chapel Island. Besides the reserves, there are several villages around the lake. The **Bras d'Or Scenic Drive** ★ *(follow the signs marked with a bald eagle)* goes all the way around the lake.

From St. Peters to Sydney

The fastest way to Sydney is along Hwy. 4.

The road to Sydney passes through small towns along the shores of Bras d'Or Lake, as well as through some Aboriginal reserves.

Another option from St. Peters is to take Hwy. 247 along the ocean. At Marion Bridge, take Hwy. 327 to Sydney.

This road winds along the coast and passes through several charming fishing villages, including L'Archevêque. Unfortunately, the road is in poor condition.

Sydney

With a population of 25,000, Sydney is the largest town in the area. J.F.W. DesBarres, a Loyalist from the United States, founded the town in 1785. A few years later, Scottish immigrants settled here. Sydney grew quickly at the beginning of the 20th century, when coal mining industries were established here. Coal mining is still Sydney's primary industry. The town has all the necessary services to accommodate visitors, and is a good place to stop for a rest before going on to Louisbourg. Otherwise, Sydney offers few attractions.

Cossit House Museum *($2; Jun to mid-Oct, Mon-Sat 9:30am to 5:30pm, Sun 1pm to 5:30pm; 75 Charlotte St., ☎539-7973)* is located in the oldest house in town. Restored and decorated with period furniture, it looks just as it did long ago. Guides dressed in period costumes lead tours through the house and are available to answer any questions.

Nearby is the **Jost Heritage House** *(Jun to Oct, Mon-Sat 9:30am to 5:30pm; 54 Charlotte St., ☎539-0366)*, which was the home of a rich merchant.

To find out more about Sydney's history, visit the **St. Patrick's Church Museum** *(87 Esplanade, ☎562-8237)*. Built in 1828, this Catholic church is the oldest in Cape Breton. It features an exhibit on the town's past.

Take Hwy. 22 to Louisbourg.

Louisbourg

Visitors are drawn to Louisbourg by the nearby Fortress of Louisbourg, which is the area's main attraction. Many of the local businesses, including hotels, motels and restaurants, are geared towards tourists. It takes a full day to see the fortress; the town itself offers few attractions.

The **Fortress of Louisbourg National Historic Site ★ ★ ★** *($13.50; Jul and Aug, 9am to 6pm; Jun and Sep, 9:30am to 5pm; May and Oct by appointment; ☎773-2280)* was strategically built at the water's edge, from where enemy ships could be seen and attacks could be countered.

The fortress was built outside of the town itself and, today, is removed from all modern development, making it easier to recreate the atmosphere of the fledgling French colony back in 1744. Furthermore, cars are not permitted near the fortress; a bus provides transportation to the site.

During the 18th century, France and England fought over territory in America. The French lost Acadia, which then became Nova Scotia. It was during this turbulent period in 1719 that French authorities decided to build a fortified city on Île Royale and began constructing the Fortress of Louisbourg. As the most complex system of fortifications in New France, this undertaking presented some major challenges.

Besides being a military stronghold, Louisbourg was also a fishing port and commercial centre. Within a short time, its population

Fortress of Louisbourg

had grown to 2,000 inhabitants. Everything was designed to enable colonists and soldiers to adjust to their new environment, where houses and garrisons were erected. Nevertheless, conditions were rough, and colonists had some difficulty adapting. Despite these hardships, the colony grew and local business flourished.

The French presence on Île Royale was a thorn in the side of the British colonies stationed further south. In 1744, when war was declared in Europe between France and England, the Louisbourg garrison attacked the British villages in the area. As a result, they took over a British outpost. This situation incensed the British in New England, provoking William Shirley, then governor of Massachusetts, to send his troops to attack the French bastion in 1745.

Four thousand New England soldiers ventured an attack on the supposedly impenetrable Fortress of Louisbourg. Despite their reputation, the French troops were underequipped and poorly organized. They had never even imagined such an attack possible, and could not defend themselves. After a six-week long siege, the Louisbourg authorities surrendered to the British troops.

A few years later, in 1748, Louisbourg was returned to France when the two nations signed a peace treaty. Life carried on in the fortress, and within a

year, Louisbourg was as active as before. This renewed prosperity was short-lived, however, since the fortress was conquered once and for all by British troops in 1758, ending the French presence in the area.

Hardly 10 years after this conquest, the fortress was left to ruin, and was only rebuilt much later. Today, almost one quarter of the fortress has been restored and, during the summer, people wearing period dress bring it back to life, recreating the Louisbourg of long ago. There are soldiers, a baker and a fisherman with his family. The scene is most convincing, and a stroll down the streets of this old French fortress is a fascinating experience.

To get to Glace Bay, return to Sydney, and take Hwy. 4 from there.

Glace Bay

Glace Bay lies on the Atlantic coast and is rich in coal, which is the basis of Glace Bay's economy. The town's name is of French origin and refers to the pieces of ice (*glace*) that can be seen drifting along the coast. This small town, which has a population of about 20,000, is home to two interesting attractions.

Guglielmo Marconi (1874-1937) became famous for proving that it was possible to send messages using a wireless telegraph. At the age of 22, Marconi had already developed a wireless station from which

messages could be sent over a short distance. In 1902, he sent the first trans-Atlantic message from his transmitting station at Table Head. At the **Marconi National Historic Site** ★ *(free admission; Jun to mid-Sep, every day 10am to 6pm; Timmerman St., ☎295-2069)* visitors can learn about Marconi's discoveries and see his work table, as well as the radio station from which the first message was sent.

The Glace Bay area's mining industry dates back many years. As long ago as 1790, French soldiers from Louisbourg were already coming to Port Morien for coal. The industry really took off at the beginning of the 20th century when mines were dug here, most importantly in New Waterford. Today, Glace Bay produces more coal than any other town in eastern Canada.

To learn more about this industry, visit the **Miner's Museum** ★★ *($8; Jun to early Sep, every day 10am to 6pm, Tue until 7pm; rest of the year, Mon-Fri 9am to 4pm; 42 Birkley St., ☎849-4522)*, which exhibits the various tools and techniques used in coal mining. There is also a re-creation of a typical mining town from the beginning of the 20th century. Finally, the most fascinating part of the museum is a guided tour of a coal mine.

Go back to Sydney via Hwy. 4. To reach Baddeck, take Rte. 125, then take the Trans-Canada (Hwy. 105).

Nova Scotia

Baddeck

Baddeck is a charming village, perfect for taking a stroll or enjoying a bite to eat on a terrace. Whether you decide to stay for a few days to enjoy its comfortable hotels and peaceful atmosphere, or simply stop for a few hours before heading off on the Cabot Trail, Baddeck offers many attractions that make it worth the detour. One fascinating sight is the summer home of inventor Alexander Graham Bell.

The **Alexander Graham Bell National Historic Site** ★★ *($5.75; Jun, every day 9am to 6pm; Jul to mid-Oct, every day 8:30am to 6pm; at the town's east exit, Chebucto St., ☎295-2069)* exhibits many of Bell's inventions, as well as the instruments he used in his research. Bell's life story is also told. Visitors will learn, for example, that after teaching sign language for many years, he created an artificial ear that recorded sounds. This experiment led to his invention of the telephone.

From Baddeck, the Cabot Trail is the only road that goes around this part of the island. Take this route north towards Ingonish.

The Cabot Trail

Dotted with picturesque little villages, the Cabot Trail follows precipitous cliffs that jut out over the

Alexander Graham Bell

Alexander Graham Bell was born in 1847 in Edinburgh, Scotland. He settled in Brantford, Ontario with his parents in 1870. From very early on, the brilliant inventor shared his father's interest in teaching sign language to the deaf. Bell's research led him to teach at the University of Boston, where he trained teachers to work with the deaf. He created an artificial ear that could record sounds, which led to his invention of the telephone in 1876. Bell became rich and famous and spent a number of years with his wife Mabel, herself deaf, at his summer home in Baddeck (Nova Scotia), where he continued to do research in various fields.

Atlantic Ocean. Leaving Baddeck, the road follows the shore before climbing up to the plateau on the north end of the island. The many lookouts along this road offer magnificent panoramic views. It's worth taking the time to stop and appreciate the beauty of the landscape, where a restless sea, steep hills and a dense forest are home to a variety of animal species.

The first village after Baddeck is tiny **South Gut St. Ann's**, home to the **Gaelic College**, an institution devoted to the survival of Gaelic culture in North America. Courses are offered on the Gaelic language, singing and bagpipe playing.

The road continues along the coast to **Ingonish Ferry**, where it begins to mount the vast plateau

that occupies the north end of the island, at an elevation of 366m. The natural scenery grows more and more spectacular as you go on.

Cape Breton Highlands National Park ★★★ begins here (see p 187).

At Cape North the road heads back south, but you can continue further north by taking the small road that leads to Meat Cove.

This road leads first to the charming fishing village of **Bay St. Lawrence** ★. Built at the water's edge, the village has little wooden houses and a picturesque port, where cormorants can be seen gliding above the waves. The road climbs along the **cliffs** ★★ and winds its way to **Meat Cove**, a perfect place to stop for a picnic and enjoy the superb view ★ over the ocean waves.

To get back on the Cabot Trail, you will have to retrace your steps.

The road continues west. From Cape North to **Pleasant Bay**, visitors can gaze at the canyon formed by the sides of the hills. The **view** ★★ here is stunning. After being on the move for a while, Pleasant Bay is a welcome and enjoyable spot to rest.

The plateau ends near **Petit Étang**. The road then heads back down and follows the Gulf of St. Lawrence to the Acadian region of Cape Breton. The landscape is surprising, as forests and steep cliffs give way to a barren plateau studded with Acadian villages. Among these is **Chéticamp**, a quiet village with simple houses and a fishing port. It is a departure point for seal- and whale-watching excursions. More villages with French names follow, including Grand Étang, Saint-Joseph-du-Moine, Cap-Lemoine and Belle-Côte.

The western part of the Cabot Trail ends at Margaree Harbour. You can continue your journey by cutting across the plateau back to Baddeck. The highlight along this route is the **Margaree Salmon Museum** *($1; mid-Jun to mid-Oct, 9am to 5pm; 60 E. Big Interval Rd.,* ☎*248-2848)* in **Northeast Margaree**. The museum displays the various implements used for salmon fishing.

To leave Cape Breton Island from Baddeck, take the Trans-Canada (Hwy. 105). You can also continue along the western coast of the island.

Ceilidh Trail

The road along the western coast of the island leads to the Ceilidh Trail. This region was settled by Scots, and vestiges of Gaelic culture still remain. More than anywhere else on Cape Breton Island, the villages along the Ceilidh Trail offer an excellent opportunity to discover the region's Scottish heritage. Gaelic music can be heard throughout this region, and a few musicians from here are now famous on the national and international music scenes. Furthermore, the warm waters here wash up against a few of the island's beautiful beaches, especially near **Mabou** ★. There are a number of modest little villages along the Gulf of St. Lawrence, but Mabou is definitely the nicest place to stay. A few kilometres past Mabou is

the **Glenora Distillery** *(mid-May to Oct;* ☎*258-2662, www.glenora distillery.com)*, which produces a single malt whisky. There is also an inn and a pub here (see p 193).

This road leads to Port Hastings, where you can get back on the Trans-Canada Hwy.

Parks

Cape Breton Highlands National Park ★★★ *(*☎*285-2691)*, created in 1936, protects 950km² of wilderness and is ideal for fans of wide-open spaces. A wide range of activities is offered throughout this park, the oldest in eastern Canada. Just about everything is available for outdoor enthusiasts: magnificent views, a forest teeming with fascinating animal life, beaches, campgrounds, 25 hiking trails and even a golf course.

Beaches

There are lovely beaches near **Mabou** and in **Trout Brook Park**, **Inverness** and **Ingonish**.

Along the Northumberland Strait, **Lavilette Beach** is a particularly noteworthy spot on the northern coast of the island. This lovely 1.5km ribbon of sand is located in the park of the same name.

Nova Scotia

Outdoor Activities

Cycling

Bike Rentals

Auberge Gisèle Country Inn
387 Shore Rd., PO Box 132
Baddeck, B0E 1B0
☎295-2849

Sea Spray Outdoor Adventures
RR2, Dingwall, B0C 1G0
☎/≈383-2732
www.cabot-trail-outdoors. com

Hiking

Visitors can explore **Cape Breton Highlands National Park** by hiking along one of its 25 trails. There is something for everyone here, from short trails that take about 20min to long excursions that lead to the top of steep hills. The tourist information centre distributes a pamphlet entitled *Walking in the Highlands*.

Bird-Watching

Cape Breton is an excellent location for bird-watching. From cormo-

The Bald Eagle
(Haliaeetus Leucocephalus)

The bald eagle, the emblem of the United States, is the only eagle found solely in North America. Bald eagles can be seen in various areas of Canada, such as on Cape Breton Island, near large stretches of water, where they draw their basic diet of fish. This imposing bird has a wingspan of up to 2.5m, a weight of up to 7kg and a lifespan of up to 40 years. It is monogamous and stays faithful to its partner until death.

rants and kingfishers to impressive bald eagles, a variety of species can be spotted near the coast, around **Bras d'Or Lake** and in **Cape Breton Highlands National Park**.

It is also possible to take a trip to the coast of Bird Island, where you can see the Atlantic puffin. These small marine birds come here to nest between May and August. Some excursions offer a chance to observe other species as well, such as the black guillemot, the razorbill and the great blue heron.

Puffin Boat Tours
departures from English-town, near Baddeck
☎929-2563

Whale-Watching

Atlantic Whale Watch
three departures daily
Ingonish Beach
☎285-2320

Whale and Seal Cruise
departures at 9am, 1pm and 6pm
Pleasant Bay
☎ *224-1316 or 888-754-5112*

Seaside Whale & Nature Cruises
three departures daily
Laurie's Motor Inn, Chéticamp
☎ *224-2400 or 800-959-4253*
www.lauries.com

Whale Cruisers
$25
three departures daily
Chéticamp
☎ *224-3376 or 800-813-3376*
www.whalecruises.com

Kayaking

The rugged coastlines of Cape Breton Island offer incredible panoramic views. Kayak trips are a particularly good way to observe the scenery from another vantage point.

Experience Kayaking
North River
☎ *567-2322*

Golf

In **Cape Breton Highlands National Park**, visitors will find the magnificent **Highland Links** *(Ingonish,* ☎ *285-2600 or 800-441-1118, www.highlandslinks golf.com)*, which ranks among Nova Scotia's most spectacular golf courses.

Deep-Sea Fishing

Various outfits organize deep-sea fishing expeditions. Participants are provided with all necessary equipment and instruction.

Whale Island
$25
Ingonish
☎ *285-2338 or 800-565-3808*
⇄ *285-2338*

Deep-Sea Fishing Chéticamp
$25
PO Box 221, Chéticamp, B0E 1H0
☎ *224-3606*

Accommodations

Liscomb Mills

Liscombe Lodge
$$$$
ℜ, ≈, ☺, ◠, ⊛, ✗
65 lodges and cottages
2884 Rte. 7, B0J 2A0
☎ *779-2307 or 800-665-6343*
⇄ *779-2700*
The Liscombe Lodge is a true paradise for nature

lovers, as it is located on the edge of the water, perfect for fishing and canoeing, among other activities. The area is peaceful, the rooms are comfortable, and the grounds are magnificent.

Sydney

Cambridge Suites Hotel
$$$ bkfst incl.
≈, ℜ, ◠, ☺, ≡, ✗, K
149 rooms
380 Esplanade, B1P 1B1
☎ *562-6500 or 800-565-9466*
⇄ *564-6011*
Right next door to the Delta Sydney is the Cambridge Suites Hotel, which is about as comfortable as the Delta, though more care has been taken with the decor. The rooms are actually small apartments equipped with kitchenettes. The hotel is also home to an excellent restaurant called Goody's.

Delta Sydney
$$$
≈, ℜ, ◠, ☺, ⊛, ≡, ✗, ♿
152 rooms
300 Esplanade, B1P 1A7
☎ *562-7500 or 800-268-1133*
⇄ *562-3023*
Downtown Sydney consists mainly of a few streets alongside the river, and most of the town's hotels are located here. One of these is the Delta Sydney, whose facade overlooks the Sydney River. The rooms are a bit low on charm, but thoroughly functional. As a bonus, the hotel features a great swimming pool with a slide–sure to be a hit with the children.

Louisbourg

Point of View Suites
$$$
ℜ, K
16 rooms
15 Commercial St., B1C 2J5
**☎733-2080 or
888-374-8439
*www.louisbourgpointof
view.com***
Located near the Louis-
bourg Fortress, this lovely
establishment has attrac-
tively designed modern
rooms and a warm ambi-
ance. Each room has a
kitchenette and a balcony.
There is also a restaurant
that serves excellent
dishes, such as snow crab
(in season). As its name
suggests, this place offers a
magnificent view of the
sea.

Baddeck

Silver Dart Lodge
$$
≈, ℜ, ≡, 🐾, K
84 rooms
Exit 8 off Hwy. 205, B0E 1B0
**☎295-2340 or
888-662-7484
⇄295-2484**

and

MacNeil House
$$$$
≡, K, ℑ
6 rooms
These two establishments
share a magnificent park
covering about 38ha that
looks out onto beautiful
Bras d'Or Lake. Given the
exquisitely peaceful setting,
this is the perfect place to
relax. The Silver Dart has
pretty, comfortable rooms
and several cottages, some
with fireplaces, while
McNeil house offers luxu-
rious rooms, some of

which also feature fire-
places.

🦞 Duffus House
$$$ bkfst incl.
7 rooms
108 Water St., B0E 1B0
☎295-2172
Visitors will enjoy the
particularly relaxing atmo-
sphere at one of a handful
of charming inns along the
waterfront, including
Duffus House, one of the
oldest residences in town.
Built in the 19th century, it
is nicely furnished with
antiques and boasts a
lovely garden.

Auberge Gisele's Country Inn
$$$
ℜ, ⊛, ≈, △, ≡
early May to late Oct
75 rooms
387 Shore Rd., B0E 1B0
**☎295-2849 or
800-304-0466
⇄295-2033
*www.giseles.com***
On the shores of Bras
d'Or Lake, Auberge
Gisele's Country Inn offers
rooms with a pleasant
view, and is a good place
to keep in mind. Upon
arrival, visitors will be
enchanted by the pine-
bordered lane that leads
up to this lovely residence,
whose rooms are all at-
tractively decorated. There
are also a few modern
rooms in a motel-style
annex.

Telegraph House
$$$
ℜ
43 rooms
205 Chebucto St., Exit 9 off Rte.
205, B0E 1B0
**☎295-1100 or
888-263-9840**
The Telegraph House is a
fine-looking Victorian
house set in the heart of

town. Its 43 rooms, which
have a slightly old-fash-
ioned charm about them,
are pleasant and comfort-
able.

Inverary Resort
$$$
ℜ, ≈, △, ≡, ℑ
138 rooms
Exit 8 off Hwy. 105, B0E 1B0
**☎295-3500 or
800-565-5660
⇄295-3527
*www.inveraryresort.com***
At the cozy Inverary Re-
sort, guests can stay in
either the main building or
in charming little wooden
cottages. The decor and
the vast grounds give this
place a rustic feel well-
suited to the Nova Scotian
countryside.

Ingonish Beach

There are several camp-
grounds in **Cape Breton
Highlands National Park**
(no reservations; ☎285-
2329 or 888-773-8888).
Average rates are about
$14 for a tent and $20 for
a trailer.

Castle Rock Inn
$$
ℜ
15 rooms
RR1, B0C 1L0
**☎285-2700 or
888-884-7625
⇄285-2525**
This beautiful Georgian
home, which was con-
verted into an inn, is ideally
located with an excellent
view of the surrounding
area. The place is very
peaceful and is ideal for
nature lovers. The rooms
are attractive, although the
decor is rather drab.
Guests can relax on a
pretty terrace.

Ingonish Chalets
$$ room
$$$ cottage
K, 🐾, ♿
7 cottages, 5 rooms
PO Box 196, B0C 1L0
☎*285-2008 or*
888-505-0552
This little establishment, which is composed of cottages and motel rooms, is right near one of the most beautiful beaches on this part of the island. The cottages and the rooms are comfortable, clean and welcoming.

Keltic Lodge
$$$-$$$$
≈, K, ℜ, ℑ, 🐾, ♿
92 rooms
Jun to Oct and Jan to Mar
Middle Head Peninsula, B0C 1L0
☎*285-2880 or*
800-565-0444
⇄*285-2859*
The Keltic Lodge is very well located alongside a cliff overlooking the sea. In a tranquil environment slightly removed from the access roads, the Keltic Lodge offers top-notch accommodation just a short distance from the Cabot Trail. The buildings are handsome and the rooms, some of which are in cottages, are both charming and comfortable. The dining room features a gourmet menu.

Dingwall

Markland Coastal Resort
$$$
K, ℜ, ≈, 🐾
25 cottages
3km from Dingwall, B0C 1G0
☎*383-2246 or 800-872-6084*
⇄*383-2092*
www.marklandresort.com
An excellent place to relax, admire the sea, walk along

the beach or depart from to explore the Cabot Trail, the Markland Coastal Resort offers comfortable accommodation in wooden cottages with a cozy interior. Each cottage has several rooms equipped with a terrace. The large, grassy space opposite the cottages leads to an untouched beach. The Markland is an ideal spot for couples or families who prefer a peaceful, secluded setting and the outdoors. The fine food served in the dining room (see p 192) hits the spot after a long day in the fresh air.

Chéticamp

Laurie's Motor Inn
$$-$$$
K, ℜ, 🐾, ⊛
61 rooms
Main St., B0E 1H0
☎*224-2400 or*
800-959-4253
⇄*224-2069*
www.lauries.com
There are several places to stay in the centre of the Acadian community of Chéticamp. One of these is Laurie's Motor Inn, a motel stretching alongside the Gulf of St. Lawrence. Although the decor is not very original, the rooms are clean and comfortable. To enjoy a satisfying meal, stop in at the motel's dining room (see p 193),

which has a very decent menu. The seafood is especially good.

L'Auberge Doucet Inn
$$$
ℜ, ♿, 🐾
11 rooms
on the way out of Chéticamp, B0E 1H0
☎*224-3438 or*
800-646-8668
⇄*224-2792*
www.aubergedoucetinn.com
L'Auberge Doucet Inn, which stands on a hill at the edge of town, rents out large, comfortable rooms. Although the front garden is somewhat disappointing, the inn boasts a lovely setting that affords beautiful views of the Gulf of St. Lawrence.

Margaree Valley

Normaway Inn
$$
ℜ, ℑ, 🐾, ⊛
28 rooms
mid-Jun to Oct
Egypt Rd., B0E 2C0
☎*248-2987 or*
800-565-9463
⇄*248-2600*
www.normaway.com
The Normaway Inn has been welcoming vacationers for over 60 years. The place has a great deal of charm, thanks to its magnificent garden which stretches across several hundred hectares, creating a pastoral atmosphere. Appropriately, the main building looks somewhat like a farmhouse. The rooms are located inside this building and in a number of cottages. Some of them include fireplaces and whirlpool baths. Guests also have access to a cozy living room.

Nova Scotia

Restaurants

Sydney

On Charlotte Street, there are a number of little snack-bars serving hamburgers and fries.

Island Mermaid
$$
Delta Sydney, 300 Esplanade
☎562-7500
The Island Mermaid has a very decent menu featuring a fair number of fish dishes. With its large picture windows looking out onto the water, the place boasts a lovely view. Breakfast served.

Joe's Warehouse
$$-$$$
424 Charlotte St.
☎539-6686
Don't be turned off by the Western look of Joe's Warehouse, which happens to be a local institution. Although the decor is not exactly sophisticated and the music sounds like what you'd hear in a shopping mall, the atmosphere is still very inviting. People come to Joe's for the generous portions of delicious prime rib. Seafood is also included on the menu.

Louisbourg

At the fortress, a restaurant has been set up in one of the buildings facing the water. The food is no better than decent, but at least visitors can eat lunch without leaving the site.

Grubstake
$$
1274 Main St.
☎733-2308
Another possibility is the Grubstake, whose specialty is seafood. For those who prefer grilled meats or poultry, the menu also lists steak and chicken dishes.

Baddeck

McCurdy's
$$
Silver Dart Lodge, Shore Rd.
☎295-2340
The **Silver Dart Lodge** (see p 190) is pleasantly located on the shores of Bras d'Or Lake. Its restaurant, McCurdy's, which looks out onto this magnificent body of water, offers an unbeatable atmosphere. In addition to the view, people come here to sample tasty seafood dishes and savour Scottish cuisine.

Baddeck Lobster Suppers
$$-$$$
17 Ross St.
☎295-3307
If you are hungry for lobster, head over to Baddeck Lobster Suppers. The main dish includes lobster and unlimited seafood chowder, mussels, salad and dessert.

Ingonish Beach

Purple Thistle Dining Room
$$$-$$$$
☎285-2880
The Purple Thistle Dining Room is the restaurant at the splendid **Keltic Lodge** (see p 191). In a refined atmosphere, guests can

taste a variety of specialties, many of which are made with seafood. The hotel has another, simpler restaurant, the **Atlantic** (*$$*), which is a good place for lunch.

Ingonish Ferry

Castle Rock
$$$
RR 1
☎285-2700
The Castle Rock offers good food in a quiet, relaxing location. Its menu includes an excellent selection of delicious fish and seafood.

Cape North

Morrison's Restaurant
$-$$
☎383-2051
You can't miss Morrison's Restaurant, a wooden building located right alongside the road. Despite its modest appearance, it is one of the better family-style restaurants in the area. The food is simple (seafood chowder, beef stew, etc.) but good.

Dingwall

Markland
$$-$$$
802 Dingwall Rd.
☎383-2246
The restaurant at the **Markland Coastal Resort** (see p 191) has a pine-panelled dining room with a stylish, if not extravagant, decor. The menu is extremely interesting, and simply reading it over will whet your appetite. The offerings include grilled salmon with mousseline

sauce and grilled filet of pork with plums in a red-wine and onion sauce.

Pleasant Bay

Rusty Anchor
$$
☎224-1313
This small restaurant's deck, which faces the ocean, is a great place to be on gorgeous summer evenings. The menu includes expertly prepared fresh seafood.

Chéticamp

Harbour Restaurant & Bar
$-$$
☎224-2042
The Harbour Restaurant, which has a great view of the coast, is a good place to dine after an excursion on the Cabot Trail. The place has a friendly atmosphere and is decorated with old black-and-white photos of Chéticamp. The menu includes a variety of scrumptious dishes, such as the lobster on a Kaiser bun, the hot chicken sandwich, the fresh Atlantic salmon and the sirloin.

Laurie's
$-$$
☎224-2400
At Laurie's, visitors might be surprised to discover that the menu lists both lobster and hamburgers. This restaurant has something for everyone, in terms of both taste and budget. Guests can try such succulent dishes as the fisherman's platter, which includes lobster, crab and shrimp. The Acadian staff is as friendly as can be, amiably telling their guests to "enjoy *le repas*."

Mabou

Duncreigan Country Inn
$$$
Hwy. 19
☎945-2207
Mabou has a few good restaurants. The Duncreigan Country Inn offers several regional and international classic gourmet dishes, which are all deliciously prepared, including fresh halibut, scallops in basil cream sauce and rosemary lamb. Its pleasant dining room, which

opens onto the harbour, is accented with flowers, and, if the temperature warrants it, a cozy fire. The lunch menu offers light, healthy fare, such as salads, vegetarian dishes and sandwiches. The dining room is open year-round.

Glenville

Glenora Inn & Distillery Resort
$$$
☎258-2662
Along the road near Mabou is one of the best-known establishments on Cape Breton Island, the Glenora Inn, which is both an inn and a distillery that makes pure malt whiskey. Here you can enjoy seafood chowder, trout, salmon or lamb, while listening to Celtic music in the dining room.

Shopping

Baddeck

In the centre of town, visitors will find the **Village Shops**, which include an attractive craft shop with articles by local artisans.

Cabot Trail

Visitors will find a number of stores selling local and Aboriginal crafts along the Cabot Trail. Quilts, wooden sculptures and pottery are among the available products.

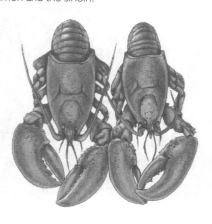

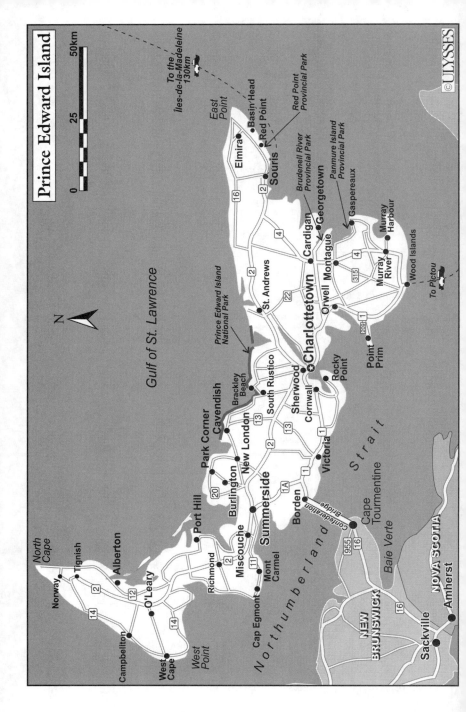

Prince Edward Island

© ULYSSES

0   25   50km

N

Gulf of St. Lawrence

North Cape
Norway
Tignish
Alberton
O'Leary
Campbellton
West Cape
West Point
Cap Egmont
Mont Carmel
Richmond
Miscouche
Port Hill
Burlington
Summerside
Borden
New London
Park Corner
Cavendish
Brackley Beach
South Rustico
Sherwood
Cornwall
Victoria
Rocky Point
Charlottetown
Sherwood
St. Andrews
Prince Edward Island National Park

Elmira
East Point
Basin Head
Red Point
Red Point Provincial Park
Souris
Brudenell River Provincial Park
Cardigan
Georgetown
Panmure Island Provincial Park
Gaspereaux
Orwell
Montague
Murray Harbour
Murray River
Wood Islands
Point Prim

To the Îles-de-la-Madeleine 130km

To Pictou

Northumberland Strait

Baie Verte
Cape Tourmentine
Confederation Bridge

NEW BRUNSWICK
NOVA SCOTIA
Sackville
Amherst

Prince Edward Island

Mention Prince Edward

Island and many people envision a rare harmony of rural and maritime landscapes, the epitome of serene country life.

Set back from the peaceful roads and tucked away behind rolling valleys of farmland lie picturesque little fishing villages, adorable white clapboard churches, and the pulsing glow of a lighthouse towering over the sea from isolated rocky outcrops. Most striking in these charming scenes is the brilliant palette of colours: the vibrant yellow and green of the fields falling over the cliffs of deep rust red into the lapis blue of the sea.

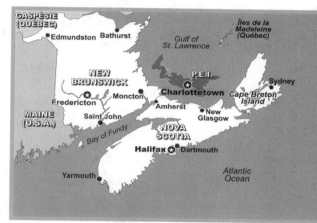

Bathed to the north by the Gulf of St. Lawrence and to the south by the Strait of Northumberland, this island is above all known for its magnificent white-sand dunes and beaches, often deserted and extending between sea and land as far as the eye can see. These ribbons of sand are among the most beautiful on the east coast of the continent. They offer great spots for

swimming, long walks and discoveries. The beaches may be what initially attracts most visitors, but they quickly discover the many other treasures Prince Edward Island (P.E.I.) has to offer. For starters, the small capital city of Charlottetown, whose architecture and unique atmosphere give it an antique charm; from there, the possibilities are virtually endless: the friendliest fresh lobster feasts you can imagine, the storybook world *Anne of Green Gables*, the kindness of the inhabitants, and the

richness of the magnificent plants and wildlife of Prince Edward Island National Park.

Prince Edward Island is about 255km long, making it the smallest Canadian province. It was originally christened «Île Saint-Jean» by explorer Jacques Cartier, who sailed along its shores in 1534. Acadians began colonizing what were originally Mi'kmaq grounds in 1720, continuing until 1758, when the island fell into the hands of the British, who rechristened it in

---

honour of the son of King George III.

As in other Atlantic provinces, the ship-building years were a veritable golden age that ended in the second half of the 19th century. At the same time, negotiations began between the North American British colonies about the possibility of creating a confederation. It was in Charlottetown in 1864 that delegates from each of these colonies finally met, and three years later that the Dominion of Canada was born as a result of this conference. Today, islanders are proud to remind you that their province was literally the birthplace of Canadian Confederation.

Finding Your Way Around

We have divided Prince Edward Island into four tours:

Tour A:
Charlottetown ★★

Tour B:
Central P.E.I. ★★

Tour C:
Eastern P.E.I. ★

Tour D:
Western P.E.I. ★

By Car

P.E.I. has a good road network. Due to the lack of adequate public transit, the best way to tour the island is either by bike or by car.

The island is accessible from Cape Tormentine, New Brunswick, via the 13km-long **Confederation Bridge** (*$39/car, round-trip;* ☎902-437-7033 *or* 888-437-6565, *www. confederationbridge.com*), which spans Northumberland Strait. For islanders, the bridge's inauguration in 1997 marked a veritable revolution: crossing the strait now takes 10min by car compared to a half hour by ferry. You can pay the toll with cash, or by credit or debit card.

By Plane

Visitors flying to the island arrive at **Charlottetown Airport**, about 4km north of downtown Charlottetown, in Sherwood (☎902-566-7997, *www.flypei. com*). **Air Canada** (☎902-894-5238, *www.aircanada.ca*) and **Air Canada Jazz** (*www.flyjazz.ca*) are the major airline companies serving this airport. Four car-rental agencies have offices in the airport, including **Budget** (☎902-566-5525).

By Ferry

From May to December, you can reach P.E.I. by taking the **Northumberland Ferries**, which link Caribou (Nova Scotia) to the Wood Islands (*May to Nov, no reservation; cars $53 round-trip;* ☎888-249-7245, *www.nfl-bay.com*). The trip takes 75min and there are between three and nine departures every day, depending on the season.

P.E.I. is also accessible by ferry from the Îles-de-la-Madeleine (Québec) aboard the **Madeleine** (*cars $70, adults $37; one ferry/day, reserve if possible;* ☎418-986-3278), which arrives in Souris, near the northeastern point of the island.

By Bus

Prince Edward Island has limited bus service. However, a bus does link Cavendish to the big hotel chains in downtown Charlottetown (*departure 9am, return 6pm*).

Practical Information

Area code: **902**

Tourist Information

The island's main provincial tourist information office is in Borden-Carleton, right at the foot of the Confederation Bridge.

☎**437-8570 or 800-PEI-PLAY** *www.peiplay.com*

A Bridge to the Island

It had been discussed for years, but, following an election promise by the then-current federal government, the old dream of a bridge linking Prince Edward Island to the mainland finally came true in 1997. The Confederation Bridge between Cape Tourmentine (N.B.) and Borden (P.E.I.) spans 12.7km across the Strait of Northumberland. This bold project required the latest technology and the hiring of 1,000 local workers. The building of a bridge, however, did not please everyone on the island.

Throughout its construction, a good many islanders took action to condemn a project they believed would lead to the end of their unique way of life. A few years after the end of the project, however, the controversy died out. The bridge allows for easier access to the island and its bucolic character has remained intact; Prince Edward Island remains the most peaceful of the Canadian provinces.

www.confederation bridge.com

For information on the province's parks:
www.gov.pe.ca

A hotel reservation service is also available at:
☎*888-268-6667*

Tour A: Charlottetown

Charlottetown
corner of Water and Prince Sts.
☎*368-4444*

Tour B: Central P.E.I.

Borden-Carleton
100 Abegweit St., at the foot of the Confederation Bridge
☎*437-8570*

Cavendish
Rte. 6
☎*963-7830*

Brackley Beach
Rte. 15
☎*672-7474*

Tour C: Eastern P.E.I.

Poole's Corner
intersection of Rtes. 3 and 4
☎*838-0670*

Wood Islands
on the road that leads to the ferry
☎*962-7411*

Souris
95 Main St.
☎*687-7030*

Tour D: Western P.E.I.

Summerside
Rte. 1A
☎*888-8364*

Mount Pleasant
Rte. 2
☎*831-7930*

Exploring

Tour A: Charlottetown

Charming and quaint, Charlottetown has a unique atmosphere. Despite its size, it is more than just a small, typical Maritime town—it is a provincial capital with all the prestige, elegance and institutions one would

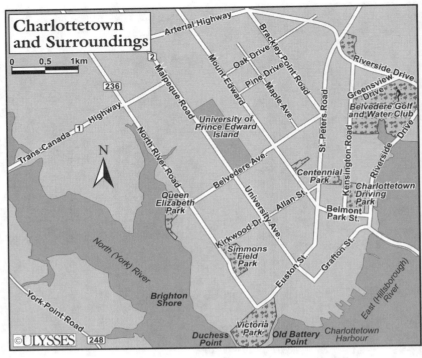

expect from a town of its status. Though everything here seems decidedly scaled down, the capital of Prince Edward Island has its parliament buildings and sumptuous lieutenant-governor's residence, a large performance and visual-arts complex, pretty parks and rows of trees concealing beautiful Victorian homes, the prestigious Delta Prince Edward hotel and several fine restaurants. Adding to its charm is its picturesque location on the shores of a bay at the confluence of the Hillsborough, North and West rivers.

A meeting place for the Mi'kmaq, the site was known to explorers and French colonists in the 18th century. It was not until 1768, however, that British settlers actually founded the city, naming it Charlottetown in honour of the wife of King George III of Great Britain. Less than a century later, Charlottetown made its way into the history books as the cradle of Canadian Confederation. It was in this little town, in 1864, that delegates of the North American British colonies met to discuss the creation of the Dominion of Canada.

The **Confederation Centre of the Arts ★ ★** *(free admission; every day 9am to 5pm; 145 Richmond St., ☎628-1864 or 800-565-0278, ≈566-4648, www.confederationcentre. com)* was built in 1964, one century after the decisive meeting of the Fathers of Confederation in Charlottetown. The complex was designed to increase public knowledge of current Canadian culture and its evolution over

Confederation Centre of the Arts

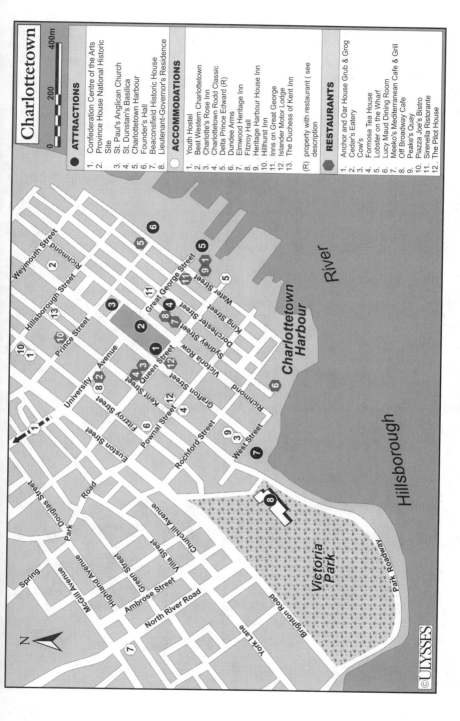

Charlottetown

0   200   400m

● **ATTRACTIONS**

1. Confederation Centre of the Arts
2. Province House National Historic Site
3. St. Paul's Anglican Church
4. St. Dunstan's Basilica
5. Charlottetown Harbour
6. Founder's Hall
7. Beaconsfield Historic House
8. Lieutenant-Governor's Residence

○ **ACCOMMODATIONS**

1. Youth Hostel
2. Best Western Charlottetown
3. Charlotte's Rose Inn
4. Charlottetown Rodd Classic
5. Delta Prince Edward (R)
6. Dundee Arms
7. Elmwood Heritage Inn
8. Fitzroy Hall
9. Heritage Harbour House Inn
10. Hillhurst Inn
11. Inns on Great George
12. Islander Motor Lodge
13. The Duchess of Kent Inn

(R) property with restaurant (see description

◆ **RESTAURANTS**

1. Anchor and Oar House Grub & Grog
2. Cedar's Eatery
3. Cow's
4. Formosa Tea House
5. Lobster on the Wharf
6. Lucy Maud Dining Room
7. Meeko's Mediterranean Cafe & Grill
8. Off Broadway Cafe
9. Peake's Quay
10. Piazza Joe's Bistro
11. Sirenella Ristorante
12. The Pilot House

© ULYSSES

the last 135 years. The Centre of the Arts has many facets, including a museum with several impressive exhibits, an art gallery and a public library. There are also several beautiful auditoriums where visitors can take in a performance of *Anne of Green Gables* during the summer. Presented every summer for more than three decades now, this musical is a fun way to spend an evening in Charlottetown and discover in the world of Prince Edward Island's most famous author, Lucy Maud Montgomery.

The **Province House National Historic Site** ★★ *(free admission; Jun and Sep to mid-Oct, every day 8:30am to 5pm; Jul and Aug, every day 8:30am to 6pm; mid-Oct to Jun, Mon-Fri 9am to 5pm; 165 Richmond St., ☎566-7626)* can honestly be considered the cradle of Canadian

Confederation. It was here that the 23 delegates from United Canada (present-day Ontario and Québec), Nova Scotia, New Brunswick and Prince Edward Island assembled in 1864 to prepare the Confederation of 1867. Ironically, the host of this decisive conference, Prince Edward Island, did not join the Dominion of Canada until a few years later, in 1873. Visitors can see the rooms where the Canadian Confederation was worked out and watch a short film explaining the significance of the event. Province House is now the seat of the Legislative Assembly of Prince Edward Island.

St. Paul's Anglican Church ★ *(free admission; corner of Grafton and Prince Sts.)* was erected in 1896 to replace several Anglican churches built in the previous century. Its interior is splendid, especially the wooden vault and stained-glass windows.

St. Dunstan's Basilica ★ *(free admission, donations accepted; corner of Great George and Sydney Sts.)*, a beautiful example of the Gothic style, is the most impressive religious building on Prince Edward Island. Its construction began in 1914, on the same site that was successively occupied by three Catholic churches during the previous century.

Pretty Great George Street, where you can browse through many shops and second-hand stores, ends at the small **port of Charlottetown**, a pleasant area where visitors will not only find a park and marina but also **Peake's Wharf** ★ *(at the end of Great George St.)*, a collection of shops in charming, renovated old buildings. Close by stands the classy **Delta Prince Edward** hotel (see p 219), as well as a few restaurants.

Province House National Historic Site

The port of Charlottetown is also home to **Founders' Hall** ★ *($7; May to late Jun and Sep to mid-Oct, Mon-Sat 9am to 5pm, Sun 9am to 4pm; late Jun to Aug, Mon-Sat 9am to 8pm, Sun 9am to 4pm; ☎368-1864, www.founders-hall.ca)*. This facility spotlights Canadian history, from the time of the Fathers of Confederation to the present day, though the use of impressive displays, multimedia features and the latest technology.

Beaconsfield Historic House ★ *($4.25; Jun, Sep and Oct, 10am to 4pm; Jul and Aug, 10am to 5pm; Nov to mid-May, Wed and Thu 10am to 4pm; 2 Kent St., ☎368-6603, www.pei museum.com)* was built in 1877 for wealthy shipbuilder James Peake and his wife Edith Haviland Beaconsfield. It is one of the most luxurious homes in the province, with 25 rooms and nine fireplaces. After James Peake declared personal bankruptcy in 1882, his creditors, the Cunall family, moved in. The family had no descendants, so Beaconsfield House served as a training school from 1916 on, before being converted into a museum in 1973.

On the other side of Kent Street, shielded behind a stately row of trees, stands the splendid **Lieutenant-Governor's residence** *(corner of Kent St. and Pond Rd.)*. It has been the official residence of the British crown's representative on Prince Edward Island since 1835. Magnificent, beautifully designed

Victoria Park ★, which spreads out before the residence, is a lovely place for a stroll.

Tour B: Central P.E.I.

This section covers the central region of the island, including the regions known as "Anne's Land" and "Charlotte's Shore." It extends from the southern coast along the Strait of Northumberland, east of Charlottetown to the northern shores of the Gulf of St. Lawrence, an area stretching from the town of Malpeque to Tracadie. This beautiful farming region is relatively flat along the southern coast, while towards the northern coast it offers pretty landscapes of valleys and rolling farmland that leads to splendid steep cliffs and some of the most beautiful fine- sand beaches on the island. A unique ecosystem makes up an important part of this coastline, protected by Prince Edward Island National Park.

The northern coast is called "Anne's Land" because it was here, in New London, that Lucy Maud Montgomery was born and it was this idyllic corner of the island that inspired *Anne of Green Gables*. Montgomery fans from around the world make pilgrimages to the spots that marked the childhood of the island's biggest star. The southern region is nicknamed "Charlotte's Shore" and its biggest attractions are the

little villages, including the adorable town of Victoria, that dot its coast.

Take the Trans-Canada Hwy. from Charlottetown to Cornwall, then Rte. 19 (follow the signs for the Blue Heron Tour) south to Rocky Point.

★
Rocky Point

Rocky Point is located at the end of a strip of land, at the mouth of the West River and facing the Hillsborough River, which was always a strategic point in the defence of Charlottetown and the back-country against a possible attack from the sea. Early on, this site was of particular interest to the colonial empires, who battled for control of the island.

The French were the first to establish themselves here in the 1720s, by founding Port La Joye, which was then captured in 1758 by the British who then founded Fort Amherst. The fine-tuning of the fort came that same year when the war between France and England began in earnest.

The British garrison had the important role of protecting the island from French invasion and controlling maritime traffic in the Northumberland Strait throughout the whole war. However, with the end of the war, in 1763, the fort's importance decreased significantly and was abandoned by the British in 1768.

The **Port La Joye–Fort Amherst National Historic Site ★** *($3.50; mid-Jun to early Sep, every day 9am to 5pm; Rte. 19, ☎566-7626)* houses a small interpretive centre presenting an exhibit on the various documents related to the French colony (Port La Joye) and the British presence at the site (Fort Amherst). There is also a short documentary film on the history of the Acadians of Prince Edward Island. Very little remains today of Fort Amherst. This site does, however, offer a lovely view of the surrounding fields and the city of Charlottetown.

The road from Rocky Point to Victoria is calm and there are several great views of the strait along the way. This tranquil country region consists essentially of farms, small peaceful hamlets and provincial parks. Here and there along the road are the small fruit and vegetable stands of farmers selling produce from their harvest.

★
Victoria

The beautiful homes lining the streets of this charming and peaceful coastal town attest to the opulence of another era. Founded in 1767, this seaport played a significant role in the local economy up until the end of the 19th century, when the island's new railway rendered it obsolete. Fishing trawlers can still be seen, however, bobbing about just beyond the once busy harbour. Today, Victoria's

interest lies mainly in its old-fashioned character and the friendliness of its residents. Country life on the island is best represented here. The town numbers two inns, a few restaurants, and a reputed chocolatier.

When arriving from the east you'll first come to **Victoria Provincial Park**, which extends to the water and includes a small beach and a picnic area. The **Victoria Seaport Museum** *(free admission; Jul to early Sep, Tue-Sun 10am to 5pm; Rte. 116, ☎658-2602)* is located close by in a lighthouse. There are several photographs of Victoria on display, and you can climb to the top of the lighthouse for a view of the village, the coast and the surroundings.

Just a few streets make up the centre of Victoria. There are several shops and restaurants, as well as **The Victorian Playhouse** *(☎658-2025)*, which presents topnotch concerts and theatrical plays all summer long, further adding to the charm of the town.

Borden-Carleton

This town has little to offer visitors. It is, however, one of the most visited spots on the island, since this is the starting point of the Confederation Bridge, which links Prince Edward Island to New Brunswick (see p 47). There are several businesses and restaurants here, as well as a good tourist information centre.

You can also visit an **interpretation centre ★** that presents an interesting exhibit on the population, culture and history of the island. It is an excellent introduction to the life of the islanders.

If you are not continuing west to Summerside (see Tour D: Western P.E.I.) from Victoria or Borden-Carleton, we suggest taking the secondary road, Rte. 231, which joins Rte. 2 to reach Kensington.

Kensington

Kensington is one of the larger communities of this part of the island. Situated at the junction of routes 2 and 20, it is the entrance to "Anne's Land." Information on the town and its surroundings is available at the tourist information office at the **Kensington Railyards & Welcome Centre** *(Jun to Oct, 9am to 9pm; Rte. 20, ☎836-3031, www.kata.pe.ca)*, which happens to be one of the prettiest on the island. The main attraction in Kensington is the **Kensington Water Gardens** *($6; Summerside Rd., ☎836-3336, www.kata.pe.ca/attract/water/water.htm)*, which consists of a series of miniature reconstructions of famous buildings, all of them set in gardens.

Burlington

One of the most popular attractions as far as children are concerned is **Woodleigh ★** *($8.50; Jun, Sep and Oct, every day 9am to 5pm. Jul to Aug, every day 9am to 7pm; Rte. 234; ☎836-3401, www.woodleighreplicas.com)*, the brainchild of Col. Ernest Johnstone, who constructed replicas of famous buildings and monuments on his property after his return from the First World War up until his death 50 years later.

The site opened in 1958 and now includes some 30 wooden and stone buildings, several of which can be visited, and a variety of other monuments dispersed across this lovely, wooded property. The most impressive building is probably the replica of the Tower of London. Celtic music shows are held here, usually on Sundays.

Indian River

Indian River was a Mi'kmaq meeting place up until 1935, hence the apparent origin of the town's name. Today, Indian River is neither a town nor even a village, but it is still the site of the impressive **St. Mary's Roman Catholic Church** ★ *(Rte. 104)*. Built between 1900 and 1902, St. Mary's is the most famous work of island architect William C. Harris and the largest wooden church on the island, with a seating capacity of up to 600 people. Its Gothic Revival altar and elegant belltower are particularly remarkable.

Malpeque

Malpeque, which means "large bay" in Mi'kmaq, is a pretty little community bordered by expanses of water. The town is world-famous for the celebrated

Lucy Maud Montgomery

Lucy Maud Montgomery was born on November 30th, 1874 in New London, P.E.I. Early in her childhood she left New London for Cavendish, to live with her grandparents, Alexander and Lucy MacNeill, who raised her after the death of her mother. Her first novel, *Anne of Green Gables*, inspired by her own orphan life, was a huge success as soon as it appeared in 1908. It has since been translated into 16 languages. L.M. Montgomery went on to publish 23 novels before her death in 1942. Her most famous work, however, remained the story of Anne, the enchanting little orphan with the red hair and freckled face.

oysters that are gathered in its bay. The best place from which to admire the bay is **Cabot Beach Provincial Park**, whose beaches are usually completely deserted.

Park Corner

Park Corner was granted to James Townshend in 1755 as compensation for his service in the British army, and was put on the map by one of his direct descendants, Lucy Maud Montgomery.

The **Anne of Green Gables Museum at Silver Bush** ★ *($2.55; Jul and Aug, every day 9am to 5:30pm; Jun and Sept, every day 9am to 5pm; Oct, every day 10am to 4pm; ☎886-2807)* was actually a favourite house of Lucy Maud Montgomery. It belonged to her aunt and uncle, Annie and John Campbell. She

adored it and was married here in July, 1911. Today it is a historic house, decorated with period furniture and many of the author's and her family's personal effects.

New London

The small community of New London has the distinguished honour of being the birthplace of the writer who has made Prince Edward Island famous internationally. The main attraction is the house where she was born, the **Lucy Maud Montgomery Birthplace** *($2; late May and Jun and Sep to mid-Oct, every day 9am to 5pm; Jul and Aug, every day 9am to 6pm; intersection of Rtes. 6 and 8, ☎886-2099 or 436-7329)*. Personal objects, includ- ing L.M. Montgomery's wedding dress, can be viewed in this unassuming house.

Cavendish:
The ideal family destination

The Cavendish region is the ideal family vacation spot. First of all, Prince Edward Island National Park is located here and has sandy beaches that make a great natural playground. Also nearby are all the tourist attractions related to the *Anne of Green Gables* children's novel as well as a whole array of activities to enliven a vacation with children.

There are amusement parks like the **Burlington Amusement Park & Go-Karts** *(Rte. 234, Burlington, ☎836-3098)*, the **Rainbow Valley Family Fun Park** *(Cavendish, ☎963-2221)* and the **Brackley Beach Drive-In Theatre and Fun Park** *(Rte. 15, Brackley Beach, ☎672-3333)*, theme museums like the **Ripley's Believe It or Not Museum** *(Rte. 6, Cranberry Village, Cavendish, ☎963-2242)* and the **Royal Atlantic Wax Museum** *(at the intersection of Rtes. 6 and 13, Cavendish,* ☎963-2350*)*, various worthwhile attractions such as the **Woodleigh Replicas & Gardens** *(Rte. 234, Burlington, ☎836-3401)* and the **Kensington Towers & Water Gardens** *(Rte. 2, Kensington, ☎836-3336)*, drive-ins, minigolf, a heap of family restaurants and the list goes on. With all its attractions, more and more families are choosing the Cavendish region as the destination for their summer holidays.

★
Cavendish

The Cavendish area is a sacred spot for tourists on Prince Edward Island. Located next to some of the most beautiful beaches on the island and several big tourist attractions, Cavendish offers many lodging options, restaurants and shops. It is for many a gateway to the national park, and has an excellent tourist information centre.

Green Gables ★ *($4.50; May, Jun, Sep and Oct, every day 9am to 5pm; Jul and Aug, every day 9am to 8pm; Rte. 6, west of Cavendish, ☎963-7874)* is the house that Lucy Maud Montgomery used as the main setting for her famous novel, *Anne of Green Gables*. Built in the mid-1800s, the house belonged to David and Margaret MacNeil, the author's older cousins.

L.M. Montgomery used to love strolling down "lover's lane," located in the woods on her cousins' property. She was so inspired by the surroundings that it became the backdrop for her novel. In 1936, the site was included in Prince Edward Island National Park.

A visit to the island would not be complete without at least a one-day trip to

Green Gables

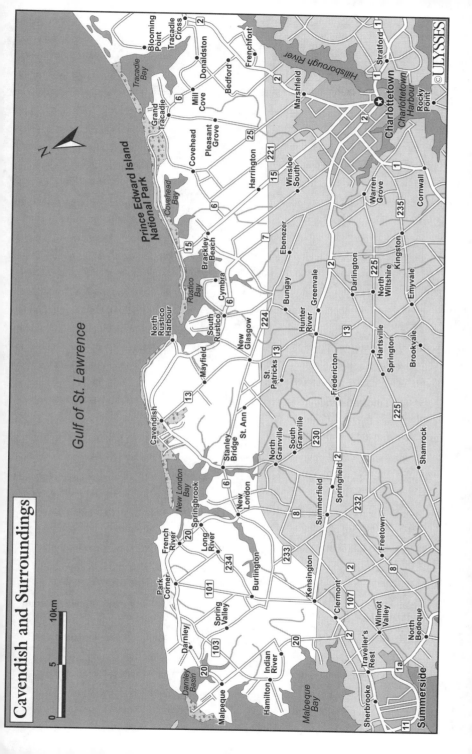

Cavendish and Surroundings

Gulf of St. Lawrence

Prince Edward Island National Park

Hillsborough River

Charlottetown Harbour

Tracadie Bay
Covehead Bay
Rustico Bay
New London Bay
Darnley Basin
Malpeque Bay

Blooming Point
Tracadie Cross
Tracadie
Donaldston
Frenchfort
Bedford
Mill Cove
Grand Tracadie
Covehead
Pleasant Grove
Marshfield
Harrington
Winsloe South
Warren Grove
Rocky Point
Cornwall
Kingston
Emyvale
North Wiltshire
Darlington
Brookvale
Springton
Hartsville
Ebenezer
Bungay
Greenvale
Hunter River
Fredericton
Shamrock
Brackley Beach
Cymbra
New Glasgow
St Patricks
North Rustico Harbour
South Rustico
Mayfield
Cavendish
Stanley Bridge
St. Ann
North Granville
South Granville
Springfield
Summerfield
Freetown
Wilmot Valley
North Bedeque
Traveller's Rest
Sherbrooke
Summerside
Kensington
Clermont
Burlington
New London
Long River
French River
Springbrook
Park Corner
Spring Valley
Darnley
Malpeque
Hamilton
Indian River

Stratford
Charlottetown

© ULYSSES

0 5 10km

N

The Piping Plover

In all of Prince Edward Island National Park, there are only 25 pairs of piping plovers, little birds that measure about 19cm and have a sandy beige plumage, with a few black feathers on their head and neck.

The piping plover feeds on insects and tiny crustaceans, and can often be seen combing the beach in search of nourishment. It also builds its nest in the sand, a little bit above the waterline at high tide.

During the 28-day incubation period of their eggs, and until the baby birds set off on their own at the end of July, the parents watch over the nest, which is well-hidden in the sand, safe from predators.

Unfortunately, the nests are also well-hidden from people strolling along the beach, who can inadvertently cause irreparable damage to them. The number of piping plovers has diminished greatly over the past decade, and if the population is to grow, the nests must be protected from any disturbance. While walking along the beach, therefore, it is crucial that visitors pay careful attention to all signs.

Prince Edward Island National Park ★★★

(three welcome centres: Cavendish, near the intersection of Rtes. 6 and 13; opposite the Dalvay-by-the-Sea Hotel; Brackley, at the intersection of Rtes. 6 and 15; ☎672-6350), which stretches for several kilometres along the northern coast of the island, from Blooming Point to New London Bay. The park was created in 1937 with the goal of preserving a unique natural environment that includes sand dunes and their fragile ecosystem, red-sandstone cliffs, magnificent beaches and saltwater marshes.

While exploring the park from the trails that crisscrossed it, visitors will be constantly delighted by stunning views of the sheer coastline, the sudden appearance of a red fox or one of the many activities that may be enjoyed here.

In February 1998, the park was expanded to include the Greenwich Peninsula, which stretches to the east of **St. Peters Bay** (see p 211).

The beaches here are also terrific for families. Be careful around the neighbouring sand dunes, however, since the piping plover, a small, endangered species of bird, sometimes nests there. Footbridges have been laid out in order to protect this fragile environment; please respect the signs.

There are four **camping sites** within Prince Edward Island National Park. The one on Robinson Island (previously known as Rustico Island) is ideal for peaceful, rustic camping. The **Cavendish** campground, located closer to the ocean, offers full service amenities. Several different types of campsites can be found within the **Stanhope** campground. The fourth campground, **Brackley Group Tenting**, only accepts groups of campers *(reservations required)*. For information and reservations for these four campgrounds, call ☎672-6350 or 800-414-6765.

Avonlea Village of Anne of Green Gables ★ ($16.95; Jun to Sep, everyday 9am to 5pm; centre of Cavendish, ☎963-3060, www.avonlea.ca)

is located in the heart of Cavendish. The site features a dozen buildings, either reconstructed or original, which are reminiscent of the village of Avonlea. Actors liven up the surroundings by bringing to life some of the characters from the stories of Avonlea. In addition to touring the site, visitors can enjoy musical performances, storytelling and carriage rides. There are also several shops that offer local products. This makes for a great family activity.

★ New Glasgow

From Cavendish, the route travels through beautiful landscapes of rolling hills to New Glasgow, a picturesque little village whose handsome houses rise from either bank of the Hunter River. New Glasgow is mainly appealing for its rural charm, but its pleasant restaurants, especially the **P.E.I. Preserve Co.** (Rte.13, at the intersection of Rtes. 224 and 258, ☎964-4300), which houses a shop that sells various homemade provisions (jams, jellies, teas, honey) and an excellent dining room, are equally attractive.

★ North Rustico

North Rustico, a charming village where the main activities are fishing and, more specifically, lobster-

trapping, overlooks both Rustico Bay and the Gulf of St. Lawrence. One of the national park's beautiful sandy **beaches ★★** is directly accessible from this village. Nearby, North Rustico Harbour is an equally enticing destination that offers beautiful maritime scenery.

★ South Rustico

Once a large Mi'kmaq settlement known as *Tabooetooetun*, the region of Rustico Bay was one of the first parts of the island to be colonized by the French and a good number of their descendants still reside in the South Rustico region. The name Rustico derives from the gradual transformation of the name of the first French man to settle in the area, René Rassicot. **Café St-Jean** (see p 229), in Oyster Bed Bridge, is a local hub of Acadian culture.

South Rustico itself is actually a crossroads in the middle of the countryside, around which stand the main institutions of the local Acadian community: the church, the presbytery, the cemetery, the school and the **Farmer's Bank of Rustico ★** ($1; Jun to Sep, Mon-Sat 9:30am to 5:30pm, Sun 1pm to 5:30pm; Rte. 243, ☎963-3168). This farmer's bank was founded in 1864 by Father George-Antoine Belcourt to give Acadians the opportunity to participate in the economy. It was the first people's bank in the country, and for a certain time, the smallest

chartered bank in Canada. It is now a museum that explains Father Belcourt's work. Right next door, the modest **Saint Augustine Church** (Church St.) is the oldest Acadian church on the island.

Brackley Beach

This small hamlet on the shores of Rustico Bay is worth a visit to see the **Baywatch Lighthouse** ($2; early Jun to mid-Sep, 10am to 10pm; at the intersection of Rtes. 15 and 16, ☎672-3478) and its exhibit of photographs of island lighthouses. Another recommended stop close by is **The Dunes Studio Gallery** (free admission; May, 10am to 6pm; Jun to Sep, 9am to 10pm; May and Oct, 10am to 5pm; Rte. 15, ☎672-2586), where the works of the greatest artists of the island are on display. The gallery also houses a charming little restaurant. With Prince Edward Island National Park right nearby, Brackley Beach provides plenty of accommodation options.

Tour C: Eastern P.E.I.

Extending to the east of Charlottetown is a lovely rural region that will delight visitors seeking the tranquillity of its deserted beaches, the busy atmosphere of its small fishing villages and the beauty of the enchanting bays that appear around every bend in the road. Somewhat hilly to the north, this region presents a varied landscape that may not always be spectacular, but is often pretty and harmonious.

None of the communities in this part of the island have more than a few hundred inhabitants, and life here revolves mainly around fishing and agriculture. A tour of eastern Prince Edward Island thus offers visitors an opportunity to discover a lovely part of the province while experiencing a way of life that remains directly linked to nature.

Orwell Corner

A visit to the **Orwell Corner Historic Village** ★ (*$5; mid-May to mid-Jun and Oct, Mon-Fri 10am to 5pm; mid-Jun to Sep, every day 9am to 5pm; Trans-Canada Hwy., 30km east of Charlottetown, ☎651-8510*) is a must for anyone interested in discovering what life was like in rural Prince Edward Island back in the 19th century. This delightful village is made up of restored buildings, including a pretty little school that looks as if it came straight out of an L.M. Montgomery novel, a church, a shingle factory, several barns, a forge and a farmhouse that doubles as a general store and post office.

The atmosphere is enlivened by characters in period dress who are available to answer visitors' questions. Orwell Corner may be smaller than other similar historic villages such as Kings Landing in New Brunswick, but its size gives it a charming authenticity.

A few hundred metres from Orwell Corner, tucked away in an enchanting setting, lies the **Sir Andrew Macphail Homestead** (*free admission, donations are welcome; late Jun to early Oct, Sun-Fri 10am to 8:30pm; 30km east of Charlottetown, Rte.1, ☎651-2789*). A native of Prince Edward Island, Andrew Macphail (1864-1938) had an extraordinary career in the fields of research and medicine, as well as in writing and journalism. His house, furnished as it was a century ago, is a lovely part of the local heritage. There is a small dining room where light meals are served. Visitors can also explore the vast grounds by taking a pleasant walk along a 2km trail.

Point Prim

Not far from the village of Eldon, Route 1 intersects with Route 209, a small road leading to the **Point Prim Lighthouse** (*free admission, donations are welcome; Jul and Aug, 9am to 7pm; Rte. 209, ☎659-2412*), designed and built in 1845 by Isaac Smith, the architect of Charlottetown's Province House. The lighthouse is open to the public, and the surrounding area is perfect for a picnic. The **view** ★ of the sea is worth the short detour.

Wood Islands

Wood Islands, the departure point for the ferry to Pictou, Nova Scotia (see p 140), has a large tourist information centre. The village's setting is very

pretty and offers a beautiful **view** ★ of Northumberland Strait.

Very close by, there are beautiful **beaches** that are ideal for swimming and are often deserted. It is also possible to swim at the beach at **Wood Islands Provincial Park**, a few kilometres further east. Keep in mind that although the beaches along the shore of Northumberland Strait are often less spectacular than those on the Gulf of St. Lawrence, the water here is significantly warmer. The park's vegetation is mainly composed of leafy trees.

Little Sands

At Little Sands, on a small plateau overlooking the waters of Northumberland Strait, the vineyards of the **Rossignol Estate Winery** ★ (☎962-4193), the island's only vineyard, suddenly appear before your eyes. The Rossignol family produces seven table wines, a cider and a few fruit liqueurs here, all of which may be savoured on the spot, and they happily explain the processes by which the fruit is cultivated and pressed and how their wines are stored. The winery shop also displays lovely crafts, as well as the paintings of Little Sands artist Nancy Perkins.

Murray Harbour

Murray Harbour, which rises on the banks of the Murray River, is home to a few pretty period houses and a charming little harbour. Antique lovers should stop by the **Log Cabin Museum** *($2.50; Jul to early Sep, 9am to 6pm; Rte. 18A,* ☎*962-2201)*, which displays a curious collection of original items.

Murray River

Murray River is a vibrant little community that has a few restaurants and some attractive local craft shops, including **The Old General Store** *(*☎*962-2459)*. Near Murray River is the beach at **King Castle Provincial Park**, a pleasant recreation area that also has a small playground. Seal- and bird-watching tours depart from Murray River (see p 217).

★
Panmure Island

A turnoff from **Gaspereaux**, a picturesque lobster-trapping village, leads to Panmure Island. **Panmure Island Provincial Park ★**, located along the road to the island, encloses some of the most splendid sand **beaches ★** on Prince Edward Island. Stretching on for kilometres, these dune-bordered beaches are often practically deserted. The lighthouse on Panmure Island offers a gorgeous panoramic view.

★
Montague

Montague might not be very big, but it is nevertheless one of the largest communities in the eastern part of the province. It is home to several businesses, shops and restaurants, as well as the inter-esting **Garden of the Gulf Museum ★** *($3; Jun to late Sep, Mon-Sat 9am to 5pm; 2 Main St. S.,* ☎*838-2467)*, set up inside a former post office. The exhibit deals with both local and military history. Montague is also the point of departure for excursions organized by **Cruise Manada Seal Watching Boat Tours** (see p 217). Other excursions start at the Brudenell Marina.

Georgetown

The small fishing port of Georgetown witnessed the golden age of wooden ship-building. In that era, Georgetown's natural port, which, in addition to being well protected, is the deepest on the island, was a distinct advantage. Today, numerous boutiques and cafés can be found close to the port, making it a particularly pleasant area.

Right before Georgetown, stretching along the banks of the river for which it was named, is the superb **Brudenell River Provincial Park**. This park offers a stunning view of the water, a beach, a beautiful golf course, an interesting hiking trail that runs along the river all the way to Georgetown, a good hotel and a number of campgrounds.

Cardigan

A small community looking out onto the bay of the same name, Cardigan was a ship-building centre in the 19th century. It is now home to several interesting craft shops.

Souris

The little town of Souris, with its 1,600 or so inhabitants, is the largest community on the eastern part of Prince Edward Island. Accordingly, it offers a wide range of services, several restaurants and hotels and a tourist information centre. Not far away lies **Souris Beach Provincial Park**, with a picnic area and an unsupervised beach. The town's Main Street is graced with several pretty buildings that bear witness to Souris's prominent role in this region. The most striking of these are the **Town Hall** and **St. Mary's Church**. The town's port is the boarding point for the ferry (see p 196) to Québec's Îles-de-la-Madeleine, situated in the heart of the Gulf of St. Lawrence.

Red Point

Red Point Provincial Park ★ was created to protect the island's magnificent red sandstone cliffs, and some of the views here are picture-perfect. Visitors will also be charmed by the **beach ★**, a long strip of fine sand along the Northumberland Strait. The park has lovely picnic areas, too, and campers are welcome at the excellent campground.

★
Basin Head

Ideally located on one of the island's loveliest **sandy beaches ★★**, not far from some magnificent

The Golden Era of the Railway

The history of the railway is closely linked to that of Prince Edward Island and its adherence to the Canadian Confederation. In the 1860s and 1870s, the island's inhabitants began demanding a railway, which in those years was the most efficient means of communication and transport throughout North America, as well as a virtual guarantee of economic growth.

In August of 1871, the island's government passed the Railroad Act, and construction of the railway began two

months later. By the following year, however, construction costs had led to an unprecedented crisis in the island's public finances. On the verge of bankruptcy, the government had no other option but to transfer its debt to the Canadian government and join the Canadian Confederation in July 1873.

Two years later, the island's railway began operating. Its main track linked Alberton, in the west, to Georgetown, in the east, later continuing to Elmira. Another line

linked Tignish, in the west, to Souris, in the east. For nearly a century, the railway was the backbone of the island's development.

Starting in the 1960s, however, the emergence of new and more efficient means of transportation forced the Canadian National railway company to cut back its services all over the country, including on Prince Edward Island. In 1989, the island's last line was closed, bringing the golden era of the railway to an end.

dunes, the **Basin Head Fisheries Museum ★ ★** *($3; mid-Jun and late Sep, Mon-Fri, 10am to 5pm; Jul and Aug 10am to 7pm; Rte. 16, ☎357-7233)* offers visitors an opportunity to learn about all the different facets of the wonderful world of fishing around the island.

The museum displays an interesting collection of artifacts related to the lives and occupation of the fishermen of old. The building itself is flanked by sheds in which vessels of various sizes and periods are displayed, as well as a workshop where local artisans make wooden boxes like those that were

used in the past for packing salted fish. An old canning factory stands a little farther off. In all respects, this is one of the most interesting museums in the province. To make the most of your visit, however, take a stroll along the neighbouring beaches and dunes as well.

East Point

For a magnificent view of the ocean and the area's coastal landscape, head to the **East Point Lighthouse ★** *(guided tours $3; Jul to mid-Aug; Rte. 16, ☎357-2718)*, which stands on the easternmost tip of the island. During summer, visitors can climb to

the top of this old lighthouse, which dates back to 1867.

Elmira

A tiny rural village near the easternmost tip of the island, Elmira is home to one of the six museums of the Prince Edward Island Museum and Heritage Foundation, the

Elmira Railway Museum ★ *($2; mid-Jun to early Sep, every day 10am to 6pm; Rte. 16A, ☎357-7234)*. Located in a bucolic setting, it occupies the town's former train station, which has been closed since 1982. In addition to the main building, there is a warehouse and a railway car stationed on one of the tracks. This museum's excellent exhibit is a reminder of the glorious sense of adventure that accompanied the construction of the island's railway.

★
St. Peters

St. Peters was the site of the very first French establishment on Prince Edward Island (then known as «Île Saint-Jean»), when two Norman mariners, Francis Douville and Charles Carpentier, arrived here after their ship ran aground at Naufrage, a little further east. The site was named «Havre Saint-Pierre»; its population prospered thanks to fishing, growing to about 400 colonists by the time of the Acadian deportation in 1755.

Today, St. Peters is a very pretty village whose sumptuous residences stretch along the shores of the bay.

In February 1998, the Greenwich Peninsula was annexed to **Prince Edward Island National Park** ★★★ in order to protect and preserve its natural resources and cultural riches.

The area comprises a vast network of fragile coastal sand dunes, wetlands and various ecosystems harbouring an abundance of rare plant life. Among Greenwich's most spectacular protected natural features are the high, shifting parabolic dunes, as

The Acadian Presence

Although Acadians didn't settle in the Evangeline region until 1812, their presence on Prince Edward Island dates back to the 1720s, when the island was a French colony named "Île-Saint-Jean."

These first colonists, who came from the area then known as Acadia (present-day Nova Scotia), founded the settlements of Port-La-Joye, Pointe-Prime and Malpèque, among others. In the following decades, the Acadian population gradually increased, then began growing rapidly in 1755,

with the arrival of refugees fleeing deportation from Acadia. In 1758, however, Île-Saint-Jean also fell to the British, who deported some 3,000 of the 5,000 Acadians living on the island.

After the war, the remaining Acadians, along with those who had returned to the island, settled mainly in the area around Malpèque Bay. It wasn't until 1812 that some families left this region to settle in the southwest, founding La Roche (Baie-Egmont) and Grand-Ruisseau (Mont-Carmel).

well as the counter ridges, or low dune ridges, a very rare sight in North America. Moreover, the area serves as a habitat for the endangered piping plover, a small shore bird.

Equally remarkable are Greenwich's cultural heritage and history. The area contains vestiges of the major cultures that have populated Prince Edward Island over the last 10,000 years, notably the first Aboriginal peoples, the Mi'kmaq, the French and Acadian colonists, as well as the Scottish, Irish and British immigrants.

At the **Greenwich Interpretive Centre** (*May to mid-Jun and Sep to Oct, every day 9am to 5pm; mid-Jun to Aug, every day 9am to 8pm*), visitors learn about the importance of protecting the area's precious natural and cultural resources. The large exhibit hall features various interactive montages and pannels highlighting the region's unique natural characteristics, a 3-D model of the Greenwich Peninsula and a multimedia program on Greenwich's human history.

The site also offers three self-guided, interpretive

walking/hiking trails, as well as daily interpretive activities in July and August. For more information, consult the bulletin boards or request the program of activities. The beach facilities, which include a lookout, cabins and showers, are located in the central area. Lifeguards are on duty from late June to late August.

St. Andrews

After Elmira, the Trans-Canada Highway passes through several tiny rural communities. A brief stop in St. Andrews is a must to visit its little **chapel** *(free admission; late Jun to early Sep, 10am to 7pm)*, which has been moved twice. Built in 1803 on its present site, it was transported down the frozen Hillsborough River to Charlottetown in the winter of 1964, where it was used as a girls' school. It was restored in 1988 and moved back to its original site two years later.

Tour D:
Western P.E.I.

The western part of Prince Edward Island is home to the province's second-largest town, Summerside, as well as its most isolated area, the northwest. Southwest of Summerside, visitors can explore the Acadian region of Prince Edward Island, the domain of the Arseneault, Gallant and Richard families, among others, who live in a string of tiny coastal villages with colourful

names like Baie-Egmont, Saint-Chrysostome, Mont-Carmel and Maximeville.

Here, in the Evangeline region, inhabitants proudly preserve the French language and Acadian culture that was passed down to them by their ancestors. A tour of the western part of the island offers visitors an opportunity to discover this Acadian legacy, while visiting a peaceful, picturesque region whose inhabitants live mainly on fishing and potato-farming. The scenery is pretty and sometimes even spectacular, especially near North Cape.

★
Summerside

With a population of around 10,000 inhabitants, Summerside is Prince Edward Island's second-largest town. It is presently experiencing an economic boom, due to the nearby Confederation Bridge that links the island to New Brunswick, completed in 1997. It is a pleasant town, graced with lovely Victorian residences and a pretty waterfront. As the chief urban centre on the western part of the island, Summerside also has a number of shops, restaurants and places to stay.

Spinnakers' Landing ★ *(free admission; Harbour Dr., ☎436-6692)* constitutes a good place to start off a visit of Summerside. This pleasant promenade, laid out near the town's port, numbers a few beautiful shops and offers a wonderful view. Harbour cruises leave from Spinnakers' Landing.

Eptek Art & Culture Centre *($3.50; Jul to early Sep, every day 9am to 5pm; Sep to Jun, Tue-Fri 10am to 4pm; 130 Harbour Dr., ☎888-8373)* is a national exhibition centre that presents travelling exhibits of Canadian art. The same building also houses the **Prince Edward Island Sports Hall of Fame** *(☎436-0423)*.

For a lovely exploration of part of Summerside's history, head to the **Wyatt Heritage Properties ★** *(Jun to Sep, Mon-Sat 9am to 5pm; Oct to May, Tue-Fri 9am to 5pm; 85 Spring St., ☎432-1327, www.wyatt heritage.com)*. The site, which opened in 2000, includes three properties all located close to one another. The **Wyatt House** *(85 Spring St.)*, a lovely residence built in 1867, once belonged to one of the most important families on the island. Today, visitors can tour the house and learn about the lifestyle of a bygone era. The **MacNaught History Centre** *(75 Spring St.)*, dating from 1887, is an archival and historical centre where you can admire an exhibit consisting of vintage objects. Finally, you can also visit the **Lefurgey Cultural Centre** *(205 Prince St.)*, which was recently restored after a fire had damaged it in March 2004.

Through a collection of photographs and other articles, the **International Fox Museum ★** *(free admission, donations are welcome; Jun to Sep, 10am to 6pm; 286 Fitzroy St., ☎436-2400)* traces the history of fox-breeding on Prince Edward Island. After a timid start at the end of the 19th century, this activity came to represent 17% of the province's economy by the 1920s. In those years, a pair of silver foxes could fetch as much as $35,000. Efforts are now being made to revive this once prosperous industry.

By visiting **Cavendish Figurines** *(149B Industrial Cr.)* you can see how the *Anne of Green Gables* dolls are manufactured. Or head to the **College of Piping** *(free admission; 619 Water St. E., ☎436-5377)* for an introduction to traditional Scottish music.

Miscouche

In Miscouche, barely 8km west of Summerside, the **Acadian Museum of Prince Edward Island** ★ *($3.50; Jul to Aug, every day 9:30am to 7pm; Sep to Jun, Mon-Fri 9:30am to 5pm, Sun 1pm to 4pm; Rte. 2, ☎432-2880)* offers an excellent introduction to the world of the local Acadians. The museum's exhibit recounts the history of the island's Acadian community, from 1720 to the present day, with the help of artifacts, writings, numerous illustrations and an audiovisual presentation, shown on request, which lasts about 15min. The museum also houses Prince Edward Island's Acadian Research Centre, which has a library and archives that may be used for genealogical research.

Wellington

From Miscouche you can head to the small community of Wellington, where

the interesting **Econo-musée de la Courtepointe** *(Promenade Acadienne, ☎854-2614, www.econo-musee-atl.com)* is located. This economuseum is situated in the Promenade Acadienne, a pretty little shopping complex with arts-and-crafts boutiques, built inside replicas of 19th-century buildings.

Mont-Carmel

Mont-Carmel, known for many years as «Grand-Ruisseau», was founded in 1812 by the Arseneault and Gallant families. The splendour of the **Église Notre-Dame-du-Mont-Carmel** ★ *(Rte. 11, ☎854-2208)*, which lies in the heart of the parish, bears eloquent witness to the prominent role played by Catholicism in Acadian culture.

Located on the site of the very first settlement of Grand-Ruisseau (now known as «Mont-Carmel»), the **Acadian Pioneer Village** ★ *($3.50; Jun to mid-Sep, 9am to 7pm; Rte. 11, 1.5km west of the church, ☎800-567-3228)* recreates the rustic lifestyle of early 19th-century Acadians. The village includes a church and presbytery, two family homes, a smithy, a school and a barn. Most of the furniture in the buildings was donated by the citizens of neighbouring villages. There is a comfortable hotel at the entrance to the pioneer village, as well as the restaurant **Étoile de Mer** (see p 231), which offers visitors a unique opportunity to enjoy Acadian cuisine.

Cap-Egmont

A pretty fishing village looking out on the Northumberland Strait, Cap-Egmont, often referred to locally as «Grand-Cap», lies in the most peaceful setting imaginable. Visitors can stop at the **Bottle Houses** *($4; Jul and Aug, every day 9am to 8pm; Jun and Sep, every day 10am to 6pm; Rte. 11, ☎854-2987)*, three buildings made out of a total of 25,000 bottles, set in the midst of a park filled with flowers.

O'Leary

A village typical of this region which produces masses of potatoes, O'Leary is home to the **Prince Edward Island Potato Museum** ★ *($5; mid-May to mid-Oct, Mon-Sat 9am to 5pm, Sun 1pm to 5pm; 22 Parkview Dr., ☎859-2039, www.peipotato museum.com)*, the only museum in Canada devoted to the history of potato-growing. The well-designed exhibit clearly illustrates this tuber's role in the history of food. Visitors will also learn the various techniques used to grow potatoes. This is an excellent and interesting museum, despite the peculiar nature of its subject matter.

★
West Point

A stop at West Point offers an opportunity to explore one of the most peaceful and picturesque spots on the island, **Cedar Dunes Provincial Park** ★ *(Rte. 14)*, which features endless deserted beaches and dunes and constitutes an excellent spot for observing wildlife and vegetation. Another interesting spot nearby is the **West Point Lighthouse** *($2.50; early Jun and Sep, every day 8am to 8pm; mid-Jun to Aug, every day 8am to 9:30pm; Rte. 14, ☎859-3606, www.westpointlighthouse.com)*, which dates back to 1875 and is one of the largest in the province. In addition to housing a museum and a restaurant, it is the only lighthouse in Canada that is used as an inn.

★
North Cape

West Point Lighthouse

The scenery around North Cape, the northernmost tip of the island, is not only pretty, but often spectacular, with red sandstone cliffs plunging into the blue waters of the Gulf of St. Lawrence. North Cape itself occupies a lovely site along the coast. Here, visitors will find the **North Cape, Nature and Technology in Perfect Harmony** *($5; mid-May to end of Jun and early Sep to mid-Oct, every day 10am to 6pm; Jul to early Sep 9am to 8pm; at the end of Rte. 12; ☎882-2991 or 882-3535)* interpretive centre, where wind technology is tested and evaluated. A small exhibit explains the advantages of using this type of energy.

Alberton

In 1534, during his first trip along the coast of what would eventually become Canada, Jacques Cartier apparently stopped at the present-day site of Alber-

ton, an attractive little village which is now adorned with a number of pretty buildings. Set up inside the former courthouse, built in 1878 and now a historic site, the **Alberton Museum** ★ *($3; Jun to Sep, Mon-Sat 10am to 5:30pm, Sun 1pm to 5pm; Church St., ☎853-4048)* offers a wonderful introduction to the history of this region. The collection on display includes such varied objects as furniture, dishes and old farming instruments.

Located at the mouth of Mill River, where it flows into Cascumpec Bay, **Mill River Provincial Park** stretches forth like a huge garden. It also features a superb golf course.

Tyne Valley

The region of Tyne Valley, on the edge of Malpeque Bay, offers some of the most beautiful rural landscapes on the island.

When passing through the village itself, the **Shoreline Lobster Pattern Sweaters** *(Rte. 12, ☎831-2950)* shop is a must to visit; splendid wool sweaters in original designs are made right on the premises. A few kilometres north of Tyne Valley, the **Green Park Shipbuilding Museum** ★ *($2.50; Jun to early Sep, 9am to 5pm; Rte. 12, Port Hill, ☎831-7947)* reminds visitors that shipbuilding was the mainspring of Prince Edward Island's economy for the greater part of the 19th century.

The museum presents an exhibit on the history and the various techniques used in shipbuilding. The site includes a reconstructed shipyard, complete with a ship in progress. Right nearby stands the **Yeo house**, the lovely former home of James Yeo Jr., who owned a shipyard here in the 19th century.

Parks and Beaches

The craggy, breathtakingly beautiful landscapes, endless beaches and unique plant and animal life are among the most spectacular attractions of this red crescent-shaped island that lies 40km east of continental Canada. A number of parks have been created to highlight the natural beauty of parts of the island.

The most renowned is Prince Edward Island National Park, but there are also some 30 provincial parks. More than 40 lovely beaches with sands in countless shades of pink also help make this island a veritable paradise for vacationers.

Parks

The province's parks provide all sorts of services for vacationers (campgrounds, picnic areas, supervised beaches) and feature a variety of activities intended to familiarize visitors with various natural settings; nature trails and welcome centres offer information on the local plant and animal life. These parks are an inexhaustible source of discovery for the entire family.

About 15 of the provincial parks have **camping** facili-

ties (☎859-8790 *for reservations).* Visitors can also camp in the national park, where camping conditions vary (see p 206).

Beaches

The island is fringed by a series of exquisite white- and red-sand beaches, especially along the north coast. Magnificent sandy **beaches ★**, which are ideal for swimming and undoubtedly among the most beautiful on the eastern coast of North America, run along the entire shoreline of **Prince Edward Island National Park** *(☎672-6350).* Some have been landscaped and are supervised; they usually have showers, changing rooms and little restaurants. Other beaches, just as beautiful but unsupervised, stretch as far as the eye can see. The eastern part of Prince Edward Island boasts equally beautiful sandy beaches.

The splendid **beach ★** at **Basin Head**, also accessible from **Red Point Provincial Park**, stretches several kilometres. Another exceptional **beach ★** is located at **Panmure Island Provincial Park**, in the eastern section of the island. Along Northumberland Strait, where the water is considerably warmer than it is in the Gulf of St. Lawrence, there are also a few lovely beaches. **Wood Islands Provincial Park**, in the southeast, is a very pleasant place to swim.

Outdoor Activities

Hiking

The railway line of yesteryear which crisscrossed the island has found a new purpose: it has been filled with crushed stone and transformed into several hiking and cycling paths. This 270km network of paths is called the **Confederation Trail**. A branch of the trail heads towards the western part of the island, from Kensington to Tignish, where beautiful scenery can be enjoyed along the way. It also passes through a number of towns, including Summerside and Wellington.

Another section of the trail crisscrosses the eastern part of the island, from Mount Stewart to Elmira. It runs along St. Peters Bay, offers magnificent views of the dunes on Greenwich Peninsula, and crosses wooded areas and wetlands, where you can observe many different species of birds, such as the Canada goose. The trail also leads to Souris and Borden-Carleton.

The various trails in **Prince Edward Island National Park** allow hikers to learn about the plant and animal life that have developed in this part of the island.

The **Reeds and Rushes Trail** (0.5km) leads through the forest to a marsh spanned by a wooden footbridge, from which hikers can observe a wide variety of insects, plants and animals.

The **Farmlands Trail** (2km) leads into the heart of the park, passing through different types of vegetation, including a spruce forest.

The **Bubbling Springs Trail** (2km) also passes through a spruce forest, then leads to an observation post on the banks of a pond, where visitors can observe various species of water birds.

There are three other trails to help you discover the forest: **Homestead** (5.5 to 8km), **Haunted Wood** (1.6km) and **Balsam Hollow** (1km).

There are also hiking trails in the provincial parks, particularly the **Mill River**, **Brudenell** and **Strathgartney** parks.

Bird-Watching

More than 300 different species of birds can be observed along the shores of the island. From the remarkable great blue heron to the kingfisher, blue jay (the provincial emblem) and rare piping plover, the island has plenty to offer amateur ornithologists. In **Prince Edward Island National Park**, there are observa-

Blue jay

tion points at **Brackley Marsh**, **Orby Head**, **Covehead Pier** and all along the **Rustico Island floating bridge**. It is not necessary to go to a park to observe many of these birds; they can be spotted in many different parts of the island–just keep your eyes peeled.

Cycling

The island is a marvellous place to cycle, since the traffic is never heavy and there are many quiet roads crisscrossing the fields. In **Prince Edward Island National Park**, cyclists can enjoy magnificent scenery without having to worry about cars.

Cycling enthusiasts will be delighted to learn that they can pedal across the island thanks to the **Confederation Trail** (see p 215), which runs through the island, from Tignish in the west to Elmira in the east.

For information on cycling excursions, contact **Sport PEI** (☎*368-4110*).

The following establishments offer tours and bike rentals:

Charlottetown

Smooth Cycle
$17/half-day, $25/day
172 Prince St.
☎*566-5530*

MacQueen's Island Tours
$25/day
430 Queen St.
☎*368-2453 or*
800-969-2822
⇗*894-4547*
www.macqueens.com

North Rustico

Outside Expedition
$25/day
☎*963-3366 or*
800-207-3899
⇗*963-3322*
www.getoutside.com
Outside Expedition offers bike tours that last a few days, allowing you to explore some of the most picturesque regions in the province.

Summerside

Papa Whealie's Bike Rentals
$25/day
Harbour Dr.
☎439-3346

Souris

Venture Out Cycle & Kayak
$12/half-day
☎687-1234 or
877-473-4386

Brackley Beach

Brackley Beach Freewheeling Adventures
☎857-3600 or
800-672-0775
www.freewheeling.ca

North Shore Rentals
$20/day
☎672-2022

Golf

Prince Edward Island has a lot to offer golfers. It features several excellent greens, laid out on sites that not only make for a good game, but also offer breathtaking views of the sea and the cliffs.

The 18-hole **Green Gables Golf Course** *($42; Cavendish,* ☎963-2488) is located in **Prince Edward Island National Park**.

In **Mill River Provincial Park** *($40;* ☎859-8873), there is an 18-hole golf course that stretches 5,944m along the banks of the Mill River.

Built around dunes, **Links at Crowbush Cove** *($60;* ☎961-7300) is one of the most beautiful golf courses in the province, or perhaps the entire country. It offers a breathtaking view of the sea along its 18-hole course.

The 18-hole golf course in **Brudenell River Provincial Park** *($50; Roseneath,* ☎652-8965 or 800-235-8909) also boasts a lovely site. Golfers get to enjoy the vast, peaceful park surrounding the green.

For more information on the island's golf courses, consult the *Golf Prince Edward Island* brochure or write to:

Golf PEI
Charlottetown
☎888-734-7529
information
☎866-465-3734
reservations
www.golfpei.com

Cruises

Visitors wishing to head out to sea can take part in one of a variety of short cruises offered by the following local companies:

Charlottetown

Peake's Warf Boat Cruises
various excursions from $16
☎566-4458

Cardigan

Cardigan Sailing Tours
$60/day
☎583-2020

Seal-Watching

Groups of seals regularly swim near the shores of the island. Visitors interested in observing these large sea mammals can take part in a seal-watching tour.

Cruise Manada
$20, $10 children under 12
☎838-3444 or
800-986-3444
Departures: From the Montague Marina; mid-May to late Jun and early Sep to early Oct, every day 10am and 2pm; early Jul to late Aug, every day 10am, 1pm, 3:30pm and 6:30pm; Jul and Aug, every day 2:30pm.

Garry's Seal Cruises
$17, children $8.50
☎962-2494 or
800-561-2494
Departures: Murray River pier; May to mid-Jun, every day 1pm, 3:30pm and 6:30pm; mid-Jun to mid-Sep, every day 8:30am, 10:30am, 1pm, 3:30pm and 6:30pm; mid-Sep to late Oct, 10:30am, 1pm, 6:30pm.

Murray Harbour Seal & Bird Watching Tours
$15, children $10
Murray Harbour
☎962-3163
Jul to mid-Sep, every day 9am, 1pm and 6pm.

Deep-Sea Fishing

Several companies offer deep-sea fishing excursions, giving visitors a chance to test their fishing skills while enjoying an exciting outing on the water.

Excursions of this type set out from different places on the island:

Covehead Harbour

Richard's Deep-Sea Fishing
☎672-2376

Salty Seas Deep-Sea Fishing
☎672-3246

Alberton

Andrew's Mist
☎853-2307

North Rustico

Aiden Deep-Sea Fishing
☎963-3522

Kayaking

Outside Expeditions
☎963-3366
www.getoutside.com
The tours organized by this company offer magnificent views of the island's coastal region, along the red cliffs of the north or down Murray River. These trips will also delight bird lovers, since they cross several prime bird-watching areas.

Accommodations

Tour A: Charlottetown

Youth Hostel
$
153 Mount Edward Rd.
☎894-9696
The youth hostel provides the least expensive lodging in the provincial capital region. It's a friendly spot set up in a barn-like building about 3km west of downtown, near the university. During summer, rooms are also available at the **University of Prince Edward Island** (*$;* ☎566-0442).

The Duchess of Kent Inn
$$-$$$
4 rooms
218 Kent St., C1A 3W6
☎566-5826 or
800-665-5826
The Duchess of Kent Inn occupies a lovely old house built in 1875. This charming inn is located downtown, near most of Charlottetown's principal attractions.

Heritage Harbour House Inn
$$$ bkfst incl.
pb/sb
11 rooms
9 Grafton St., C1A 1K3
☎892-6633 or
800-405-0066
≈892-8420
The Heritage Harbour House Inn is an excellent bed and breakfast located on a residential street, just a stone's throw from the Confederation Centre of the Arts. The rooms are impeccably clean, as are the shared bathrooms. The house itself is warm and inviting, and guests have use of a day room where they can relax, read or watch television. Each morning, Bonnie, the owner and charming hostess, serves a continental breakfast.

Elmwood Heritage Inn
$$$ bkfst incl.
ℑ
PO Box 3128, 121 North River Rd., C1A 3K7
☎368-3310 or
877-933-3310
≈628-8457
www.elmwoodinn.pe.ca
At the end of an elm-lined lane stands the Elmwood Heritage Inn, a lovely Victorian house built in the 1880s by celebrated architect William C. Harris. Set in tranquil surroundings, about 15min on foot from downtown Charlottetown, this inn offers a few very well-decorated rooms and suites furnished with antiques. All of them have private washrooms and balconies. Each of the two suites has a fireplace, as does the living room. Bicycles, a very pleasant means of touring the city and its outskirts, are available for guests' use.

Hillhurst Inn
$$$ bkfst incl.
ℜ
181 Fitzroy St., C1A 1S3
☎894-8004
≈892-7679
www.hillhurst.com
The Hillhurst Inn is one of the most beautiful hotels on the island. Built in 1897, this sumptuous residence once belonged to a man named George Longworth, a local merchant who amassed a fortune through shipbuilding, trade and, so it is said,

bootlegging. Once you see how splendid looking this house is, there will certainly be no doubt in your mind as to Longworth's wealth.

The richly ornamented dining room and entrance hall are particularly lovely and are furnished, as is the rest of the house, with antiques. Each guest room, located on the upper floors, is unique, comfortable, very well decorated and equipped with a private bathroom. Guests are accorded a very friendly welcome; breakfast is copious and delicious.

Charlotte's Rose Inn
$$$ bkfst incl.
4 rooms
11 Grafton St., C1A 1K3
☎*892-3699 or*
888-237-3699
⇆*894-3699*
The Charlotte's Rose Inn is an elegant, 19th-century Victorian home. Originally built in 1884, it has since been meticulously renovated. In addition to its old-world charm, its rooms are furnished with antiques and private bathrooms. Great location on a peaceful street in the old part of town.

Fitzroy Hall
$$$ bkfst incl.
⊗
8 rooms
45 Fitzroy St., C1A 1RA
☎*368-2077*
Charlottetown has preserved a few beautiful Victorian homes, many of which have been converted into B&Bs. One example is Fitzroy Hall. Originally built in 1872, this impeccably decorated house could very well serve as a small museum. Each room is filled with

antiques and 19th-century photos, pleasantly re-creating the charm of a bygone era. The owners can also tell you a few haunting stories about this home.

Best Western Charlottetown
$$$
≈, ℜ, △, 🐾, ⊘
238 Grafton St., C1A 1L5
☎*892-2461*
⇆*566-2979*
Located in the heart of Charlottetown, the Best Western Charlottetown offers comfortable rooms and suites that were renovated just a few years ago. Amenities of note include a family restaurant and an indoor swimming pool.

Islander Motor Lodge
$$$
ℜ
50 rooms
146-148 Pownal St., C1A 3W6
☎*892-1217 or*
800-268-6261
⇆*566-1623*
The Islander Motor Lodge offers motel-style accommodation, but in pleasantly furnished, quality rooms. This is a convenient place for families, since it's just a few steps from the main attractions and has a small, inexpensive restaurant. If you are travelling on a low budget, reserve in advance to get the less expensive rooms.

Dundee Arms
$$$
ℜ, 🐾
18 rooms
200 Pownal St., C1A 3W8
☎*892-2496 or*
877-638-6333
⇆*368-8532*
www.dundeearms.com
The Dundee Arms, built in 1903, is an elegant inn set

up inside a large Queen Anne–style residence built in the early 1900s. The beautifully decorated bedrooms and common rooms will take you back in time. The inn also features a highly reputed dining room. Finally, there are comfortable, slightly less expensive motel rooms available in an adjoining building.

Charlottetown Rodd Classic
$$$$ bkfst incl.
ℜ, ≈, ⊘, △, 🐾
115 rooms
75 Kent St.
☎*894-7371 or*
800-565-7633
⇆*368-2178*
The Charlottetown Rodd Classic is an excellent downtown hotel with a rather stately appearance, built to meet the needs of both business travellers and vacationers. Renovated in 1998, the inviting rooms are modern and tastefully furnished. The hotel also houses a good restaurant.

🌴 Delta Prince Edward
$$$$
ℜ, ≈, △, ⊘, 🐾, ♿
211 rooms
18 Queen St., C1A 8B9
☎*566-2222 or*
800-894-1203
⇆*566-2282*
www.deltaprinceedward. pe.ca
The Delta Prince Edward is without a doubt the ritziest and most comfortable hotel on the island. It is also perfectly situated, looking out over the port of Charlottetown. The interior is modern and well designed, with four restaurants and all the facilities one would expect to find in a hotel of this calibre.

Business meetings and conferences are often held at the Prince Edward. Its conference rooms can accommodate up to 650 people.

☸ Inns on Great George
$$$$-$$$$$ bkfst incl.
𝕁, ⊛, K
49 rooms
58 Great George St.
☎892-0606 or
800-361-1118
www.innsongreatgeorge.
com

Completely unique, the Inns on Great George consist of several residences located in one district, in the heart of the historic section of Charlottetown. You can choose from a lovely selection of lodging types that will satisfy the needs and budgets of one and all. The main building, the Pavilion, features 24 well-decorated rooms furnished with antiques. There are also more luxurious rooms that include, among other things, a fireplace and a whirlpool tub. The Wellington, for its part, consists of five spacious rooms and a lovely sitting room on the first floor. Those who prefer taking advantage of a full residence should opt for the Carriage House; this two-storey house features a bedroom, living room, kitchen and bathroom. The Witter-Coombs House and the Carroll House are two charming, historical residences featuring luxurious suites. The J.H. Down House and the Townhouses offer well-equipped apartments that feature one, two or three bedrooms. Breakfast is served in the friendly dining room of the Pavilion.

Cornwall

Chez Nous B&B
$$-$$$ bkfst incl.
4 rooms
Hwy. 248, Old Ferry Rd.,
C0A 1H0
☎566-2779 or
800-566-2779
⇁628-3852
www.cheznous.pe.ca

Located 15min by car from Charlottetown, Chez Nous B&B is another option for those who prefer to stay in the countryside rather than in town. Well-lit and warmly decorated with paintings and antique furniture, this home will immediately take your breath away. The owners greet their guests with a warm welcome and do everything to ensure they have an enjoyable stay in this wonderful B&B. The breakfasts are delicious.

Tour B: Central P.E.I.

Strathgartney

☸ Strathgartney Homestead Inn
$$ bkfst incl.
ℜ, sb/pb
8 rooms
Trans-Canada Hwy., C0A 1H0
☎675-4711 or
800-267-4407
www.strathgartney.com

Right near Strathgartney Provincial Park, the Strathgartney Homestead Inn is set up inside a superb upper-class home built in 1863 on a property covering about 10ha. The fine food served in the dining room adds to the charm of this magnificent house, which is adorned with period furniture. A good choice for anyone wishing to relive the charm of the Victorian era in a rural setting.

Victoria

☸ The Orient Hotel
$$ bkfst incl.
ℜ
6 rooms
mid-May to mid-Oct
Main St., C0A 2G0
☎658-2503 or
800-565-6743
⇁658-2078
www.theorienthotel.com

The Orient Hotel fits in perfectly with Victoria's historic atmosphere. Built a century ago, it is a delightful place with decorations and furniture from days gone by. It is comfortable without being overly luxurious, and guests receive a warm welcome. The Orient also has a dining room and a pretty tea room which looks out onto the street.

Sea View

Adams Sea View Cottages
$$$
K, ℜ
15 rooms
mid-May to late Sep
RR2, C0B 1M0
☎836-5259

During summer, scores of cottages are available for rent all along the north shore of the island. There are over a dozen of these at Adams Sea View Cottages, all lined up along the beach. Each cottage has two bedrooms, a kitchenette and a refrigerator. The rooms are sparsely furnished.

Cavendish

Andy's Surfside Inn
$ bkfst incl.
7 rooms
Jun to Nov
PO Box 5, C1A 7K2
☎*963-2405*
=*963-2341*
At Andy's Surfside Inn, the sea is all around you: it's the backdrop for the property, as well as the theme for the decor inside the inn, which is filled with maritime decorations in each of its rooms. As soon as you enter, you fell like you are in a sailor's hideaway. The large house is modest, but nevertheless has a certain allure.

New Glasgow Highland Camping
$
≈
34 campsites, 18 huts
RR3, C0A 1N0
☎*964-3232*
Situated in a wooded area, this campground is quite pleasant. You can pitch your tent here or stay in one of the little cabins. Near Cavendish.

Kindred Spirits Country Inn
$$ bkfst incl.
≡, ⊛
25 rooms
mid-May to Oct
Rte. 6, C0A 1N0
☎*963-2434*
=*963-2619*
www.kindredspirits.ca
Furnished with antiques and exquisitely decorated, the Kindred Spirits Country Inn offers quality accommodation less than 1km from the Cavendish beach. Guests can relax in one of several common rooms, including a superb

living room. Kindred Spirits has 25 rooms, 14 of which have whirlpool baths. The establishment also offers suites with more luxurious accommodation, as well as 12 fully equipped charming cottages, more suitable for families.

🦅 Osprey Outlook
$$ bkfst incl.
⊛
3 rooms
Hwy. 242, C0A 1X0
☎*963-3366*
=*963-3322*
www.ospreyoutlook.com
Even if it's just for one night, it sometimes feels good to be welcomed by a family when you are far away from home. If this is what you seek, you will feel right at home at this B&B. The house is modest, but the rooms are comfortable. For longer stays, a small apartment is also available. The family organizes kayak and bike trips.

🏊 Shining Waters Country Inn and Cottages
$$ bkfst incl.
≈, ☺
10 rooms
May to mid-Oct
Rte. 13, C0A 1N0
☎/=*963-2251*
☎*877-963-2251*
Located in the heart of Cavendish, the Shining Water Country Inn and Cottages is a lovely old house with spacious porches all around. This inn features comfortable rooms and friendly service. Guests can relax in a pleasant, airy living room. There are cottages behind the house, which are available for about $15 extra.

Country House Inn
$$
K
5 rooms
RR2, C0A 1N0
☎/=*963-2055*
☎*800-363-2055*
The Country House Inn is conveniently located near Prince Edward Island Provincial Park, the main attraction in the region. This inn is also only 2min from a beautiful sandy beach on the coast. The rooms, which are filled with a variety of knick-knacks, are basic, but offer adequate comfort.

Bay Vista Motel
$$
≈, ℝ
RR6, C0A 1E0
☎*963-2225 or*
800-846-0601
www.bayvistamotorinn.
com
The Bay Vista Motel is a quiet establishment located near the main points of interest in the region. It is equipped with a pool and surrounded by a large grassy lawn where children can play in complete safety. There is a popular family restaurant nearby. The rooms are all clean, but some are more inviting than others; try to see a few before you choose one.

Cavendish Motel
$$
ℜ, ≈, ℂ
35 rooms
early Jun to mid-Sep
intersection of Rtes. 6 and 13, C0A 1M0
☎*963-2244 or*
800-565-2243
www.cavendishmotel.
pe.ca
In the centre of what could be considered the village

of Cavendish, the Cavendish Motel offers clean, pleasant, modern rooms.

Anne Shirley Motel & Cottages
$$ motel
$$$ cottage
K, ≈
Rte. 13, C0A 7T2
☎963-2224 or
800-565-2243
www.anneshirley.ca
The Anne Shirley Motel & Cottages is a fair-size establishment located near the centre of Cavendish. Various types of accommodation are available here: motel rooms, one- and two-bedroom apartments and one- and two-bedroom cottages with kitchenettes. This spot is very well kept, modern and welcoming.

Lakeview Lodges & Cottages
$$$
≈, ⊛
Rte. 6, C0A 1N0
☎963-2436 or
800-565-7550
⇌963-2493
www.lakeviewlodge.cc
Beach and golf lovers will be in seventh heaven at the Lakeview Lodges & Cottages, located at the edge of the national park and just a few hundred metres from the Green Gables Golf Course. The Lakeview offers a few motel-style rooms and about 20 cottages, each equipped with one or two bedrooms. This establishment is well maintained and surrounded by greenery.

Cladach Breagh
$$$
K, ≈
3km west of Cavendish, C0A 1E0
☎886-3313
www.cladachbreagh.com
Slightly set back from the centre of Cavendish, the Cladach Breagh numbers about 15 cottages in a beautiful setting on the edge of New London Bay. The interior design of the cottages is cozy and very inviting. Each one is equipped with a kitchenette and can house up to four people. There is a small, undeveloped beach nearby that is unsuitable for swimming but just right for long seaside walks.

Brackley Beach

North Winds Motel
$$-$$$
≈, ℝ, K
66 rooms
RR9, Brackley Beach, C1E 1Z3
☎672-2046 or
800-901-2245
The North Winds Motel is set in a peaceful environment about 2km from the entrance to the national park. Its rooms are spacious and well kept. The motel also has a lovely indoor pool.

Shaw's Hotel & Cottages
$$$$-$$$$$
ℜ, ℑ, sb/pb
99 Apple Tree Rd., C1E 1Z3
☎672-2022
⇌672-3000
Shaw's Hotel first opened its doors in 1860; since then, four generations of the Shaw family have taken the helm of this little establishment, located a 15min walk from the national park. Although the ocean is not far away, a pastoral atmosphere predominates at this hotel surrounded by

farm buildings in the open countryside. The rooms are clean and comfortable, although slightly rudimentary. Some of them have private bathrooms. It is also possible to stay in one of the nearby cottages, which are equipped with fireplaces and up to four bedrooms.

New Glasgow

My Mother's Country Inn
$$-$$$$$
K
10 rooms
Rte. 13, Hunter River
☎964-2508 or
800-272-2071
⇌964-2606
www.mymotherscountry inn.com
Located in a peaceful and pleasant spot, My Mother's Country Inn is housed in an elegant residence that was built in the middle of the 18th century. This stylish inn offers rooms and suites that are both comfortable and modern. Guests can also stay in fully equipped cottages featuring two or three bedrooms that are ideal for families. The surroundings are simply wonderful.

New Glasgow Inn
$$$ bkfst incl.
6 rooms
Rte. 13
☎964-2315 or
877-862-0270
New Glasgow is a charming, quaint village in the heart of a beautiful rural section of the island, only a few minutes away from the beaches and attractions of Cavendish. It is therefore a good choice for many a traveller. Indeed, the New Glasgow Inn is one of the loveliest

places in the village. It features comfortable rooms and suites furnished with antiques. The reception is very friendly and the breakfasts are delicious and unique.

South Rustico

Barachois Inn
$$$$ bkfst incl.
ℜ
8 rooms
Rte. 243, C0A 1N0
☎*963-2194*
⌐*963-2906*
www.barachoisinn.com
The heart of South Rustico is in reality a crossroads ringed by a farmers' bank, a school, a presbytery and a church—the key institutions of the local francophone community. The Barachois Inn, located nearby, is a nice addition to this pretty architectural grouping. Built in the 1870s, this lovely upper-class house was renovated just a few years ago and includes two rooms and two suites, all furnished in period style and each equipped with a private washroom. With its large porches and beautiful gardens, the Barachois is very appealing. It is especially suited to those who enjoy the charms of a quiet, country setting.

Little Rock

Dalvay-by-the-Sea
$$$$
ℜ, ≈
PO Box 8, C0A 1P0
☎*672-2048*
www.dalvaybythesea.com
Dalvay-by-the-Sea is an impressive Victorian house located at the eastern tip of the park, a few hundred metres from magnificent white-sand beaches. It is

also the only lodging establishment within the perimeter of the national park. Built in 1896, the Dalvay was once the summer residence of Alexander MacDonald, one of the most powerful American industrialists of his era and a business partner of John D. Rockefeller. Nowadays, the house has 26 very elegantly decorated rooms and eight cottages, all with private bathrooms. As much because of its unique location as for its splendid design, Dalvay-by-the-Sea is one of the best hotels on the island; advance reservations for summertime stays are strongly recommended. Visitors who lodge elsewhere should still stop by for a peek at the building's splendid dining and living rooms.

Tour C: Eastern P.E.I.

Little Sands

Bayberry Cliff Inn Bed & Breakfast
$$$ bkfst incl.
4 rooms
mid-May to late Sep
Rte. 4, 8km from Wood Islands, C0A 1W0
☎*962-3395 or 800-668-3395*
www.bayberrycliffinn.com
One of the most charming establishments of its type on the island, the Bayberry Cliff Inn Bed & Breakfast offers quality accommodation. The warm interior, with its rich woodwork, was designed with taste and care, and the rooms, each different from the next, are very inviting. Large windows have been added to the back of the house to let the sun in and

provide an excellent view of the sea. The property is bordered by a red-sandstone bluff.

Montague

Windows on the Water
$$
≈
106 Sackville St., C0A 1R0
☎*838-2080*
Windows on the Water is a pleasant, charming inn with a very nice atmosphere, located in the heart of Montague. All of its rooms are carefully furnished and decorated, and offer splendid views of the river and the town's small harbour. In the morning, breakfast is served in the dining room on a pleasant terrace. Windows on the Water is equally renowned as one of the better restaurants in the area (see p 229).

Roseneath

Rodd Brudenell River Resort
$$$
ℜ, ≈, ☺, △, ⊛
99 rooms
May to Oct

PO Box 67, Roseneath, C0A 1G0
☎*652-2332 or 800-565-7633*
⌐*652-2886*
www.rodd-hotels.ca
Visitors who like to spend all day playing golf should choose the Rodd Brudenell River Resort, erected on a pretty, verdant site along a river in Brudenell River Provincial Park, right near the fantastic golf course. There are about 50 hotel rooms and 40 cottages set on the riverbank. The rooms are modern, comfortable, well-furnished and equip-

ped with balconies. The Rodd also offers family activities.

Little Pond

🐚 **Inn at Spry Point**
$$$$ bkfst incl.
ℜ, ⊛
15 rooms
mid-Jun to Oct
RR4, C0A 2B0
☎*583-2400*
⇒*583-2176*
www.innatsprypoint.com
A haven of peace, the Inn at Spry Point stands on a large property with access to a private beach. The comfortable rooms feature futons, modern furniture and large windows. One thing that sets the Inn at Spry Point apart is that most of its rooms are split-level, with the upper portion affording a lovely view. There is a pleasant restaurant on the ground floor.

Bay Fortune

🐚 **Inn at Bay Fortune**
$$$-$$$$ bkfst incl.
ℜ, ℑ
18 rooms
late May to mid-Oct
Rte. 310, C0A 2B0
☎*687-3745*
⇒*687-3540*
www.innatbayfortune.
com
One of the most sumptuous and charming inns on the island, the Inn at Bay Fortune offers high-quality food and accommodation. The building has a unique architectural design; it stands on a lovely, verdant site, offering a superb view of the bay after which it is named. The rooms are furnished in an elegant and original fashion, each one different from the last. Some even

have a fireplace. An excellent choice!

Souris

Bed & Breakfast by the Sea
$ bkfst incl
4 rooms
PO Box 223, Hwy. 16, C0A 2B0
☎*687-1527*
The Bed & Breakfast by the Sea is a peaceful accommodation option. Located in a large, gorgeous home, it has a magnificent view of the sea. The rooms are comfortable and the welcome is courteous.

Hilltop Motel
$$
12 rooms
Lea Crane Dr., C0A 2B0
☎*687-3315 or*
800-445-5734
⇒*687-3003*
The Hilltop Motel has clean, comfortable rooms and is advantageously located within a few minutes from the boarding point for the ferry to the Îles-de-la-Madeleine in Québec.

Matthew House Inn
$$$ bkfst incl.
6 rooms
15 Breakwater St., C0A 2B0
☎*687-3461*
⇒*687-5630*
www.matthewhouseinn.
com
More expensive, but also more elegant, the Matthew House Inn boast a magnificent view of the sea and a meticulous decor. A beautiful collection of antique furniture adorns this Victorian home. The inn offers all the comfort you could hope for, especially within the charming rooms. The property is surrounded by a large garden with majestic trees.

St. Peters

Inn at St. Peters
$$$$$ ½ b
≡, ℜ, ℑ
14 rooms
1668 Greenwich Rd.
☎*961-2135 or*
800-818-0925
⇒*961-2238*
www.innatstpeters.pe.ca
This magnificent residence, located right on St. Peters Bay, is one of the most luxurious lodging establishments in this part of the island. Its 14 beautiful rooms all feature a fireplace, a living room and a private terrace. The inn also features a remarkable fine-cuisine restaurant (see p 230). The establishment is located near the eastern section of Prince Edward Island National Park and some excellent golf courses.

Lakeside

🐚 **Rodd Crowbush Golf & Beach Resort**
$$$$-$$$$$
≈, ≡, K, ℑ, ⊛
49 rooms
Rte. 350
☎*961-5600 or*
800-565-7633
⇒*961-5601*
www.rodd-hotels.ca
The Rodd Crowbush Golf & Beach Resort is one of the most prestigious hotel establishments on the island. It stands at the heart of the famous **Links at Crowbush Cove** (see p 217) golf course and features 25 rooms, as well as 24 suites that include a living room and a whirlpool tub. The complex also offers 32 luxurious cottages with one or two bedrooms, living room, fireplace, whirlpool tub and kitchen. The Rodd is a

fantastic place, especially since it has access to the beach.

Tour D: Western P.E.I.

Summerside

Silver Fox Inn
$$ bkfst incl.
ℜ
6 rooms
61 Granville St., C1N 2Z3
☎*436-1664 or*
800-565-4033
The beautiful Silver Fox Inn lies a short distance from the port in an old residential neighbourhood and is surrounded by a pretty little garden. All of the rooms are well furnished and inviting. Overall, the inn is elegantly decorated and has an atmosphere reminiscent of early-20th-century high-society.

Summerside Inn
$$ bkfst incl.
6 rooms
98 Summer St.
☎*436-1417 or*
877-477-1417
This large, elegant Victorian home is located in a residential district. It contains six absolutely charming rooms, each featuring a private bathroom and lovely antique furnishings.

Mulberry Motel
$$
39 rooms
6 Water St. E., C1N 1A1
☎*436-2520 or*
800-274-3825
⇌*436-4210*
At the entrance to town, there is a series of inexpensive motels. One of these is the Mulberry Motel, whose rooms offer

a fairly decent and standard level of comfort.

Quality Inn – Garden of the Gulf
$$$
ℜ, ≈
95 rooms
618 Water St. E., C1N 2V5
☎*436-2295 or*
800-265-5551
⇌*436-6277*
The Quality Inn – Garden of the Gulf features several sports facilities, including a nine-hole golf course and an indoor swimming pool. This modern hotel is pleasant and well-designed, making good use of natural lighting.

Loyalist Country Inn
$$$
ℜ, △, ⊘, ⊛
94 rooms
195 Harbour Dr., C1N 5R2
☎*436-3333*
⇌*436-4304*
The most comfortable hotel in Summerside, the Loyalist Country Inn boasts an excellent location in the heart of town, with a view of the nearby port. Although they are modern, the rooms still have character and are tastefully furnished. This hotel is a real favourite with business travellers. Its restaurant, the **Prince William Dining Room** (see p 230), is highly recommended.

Mont-Carmel

Hôtel Village sur l'océan
$$-$$$
ℜ, ≈
late May to late Sep
30 rooms
Rte.11, C0B 2E0
☎*854-2227 or*
800-567-3228
⇌*854-2304*
There is no hotel more luxurious in the Evangeline

region than the Hôtel Village sur l'océan, located beside the **Acadian Pioneer Village** (see p 213) and the famous **Étoile de Mer** (see p 231) restaurant. The place is actually too big for the number of tourists who visit this region, so its clean, comfortable rooms are often empty.

West Point

West Point Lighthouse
$$
ℜ
9 rooms
late may to late Sep
O'Leary, RR2, C0B 1V0
☎*859-3605 or*
800-764-6854
⇌*859-1510*
*www.westpointlighthouse.
com*
The only inn in Canada set up inside a lighthouse (only one room is actually inside the lighthouse; the others are in the adjoining building), the West Point Lighthouse is a good spot to stop for a day or two, long enough to explore the magnificent dunes and beaches along the nearby shore. This is a friendly place, and the rooms are decent.

Tignish

Tignish Heritage Inn
$$ bkfst incl.
17 rooms
PO Box 398, C0B 2B0
☎*882-2491 or*
877-882-2491
⇌*882-2500*
www.tignish.com/inn
A former convent built in 1868, the Tignish Heritage Inn has an unusual but pleasant setting. The simply furnished rooms are

adequate. Guests have access to the kitchen.

Alberton

Traveller's Inn Motel
$$
ℜ
14 rooms
Rte. 12, C0B 1B0
☎*853-2215 or*
800-561-7829
The Traveller's Inn Motel, on the edge of Alberton, is not exactly charming, but nevertheless offers acceptable accommodation for the price.

Woodstock

Rodd Mill River Resort
$$
ℜ, ⊛, △, ☺, ≈
90 rooms
Feb, Mar and May to Oct
O'Leary, RR2, C0B 1V0
☎*859-3555 or*
800-565-7633
⇄*859-2486*
www.rodd-hotels.ca
The Rodd Mill River Resort is ideal for sports buffs. Not only is there an excellent golf course nearby, but the resort itself has an indoor pool, tennis courts, a gym and squash courts. The rooms, furthermore, are very comfortable.

Tyne Valley

Doctor's Inn Bed & Breakfast
$$ bkfst incl.
ℜ
2 rooms
Rte. 167, C0B 2C0
☎*831-3057*
The Doctor's Inn Bed & Breakfast is a country home typical of the 1860s, with a pleasant garden. Its two decent, but not very luxurious rooms are available year-round. The

place is very quiet, and excellent evening meals are available.

Restaurants

Tour A: Charlottetown

Cow's
$
In front of the Confederation Centre of the Arts
Those with a sweet tooth will love Cow's, which offers wonderful ice cream and waffle cones.

Anchor and Oar House Grub & Grog
$
mid-May to mid-Oct
behind the Delta Prince Edward, Peake's Wharf
☎*894-1260*
Just outside The Delta Prince Edward hotel, on the same side as Peake's Wharf, the Anchor and Oar House Grub & Grog has a simple, inexpensive lunch menu. There is a selection of salads and sandwiches, and several fish and seafood dishes round out the offerings.

Cedar's Eatery
$
81 University St.
☎*892-7377*
Centrally located, Cedar's Eatery offers an inexpensive change of pace. *Kebab, falafel, shawarma* and *shish taouk*, Lebanese cuisine's most famous exports, are the headliners. The atmosphere is young, friendly and unpretentious, and the portions are generous.

Formosa Tea House
$
86 Prince St.
☎*566-4991*
A colourful place that some might even describe as strange, the Formosa Tea House only offers a few dishes, which are actually more snacks than actual meals. The place is popular for tea time in an Asian-style decor.

Peake's Quay
$-$$
May to Sep
36 Water St.
☎*368-1330*
www.peakesquay.com
Peake's Quay could win the trophy for the best-situated restaurant in Charlottetown. Its pleasant terrace looks directly out over the city's marina. An economical menu of simple dishes, including excellent seafood crepes, is offered at breakfast time. In the evening, the menu is more elaborate but still affordable. You can savour, among other dishes, a delicious plate of lobster for a decent price. Peake's Quay is also a pub where people can linger over a drink or two.

The Pilot House
$$
70 Grafton St.
☎*894-9222*
A fun and cozy pub with a wood decor, the Pilot House offers quality fare at reasonable prices. Hearty portions of various offerings, mainly pasta, meat and seafood dishes are served here. The atmosphere is quieter than you'd usually expect from a pub.

Lobster on the Wharf
$$
2 Prince St.
☎368-2888
This restaurant is blessed with a fabulous location, right next to the water at Confederation Landing Park. As is to be expected, the menu here is largely made up of seafood, although you can also enjoy steak or pasta. This place is especially popular with families. In addition to the restaurant, the establishment features a fish market for those who prefer take-out.

Off Broadway Cafe
$$
125 Sydney St.
☎566-4620
Perhaps surprisingly for a city of this size, Charlottetown does hide a few gems in terms of restaurants, one of them being the Off Broadway Cafe. Its relaxing, romantic and tasteful atmosphere and its excellent, delicious menu make it the hottest restaurant in town. A variety of dishes, many with a European touch, are served. Seafood connoisseurs will not be disappointed by the main dishes and appetizers. Rounding up the menu is a choice selection of desserts, including many crepes.

Piazza Joe's Bistro
$$
189 Kent St.
☎894-4291
Piazza Joe's Bistro offers pizza baked in a wood burning oven, lasagna *au gratin* and *bruschetta*. It's a great place for lovers of Italian cuisine. The relaxed atmosphere, generous portions and reasonable prices make this place an excellent choice for families and groups of friends.

Meeko's Mediterranean Cafe & Grill
$$-$$$
146 Richmond St.
☎892-9800
There's an exotic feeling in the air at Meeko's, one of the few Greek restaurants on the island. Tzatziki, souvlaki and moussaka are featured on the menu, as well as some Italian specialties and steak for those looking for a more conventional option. The dining room decor transports you to Greece. Children's portions are also available.

Sirenella Ristorante
$$-$$$
83 Water St.
☎628-2271
A little establishment that is easy to miss, Sirenella Ristorante is in fact one of the best restaurants in Charlottetown. The menu is made up of Italian specialties, of which fresh pasta and meat are the essential elements. The dessert menu includes some succulent Italian ice creams. The Sirenella also has a small patio.

Lucy Maud Dining Room
$$$
4 Sidney St.
☎894-6868
The Atlantic Tourism & Hospitality Institute offers a variety of programs for young people who want to specialize in tourism or the hotel business. Among them, the cooking program merits particular mention. It not only includes cooking courses but also food-service training, and a dining room has been opened which now welcomes guests so students can practice their skills. Although it is a training school, visitors can expect good service and quality food—a good opportunity to discover the talents of budding chefs while enjoying a good meal. The menu offers French and Italian specialities. Reservations are required.

The Selkirk
$$$
18 Queen St., Delta Prince Edward
☎894-1208
The Selkirk offers a varied menu featuring several seafood dishes. Among the appetizers, the lobster-garnished linguine is particularly succulent. The main dishes, including parboiled Atlantic salmon, Atlantic halibut filet and duck roasted with red pepper are all excellent. The ambiance at the Selkirk is, of course, very chic, but inviting.

Tour B: Central P.E.I.

Victoria

Landmark Cafe & Craft
$-$$
mid-Jun to Sep
Main St.
☎658-2286
In the centre of the charming little village of Victoria, near the two inns and almost directly opposite the chocolate shop, visitors will find the Landmark Cafe & Craft an extremely friendly, warm and simple place whose walls are adorned with pretty handicrafts. The menu consists

of light homemade dishes–quiche, *tourtière* (meat pie), pasta, salads and desserts, amongst others.

Mrs. Profitt's Tea Shop
$$
Main St., Orient Hotel
☎658-2503
For afternoon tea or a more substantial meal, head to Mrs. Profitt's Tea Shop, in the charming setting of Victoria's historic **Orient Hotel** (see p 220). The menu is not very elaborate, but does include a variety of sandwiches and desserts, as well as fresh lobster, lobster salad and lobster quiche.

Margate

Shipwright's Cafe
$$-$$$
11869 Rte. 6
☎836-3403
This café is housed in a beautiful residence dating from the 18th century that stands in the middle of a lovely garden. The menu features a selection of island products, with an emphasis on fish and sea-food dishes. The dining room offers a great view of the pretty landscaping behind the establishment.

New London

Catherine McKinnon's Spot O'Tea
$$$
RR6
☎886-3346
Catherine McKinnon's Spot O'Tea, a pretty res-taurant, offers dinner-theatre, a popular form of entertainment on the island. In addition to a good meal, guests can enjoy an entertaining show. On beautiful sum-mer nights, those who prefer to watch nature's own spectacle can sit on the terrace facing the Stanley River.

St. Ann

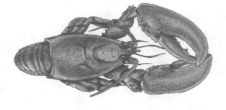 ## St. Ann's Church Lobster Supper
$$
Jun to Oct
Rte. 224
☎621-0635
For more almost 50 years now, St. Ann's Church Lobster Supper, a non-profit organization, has been serving lobster every day from 4pm to 9pm. The menu, like those of other similar local restau-rants, includes a salad, fish soup, mussels, lobster and dessert. This is the type of tradition that visitors to Prince Edward Island should definitely not miss out on.

New Glasgow

Olde Glasgow Mill
$-$$
☎964-3313
Some high-calibre restau-rants attract evening visi-tors to New Glasgow, one of the most picturesque villages on this part of the island. One of these little gems is the Olde Glasgow Mill, which offers an inex-pensive varied menu mainly composed of sea-food and fish dishes.

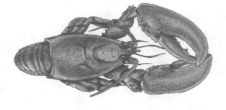 ## Cafe on the Clyde
$$
Rte. 224, at the intersection of Rte. 258
☎964-4300
Cafe on the Clyde, on the premises of the P.E.I. Pre-serve Co., is a great place to linger, as much for the cuisine as for the ambi-ance. Its pretty dining room overlooking the river makes diners feel right at home. The evening menu offers a good selection of local specialties, namely seafood and fish. The café is open for breakfast and light meals are served all day long. The temptation to while away some time before or after a meal at the P.E.I. Preserve Co. shop, which sells a variety of homemade food prod-ucts, is practically irresist-ible.

New Glasgow Lobster Suppers
$$
Jun to mid-Oct
Rte. 258
☎964-2870
Overlooking the Clyde River, the New Glasgow Lobster Suppers is one of the island's classic eater-ies–it has served over a million customers! During summer, hundreds of people pass through its two dining rooms every evening between 4pm and 8:30pm. The charm of this place lies in its simplicity; in

the dining rooms, there are rows of plain tables covered with red-and-white-checkered tablecloths. The menu, obviously, revolves around lobster. Each meal includes an all-you-can-eat appetizer, one lobster and a homemade dessert. Prices vary depending on the size of the lobster you choose.

North Rustico

 Fisherman's Wharf Lobster Suppers
$$
mid-May to mid-Oct
Rte. 6
☎*963-2669*
A well-known local institution, Fisherman's Wharf Lobster Suppers also serves traditional lobster meals, including unlimited fish and seafood soup, a vast choice of salads, bread, lobster and dessert. The place can seat approximately 500 people, which doesn't exactly make it intimate, but that's part of its charm.

Oyster Bed Bridge

Café St-Jean
$$
early Jun to late Sep
Rte. 6
☎*963-3133*
Both elegant and inviting, the Café St-Jean is a small restaurant set up inside a rustic looking house that looks out on the Wheatley River. In the evening, the food is fairly elaborate, with not only seafood on the menu, but also a fair number of other well-prepared, original dishes and Cajun specialties. The less expensive lunch menu offers light dishes. The name of the café refers to the time before the British

conquest, when the island was known as Île St-Jean and the Acadian presence was very strong in this region.

Brackley Beach

Dunes Cafe
$$
mid-Jun to Oct, 11:30am to 9pm
Rte. 15
☎*672-2586*
The Dunes Cafe is the only place of its kind on the island. Set up in a complex of original, contemporary design, which also houses a remarkable art gallery, it serves Asian cuisine with strong Vietnamese influences. The dishes offer a most interesting and innovative blend of fragrances and flavours. In the back garden, you'll find sculptures representing elements from Buddhist and Hindu temples.

Tour C: Eastern P.E.I.

Orwell Corner

Sir Andrew Macphail Restaurant
$$
mid-Jun to mid-Sep
Rte. 1
☎*651-2789*
Located on the historic site of the Sir Andrew Macphail Homestead, the Sir Andrew Macphail Restaurant is a pleasant place to enjoy a good, light meal at lunchtime or take a break in the afternoon. Though the menu is simple, the food is tasty. Reservations are required for dinner. The elegance and atmosphere of the Macphail Homestead make this a very appealing little restaurant.

Montague

Lobster Shanty Restaurant
$$
Rte. 17
☎*838-2463*
In the purest Prince Edward Island tradition, the Lobster Shanty Restaurant offers first-rate lobster suppers that include a seafood appetizer, a lobster and a dessert, for about $20. Guests sit in a simply decorated dining room overlooking the Montague River. This restaurant had the honour of serving Her Majesty Queen Elizabeth II and Prince Philip in 1973, as well as Prince Charles and Lady Diana in 1983. In addition to its seafood, the place is also known for its char-broiled steaks.

Windows on the Water Cafe
$$-$$$
106 Sackville St.
☎*838-2080*
The Windows on the Water Cafe is a thoroughly enjoyable spot, especially when the weather allows for dining *al fresco* on its pretty terrace overlooking Montague's little harbour. The main elements on the lunch menu are sandwiches, salads, soups and pasta dishes. In the evening, there is generally a selection of about 10 seafood, fish, poultry and meat dishes.

Cardigan

Cardigan Craft Centre & Tea Room
$
Rte. 4
☎*583-2930*
Set up inside the former railway station, the Cardigan Craft Centre & Tea

Prince Edward Island

Room has a simple, inexpensive menu made up of sandwiches, salads and other light dishes.

Cardigan Lobster Suppers
$$
late Jun to late Sep
Rte. 311, at the intersection of Rtes. 3 and 4
☎*583-2020*
Set up inside a century-old general store, Cardigan Lobster Suppers serves traditional lobster meals at reasonable prices, from 5pm to 9pm every night. This type of supper, consisting of a seafood appetizer, a lobster and a dessert, is an island tradition that is not to be missed.

Bay Fortune

Inn at Bay Fortune
$$$
May to mid-Oct
Rte. 310
☎*687-3745*
Without question one of the finest restaurants in the region, the dining room of the **Inn at Bay Fortune** (see p 224) has a beautiful layout and offers a magnificent view of the bay. The chef is one of the best in the province, and dishes are prepared from market-fresh ingredients. The cuisine is both exquisite and original, and the service is highly professional.

Clear Spring

The Carousel
$$
mid-Jun to Sep
Hwy. 16
☎*687-4100*
You won't find fries or soft drinks on the menu at The Carousel. Instead, you will notice a healthy selection of foods: organic fruits and vegetables, seafood and

homemade cakes and pies. The selection of fresh produce, which varies according to the season, guarantees the success of this establishment. This place concocts simply prepared, quality dishes every day. Nestled in the middle of the forest with a magnificent view of its natural setting, this restaurant has much to offer.

St. Peters

Rick's Fish and Chips & Seafood House
$-$$
Rte. 2
☎*961-3439*
In St. Peters, the spot to satisfy your hunger without breaking your piggy-bank is Rick's. The atmosphere is unpretentious and the decor is simple, but the variety of dishes that are served here is well worth the trip.

Inn at St. Peters
$$$
1668 Greenwich Rd.
☎*961-2135*
Undoubtedly one of the top dining establishments on the island, the restaurant at the **Inn at St. Peters** (see p 224) offers refined cuisine that will please the foodie in you. The dishes, which are all delicious, are concocted according to the chef's inspiration from the freshest of local products. Various fine cheeses and alcoholic beverages round out the menu. You'll spend a lovely time here in the wonderful dining room, with the large fireplace and huge windows overlooking the bay and beautiful outdoor gardens.

Tour D: Western P.E.I.

Summerside

Deckhouse
$-$$
Spinnakers' Landing
☎*436-0660*
Laid out in one of the buildings on Spinnakers' Landing, the Deckhouse is a pleasant pub that serves light meals. The upstairs terrace offers a lovely view of the port and the town.

Brothers Two
$-$$
618 Water St. E.
☎*436-9654*
With its extremely relaxed pub atmosphere, the Brothers Two is one of the liveliest and most popular spots in Summerside. People come here to eat or simply have a drink. As in many restaurants on the island, fish and seafood are highlighted on the menu, which nevertheless lists a variety of other specialties as well. The portions are generous.

Prince William Dining Room
$$
195 Harbour Dr., in the Loyalist Country Inn
☎*436-3333*
The Prince William Dining Room offers well-prepared food and a fairly elaborate menu, including a wide choice of appetizers and main dishes. Seafood and fish make up a good part of the offerings, but various steak and chicken dishes are also available. There are occasional evening specials, such as the excellent surf and turf, consisting of a

small steak and a lobster tail. The service is courteous and the atmosphere is elegant but relaxed.

Mont-Carmel

L'Étoile de mer
$-$$
mid-Jun to Sep
Rte. 11
☎*854-2227*
A visit to the Evangeline region offers a good opportunity to enjoy a meal at the most famous Acadian restaurant on the island, L'Étoile de mer, located at the entrance to the Acadian Pioneer Village. Dishes prepared according to the best-known Acadian recipes, such as *râpure*, *fricot au poulet*, *fricot aux palourdes* and *pâté acadien*, are served in a cozy dining room. The menu also lists a good number of other (more expensive) dishes, mostly lobster and other types of seafood and fish. This is a good place to familiarize yourself with the island's Acadian community.

West Point

West Point Lighthouse
$-$$
late May to late Sep
Rte. 14
☎*859-3605*
A good place to stop for a break during a tour of western Prince Edward Island, the West Point Lighthouse is an inn (see p 225) whose restaurant is open from daybreak to 9:30pm. The lunch menu consists of a variety of light dishes, including the usual lobster rolls, chowders and other seafood. In the evening, the cuisine becomes a bit more sophisti-

cated, with more elaborate appetizers and main courses, such as a fisherman's platter that includes five different kinds of seafood or fish. The menu also lists steak, chicken Kiev and pasta. The restaurant is laid out in a simple fashion in the building adjoining the lighthouse. Guests can also eat on the terrace outside.

North Cape

Wind & Reef
$$
at the end of Rte. 12
☎*882-3535*
Located on the site of the **North Cape, Nature and Technology in Perfect Harmony** (see p 214) centre, the Wind & Reef is a perfect place to dine on seafood and fish. The menu includes other dishes as well, but people come here mainly for the lobster, shrimp, oysters and fisherman's platter. Although the prices are not exorbitant, you do have to pay a little extra for the lovely setting. Lighter, less expensive meals are also available at lunch time.

Entertainment

Tour A: Charlottetown

Buzz magazine, published monthly, is a good source of information on the cultural events in town, such as film, theatre, music, bars and nightclubs.

Each summer, for more than three decades now, the Confederation Centre of the Arts has presented the ***Anne of Green Gables*** *(Confederation Centre of the Arts,* ☎*628-1864 or 800-565-0278, www. confederationcentre.com)* musical, inspired by the work of Prince Edward Island's favourite daughter, Lucy Maud Montgomery. Both funny and touching, the story of little "Anne with an *e*" is now a classic of children's literature known all over the world. It is amazing to see to what point Anne has affected Japanese youth, who now make up a significant percentage of tourists to the island. The musical is well staged and makes for a fun night out.

At the **Festival Dinner Theatre** *(Charlottetown Hotel,* ☎*892-6633)* guests can enjoy a meal while watching (and sometimes even participating in!) an entertaining play. You'll laugh with, and at, everyone. The young actors wait the tables, sing and play music.

For fans of Irish music, the **Olde Dublin Pub** *(131 Sydney St.,* ☎*892-6992)* is the place to be for a pint of Guinness and a jig. There is often live music, and simple meals are also served in this popular spot.

Cedar's Eatery *(81 University St., 2nd floor)* regularly showcases popular bands on the weekends. You can also check out the **Off Broadway Cafe** *(125 Sydney St.),* which hosts jazz concerts.

Myron's *(161 Kent St.,* ☎*892-4375)* is one of the most popular spots for a night out in Charlottetown. This vast complex includes a pool room in the basement, a performance hall, a small dance floor on the first floor and a larger one on the second floor.

The **St. James' Gate** *(129 Kent St.,* ☎*892-4283)* is a lovely restaurant that becomes a bar at night. Musical performances are often presented here. This is a popular spot with residents who come to discover local talent.

The **Merchantman Pub** *(23 Queen St.,* ☎*892-9150)* is housed in a brick building with large windows. It includes three rooms, as well as a terrace at the back. This place is rather quiet, without the typically noisy ambiance of a pub.

An especially friendly place to have a drink, **Gahan House** *(126 Sydney St.,* ☎*626-2337)* is located in a quaint building with a warm atmosphere. People come here to savour beer brewed on site.

Horse-racing fans can get their fix at the **Charlottetown Driving Park** *(Kensington Rd.,* ☎*892-6823)*. Races are held two to four times a week during the summer.

Tour B: Central P.E.I.

Victoria

Almost every night in July and August, the **Victoria Playhouse** *(about $12;*

☎*658-2025 or 800-925-2025, www.victoriaplayhouse.com)* presents entertaining plays and concerts in its little theatre. With its quality performances, the Victoria Playhouse is as charming as the city itself.

Tour D:
Western P.E.I.

Summerside

At the **Feast Dinner Theatre** *(Water St. E., Brothers Two restaurant,* ☎*888-2200 or 800-748-1010, www.feastdinnertheatres.ca)*, which has been presented on summer evenings *(starting at 6:30pm)* for the past 20 years or so, diners enjoy their meal while delighting in a humorous non-stop blend of music, songs and theatre.

Mont-Carmel

The **Cuisine à Mémé** *(Rte. 11, Acadian Pioneet Village,* ☎*854-2227 or 800-567-3228)* brings Acadian Prince Edward Island to life through songs, music and theatre. These shows, held in the evening, are combined with a meal.

Shopping

Tour A:
Charlottetown

In Charlottetown, visitors can go to **Peake's Wharf** to stroll along the pier and enjoy the seashore while doing some shopping in the pretty boutiques.

There is something for everyone here–crafts, souvenirs, T-shirts, etc.

PEI Factory Shops
Trans-Canada Hwy.
Those who want to buy well-known brand names such as Jones of New York, Liz Claiborne, Levi's, Island Beach Co. T-shirts with pretty island logos, or Paderno pots and pans, should head to the PEI Factory Shops, where there are good bargains to be had.

Confederation Court Mall *(corner of Ken St. and University Ave.,* ☎*894-9505)* has 90 stores, with something for everyone.

Both children and their parents will enjoy picking out one of the funny T-shirts and sweatshirts available at **Cow's** *(opposite the Confederation Centre of the Arts)*. Make sure to sample the store's excellent ice cream too!

Visitors looking for warm woolens should head over to the **Wool Sweater Factory Outlet** *(at the Delta Prince Edward and 133 Queen St.,* ☎*566-5850)*, which offers a lovely selection of high-quality, casual sweaters.

All sorts of beautiful crafts, books and souvenirs are available at **The Two Sisters** *(150 Richmond St.,* ☎*894-3407)*.

P.E.I. has inspired many an artist. The **Island Craft Shop** *(156 Richmond St.,* ☎*892-5152)* presents some beautiful creations by members of the PEI Craft Council, an organization that promotes local artists. Sculptures, pottery, wool sweaters and other quality crafts are sold here.

The charming **Island Poster** (*142 Richmond St.*, ☎566-5642) shop sells wonderful mementoes of your stay in the province–namely large, beautiful posters.

Anne of Green Gables fans can poke around in the **Anne of Green Gables Store** (*110 Queen St.*, ☎368-2663).

The Book Emporium (*169 Queen St.*, ☎628-2001) offers a great selection of new and used books, as well as works by regional authors.

Tour B: Central P.E.I.

Victoria

The melt-in-your-mouth homemade chocolates at **Island Chocolate** (*Main St.*, ☎658-2320) are an absolute delight.

Borden-Carleton

Those who appreciate craft shops should check out **The Official Island Store** (☎437-6421), which has, without a doubt, the loveliest crafts on the island.

Kensington

Who doesn't know Geppeto? On the island, his name is synonymous with home-made toys–wooden toys, of course. The puppets at **Geppeto's Workshop** (*Hwy. 238*, ☎886-2339) are all masterpieces.

New Glasgow

If you couldn't find the toy of your dreams at Geppeto's, you can always try another little factory that makes amusing wooden toys: **The Toy Factory** (*Hwy. 13*, ☎964-2299), in New Glasgow.

The **Prince Edward Island Preserve Co.** (*at the intersection of Rtes. 224 and 258*; ☎964-4300) sells a wide selection of excellent jams that contain very little sugar.

South Rustico

The pottery made on the island has become quite well known. If you are looking to buy some, **The Old Forge Pottery** (*Hwy. 6, at the intersection with Hwy. 243*, ☎963-2878) is a must.

Cavendish

The **Cavendish Boardwalk** (*Rte. 6*) has all kinds of adorable little shops, some specializing in T-shirts and souvenirs. Visitors will also find a branch of **Roots** (sportswear) and **Cow's**, with its cute clothing and terrific ice cream. At the front of the store, you'll find a selection of slightly defective Cow's clothing at reduced prices.

The **Island Treasures** (*at the intersection of Rtes. 6 and 13*, ☎963-2350) shop is another good place to purchase local crafts and many other articles for the house.

Tour C: Eastern P.E.I.

Murray River

Those who enjoy exploring cute little souvenir and craft shops should make sure to stop by Murray River, which boasts two of the loveliest craft shops in the region, if not on the entire island.

The Old General Store
Main St.
☎962-2459
The Old General Store features a delightful selection of housewares and quilts.

The Primrose Path
Rte. 3
☎838-3707
The Primrose Path is a worthy competitor to the Old General Store.

Tour D: Western P.E.I.

Summerside

In summer, there is nothing more pleasant than strolling about **Spinnaker Landing**, with its pretty string of shops along the waterside. This complex, built on piles, also has a little outdoor theatre where a variety of activities are organized.

Tyne Valley

Shoreline Lobster Pattern Sweaters (*Rte. 12*, ☎831-2950) is a shop where visitors will find top-quality wool sweaters hand-knit on the premises, as well as a variety of souvenirs.

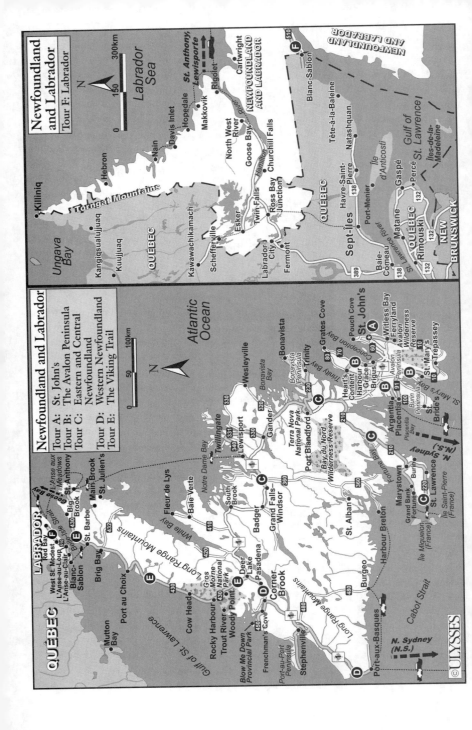

Newfoundland and Labrador

Tour A: St. John's
Tour B: The Avalon Peninsula
Tour C: Eastern and Central Newfoundland
Tour D: Western Newfoundland
Tour E: The Viking Trail

Newfoundland and Labrador
Tour F: Labrador

Newfoundland
and Labrador

Still a little-known corner

of the world, Newfoundland and Labrador is very different from Canada's other Atlantic provinces—not just geographically, but historically and culturally as well.

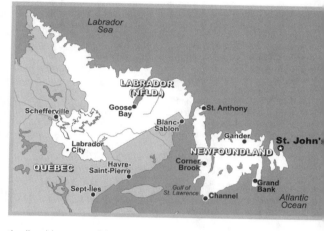

The province's geographical isolation, at the northeastern most edge of North America, has helped forge its unique character. "The Rock," as it is aptly nicknamed, is a rocky island whose landscape, often very rugged, is so splendid that you can't help but stand back and marvel.

The western part of the island is shaped by the ancient Long Range Mountains, the tail end of the Appalachians. Gros Morne National Park, a UNESCO World Heritage Site, offers visitors a remarkable opportunity to explore these mountains, which in many places plunge straight into

the limpid waters of the deep fjords.

Farther north, towards L'Anse aux Meadows, the former site of a Viking camp, the road runs along flat and strikingly desolate coastal landscapes. Elsewhere, lofty cliffs, pebble beaches and tiny fishing villages, known as outports, punctuate the shore, providing scenes of picturesque enchantment.

The capital of the province, St. John's, lies in a magnificent natural setting on the shores of a long

harbour rimmed with high, rocky hills.

In addition to the island of Newfoundland, the province also includes Labrador, covered with subarctic forests and tundra. Labrador, sparsely populated with just a few thousand inhabitants, covers nearly 300,000km². Both the island of Newfoundland and Labrador, far off the beaten tourist track, offer outdoor enthusiasts countless opportunities to explore a rich wilderness. Without much difficulty, visitors can observe caribou and moose, colonies of puffins and gannets, and, from the coast, whales swimming about and icebergs slowly drifting by.

The numerous traces of Aboriginal communities that have been discovered along its shores indicate that this province has been inhabited almost continuously, for over 8,000 years.

The first people to settle here belonged to the Maritime Archaic tradition. Paleoeskimo groups (Dorset and Groswater) arrived here about 3,000 years ago. The first people encountered by European explorers, however, were the Beothuk, whose ancestors are thought to have come to Newfoundland 3,500 years ago. Due to its relative proximity to the European continent, the island of Newfoundland was one of the very first places in the New World to be known to Europe.

Legend has it that at the end of the 5th century, St. Brendan, an Irish abbot, crossed the Atlantic in his search for new peoples to convert to Christianity and landed on this island.

The first Europeans whose presence here can actually be proven, however, were the Vikings, who, around the year 1000, apparently used the island as a base for exploring the continent. Leif's camp, in L'Anse-aux-Meadows, is the oldest known European site in North America.

It wasn't until several centuries later that Europeans rediscovered Newfoundland. In the 15th century, Europe learned of the teeming waters that surround the island through Basque fishermen. Each summer the Basques would come to this region to fish cod in the Grand Banks and hunt whales in the Strait of Belle Isle. The Basque whaling station in Red Bay, Labrador, dates from the 16th century.

Officially, however, the credit for discovering Newfoundland goes to Giovanni Caboto (John Cabot), who came here in the service of England in 1497. Over the following centuries, the French and the English competed for control of Newfoundland and the rest of North America. In 1558, the English founded their first permanent settlement in

Trinity, on the Bonavista Peninsula.

Then, in 1583, Sir Humphrey Gilbert officially claimed St. John's harbour and the rest of the island of Newfoundland for Queen Elizabeth I of England. This did not, however, prevent the French from establishing their own permanent settlement, known as Plaisance (now Placentia), on the coast of the Avalon Peninsula in 1662.

Plaisance remained the capital of the French colony of Terre-Neuve (Newfoundland) until the signing of the Treaty of Utrecht in 1713. Though the island was ceded to England under this treaty, the French continued to take an interest in it; in fact, the last battle of the Seven Years' War (or French and Indian War) took place in St. John's. The war ended with the signing of the Treaty of Paris in 1762, under which France lost its North American empire. Over the following centuries, more people, many from Ireland, came to settle along the coasts of Newfoundland. In 1867, the year the Canadian Confederation was created, the islanders decided that

Newfoundland should remain a British colony. It wasn't until 1949 that Newfoundland became the tenth and final province to join Canada.

The official name of the province has recently been changed from "Newfoundland" to "Newfoundland and Labrador".

Finding Your Way Around

This chapter is divided into six tours: five for Newfoundland and one for Labrador:

Tour A: St. John's ★★

Tour B: The Avalon Peninsula ★★

Tour C: Eastern and Central Newfoundland ★

Tour D: Western Newfoundland ★

Tour E: The Viking Trail ★★★

Tour F: Labrador ★

By Ferry

Island of Newfoundland

The island of Newfoundland is accessible by ferry from North Sydney, on Cape Breton Island, Nova Scotia. These ferries, op-erated by **Marine Atlantic** (*www.marine-atlantic.ca*, ☎800-341-7981), offer service to Port aux Basques (in southwestern Newfoundland) and Argentia (on the Avalon Peninsula, in southeastern Newfoundland). The crossing between North Sydney and Port aux Basques usually takes about 5hrs. With a few exceptions, there is at least one crossing per day, each way, between North Sydney and Port aux Basques. One-way fare costs approximately $76.50 per car or $27 per adult.

It takes about 14hrs to travel between North Sydney and Argentia. There is at least one crossing each way, every Monday, Wednesday and Friday from June to September. The one-way fare is $157 per car or $75.50 per adult.

It is also possible to take the ferry from Goose Bay, Labrador to the island of Newfoundland. This ferry, which travels to Lewisporte, in north-central Newfoundland, runs several times a week from the beginning of June to the beginning of September (*Reservations:* ☎866-535-2567). There is an un-paved road that leads from Goose Bay to Churchill Falls and Labrador City, then on to Baie Comeau (Québec).

Labrador

Two or three times a day, from May to October, a ferry travels between St. Barbe, on the "Viking Trail," and Blanc Sablon (Québec), on the Strait of Belle Isle. Blanc Sablon is only 3km from the Labrador border, and a paved road connects it to Red Bay. The ferry schedule makes it possible to make a day trip to Labrador. Reservations: ☎**866-535-2567**.

A cargo ship sets out each week from St. Anthony, at the end of the "Viking Trail," to bring supplies to some 48 communities along the coast of Labrador. The ship also doubles as a cruise boat for visitors who would like to discover Labrador's beautiful coastline. The round trip takes about 3 weeks. Reservations: ☎**800-563-6353**.

By Plane

Island of Newfoundland

Air Canada (☎888-247-2262, *www.aircanada.com*) offers direct flights between St. John's and a number of large Canadian cities, including Halifax, Montréal and Toronto. Air Canada also offers direct service to St. John's from London, England. The airport is only 6km from downtown St. John's.

Labrador

Airplanes fly into the Wabush, Churchill Falls and Goose Bay airports from outside Labrador (mostly from the island of Newfoundland). The main airlines serving Labrador are **Air Canada** (☎888-247-2262, www.aircanada.ca), **Westjet** (☎888-448-8888, www.westjet.com), **Provincial Airlines** (☎709-576-1666, www.provair.com) and **Air Labrador** (☎800-563-3042, www.airlabrador.com).

By Train

Labrador

Rail service between Labrador City (Labrador) and Sept-Îles (Québec) is provided by **Quebec North Shore & Labrador Railways** (☎418-968-7808).

Car Rentals

The following car rental companies have branches in St. John's and the other major towns in the province:

Avis
☎800-437-0358

Budget
☎800-268-8900

Hertz
☎800-263-0600

National
☎800-387-4747

Thrifty
☎800-847-4389

Labrador

There is an unpaved road that leads from Baie Comeau (Québec) to Labrador City, Churchill Falls and Goose Bay. From Goose Bay, motorists can take the ferry to Lewisporte, in the north-central part of the island of Newfoundland. There are limited services from Baie Comeau to Labrador so be sure to have a full tank of gas.

Practical Information

Area code: **709**

Tourist Information

Tourism Newfoundland and Labrador
PO Box 8730, St. John's, A1B 4K2
☎729-2830 or
800-563-6353
≠729-0057
www.gov.nl.ca/tourism

There are about 30 tourist information centres scattered across the province, notably in St. John's and in the major ports of entry.

Exploring

Tour A: St. John's

St. John's, the provincial capital, occupies a spectacular site on the Avalon Peninsula, at the eastern tip of the island. The city is built like an amphitheatre around a well-protected harbour that opens onto the Atlantic Ocean by way of a narrow channel, aptly known as the Narrows, and is flanked on either side by tall, rocky peaks. About 1.6km long and 800m wide, St. John's harbour is an excellent inland port which is frequented by ships of all sizes, flying the flags of various countries. Hidden behind the port installations lies a charming city whose winding streets are lined with pretty, brightly coloured wooden houses.

European fishers of various nationalities were already coming regularly to the site of modern-day St. John's as early as the 15th century. In 1583, Sir Humphrey Gilbert officially claimed the harbour and the rest of the island of Newfoundland for the Queen of England. Later, St. John's was often at the centre of rivalries between the French and the English, falling into the hands of the French on three different occasions. Signal Hill was subsequently fortified to protect the city.

Commissariat House ★ (*$2.50; Jun to Oct; King's Bridge Rd.*, ☎729-6730). This Georgian-style wooden building, completed in 1821, was first used as the residence of the commissariat of the local military base, and then served as the rectory of **St. Thomas Anglican Church** (*Military Rd.*). This church, also known as "Old Garrison Church" (1836), was the chapel of the British garrison of Fort William.

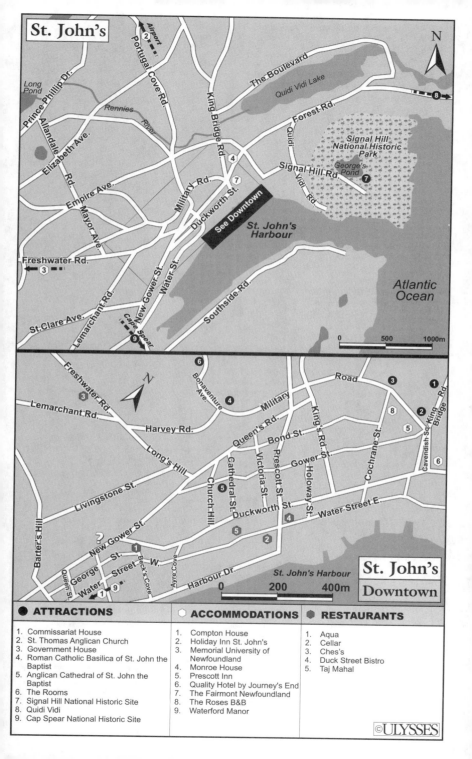

St. John's

N

- Airport
- Portugal Cove Rd.
- The Boulevard
- Quidi Vidi Lake
- Prince Phillip Dr.
- Long Pond
- Allandale Rd.
- Rennies River
- King Bridge Rd.
- Forest Rd.
- Signal Hill National Historic Park
- George's Pond ⑦
- Elizabeth Ave.
- Empire Ave.
- Military Rd.
- ④
- ⑦
- Duckworth St.
- Signal Hill Rd.
- Quidi Vidi Rd.
- Mayor Ave.
- See Downtown
- St. John's Harbour
- Freshwater Rd. ③
- Water St.
- New Gower St.
- Lemarchant Rd.
- St. Clare Ave.
- Southside Rd.
- Atlantic Ocean
- Cape Spear ⑨

0 · 500 · 1000m

St. John's Downtown

N

- Freshwater Rd. ③
- Lemarchant Rd.
- ⑥
- Bonaventure Ave.
- ④
- Military Road
- ③
- ①
- Harvey Rd.
- Queen's Rd.
- Bond St.
- ⑧
- ②
- ⑤
- King Bridge Rd.
- Cavendish Sq.
- Long's Hill
- King's Rd.
- Victoria St.
- Prescott St.
- Gower St.
- Holoway St.
- Cochrane St.
- ⑥
- Livingstone St.
- Cathedral St.
- ⑤
- Church Hill
- Duckworth St.
- ④
- Water Street E.
- Barter's Hill
- ⑤
- ②
- New Gower St.
- ①
- Beck's Cove
- George St.
- W.
- Ayre Cove
- Harbour Dr.
- St. John's Harbour
- Queen St.
- Water Street
- ① ⑨

0 · 200 · 400m

● ATTRACTIONS	○ ACCOMMODATIONS	● RESTAURANTS
1. Commissariat House	1. Compton House	1. Aqua
2. St. Thomas Anglican Church	2. Holiday Inn St. John's	2. Cellar
3. Government House	3. Memorial University of Newfoundland	3. Ches's
4. Roman Catholic Basilica of St. John the Baptist	4. Monroe House	4. Duck Street Bistro
5. Anglican Cathedral of St. John the Baptist	5. Prescott Inn	5. Taj Mahal
6. The Rooms	6. Quality Hotel by Journey's End	
7. Signal Hill National Historic Site	7. The Fairmont Newfoundland	
8. Quidi Vidi	8. The Roses B&B	
9. Cap Spear National Historic Site	9. Waterford Manor	

©ULYSSES

Commissariat House and St. Thomas Church are among the few buildings in downtown St. John's to have survived the great fires of 1846 and 1892. Now a provincial historic site, Commissariat House was restored and furnished in the style of the 1830s.

Government House *(Military Rd.,* ☎ *729-4227)*, another building that escaped the great fires, was erected in 1831 as the official residence of the governor of Newfoundland. It has served as the lieutenant-governor's house since the province joined the Canadian Confederation. The beautifully landscaped grounds are open to the public every day, but the house itself may only be visited by appointment. The frescoes adorning the ceiling were executed by Polish painter Alexander Pindikowski in 1880 and 1881. He would paint during the day then return to the local prison at night, where he was serving a sentence for counterfeiting.

Built on a promontory overlooking the city, the **Roman Catholic Basilica of St. John the Baptist ★** *(Military Rd.)* was designed by Irish architect John Jones in 1855. Originally a cathedral, it was converted into a basilica in 1955. Its facade is graced with two 43m-high towers. The interior is richly decorated; the left transept contains a statue of Our Lady of Fatima, a gift from some Portuguese sailors who had survived a shipwreck on the Grand Banks. The

front of the basilica is a splendid vantage point from which to view the city.

The elegant **Anglican Cathedral of St. John the Baptist** *(at the corner of Church Hill and Gower St.)*, with its pure Gothic lines, was designed by English architect Sir George Gilbert Scott in 1847. It was completed in 1885 but totally destroyed by a fire in 1892. The cathedral was rebuilt a few years later under the supervision of Sir George's son. Its magnificent stained-glass windows are particularly noteworthy. Established in 1699, the parish of St. John the Baptist is the oldest Anglican parish in Canada.

Inauguration of **The Rooms ★★** *(9 Bonaventure Ave.,* ☎ *747-8070)* is expected to take place in June of 2005. This new modern centre will house some of the province's most important institutions, namely the **Provincial Museum**, the **Provincial Archives** and the **Art Gallery of Newfoundland and Labrador**. The Rooms will also welcome travelling exhibitions from elsewhere in Canada and around the world.

Presently located in an old building on Duckworth Street while they await the opening of the new facilities, the Provincial Museum's collections offer an excellent overview of the province's human history. The Provincial Museum's collections also examine the way of life of the six Aboriginal nations who live

or once lived in these regions: the Maritime Archaic who left traces of their passage in Port au Choix, among other places; the Dorset, who lived on the shores of the island until beginning of the first century AD; the Beothuk, the predominant Aboriginal nation in Newfoundland when the Europeans arrived, who have since been completely wiped out; the Mi'kmaq, the largest Aboriginal nation in Atlantic Canada; the Inuit, once called Eskimos, who still inhabit the northernmost shores of Labrador; and the Montagnais, who live in Labrador, along the shores of the Gulf of St. Lawrence. The exhibitions also explore the lives of 19th-century settlers and fishers.

The Provincial Archives, which collect historically significant governmental and private documents, will also be moving from their current location in the Colonial Building to The Rooms. The Archives' collection of historic photographs is particularly rich.

The Art Gallery of Newfoundland and Labrador's collections will also be relocated to The Rooms from their current home at Memorial University.

Signal Hill National Historic Site ★★, visible from all over St. John's, is a rocky hill topped by a tower, which looks out over the mouth of the harbour. The hilltop commands magnificent **views ★★** of the Atlantic, the harbour and the city, both day and night. Be

At the far end of Île Miscou stands one of New Brunswick's oldest lighthouses. -
New Brunswick Department of Tourism and Parks

Bouctouche's Pays de la Sagouine presents writer Antonine Maillet's universe
through a mixture of music, theatre and Acadian legends. - *Gilles Daigle*

The Atlantic puffin's distinctive beak has earned
it the nickname "parakeet of the sea". - *P. Quittemelle*

cause of its strategic location, Signal Hill was long used as an observation and communications post. As early as 1704, flags were flown here to inform the military authorities and merchants of St. John's when ships were arriving. It was also on Signal Hill that the city's defences were erected, from the 18th century to the Second World War.

Vestiges of 19th-century military installations can still be found here. In 1762, Signal Hill was the scene of the final North American battle of the Seven Years' War (also known as the French and Indian War). The French, who had been defeated in Québec City and Louisbourg several years earlier, managed to seize St. John's for a few months, after which they were ousted by English troops led by Lieutenant-Colonel William Amherst. During the summer, visitors can see the **Signal Hill Tattoo**, a re-enactment of 19th-century military exercises, complete with period costumes and gun and cannon salvos.

At the Signal Hill welcome centre, there is a small **museum** *($3.50; mid-Jun to early Sep, every day 8:30am to 8pm, rest of the year 8:30am to 4:30pm; ☎772-5367)* with an exhibition on fishing and the history of St. John's and Newfoundland. **Cabot Tower**, the main building on Signal Hill, was erected in 1897 in honour of the 400th anniversary of John Cabot's arrival in North America and Queen Victo-

ria's diamond jubilee. The tower served as a maritime signal station until 1960 and now houses an exhibition on the history of maritime signalling on this hill.

The exhibit also takes a close look at the life of Guglielmo Marconi, who, on December 12 1901, received the first transatlantic wireless message at Signal Hill. This message, an *S* in Morse code, was sent from Cornwall, England. From the top floor of Cabot Tower, visitors can enjoy a splendid view of the ocean.

For a view of the harbour, head to the ruins of the **Queen's Battery**. From the foot of the cliff, you can see the rock to which the chain used to seal off the harbour in the 18th century was fastened. On the other side, you'll see the ruins of Fort Amherst, now topped by a lighthouse. Signal Hill's well laid out paths make it a pleasant place for a walk. Another trail runs along the harbour from Signal Hill to St. John's.

Standing proudly at the foot of Signal Hill and flanked by rock walls is **Quidi Vidi**, one of the most picturesque villages in the province. It is made up of a few dozen brightly coloured houses, a small chapel and, of course, a fishing port, which has been in use since the 17th century. Nearby **Quidi Vidi Lake** is the scene of the annual **St. John's Regatta**, held on the first Wednesday of August. On a nearby promontory,

visitors will find the remains of the **Quidi Vidi Battery** *(free admission; Jun to Oct, every day 10am to 5:30pm; ☎729-2977)*. Built in 1762 by the French, who occupied St. John's and its surrounding area for several months, this battery was later used by the British and was only abandoned in 1870.

The **Cape Spear National Historic Site ★★** *($3.50; mid-May to mid-Oct, every day 10am to 6pm; 11km south of St. John's on Hwy. 11, ☎772-5367)* is the site of the easternmost point on the North American continent. It was thus graced with a lighthouse (1863), which became the most important one in the province after the lighthouse in St. John's harbour.

Originally, the lighthouse was a square structure built around a tower, at the top of which were seven parabolic reflectors that reflected the light from seven lamps. The lighthouse was modernized over the years and a new one was erected right nearby in 1955. The **old lighthouse** *($2.50; year-round, every day 9am to 5pm)*, furnished the way its keeper's house was in 1939, is open to the public. Close by, visitors can see the remnants of the extensive military installations that were built here during the Second World War. Cape Spear is another pleasant place to stroll along the shore. In fine weather, the view of the ocean and the coast is spectacular.

Newfoundland and Labrador

Lighthouses

Until the 19th century, trade within Canada or with the rest of the world was mainly done by boat. In some parts of the country, fishing was one of the principal means of subsistence, and many little boats sailed the coastal waters. It soon became the governments' chief priority to build a network of lighthouses along the coasts and the main waterways to ensure safety.

These lighthouses were erected on rocky headlands and islands and required some ingenuity on the part of their builders. The very first ones to be built were essentially robust stone towers topped with a light. The Sambro Island Lighthouse, near Halifax, the oldest lighthouse in Canada still in use, is a good example of this type of lighthouse.

These tall towers that dominated the horizon were the most practical, but, when a lighthouse could be built on a natural headland, builders would opt for a simpler model: a house (for the lightkeeper), on top of which a light was placed. The Cape Spear Lighthouse, built on the coast of Newfoundland between 1834 and 1836, is a good example.

All of these lighthouses, especially those built at the extremities of Canada, were meticulously maintained and symbolized, among other things, a willingness to assure a presence *Amari usque ad mare* (from sea to sea).

Tour B: The Avalon Peninsula

Hwy. 10 leads south from St. John's to Witless Bay.

Witless Bay

The **Witless Bay Ecological Reserve** (see p 253) comprises three islands located offshore from the villages of Witless Bay and Bauline. Each summer, these islands serve as a refuge for hundreds of thousands of seabirds, who come here to lay their eggs and raise their nestlings.

From Witless Bay, Hwy. 10 leads south to Ferryland.

Ferryland

A pretty fishing village that feels as if it has been left behind by time, Ferryland was the site of one of the first English colonies in North America (1621). The settlers were sent here by George Calvert, who only stayed here for a few years before moving on to present-day Maryland, thus becoming the first Lord Baltimore. Calvert's departure did not mean the end of the colony of Ferryland, however, which was taken in hand by English navigator David Kirke. At the

Colony of Avalon Archaeology Site (*$3; late May to mid-Oct, every day 9am to 7pm; Hwy. 10, ☎432-3200*), where excavations have been carried out over the past few summers, visitors can see the foundations of the colony and tour the research and analysis facilities.

To learn more about the history of Ferryland and its surrounding area, head to the **Historic Ferryland Museum** (*free admission; mid-Jun to early Sep, every day 9am to 5pm; Hwy. 10, ☎432-2711*), whose exhibitions deal, most notably, with the colony's earliest days.

Caribou

The 1,070km² **Avalon Wilderness Reserve ★**, located in the southeastern part of the Avalon Peninsula, attracts fishing buffs and hikers. To visit the reserve, you must first obtain a permit at La Manche Provincial Park *(Hwy. 10, 11km from Cape Broyle)*. The Avalon Wilderness Reserve is the natural habitat of tens of thousands of caribou. In the southernmost part of the reserve, families of caribou can frequently be seen crossing Highway 10.

Cape St. Mary's is located at the southwesternmost tip of the Avalon Peninsula.

Cape St. Mary's

The **Cape St. Mary's Ecological Reserve ★★** *(May and Sep to mid-Oct, every day 9am to 5pm; Jun to Sep, every day 8am to 7pm; along Hwy. 100, ☎277-1666)* protects the most spectacular and most easily accessible colony of sea birds in North America (see p 253).

From Cape St. Mary's, Hwy. 100 leads to Placentia, on the western coast of the Avalon Peninsula.

★
Placentia

This picturesque village on the shores of Placentia Bay became closely associated with the European presence on the island at a very early date. Basque fishers were already stopping here by the early 16th century, as its pebble beach proved a particularly suitable spot for drying cod. Later, in 1662, the French established the first permanent settlement here.

Known as "Plaisance", it was the capital of the French colony of Terre-Neuve until the signing of the Treaty of Utrecht in 1713. Under the French Regime, Plaisance's role was to contain English expansion in Newfoundland, defend the French fleet based in Newfoundland, and protect Canada

from invasion in times of war. France kept only limited military forces in Plaisance, which did not stop the little garrison from attacking St. John's, the English capital of Newfoundland, three times, in 1696, 1705 and 1709. The 1705 expedition was the only one on which the French failed to seize Fort William, which overlooked St. John's, though they did still manage to burn the city.

Castle Hill National Historic Site ★ *($3.50; mid-May to mid-Oct, every day 10am to 6pm; on Hwy. 100, ☎227-2401)* protects the ruins of various 17th- and 18th-century French and English fortifications. To defend Plaisance, the French built the Vieux Fort in 1662, Fort Louis in 1691 and Fort Royal in 1693. After seizing control of the region, the British erected little Fort Frederick in 1721, and, during the War of the Austrian Succession (1740-1748), the New Fort. Castle Hill commands an outstanding view of Placentia and its bay.

From the Trans-Canada Hwy., Rte. 80 leads north to Heart's Content.

Heart's Content

Heart's Content is another testimony to the pivotal role long played by Newfoundland in communications between Europe and the New World. The invention of the telegraph (1837) revolutionized communications; within a few years, the main urban centres within North America and Europe were linked by telegraph lines. There was soon talk of linking the two continents by a telegraph line, but doing so presented a major technological challenge.

An American by the name of Cyrus W. Field decided to give it a try. In 1856, the Field New York, Newfoundland and London Telegraph Co. succeeded in installing an underwater cable between Nova Scotia and Newfoundland, at a total cost of $1 million. Laying out a transatlantic cable between Newfoundland and Europe was a much more formidable task, given the distance, the strong ocean currents and the depth of the water.

It took seven fruitless attempts before Field's Atlantic Telegraph Company succeeded, in 1866, in installing a cable between Heart's Content and Valentia, Ireland, which was the greatest technological feat of the day. The original **Heart's Content Cable Station** ★ *($2.50; Jun to Oct, every day 10am to 5:30pm; Hwy. 80, ☎583-2160)*, now a provincial historic site, remained in operation until 1965. Today, it houses an interesting well-designed exhibition on the history of the Heart's Content transatlantic cable and, more generally, on world communications, replete with all sorts of 19th-century equipment.

From Heart's Content, take Rte. 74 and then Rte. 70 to Harbour Grace, on Conception Bay.

Harbour Grace

This tiny village earned a certain amount of notoriety in the 17th century, when it was the home base of English pirate Peter Easton. However, Harbour Grace became best known not as a sea port, but rather as the point of departure for some of the first transatlantic flights. Starting in 1919, a number of pilots tried to fly to Europe from Harbour Grace, the most notable being Amelia Earhart, the first woman to accomplish this feat in 1932.

To learn more about these pilots, stop by the **Conception Bay Museum** *($2; Jun to early Sep, 10am to 5pm; Water St., ☎596-5465)*. Its collection consists mostly of photographs and other representations of the most famous planes that stopped over at Heart's Content.

Hwy. 70 runs along Conception Bay to Brigus.

★
Brigus

Located on the shores of a pretty little bay, the striking village of Brigus boasts a large number of Victorian houses whose imposing silhouettes make it look like a New England town. It was the birthplace of Captain Robert Bartlett (1875-1946), one of the great Arctic explorers. Bartlett's father and grandfather also were navigators and explorers who had ventured to the Arctic Ocean. Robert Bartlett pushed farther, becoming ship's captain for

Robert Peary, who led some of the most important Arctic expeditions in history. Bartlett's former home is now the **Hawthorne Cottage National Historic Site** ★ *($3; mid-May to mid-Oct, 10am to 6pm; ☎753-9262)*. The house has retained its original splendour and now houses an exhibition on Bartlett's life and exploits.

Tour C: Eastern and Central Newfoundland

The Burin Peninsula

Along this lengthy, isolated peninsula, flanked by Fortune and Placentia bays, visitors can take in some rocky scenery and lovely sea views. The proximity of the Grand Banks, once teeming with fish, led to the development of sizable local fishing and shipbuilding industries here.

Marystown, the main town on the peninsula, has several restaurants, an excellent motel and other services. From Marystown, the highway leads to the pretty village of **Burin**, which occupies a very steep site on the shores of a bay strewn with tiny rocky islands.

Burin was founded at the beginning of the 18th century and served as Captain James Cook's base when he was exploring the shores of Newfoundland in the 1760s. The village boasts a number of lovely homes, including the **Burin Heritage Museum** ★ *(free admission; May, Jun, Sep and Oct, every day 8:30am to 5pm; Jul and Aug, every day 10am to 8pm; ☎891-2217)*, now a museum with about a dozen rooms devoted to local history, antiques and works by regional artists.

To the south, Highway 220 runs through tiny communities with only a few houses built on a rocky plateau. In many places, the coast is punctuated by tall cliffs.

The road continues to **Fortune**, where you can take a ferry to the French islands of Saint-Pierre and Miquelon, then continues to **Grand Bank**, which has a few restaurants and places to stay, a **museum** focussing on local history and an impressive **lighthouse**. A number of trails have been cleared nearby, making it possible to take in the local scenery. At the **Southern Newfoundland Seamen's Museum** ★ *($2.50; mid-Jun to early Sep, 9:30am to 4:45pm; May to mid-Jun and Sep to late Oct, every day 9am to 4:45pm; Marine Dr., ☎832-1484)*, visitors can learn about the history of the local fisheries through photographs, models of old ships and various other objects. Yugoslavia's pavilion for Expo '67 was moved here from Montréal to house the collection.

★
Saint-Pierre and Miquelon

The islands of Saint-Pierre and Miquelon are the last remnants of France's North American empire. In 1763, under the Treaty of Paris, France ceded all its possessions to England, except for these two islands, which are now a *département d'outremer* (DOM), or overseas department, with representation in the National Assembly in France.

The local inhabitants, who only number a few thousand, are of Acadian, Basque and Breton descent. Most live in Saint-Pierre, a pretty little town made up of stone houses alongside a natural harbour on the island of the same name. Though the islands are only 25km from the Burin Peninsula, their atmosphere and residents' way of life is far more typical of metropolitan France than North America.

The ambiance and cuisine of its bistros and cafés are French, and many products—everything from wine and spirits to cars and motorcycles—are imported directly from France. These two islands cover an area of 242km². The larger and less populous of the two, Miquelon, has some lovely beaches and powdery dunes.

On Saint-Pierre, the gateway to the archipelago, visitors can sample French food, stroll along the narrow streets of the town, visit a small museum devoted to the history of the two islands or simply mingle with the friendly local residents. From the end of June to the beginning of September, there is **ferry service** from Fortune, on the Burin Peninsula *(☎832-0429 or 800-563-2006)* to Saint-Pierre. The trip takes about 2hrs and a return adult ticket costs $67.95. The ferry is for passengers only.

Canadian and U.S. citizens need only show an ID card to visit Saint-Pierre, while citizens of the European Union and Switzerland have to show their passport. It is also possible to reach the island by **plane**, as Air Saint-Pierre offers service from Halifax, Nova Scotia *(☎902-873-3566)*. For more information on Saint-Pierre and Miquelon, contact the **Agence Régionale du Tourisme** in Saint-Pierre *(☎508-41-22-22)*.

★
Trinity

A village with particularly well-preserved 19th-century architecture, Trinity sits on a promontory alongside an excellent natural harbour on the **Bonavista Peninsula** ★ ★. The site was named by explorer Gaspar Corte Real, who explored its bay on Trinity Sunday in 1501. In 1558, the English made Trinity their first permanent settlement in Newfoundland.

Thanks to its fisheries and commercial ties with London, Trinity managed to attain a certain level of prosperity. In 1615, it became the seat of the first maritime court in Canada, hearing a case involving a conflict between local and seasonal fishermen.

Trinity offers visitors all sorts of opportunities to step back into the past: the **Trinity Museum** (*$2.50; Jun to Oct, every day 10am to 5:30pm; Hwy. 239, ☎464-2042*) boasts an excellent collection of maps, illustrations and period photographs; the **Green Family Forge** (*$3; mid-Jun to mid-Sep, every day 10am to 5:30pm; ☎464-3599*) presents an exhibition on the history of a forge dating back to the 1750s, and **Hiscock House** (*$2.50; mid-Jun to early Sep, every day 10am to 5:30pm; Hwy. 239, ☎464-2042*) is a typical early 20th-century merchant's house. The most novel way to learn about Trinity's history, however, is by attending the **Trinity Pageant** ★, a series of plays about local history, presented in different places around town. The plays are held daily during summer, starting at 2pm.

From May to August, several kinds of whales come to the waters off Newfoundland. They can often be spotted from the shore. For a closer look, we recommend going on a whale-watching excursion. Trinity is a good point of departure, and a number of tour agencies organize outings.

★
Cape Bonavista

Did John Cabot really open the way to the exploration of Canada? Newfoundlanders swear that he did, maintaining that it was at Cape Bonavista that Cabot and his crew stopped for the first time in the summer of 1497, after sailing across the Atlantic from Bristol, England. In reality, no one really knows where Cabot landed in the New World. Cape Bonavista is fighting over the claim with several other sites along the Canadian coast. In any case, it was in Cape Bonavista that Newfoundlanders celebrated, with great pomp, the 500th anniversary of Cabot's landing in 1997.

The village of Bonavista is the largest community on the peninsula. Its pretty, brightly coloured houses are surrounded by a rolling landscape that unfolds onto a bustling port. Bonavista was frequented by fishers of many different nationalities throughout the 16th century, before the English settled here around 1600.

At the beginning of the 19th century, the govern-

ment of Newfoundland started building lighthouses along the shores of the island to make the waters safer for ships. In 1843, the first lighthouse on the north shore of the island was erected on Cape Bonavista. Today, you can visit the **Cape Bonavista Lighthouse Provincial Historic Site** (*$2.50; mid-Jun to early Oct, every day 10am to 5:30pm; Hwy. 230; ☎468-7444*), which has been restored and furnished the way it was in the 1870s. It houses an exhibition on the history of lighthouses and the daily life of their keepers. The point offers a magnificent **view** ★ of the sea and the rocky shoreline.

Port Blandford

This little community is the gateway to **Terra Nova National Park** (see p 251).

Gander

This modern town, one of the largest in central Newfoundland, lies on the shores of Gander Lake. In 1935, the British government (the island was still a British colony at that time) chose Gander as the site of an international airport that would serve as a stopover for transatlantic flights.

As so often occurred in its history, Newfoundland, North America's easternmost island, thus became a pivot of sorts between Europe and the New World. During the Second World War, the military used the airport to defend the North Atlantic against German U-boats. Though Gander is still a hub for international air transporta-

Cape Bonavista Lighthouse

tion, its importance diminished with the advent of long-range aircraft.

Visitors can learn about the history of aviation in Gander at the **North Atlantic Aviation Museum** *($3; summer, every day 9am to 9pm; winter, Mon-Fri 9am to 5pm; Hwy. 1, ☎256-2923)*, which exhibits a variety of items, including pilot's uniforms, weapons and airplane engines. About 4km east of Gander, on Highway 1, stands the **Silent Witness Memorial**, erected in memory of the 256 members of the 100th Airborne Division of the U.S. Air force who died when their plane crashed right after take-off at Gander airport in 1985.

From Gander, highways 330 (North), 331 and finally 340 will take you to the **Boyd's Cove Beothuk Interpretation Centre ★** *($2.50; mid-Jun to early Oct, 10am to 5:30pm; Hwy. 340, Boyd's Cove, ☎656-3114)*. From about 1650 to 1720, Boyd's Cove was the site of a large Beothuk village. Over the past few decades, extensive archaeological excavations have been carried out in the area. The interpretation centre presents some interesting collections of artifacts, as well as a slide show on the cultural history of the Beothuk. Interpretation trails have been laid out to reveal even more about the Beothuk way of life, and visitors can also see the site where the excavations were carried out. North of Boyd's Cove is the picturesque region of **Twillingate**, a charming place during summer,

when icebergs and whales can often be spotted.

Grand Falls-Windsor

Grand Falls takes its name from the spectacular **falls** on nearby Exploits River. It has been merged with its twin, Windsor, into one town. The region's economy began to take off in 1909, when a pulp and paper mill was built here. Now owned by Abitibi-Consolidated, the mill is still a mainstay of the local economy. Earlier, the region was one of the major centres of the Beothuk, an Aboriginal group who inhabited the island of Newfoundland before the Europeans arrived, and who have since been completely wiped out. The **Mary March Regional Museum ★** *(free admission; May to Oct, every day 9am to 4:45pm; 16 Saint Catherine St., ☎292-4522)* was named after one of the last members of the Beothuk nation, who died at the beginning of the 19th century. The museum presents a short film on the Beothuk. Its collections deal with the human and natural history of central Newfoundland. Right behind the museum, visitors can tour a reconstruction of a **Beothuk village** *($2; May to Oct, every day 9am to 5pm; ☎489-3559)*.

Tour D: Western Newfoundland

The western part of the island features charming

landscapes and picturesque mountains, as well as several lovely towns such as Corner Brook, the second-largest city in the province.

Port aux Basques

Located on the southwestern tip of the island, Port aux Basques is the terminal for one of the two ferries from North Sydney, Nova Scotia (the other one goes to Argentia, on the Avalon Peninsula). The community has a few hotels and restaurants, as well as an excellent tourist information centre.

Port-au-Port Peninsula

From Highway 1, visitors can reach the Port-au-Port Peninsula by way of Stephenville. Dotting the shores of the peninsula, which offer lovely views of the ocean, are a few small fishing villages, home to the bulk of the French-speaking population of the island of Newfoundland. Port-au-Port was once part of what was known as the "French Shore," where France held fishing and fish-processing rights until 1904. The communities with the highest concentration of French-speakers on the peninsula are located near Cape St. George. The *Grande Veillée* festival, held in Cape St. George in August, is a wonderful opportunity to learn about the local culture.

★
Corner Brook

Newfoundland's second-largest town, Corner

Brook, could be termed the capital of the island's west coast. It is home to many government services, a college affiliated with Memorial University and a number of hotels, shops and restaurants. Corner Brook occupies a magnificent site on the banks of a fjord, the Humber Arm, surrounded by high hills. Though French fishers had probably known about this site for a long time before, it was Captain James Cook who first reported its existence in 1767, naming it "Corner Brook".

Development of the area began in 1864 with the construction of a sawmill. However, the local economy didn't really take off until 1923, when Corner Brook was chosen as the site of one of the largest pulp and paper mills in the world. All sorts of wonderful discoveries await nature lovers in this region. During summer, visitors can start off by taking a cruise on the Humber River. These excursions, which depart from Sandy Brook, take passengers up the river, whose shores are home to numerous species of birds.

Marble Mountain ★, see p 254.

About 60km west of Corner Brook, visitors can take in the splendours of **Blow Me Down Provincial Park ★** (see p 252).

Deer Lake

Deer Lake lies at the intersection of the Trans-Canada Highway, which runs east-west across

Newfoundland, and Highway 430, which leads to magnificent Gros Morne National Park and the "Viking Trail." A small modern town, it has several restaurants and places to stay, as well as an airport that receives flights from Newfoundland's other urban centres and from Halifax, Nova Scotia.

A number of car rental agencies have branches here, as well. If you're pressed for time, a flight from St. John's to Deer Lake will spare you nearly 650km of driving. Gros Morne National Park, one of Newfoundland's major attractions, is less than an hour's drive from Deer Lake.

Tour E:
The Viking Trail

There is an excellent road that leads from Deer Lake to **Gros Morne National Park** (see p 252). The Viking Trail runs along the west coast of Newfoundland to the Strait of Belle Isle, through strikingly desolate, rocky landscapes.

Port au Choix

Port au Choix, where fishing is still the major activity, was an important port for Basque fishers for many years. Its name comes from "Portuchoa," which means "little port" in Basque. The Basques were not the first people to take advantage of Port au Choix's excellent location, however. The **Port au Choix National Historic**

Site ★ *($5.75; Jun to mid-Oct, every day 9am to 5pm; ☎861-3522)* presents relics of the peoples who inhabited this region long before any Europeans arrived.

These vestiges were discovered during archaeological excavations. In the 1950s, in nearby Phillip's Gardens, archaeologists uncovered traces of a Dorset paleoeskimo community that occupied this site between the years 200 and 600. Dorset culture was sophisticated, as evidenced by the finely worked bone and stone carvings that were discovered here. In 1967, other major digs in the region led to the uncovering of a Maritime Archaic burial ground containing human bones, tools and weapons dating back 3,200 to 4,300 years.

The Maritime Archaic survived essentially on fishing and hunting. They developed an artistic tradition and decorated their clothing with shells, seal's claws and pendants made of bone. The tools, weapons and ornaments found in the tombs indicate that these people prepared for a life after death not unlike their life on earth.

At the Port au Choix National Historic Site, visitors can see some of the artifacts found in this area and watch a documentary on the lifestyle of these indigenous peoples. A series of hiking trails leads from the interpretation centre to the Phillip's Garden archaeological site. The trails offer visitors a chance to contemplate the region's rugged landscape.

St. Barbe

During summer, a ferry carries passengers from St. Barbe to Blanc Sablon, Québec two to three times daily. From Blanc Sablon, a paved road leads through several villages along the shores of the **Strait of Belle Isle** (see p 250), in Labrador.

★
L'Anse aux Meadows

The **L'Anse aux Meadows National Historic Site** ★ ★ *($7; mid-Jun to mid-Oct, every day 9am to 8pm; Hwy. 436, ☎623-2608),* a UNESCO World Heritage Site, is the only place where traces of Norwegian sailors–or "Vikings," as they are sometimes called in North America–have been discovered.

A group of Norwegian sailors led by Leif Eriksson came here from Greenland and set up a camp around the year 1000. This camp consisted of eight buildings and was home to an estimated 80 to 100 people. The Norwegians used it as a base for their expeditions along the Atlantic coast. According to the sagas of these expeditions, Leif Eriksson and his family discovered the shores of Labrador, Newfoundland and regions farther south, in the Gulf of St. Lawrence. Eriksson named the southernmost lands "Vinland," after the wild vines that grew there. The L'Anse-aux-Meadows site was discovered by Helge Ingstad and Anne Stisne Ingstad in 1960.

Visitors can see the foundations of the eight buildings uncovered by the Ingstads and, later, by Parks Canada. Three buildings from Eriksson's era have been reconstructed nearby. Excellent guided tours are available. The welcome centre presents an interesting exhibition on the vestiges found on the site and also shows a film on the captivating story of the Ingstads' and Parks Canada's excavations.

Viking Boat Tours ★ *($25; several departures daily from Noddy Bay, about 500m from L'Anse-aux-Meadows; ☎623-2100)* offers 2hr sea excursions aboard a superb replica of a Viking ship dating from the year 1000. The cruise is worth the cost, especially during June and July, the best times to see whales and icebergs.

★
St. Anthony

Located on the shores of an excellent inland harbour, St. Anthony is the largest community in the northern part of the peninsula. Since 1922, it has been the headquarters of Grenfell Mission, which provides medical care for the isolated communities of northern Newfoundland and Labrador.

The mission was founded by Dr. Wilfred Grenfell (1865-1940), who started developing the region's first real network of hospitals, infirmaries and orphanages in 1894. To finance his projects, Grenfell created a com-

pany called Grenfell Handicrafts, which sold clothing and crafts made by local artisans; the profits would go to the mission. Today, you can visit the **Grenfell Historic Properties** *($5; mid-May to mid-Jun and Sep, every day 9am to 5pm; mid-Jun to end of Aug, every day 9am to 8pm; Hwy. 430, ☎454-4010),* the Grenfell family's former home, which houses a collection of objects that were used by fishers a century ago. The museum's shop sells lovely winter clothing made on the premises as well as local crafts.

From the centre of St. Anthony, visitors can go to nearby **Fishing Point**, which offers a splendid **view** ★ of the ocean. Whales and icebergs can often be spotted from here during the summer. There is also a good restaurant at Fishing Point.

Tour F: Labrador

Labrador, separated from the island of Newfoundland by the Strait of Belle Isle, is a huge territory covering nearly 300,000km². It is inhabited by only a few tens of thousands of people–Inuit, Aboriginals and English- and French-speaking Canadians–most of whom live in fishing villages along the shore or in small towns in the central and western regions.

Most of Labrador remains a vast stretch of wilderness, as yet undeveloped and still full of mystery. The southern part of Labrador has a gently rolling landscape strewn with lakes and rivers. Farther north, the Torngat Mountains rise to an altitude of 1,676m at their highest point. This region is covered with a subarctic forest, shrubs and scrawny trees, and, in the northernmost parts, tundra.

These infertile lands have been inhabited for over 8,000 years. The first people to live in Labrador were the Maritime Archaic. The ancestors of the Inuit, who still live in northern Labrador, arrived about 4,000 years later. Toward the year 1000, the Vikings explored the coastline of this part of the continent, but Basque whalers were the first Europeans to set up camps along the shores of Labrador, in the 16th century.

In those days, as many as 2,000 Basque sailors would come to the Strait of Belle Isle to hunt whales each year. Red Bay, on the shores of the Strait, was one of the Basques' most important bases. French and English fishers and tradesmen were the next to arrive, though they did not really establish any permanent settlements along the shore until the end of the 19th century. In western Labrador, the 20th century has been marked by large-scale projects like the huge iron mine near Labrador City and the gigantic hydroelectric dam at Churchill Falls.

★ The Strait of Belle Isle

There is a road running along the Strait of Belle Isle, through the coastal villages from Blanc Sablon (Québec) to Port Hope Simpson and Cartwright. Visitors can take the ferry to Blanc Sablon from St. Barbe, in the northern part of the island of Newfoundland, along the Viking Trail. The road runs through a very rugged coastal landscape, passing through tiny communities that survive mainly on fishing.

L'Anse-au-Clair, the first village along the way, was founded by the French in the 17th century, as were many other coastal communities. It has a pretty fishing port and a tourist information office which is set up inside a church dating from the early 1900s. Farther along, at **L'Anse-Amour**, archaeologists have discovered the remains of a funerary monument built 7,500 years ago by the Maritime Archaic.

Nearby lies the **Point Amour Lighthouse Provincial Historic Site** *($2.50; mid-Jun to early Oct, 10am to 5:30pm; ☎927-5825)*, which, at over 30m high, is the tallest lighthouse in eastern Canada. Right near **L'Anse Au Loup**, the **Labrador Straits Museum** *($2; early Jul to mid-Sep; ☎931-2067)* recounts the history of the region and is managed by the local women's institute.

Highway 510 continues to Red Bay, home of the

Red Bay National Historic Site ★ *($7; mid-Jun to mid-Oct, 9am to 6:30; ☎920-2051)*, which was the most important fishing port for Basque whalers during the 16th century. At its peak, about 20 boats and 2,000 Basque seamen would spend the summer whale hunting in the area.

The site has two interpretation centres and presents an excellent film on the history of whale hunting in the Strait of Belle Isle. Visitors can also take a boat out to Saddle Island, where the major archaeological excavations were carried out. The road then continues—unpaved—to Port Hope Simpson and Cartwright.

★ The Labrador Coast

The Labrador coast, north of Cartwright, is still inaccessible by car, but you can get there by boat or plane. Each week, a cargo ship sets out from the port of St. Anthony, in the northern part of the island of Newfoundland to bring supplies to some 48 tiny communities on the coast (see p 237).

The boat travels as far as Nain, in northern Labrador, offering passengers a chance to take in some remarkable scenery. This part of the coast is known as "Iceberg Alley"; during spring and summer, thousands of icebergs of various sizes, including some veritable mountains of ice weighing several million tonnes, can be seen here. There are some interesting places to visit during the stops on the trip. Nain has a **museum** devoted to Inuit culture.

Hopedale is home to the **Hopedale Mission National Historic Site** (☎933-3881). The mission, established by the British government in 1782, includes a church and several other buildings that are among the oldest in the Atlantic provinces.

Mary's Harbour offers access to the **Battle Harbour National Historic Site** (*free admission; early Jun to late Sep;* ☎921-6677), where you'll find the remains of an 18th-century fishing village, including the oldest Anglican church in Labrador. Still, the coast's main appeal lies in its scenery, its isolation and its welcoming inhabitants. The round trip takes about three weeks.

Central and Western Labrador

Central and western Labrador are relatively easy to reach by car from Québec, and, during summer, by ferry from the island of

Newfoundland. This unspoiled expanse of wilderness, with its forests and myriad lakes and rivers, is a choice destination for fishing and hunting buffs. The subarctic forests are teeming with animal life, including a great many moose and the largest caribou population in the world.

Together, Labrador City and Wabush form the largest community in Labrador. A number of hotels, restaurants and services can be found here. The mainspring of the local economy is an opencast iron mine, the largest in the world. A variety of outdoor activities can be enjoyed near Labrador City and Wabush, including hiking, canoeing, scuba diving, sailing and golf. The area is also home to an excellent cross-country ski centre, which maintains about 40km of trails during winter. For a lovely view of the region, head to **Crystal Falls**. The rest of Labrador is still virtually uninhabited, aside from a few small towns, such as Churchill Falls, which was

built near a huge hydroelectric dam, and Goose Bay, located near a military base.

Parks

Tour C: Eastern and Central Newfoundland

Terra Nova National Park ★ (☎533-2801) covers just over 400km² of wooded, gently rolling terrain. It is bounded by Newman Sound and Clode Sound, which are inlets of Bonavista Bay. The park is home to numerous animal species, including moose, black bears, martens, beavers and lynxes. The waters of the sounds, particularly during May and August, attract various species of whales, including humpbacks.

The main activities that can be enjoyed in the park are camping, hiking, fishing, canoeing and, in winter, cross-country skiing; most organized outings start at Newman Sound. The Twin Rivers Golf Course is located at the park's south entrance. Two lookouts, both accessible by car, offer **panoramic views** ★ of the park: the **Blue Hill Exhibit** (*drive 7km from the north entrance, then take a side road for 1.5km*) and the **Ochre Hill Exhibit** (*drive 23km from the north entrance, then take a side road for 3km*).

Newfoundland and Labrador

Moose

Tour E:
The Viking Trail

Internationally renowned **Gros Morne National Park** ★ ★ ★ *($7.50; mid-May to mid-Oct; ☎458-2417)* boasts 1,805km² of spectacular scenery: fjords, lakes, high plateaux, coastal dunes and boreal forests. The Long Range Mountains run the entire length of the park; Gros Morne is the highest peak, at 850m. In 1987, UNESCO designated Gros Morne National Park a World Heritage Site, primarily because of its geological make-up: in the southern part of the park, **Tablelands** formed by the shifting of two tectonic plates give a good example of the continental drift. The park's landscape was also shaped by the retreat of the glaciers at the end of the Glacial Period.

Gros Morne National Park protects numerous wild mammals, including bears, moose and caribou. It is not uncommon to see moose along the park's main roads, and various species of whales can be spotted from the shore during summer. In addition to wildlife observation, other activities to be enjoyed here are camping, hiking (over 100km of trails), swimming, boat rides, fishing and, in winter, cross-country skiing. Lodgings are available at Trout River, Woody Point, Wiltondale, Rocky Harbour and Cow Head.

Its splendid scenery and distinctive geological characteristics make the park's **south sector** well worth exploring. From the south entrance, Highway 431 runs through a rolling landscape, then along one of the arms of **Bonne Bay** ★, a deep fjord surrounded by the Long Range Mountains. The road leads to **Woody Point**, a historic fishing village that is home to the newly opened **Discovery Centre** ★, which offers a very interesting introduction to the park, and then on to **Trout River Pond** ★ ★. This 15km-long freshwater fjord lies in a glacial valley at the edge of the **Gregory Plateau** and **Tablelands** ★ ★, created by the shifting of the tectonic plates about 500 million years ago. Visitors can explore this part of the park by taking a boat ride with **Tableland Boat Tours** *(mid-Jun to mid-Sep; three departures per day from Trout River; ☎951-2101).*

The landscape of the **north sector** is dominated by the Long Range Mountains. The park's welcome centre on Highway 430, a few kilometres from **Rocky Harbour**, shows an excellent documentary on the flora, fauna and geological features of Gros Morne National Park. It also provides information on the various activities to be enjoyed in the park and hosts a number of nature talks. From Rocky Harbour, the road leads to the **Lobster Cove Head lighthouse**. The old lightkeeper's house now contains an exhibition on the history of the settlement of the coastline in this area. There is a trail leading from the lighthouse to a rocky beach. Much farther north in the park, a 3km trail offers access to **West-ern Brook Pond** ★ ★, a 16km-long, 165m-deep inland fjord created during the Glacial Epoch.

The rock walls that plunge into its crystalline waters reach as high as 650m in some places. A **cruise** is the most pleasant way to take in the fjord's spectacular beauty. The outing lasts about 2.5hrs; for reservations, inquire at the Ocean View Motel *(☎458-2730)* in Rocky Harbour. Trimmed with beaches and sand dunes, **Shallow Bay**, at the north end of the park, is a good place to go swimming.

Blow Me Down Provincial Park ★ *(Hwy. 450, ☎681-2430)* lies on a hilly peninsula that stretches out into the Bay of Islands, between Lark and York harbours. The park offers a glorious view of the bay and the Blow Me Down Mountains. There is a path leading up to a lookout (about a half-hour's walk), while other trails run to the tip of the peninsula. A few campsites can also be found in the park.

Atlantic puffin

Outdoor Activities

Bird-Watching

Tour B: The Avalon Peninsula

At the **Witless Bay Ecological Reserve ★** *(May to Sep; ☎635-4522)*, the main avian attraction is the Atlantic puffin, the province's emblem. Though bird colonies can be seen from the shore, you can get a much closer look by taking a cruise. A number of tour agencies, including **O'Brien Whale & Bird Tours** *(departures every day at 9:30am, 11am, 12:30pm, 2pm, 3:30pm, and 5pm; ☎753-4850, www.obrien boattours.com)* and **Captain Murphy's Seabird & Whale Tours** *(☎334-2002)*, offer excursions from the villages along the coast.

Cape St. Mary's Ecological Reserve ★★ *(May, Jun and Sep, every day 9am to 7pm; Jul and Aug, every day 8am to 7pm; Hwy. 100, ☎277-1666)*, on the southwest tip of the Avalon Peninsula and washed by the Atlantic Ocean, is home to some 60,000 seabirds. The most interesting place to observe them is along Bird Rock, a tall rock a few metres from the shore, where a number of species nest.

Visitors will also find the largest northern gannet colony in Newfoundland, the southernmost colony of thick-billed murres in the world, and many other species of birds, including eagles. Furthermore, during July, humpback whales can be spotted offshore. The welcome centre provides fascinating information on the nature of seabirds.

Whale-Watching

Nearly 20 species of whales, including about 5,000 humpbacks, visit the coast of Newfoundland and Labrador during the summer months. The whales stay in this part of the Atlantic from May to September. They can easily be observed in June and July, when their numbers are the greatest. Though many spots along the coast are good for whale-watching, some of the best places are Gros Morne National Park on the Viking Trail as far as St. Anthony, the Twillingate area (north of Gander), the Bonavista Peninsula and the eastern shore of

the Avalon Peninsula; all are points of departure for numerous whale-watching excursions.

In Terra Nova National Park, **Ocean Watch Tours** *(☎533-6024)* hosts cruises in the sounds for people interested in observing whales and other aquatic species.

Iceberg-Watching

The icebergs drifting off the shores of Newfoundland and Labrador are surely one of the most fascinating natural phenomena a person can witness. Every year, tens of thousands of icebergs of various sizes break off from the shores of Greenland and slowly drift southward. This phenomenon starts in March and ends in November. June and July are the best times to observe the icebergs from the shores of Newfoundland and Labrador. The Labrador coast, the Strait of Belle Isle, the northern part of the island of Newfoundland (especially Twillingate) and the eastern shore of the Avalon Peninsula are usually good vantage points during this time of year.

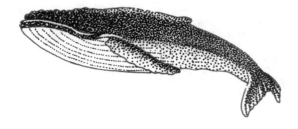

Hiking

Hiking buffs will be amazed by the possibilities available to them on the island of Newfoundland. Over the years, countless trails have been cleared along the island's spectacular coast, particularly on the Avalon Peninsula where the **East Coast Trail** (☎738-4453) has recently been completed. There are even trails in St. John's, the capital, which make for interesting outings and offer magnificent views of the ocean. If scenic variety is what you're after, head to **Gros Morne National Park**, which has some 100km of trails, some suitable for short hikes, others for four- to five-day expeditions.

Downhill Skiing

Tour D: Western Newfoundland

The **Marble Mountain Ski Resort ★** *(Hwy. 1, Steady Brook, 8km east of Corner Brook, ☎637-7600, www. skimarble.com)* is the best place for downhill skiing in the Atlantic provinces. The vertical drop is over 550m and the slopes are very steep in many places. Beginners and experts alike can enjoy the 34 trails. Aside from its excellent runs, one of Marble Mountain's major advantages is the heavy snowfall

it receives—about 4m each winter, allowing for one of the longest ski seasons in the eastern part of the continent.

Accommodations

Tour A: St. John's

Memorial University of Newfoundland
$
Memorial University Conference Office
☎737-7657
The student residences at Memorial University of Newfoundland are rented to the public from mid-May to mid-August.

The Roses B&B
$$ bkfst incl.
K, ॐ
6 rooms
9 Military Rd.
☎726-3336 or
877-767-3722
≈726-3345
Laid out in a Victorian house typical of downtown St. John's, this bed and breakfast is a friendly and very charming spot. Its high ceilings, rich mouldings and wood floors give it a warm atmosphere. Its always inviting rooms are decorated with a heterogenous mix of antiques and modern furniture. Some of the rooms are equipped with fireplaces. Days at this welcoming inn always begin on the right foot with a copious breakfast served on the top floor of the house, which affords a panoramic view of the port.

Quality Hotel by Journey's End
$$-$$$
ℜ, ≡
160 rooms
2 Hill O'Chips, A1C 6B1
☎754-7788 or
800-424-6423
≈754-5209
The Quality Hotel by Journey's End is always a sure bet. It is a welcoming, well-situated establishment near downtown that offers good value. Nevertheless, although the rooms are comfortable, well kept and functional, there is nothing especially original about them. Since it sits on a hill near the port, the Quality Hotel offers a lovely view of the bay.

Compton House
$$-$$$$ bkfst incl.
⊛, ॐ
11 rooms
26 Waterford Bridge Rd.,
A1E 1C6
☎739-5789
≈739-1770
This majestic Victorian residence converted into an inn occupies a vast, attractively landscaped property near the Waterford River valley, about 15min on foot from the centre of the city. Guests quickly feel right at home in this lovely, elegant and inviting house brimming with period charm. The front living room is particularly pleasant and has a fireplace, as do the little library and the dining room. The guest rooms are well furnished, very comfortable and all equipped with private bathrooms. If a little extra luxury is in order, visitors can stay in the suites, each of which is equipped with a balcony

or a patio, a whirlpool bath and a fireplace.

Waterford Manor
$$-$$$$ bkfst incl.
⊛, ℜ, ℨ
7 rooms
185 Waterford Bridge Rd.,
A1E 1C7
☎*754-4139 or*
888-488-4170
⇌*754-4155*
www.waterfordmanor.com
Built at the end of the 19th century for the family of a local merchant, this sumptuous Queen Anne house is now one of the province's most beautiful inns. Renovations have restored its former grandeur and adapted it to meet modern expectations of comfort. Guest rooms, each of which has its own special character, are furnished with antiques and decorated with meticulous attention to detail. They are all very pleasant, but the most beautiful of them, on the top floor, offers a fireplace and a whirlpool bath. Breakfast is served either in the guests' rooms or in the dining room on the ground floor. The Waterford Manor, tucked away in a pretty residential neighbourhood on the outskirts of the Waterford River Valley, is about a 15min walk from downtown St. John's.

Prescott Inn
$$$
K
4 rooms
21 Military Rd., A1C 2C3
☎*753-7733 or*
888-263-3786
⇌*753-6036*
www.prescottinn.nf.ca
In a beautiful Victorian house located next to the Roses B&B (see above),

the Prescott Inn is a good alternative to its neighbour. Its rooms are clean and reasonably priced. The Prescott also offers a suite equipped with a kitchenette.

Monroe House
$$$-$$$$ bkfst incl.
8A Forest Rd.
☎*754-0610*
www.monroehouse.nf.ca
Conveniently located near St. John's principal attractions, this beautiful residence was once home to Walter S. Monroe, a former Premier of Newfoundland. Elegantly furnished and comfortable, the house's rooms have a warm, homey feel.

Holiday Inn St. John's
$$$$-$$$$$
ℜ, ☉, ≈
250 rooms
180 Portugal Cove Rd., A1B 2N2
☎*722-0934 or*
800-933-0506
⇌*722-9756*
www.holidayinnstjohns.com
Located about 15min from downtown St. John's near a pretty park, the Holiday Inn has comfortable rooms with the functional layout typical of North American motels. Amenities include a lovely swimming pool and a very satisfactory restaurant.

The Fairmont Newfoundland
$$$$-$$$$$
ℜ
301 rooms
PO Box 5637, 115 Cavendish Sq., A1C 5W8
☎*726-4980 or*
800-441-1414
⇌*576-0554*
www.fairmont.com
The most prestigious establishment in St. John's,

The Fairmont Newfoundland is a modern hotel situated in the heart of the city. Its interior decor is a brilliant success: it is both original and inviting. From the lobby, visitors can go into the Court Garden, where terraced plant beds are embellished by interspersed waterfalls. The warmth and brightness of this spot are in singular contrast to the cool, rainy climate that so often shrouds the city. Guest rooms are spacious, charming and comfortable—they have been designed as much to please vacationers as to meet the needs of business travellers—and most of them offer breathtaking views of the port, the city and the bay.

Tour B: The Avalon Peninsula

Ferryland

The Downs Inn
$-$$ bkfst incl.
sb, ℨ
4 rooms
Rte. 10, A0A 2H0
☎*432-2808 or*
877-432-2808
⇌*432-2659*
Lodging is available about an hour from St. John's at The Downs Inn, a pleasant bed and breakfast laid out in an old Presbyterian convent. Erected in 1914, this building was home to some 15 nuns until the 1980s; renovation work has managed to preserve the spirit of the house. Each of the spacious, clean, comfortable rooms is equipped with a fireplace.

Trepassey

Trepassey Motel
$$
ℜ, ⚡
10 rooms
Main Rd., PO Box 22, A0A 4B0
☎*438-2934*
⇌*438-2722*
This little motel on the edge of Highway 10 at the southern tip of the peninsula occupies a very quiet setting near the Avalon Wilderness Reserve, a summer habitat for caribou. Although rather indifferently furnished, its rooms are well kept and inviting, and the fare served at the **Trepassey Motel restaurant** (see p 261) more than meets the mark.

St. Bride's

Bird Island Resort
$-$$
ℜ, K, ☉
20 cottages
Main Rd., A0B 2Z0
☎*337-2450 or*
888-337-2450
⇌*337-2903*
The Bird Island Resort is located in the tiny village of St. Bride's, not far from the ornithological reserve at Cape St. Mary's. This establishment occupies a large grassy property facing Placentia Bay. Its cottages are impeccably clean and some are equipped with kitchenettes.

Placentia

🏛 **Rosedale Manor**
$$ bkfst incl.
4 rooms
Riverside Dr., A0B 2Y0
☎*227-3613*
Guests will feel right at home at the Rosedale

Manor, one of the loveliest inns on this part of the peninsula. Located in the heart of the village, just across from the bay, this pretty historic house offers carefully decorated rooms embellished with antique furniture and equipped with private bathrooms. The owner is both attentive and discreet. If you are interested, she will be happy to fill you in on the local history.

Carbonear

NaGeira House Bed & Breakfast
$$-$$$ bkfst incl.
ℜ
4 rooms
7 Musgrave St., A1Y 1B4
☎*596-1888 or*
800-600-7757
⇌*596-4622*
www.nageirahouse.com
NaGeira House is a grand, elegant heritage home resembling an English cottage, nestled in a treed garden. Luxuriously furnished, it offers private bathrooms. The licensed dining room offers the best food in town.

Brigus

The Brittoner
$-$$ bkfst incl.
sb/pb, ⚡
5 rooms
12 Water St., A0A 1K0
☎/⇌*528-4544*
One of the prettiest towns in the province, Brigus numbers many Victorian houses, one of which is home to The Brittoner. This inn is well situated in the heart of Brigus, facing the bay, and its rooms are comfortable and well kept. Two of the

five rooms offer private bathrooms. A copious breakfast and a warm welcome pleasantly round out a stay at The Brittoner.

Tour C: Eastern and Central Newfoundland

Marystown

Hotel Marystown
$$
ℜ
131 rooms
PO Box 487, 76 Ville Marie Dr., A0E 2M0
☎*279-1600 or*
800-563-2489
⇌*279-4088*
This modern establishment located in the heart of the community of Marystown is the most comfortable on the Burin Peninsula. Its reasonably priced rooms are well maintained and conveniently designed. The hotel's enjoyable restaurant, **TJ Billington** (see p 261), serves simple but flavourful, well-prepared cuisine and is a popular meeting place for visitors from the French island of St. Pierre.

Grand Bank

The Inn By The Sea
$$ bkfst incl.
24 Blackburn Rd.
☎*832-0202*
www.theinnbythesea.com
The seaside community of Grand Bank is home to several elegant historical residences. One of them is the Inn By The Sea, which offers comfortable accommodations in its cozy, spacious rooms.

The Thorndyke B&B
$$ bkfst incl.
5 rooms
33 Water St., A0E 1W0
☎/⇄*832-0820*
☎*866-882-0820*
www.thethorndyke.com
This oceanside house was built in 1917 by John Thornhill, a fisher who was renowned as one of the best seamen in the region in his time. The old two-storey house is architecturally reminiscent of New England and, although its interior is not especially luxurious, it has a pleasant, old-fashioned allure.

Trinity

Village Inn
$$
ℜ
7 rooms
Taverner's Path, A0C 2S0
☎*464-3269*
⇄*464-3700*
Despite its relatively modest size, the Village Inn is the largest hotel establishment in Trinity. It has occupied this building in the heart of the village for a century. Its rooms vary greatly in comfort and quality. There is a good family restaurant on the premises (see p 261) and whale-watching trips are organized here.

Campbell House
$$-$$$$ bkfst incl.
ℜ
5 rooms
High St., A0C 2S0
☎/⇄*464-3377*
☎*877-464-7700*
The Campbell House is a bed and breakfast set up in a lovely house that dates from the 1840s. The old-fashioned appeal of this stately residence, which stands in the middle of the

town's historic area, has been well preserved thanks to meticulous renovation work. The rooms are charming and attractively decorated. From Campbell House there is a beautiful view of the town and the ocean.

Trinity East

Peace Cove Inn
$$-$$$ bkfst incl.
sb/pb
6 rooms
Rte. 230, A0C 2H0
☎*464-3738*
⇄*464-3010*
www.peacecoveinn.com
The Peace Cove Inn, a pretty beige and green house, occupies a beautiful spot on the shores of the bay in Trinity East, a few kilometres from the heart of Trinity's historic area. A few of its inviting, tastefully furnished and decorated rooms are equipped with private bathrooms; excellent breakfasts are served.

Port Blandford

Terra Nova Golf Resort
$$$
ℜ, ≈, ≡, ♿
95 rooms
Rte. 1, A0C 2G0
☎*543-2525*
⇄*543-2201*
www.terranovagolf.com
The Terra Nova Golf Resort stands on a large lot near the national park and close to an excellent 18-hole golf course. Naturally, it attracts golfers, but also travellers who simply want to enjoy its peaceful setting. This luxurious establishment offers all of the comforts, and the excellent cuisine served in its restaurant adds to the pleasure of staying here.

Gander

Comfort Inn
$$-$$$ bkfst incl.
ℜ, K, 🐾, ≡
63 rooms
112 Trans-Canada Hwy., A1V 1P8
☎*256-3535 or 800-424-6423*
⇄*256-9302*
The Comfort Inn offers quality accommodations.

Hotel Gander
$$-$$$$
ℜ, ≈, ≡
152 rooms
100 Trans-Canada Hwy., A1V 1P5
☎*256-3931 or 800-563-2988*
⇄*651-2641*
www.hotelgander.com
One of the many establishments in Gander, the Hotel Gander rents perfectly suitable, well-kept rooms in a slightly worn-out, two-storey building. Its restaurant is among the best in the area.

Grand Falls-Windsor

Mount Peyton Hotel
$$
ℜ, ≡
102 rooms
214 Lincoln Rd., A2A 1P8
☎*489-2251 or 800-563-4894*
⇄*489-6365*
www.mountpeyton.com
The town of Grand Falls-Windsor, situated about halfway between the east and west coasts of the island, offers numerous lodging options. Among these is the Mount Peyton Hotel, a quality establishment that offers comfortable, albeit somewhat impersonally decorated rooms.

Newfoundland and Labrador

Carriage House Inn
$$-$$$ bkfst incl.

🛪, ≡
4 rooms
181 Grenfell Heights, A2A 2J2
☎*489-7185 or*
800-563-7133
⇄*489-1990*
www.carriagehouseinn.ca
One of the best inns on this part of the island, the Carriage House occupies a beautiful, handsomely landscaped property.

Tour D: Western Newfoundland

Port aux Basques

St. Christopher's Hotel
$$
ℜ, 🐕, ≡
83 rooms
146 Caribou Rd., A0M 1C0
☎*695-7034 or*
800-563-4779
⇄*695-9841*
www.stchrishotel.com
St Christopher's Hotel, conveniently located near Port aux Basques' main attractions, offers clean, simple and spacious rooms.

Port au Port

Spruce Pine Acres
$$$-$$$$
ℜ, △, ☺, K
4 rooms, 1 cottage
PO Box 219, Rte. 460, A0M 1T0
☎*648-9273 or*
877-239-7117
⇄*648-9600*
www.spa.nf.ca
Set on a pretty, landscaped property between Stephenville and Cape St. George on the Port au Port Peninsula, Spruce Pine Acres offers top-notch lodging. Four rooms with private bathrooms

are available in the beautiful main building, or guests can stay in a cottage with two large rooms, a kitchenette and a living room with a fireplace.

Corner Brook

Bell's Inn Bed & Breakfast
$-$$ bkfst incl.
K, ⊛
8 rooms
2 Fordo Rd., A2H 1S6
☎*634-5736 or*
888-634-1150
⇄*634-1114*
www.bellsinn.ca
The Bell's Inn Bed & Breakfast occupies a comfortable modern house in a residential neighbourhood overlooking downtown Corner Brook, about 10min on foot from the town's main commercial thoroughfares. Its rooms are spacious and pleasant. In the morning, delicious breakfasts are served in a sunny kitchen at the back of the house. The welcome is friendly and the owners are both accessible and discreet.

Holiday Inn
$$-$$$
≈, ⊛, ☺, ℜ, ≡
101 rooms
48 West St., A2H 2Z2
☎*634-5381 or*
800-399-5381
⇄*634-1723*
On Corner Brook's main street, close to its main

attractions, this hotel offers spacious, functional rooms that are pretty much typical of the Holiday Inn hotel chain. The establishment is comfortable and the service is efficient and courteous.

Glynmill Inn
$$-$$$$
ℜ, ≡
81 rooms
1 Cobb Ln., A2H 6E6
☎*634-5181 or*
800-563-4400
⇄*634-5106*
www.glynmillinn.ca
The Glynmill Inn, the most famous hotel in the area, stands in the heart of Corner Brook. This beautiful Tudor building occupies a large, quiet and attractively flower-covered property that looks out over Glynmill Pond. The inn's rooms are comfortable and charming; some have been renovated. The Glynmill Inn houses two restaurants, including the elegant **Wine Cellar** (see p 262), a pleasant bar and conference rooms.

Tour E: The Viking Trail

Norris Point

Sugar Hill Inn
$$-$$$$
△, ℜ, ≡
6 rooms
PO Box 100, 115 Sexton Rd., A0K 3V0
☎*458-2147 or*
888-299-2147
⇄*458-2166*
www.sugarhillinn.nf.ca
As you approach Norris Point, in the southern part of Gros Morne National Park, the Sugar Hill—one

of the best places to stay on the western half of the island–comes into view on a beautifully landscaped hillside. All of its rooms are charming and equipped with private bathrooms. A sauna and a whirlpool are at guests' disposal and excellent fare is served in the inn's dining room.

Rocky Harbour

Ocean View Motel
$$-$$$$
ℜ
48 rooms
Main St., A0K 4N0
☎*458-2730 or*
800-563-9887
⇄*458-2841*
www.oceanviewmotel.com
The Ocean View Motel offers rooms that are spacious, comfortable and clean, but of no particular charm. This establishment is well kept and houses a good family restaurant.

Cow Head

Shallow Bay Motel & Cabins
$$-$$$
ℜ, ≈, K, △, ℑ
64 rooms
PO Box 441, Main St., A0K 2A0
☎*243-2471 or*
800-563-1946
⇄*243-1946*
www.shallowbaymotel.com
At the northern end of Gros Morne National Park, near a beautiful finesand beach, stand the few small cottages and buildings belonging to the Shallow Bay Motel & Cabins. This quiet spot offers an excellent view of the Gulf of St. Lawrence. Although the rooms and cottages are not particu-

larly luxurious, they are all comfortable. Guests have access to an outdoor swimming pool and a restaurant that serves simple, well-prepared dishes.

Main Brook

🔬 **Tuckamore Country Inn**
$$$ bkfst incl.
△, ℜ, ®
8 rooms
1 Southwest Pond, A0K 3N0
☎*865-6361 or*
888-865-6361
⇄*865-2112*
The Tuckamore Country Inn offers the luxury of first-class Scandinavianstyle accommodations in the heart of the Newfoundland wilderness. There are two main lodges, a pine A-frame and a white cedar lodge located on Southwest Pond, providing spectacular views of the lake.

L'Anse aux Meadows

Marilyn's Hospitality Home
$ bkfst incl.
3 rooms
PO Box 5, Hay Cove, A0K 2X0
☎*623-2811 or*
877-865-3958
Lodging is available at Marilyn's Hospitality Home, about 1 km from L'Anse aux Meadows, amid the few houses that make up the little community of Hay Cove. Marilyn, a very congenial woman who is always ready to share tidbits of local lore, offers slightly over-decorated but well-kept rooms and, come morning, a very generous breakfast. The service is simple and friendly.

Valhalla Lodge Bed & Breakfast
$$ bkfst incl.
ℜ, △
5 rooms
PO Box 265, Rte. 436, A0K 2X0
☎*623-2018 or*
877-623-2018
⇄*623-2144*
This cozy comfortable lodge offers friendly service and great food. There are wonderful views overlooking the Atlantic Ocean, where, in summer months, one can spot whales and icebergs. The sitting room offers an extensive library with local reading on the Vikings.

St. Anthony

Haven Inn
$$-$$$
ℜ
30 rooms
Goose Bay Rd., A0K 4S0
☎*454-9100 or*
877-428-3646
⇄*454-2270*
www.haveninn.ca
On a hill overlooking St. Anthony, the Haven Inn contains suitable yet bland rooms. St. Anthony is the largest community on this part of the island.

Cape Onion

Tickle Inn
$-$$ bkfst incl.
ℜ
4 rooms
RR1, A0K 4J0
☎/⇄*452-4321*
A little over half an hour off the road from L'Anse aux Meadows and St. Anthony is the Tickle Inn, an appealing little inn in an enchanting setting facing the ocean and surrounded by valleys. This spot is perfect for long walks and for spotting whales and icebergs on the open sea. The rooms are

well kept and inviting. The Tickle Inn's dining room serves some of the best cuisine in the area.

Tour F: Labrador

L'Anse-au-Clair

Beachside Hospitality Home
$ bkfst incl.
sb/pb
3 rooms
9 Lodge Rd., A0K 3K0
☎/≈931-2275
The few villages along the road that skirts the Strait of Belle Isle shelter many bed and breakfasts, where visitors will be warmly received; the people of Labrador are known for their friendliness. One of these is the Beachside Hospitality Home, which has inviting, well-kept rooms.

Northern Light Inn
$$-$$$$
ℜ, ≡
54 rooms
PO Box 92, 58 Main St., A0K 3K0
☎931-2332 or
800-563-3188
≈931-2708
www.northernlightinn.com
Also in L'Anse-au-Clair, the Northern Light Inn, the largest establishment on the coast, offers motel-type rooms.

West St. Modeste

Oceanview Resort
$$
≡, 🐾
10 rooms, 4 cottages
184 Main St., A0K 5S0
☎927-5288
≈927-5894
www.oceanviewresort.ca
The Oceanview Resort provides comfortable

accommodations with sweeping views of the Strait of Belle Isle. The dining facilities (see p 262) are some of the best in the region. There is also a well stocked craft shop.

Labrador City – Wabush

Wabush Hotel
$$
ℜ, ≡
65 rooms
9 Grenfell Dr., A0R 1B0
☎282-3221
≈282-3061
www.wabushhotel.com
The twin cities of Labrador City and Wabush number a few hotel establishments that offer comfortable rooms with no discernable charm. The most sizeable of these is the Wabush Hotel, whose architecture resembles that of large lodge.

Restaurants

Tour A: St. John's

Ches's
$
9 Freshwater St.
☎722-4083
≈726-3434
Ches's is without a doubt the king of fish and chips in St. John's! Having occupied the same address on Freshwater Street since 1956, this friendly little restaurant is a local institution. Their famous fish and chips, as well as hamburgers and chicken, are served at very reasonable prices in an atmosphere that couldn't be more jovial. Although the owner,

Ches Barbour, no longer hauls in the catch himself, the ambiance of those bygone days remains. There are two other Ches's in St. John's: one on Topsail Road and one on Mount Pearl.

Duck Street Bistro
$$
252 Duckworth St.
☎753-0400
The Duck Street Bistro specialises in homemade meals, fresh seafood and vegetarian dishes. You'll find warm, cozy surroundings with a friendly atmosphere. Reservations are strongly recommended.

Taj Mahal
$$
203 Water St.
☎576-5500
Lavishly decorated in Victorian style, the Taj Mahal prepares authentic Indian cuisine. Its elaborate menu highlights various tandoori specialties. The chicken tikka, the tandoori shrimp and the malai tikka fish are especially delicious. The nan bread is succulent, as is the steamed rice. Most of the main dishes cost about $10. A complete dinner for two can be enjoyed here for under $40.

Aqua
$$-$$$
310 Water St.
☎576-2782
Aqua offers big-city atmosphere with a wonderful selection of dishes with a Thai influence. The menu includes a selection of fresh seafood dishes that are sure to please. Excellent service and presentation.

Cellar
$$-$$$
Bird's Cove, 152 Water St.
☎579-8900
One of the best restaurants in the province, the Cellar earns its reputation with an innovative menu that seduces the senses. Whether in a pasta, seafood or meat dish, the originality of the flavours and the freshness of the produce are as impressive as the beautiful presentation. The pleasant atmosphere of the dining room and its low-key lighting are perfect for intimate evenings.

Tour B: The Avalon Peninsula

Trepassey

Trepassey Restaurant
$-$$
Main Rd.
☎438-2934
The magnificent restaurant in the **Trepassey Motel** (see p 256) is the perfect spot for lunch. The dishes on offer, mainly seafood and fish, are simple but well prepared and inexpensive. The layout of the restaurant is inviting and offers a pretty view of the bay.

St. Bride's

Atlantica Restaurant
$-$$
Rte. 100
☎337-2860
Vacationers can stop in St. Bride's on the way to Cape St. Mary's for a light meal at the Atlantica Restaurant. The menu lists rather simple dishes, including fish, scallops and fried shrimp. Hamburgers and other fast-food fare are also served.

Tour C: Eastern and Central Newfoundland

Marystown

TJ Billington
$$
☎279-1600
In the warm atmosphere of an English pub, its wall bedecked with a multitude of knick-knacks and framed pictures, TJ Billington cooks up the best food on the peninsula. The menu includes seafood and fish, as well as delicious steaks, ribs and chicken brochettes. Contrary to the standard practice of most Newfoundland restaurants, fresh vegetables are served here instead of the canned variety.

Grand Bank

Manuel's
$-$$
Main St.
☎832-0100
Manuel's is a family restaurant that offers fried chicken and fish, hamburgers and a few other simple dishes.

Trinity

Eriksson
$$
☎464-3698
Eriksson simmers up simple dishes, mainly composed of seafood and fish, in the warm atmosphere of a stately old home.

Village Inn
$$
☎464-3269
The **Village Inn**'s (see p 257) restaurant lovingly puts together family-style

meals that are not especially original but are good nonetheless. The restaurant is comfortable, the dishes are copious, and the atmosphere is friendly.

Tour D: Western Newfoundland

Corner Brook

Casual Jack's
$-$$
70 West St.
☎634-4242
In a young, very relaxed atmosphere, Casual Jack's serves pub-style cuisine that mainly consists of chicken dishes, ribs and steaks, accompanied by a selection of beers on tap. In lieu of entertainment, televisions do full-time duty broadcasting sporting events.

Thirteen West
$$-$$$
13 West St.
☎634-1300
Refined inspired cuisine and a tastefully decorated dining room account for the reputation of Thirteen West as one of the best restaurants in the province. Its lunch menu offers many excellent dishes for under $10. In the evening, the supper selections include a wide variety of main dishes such as seafood au gratin, linguini in clam sauce, chicken breast in white wine and roast lamb. To top it off, an excellent crème caramel and a succulent cheesecake appear on the dessert list. In the summer there is *al fresco* dining on a lovely patio.

Newfoundland and Labrador

Wine Cellar
$$-$$$
☎**634-5181**
The Wine Cellar, set up in a circular stone-walled room, is one of two restaurants at the **Glynmill Inn** (see p 258). This elegant dining room with a plush atmosphere mainly serves steak. Extensive selection of wines and spirits.

Tour E:
The Viking Trail

Rocky Harbour

Fisherman's Landing
$$
☎**458-2060**
An unpretentious family restaurant, Fisherman's Landing offers a menu of seafood and fish, with some meat and poultry items thrown in for good measure. The service is courteous, although somewhat businesslike, and the prices are reasonable. Copious breakfasts are served each morning.

St. Anthony

Lightkeepers' Cafe
$$-$$$
Fishing Point
☎**454-4900**
There could be no better location for a restaurant than that of the Lightkeepers' Cafe. Located at the very tip of Fishing Point, it offers a remarkable view of the ocean, an entrancing tableau occasionally enhanced by the slow drift of an iceberg or the to-and-fro of a whale. This beautiful panorama is happily complemented by excellent fare.

The menu mainly lists fish and seafood dishes, including succulent snow crab, and the wine list is quite varied. Sunrise over the sea is a sight that can be enjoyed here from 7am.

Tour F: Labrador

L'Anse-au-Clair

Basque Dining Room
Northern Light Inn, 58 Main St.
$$
☎**931-2332**
This is a full service restaurant that offers an excellent selection of seafood and delicious desserts.

Red Bay

Whaler's Restaurant
$-$$
☎**920-2156**
Great chowder and Canadian cuisine.

West St. Modeste

Oceanview Resort
$
☎**927-5288**
The **Oceanview Resort**'s (see p 260) restaurant offers a wonderful selection of seafood–try the Fisherman's platter. Friendly service.

Goose Bay

Mary Brown
$
Hamilton River Rd.
☎**896-8159**
For a bite to eat without taking a bite out of your wallet, Mary Brown offers good family-style fare. Nothing extravagant, but the fried chicken always hits the spot.

Also in Goose Bay, the **Labrador Inn** *($$-$$$; 380 Hamilton River Rd.,* ☎*896-3351)* and the **Aurora Hotel**'s *($$-$$$; 382 Hamilton River Rd.,* ☎*896-3398)* restaurants post varied daily menus that are sure to satisfy.

Entertainment

Tour A: St. John's

Newfoundlanders are a festive lot, and this is reflected in St. John's nightlife. There are a good many bars and nightclubs in the city, but more remarkable is the incredible number of Irish, English and Scottish pubs. The best spot for an introduction to nocturnal St. John's is unquestionably **George Street**, home to the longest uninterrupted row of pubs in Canada.

Shopping

Tour A: St. John's

Shopping Centres

The **Avalon Mall Regional Shopping Centre** *(Kenmount Rd.)* is the largest retail mall in St. John's. It encloses some 100 shops, department stores and supermarkets.

Boutiques

Water Street was apparently the first commercial thoroughfare in North America. Now it is the site of a few interesting shops. For beautiful woolen clothing, try **Annika's** *(172 Water St., ☎754-1146)* or the **Newfoundland Weavery** *(117 Water St., ☎753-0496)*.

Tour D: Western Newfoundland

Corner Brook

Nortique Specialty Gift Shop
Confederation Dr.
☎634-8334
This lovely shop located near the Corner Brook tourist information office displays an interesting

selection of souvenirs, crafts and beautiful woolen clothing.

St. Anthony

Grenfell Historic Properties
Rte. 430
☎454-4010
Crafts from all over Newfoundland and Labrador can be purchased here.

Northern gannet

Index

Index

Index

Index

Index

Travel Notes

Travel Notes

Order Form

Ulysses Travel Guides

☐	Acapulco	$14.95 CAD	$9.95 USD
☐	Alberta's Best Hotels and Restaurants	$14.95 CAD	$12.95 USD
☐	Arizona–Grand Canyon	$24.95 CAD	$17.95 USD
☐	Atlantic Canada	$24.95 CAD	$19.95 USD
☐	Beaches of Maine	$12.95 CAD	$9.95 USD
☐	Bed and Breakfasts In Ontario	$17.95 CAD	$12.95 USD
☐	Belize	$16.95 CAD	$12.95 USD
☐	Boston	$17.95 CAD	$12.95 USD
☐	British Columbia's Best Hotels	$14.95 CAD	$12.95 USD
☐	Calgary	$16.95 CAD	$12.95 USD
☐	California	$29.95 CAD	$21.95 USD
☐	Canada	$29.95 CAD	$22.95 USD
☐	Cancún & Riviera Maya	$19.95 CAD	$17.95 USD
☐	Cape Cod, Nantucket and	$17.95 CAD	$12.95 USD
☐	Cartagena (Colombia)	$12.95 CAD	$9.95 USD
☐	Chicago	$19.95 CAD	$14.95 USD
☐	Chile	$27.95 CAD	$17.95 USD
☐	Colombia	$29.95 CAD	$21.95 USD
☐	Costa Rica	$27.95 CAD	$19.95 USD
☐	Cuba	$24.95 CAD	$17.95 USD
☐	Dominican Republic	$24.95 CAD	$17.95 USD
☐	Ecuador and Galápagos Islands	$24.95 CAD	$17.95 USD
☐	Fabulous Québec	$29.95 CAD	$22.95 USD
☐	Guadalajara	$17.95 CAD	$12.95 USD
☐	Guadeloupe	$24.95 CAD	$17.95 USD
☐	Guatemala	$24.95 CAD	$17.95 USD
☐	Havana	$16.95 CAD	$12.95 USD
☐	Hawaii	$29.95 CAD	$21.95 USD
☐	Honduras	$24.95 CAD	$17.95 USD

☐ Huatulco–Puerto Escondido	$17.95 CAD	$12.95 USD
☐ Inns and Bed & Breakfasts in Québec	$17.95 CAD	$12.95 USD
☐ Islands of the Bahamas	$24.95 CAD	$17.95 USD
☐ Las Vegas	$17.95 CAD	$12.95 USD
☐ Lisbon	$18.95 CAD	$13.95 USD
☐ Los Angeles	$19.95 CAD	$14.95 USD
☐ Los Cabos and La Paz	$14.95 CAD	$10.95 USD
☐ Louisiana	$29.95 CAD	$21.95 USD
☐ Martinique	$24.95 CAD	$17.95 USD
☐ Miami	$17.95 CAD	$12.95 USD
☐ Montréal	$19.95 CAD	$14.95 USD
☐ New England	$29.95 CAD	$21.95 USD
☐ New Orleans	$17.95 CAD	$12.95 USD
☐ New York City	$19.95 CAD	$14.95 USD
☐ Nicaragua	$24.95 CAD	$17.95 USD
☐ Ontario's Best Hotels and Restaurants	$16.95 CAD	$12.95 USD
☐ Ontario	$29.95 CAD	$22.95 USD
☐ Ottawa–Hull	$14.95 CAD	$12.95 USD
☐ Panamá	$27.95 CAD	$19.95 USD
☐ Peru	$27.95 CAD	$19.95 USD
☐ Phoenix	$16.95 CAD	$12.95 USD
☐ Porto	$17.95 CAD	$12.95 USD
☐ Portugal	$24.95 CAD	$17.95 USD
☐ Provence & the Côte d'Azur	$29.95 CAD	$21.95 USD
☐ Puerto Plata–Sosua	$14.95 CAD	$9.95 USD
☐ Puerto Rico	$24.95 CAD	$17.95 USD
☐ Puerto Vallarta	$14.95 CAD	$10.95 USD
☐ Québec	$29.95 CAD	$22.95 USD
☐ Québec City	$24.95 CAD	$19.95 USD
☐ San Diego	$17.95 CAD	$12.95 USD
☐ San Francisco	$17.95 CAD	$12.95 USD